D1542871

For Joseph Fierstein
family, friend, physician

The Heirs of Stalin

DISSIDENCE AND THE SOVIET REGIME 1953-1970

by Abraham Rothberg

CORNELL UNIVERSITY PRESS | Ithaca and London

First published 1972 by Cornell University Press.
Published in the United Kingdom by Cornell University Press Ltd.,
2–4 Brook Street, London W1Y 1AA.

Quotations from *A Precocious Autobiography*, by Yevgeny Yevtushenko, translated by Andrew MacAndrew, English translation copyright © 1963 by E. P. Dutton & Co., Inc., publishers, are reprinted by permission of E. P. Dutton and The Harvill Press Ltd., London.
Quotations from *Russia Enters the 1960s*, edited, with commentary, by Harry Schwartz, copyright © 1962 by Harry Schwartz, are reprinted by permission of J. B. Lippincott Company. Quotations from *The Pasternak Affair: Courage of Genius*, by Robert Conquest, copyright © 1961 by Robert Conquest, are reprinted by permission of J. B. Lippincott Company.
Quotations from *Russia: Hopes and Fears*, by Alexander Werth, copyright © 1969 by Alexander Werth, are reprinted by permission of Simon and Schuster and Barrie & Rockliff: The Cresset Press.

International Standard Book Number 0-8014-0667-6
Library of Congress Catalog Card Number 77-164643

PRINTED IN THE UNITED STATES OF AMERICA BY VAIL-BALLOU PRESS, INC.

Librarians: Library of Congress cataloging information appears on the last page of the book.

Acknowledgments

I am grateful to the authors, editors, translators, and publishers for permission to quote from their works:

To the United States Information Agency, for quotations from *Problems of Communism* from David Burg's " 'Cold War' on the Literary Front," July–August 1962, January–February 1963; George Gibian's "Ferment and Reaction: 1956–1957," January–February 1958; and Tom Scriven's "The Literary Opposition," January–February 1958.

To *The Current Digest of the Soviet Press*, for quotations from Yevgeny Yevtushenko's "The Heirs of Stalin" and Boris Slutsky's "The Boss" and "God"; translation copyright 1962 by *The Current Digest of the Soviet Press*, published weekly at the Ohio State University, Columbus, Ohio, by the American Association for the Advancement of Slavic Studies; Leo Gruliow, editor; reprinted by permission.

To the Institute for the Study of the USSR, for quotations from Peter Benno's "The Political Aspect" and Gleb Struve's "Soviet Literature in Perspective," which were originally papers read at a symposium held under the auspices of the institute at Bad Wiessee, West Germany, in September 1963, and subsequently included in *Soviet Literature in the Sixties*, edited by Max Hayward and Edward L. Crowley, published in London by Methuen & Co., Ltd., in 1965; also for quotations from Yevgeny Yevtushenko's "The Ballad of the Poacher," Yury Krotkov's "Signs of the Times," and "Soviet Literature: To Be or Not to Be," which appeared in the institute's *Bulletin*.

To *Encounter* (London), for quotations from Khrushchev's remarks at the Manezh in the April 1963 issue, and from Richard Pipes's "Russia's Exigent Intellectuals" in the January 1964 issue.

To *The New Leader*, for quotations from "The Trial of Josif Brodsky"; reprinted with permission from *The New Leader* of August 31, 1964; copyright © 1964 by The American Labor Conference on International Affairs, Inc.

To Pall Mall Press, London, and Praeger Publishers, New York, for quotations from *In Quest of Justice: Protest and Dissent in the Soviet Union*, edited by Abraham Brumberg (1970), and from Alexander Solzhenitsyn's *For the Good of the Cause*, translated by David Floyd and Max Hayward (1964).

To Harper & Row, Publishers, for quotations from Andrei Amalrik's *Will the Soviet Union Survive until 1984?* (1970) and from Svetlana Alliluyeva's *Only One Year*, translated by Paul Chavchavadze (1969).

To Harper & Row, Publishers, and to Collins Publishers, for quotations from *On Trial: The Soviet State versus "Abram Tertz" and "Nikolai Arzhak,"* translated by Max Hayward; copyright © by Harper & Row, Publishers, Inc., 1966; reprinted by permission of the publishers.

To Random House, for quotations from *Dissonant Voices in Soviet Literature*, edited by Patricia Blake and Max Hayward, copyright © 1962 by Patricia Blake and Max Hayward, reprinted by permission of Pantheon Books, a division of Random House, Inc.; and from *Message from Moscow*, by "An Observer," copyright © 1969 by Jonathan Cape Limited, reprinted by permission of Alfred A. Knopf, Inc.

To Harcourt Brace Jovanovich and to Harvill Press, for quotations from Andrei Amalrik's *Involuntary Journey to Siberia* (1970), translated by Manya Harari and Max Hayward, copyright 1970 by Harcourt Brace Jovanovich, Inc., and The Harvill Press Ltd.

To Harvard University Press, for quotations from Harold Swayze's *Political Control of Literature in the USSR, 1946–1959* (1962).

To Columbia University Press, for quotations from Zhores Medvedev's *The Rise and Fall of T. D. Lysenko* (1969).

To Gambit, Incorporated, and to Collins Publishers, for quotations from Pavel Litvinov's *The Demonstration in Pushkin Square*, translated by Manya Harari (1969).

To The MIT Press, for quotations from *Khrushchev and the Arts*, text by Priscilla Johnson, documents selected and edited by Priscilla Johnson and Leopold Labedz, reprinted by permission of The MIT Press, Cambridge, Massachusetts; copyright © 1965 by the Massachusetts Institute of Technology.

To Holt, Rinehart and Winston and to George Weidenfeld & Nicolson Limited, for quotations from *Half-Way to the Moon* (1964), edited by Patricia Blake and Max Hayward.

To Holt, Rinehart and Winston and to Collins-Knowlton-Wing, for quotations from Viktor Nekrasov's *Both Sides of the Ocean*, translated by Elias Kulukundis (1964); copyright © 1964 by Elias Kulukundis; reprinted by permission of Collins-Knowlton-Wing, Inc., and Holt, Rinehart and Winston, Inc.

To Farrar, Straus & Giroux and to The Bodley Head, for quotations from Alexander Solzhenitsyn's *Cancer Ward*, translated by Nicholas Bethell and David Burg; copyright © The Bodley Head, 1968, 1969; front and back matter of the American edition copyright © Farrar, Straus & Giroux, 1969.

To *Survey*, for quotations from "Judgment on Pasternak" (July 1966), and Andrei Amalrik's "An Open Letter to Kuznetsov" and "I Want to Be Understood Correctly" (Winter–Spring 1970).

To Copex Establishment, for quotations reprinted with the permission of the proprietor from the article "To Boris Leonidovich Pasternak," by Svetlana Alliluyeva, in *The Atlantic Monthly* (June 1967); copyright © 1967 by Copex Establishment.

To Praeger Publishers, for quotations from Aleksandr Yesenin-Volpin's *A Leaf of Spring*, translated by George Reavey (1961).

To W. W. Norton & Company, for quotations from Andrei Sakharov's *Progress, Coexistence, and Intellectual Freedom* (1968).

To E. P. Dutton & Co., for quotations from *I Am from Moscow*, by Yuri Krotkov, English translation © 1967 by William Heinemann, published by E. P. Dutton & Co., Inc., and reprinted with their permission; and to William Heinemann Ltd, publishers of the English translation *The Angry Exile*.

ABRAHAM ROTHBERG

New York, New York

Contents

Man is born to live, not to prepare for life.

Marxism a science? . . . I don't know a movement more self-centered and further removed from the facts than Marxism. . . . As for the men in power, they are so anxious to establish the myth of their infallibility that they do their utmost to ignore the truth.

Boris Pasternak

Without the free word, there are no free people; without the independent word, there can be no mighty nation capable of internal change. "Resounding candid speech alone can satisfy a man," Herzen wrote. . . . "Muteness supports despotism."

Lydia Chukovskaya

Part I

THE BROKEN ICON:
DE-STALINIZATION

1 The Web of Politics

Everything is politics here.
Nikolay Gogol

In the more than five decades since the Bolshevik Revolution, the Soviet Union has suffered upheavals of immense magnitude, yet perhaps none has so shaken Soviet life to its roots as first the death and then the denigration of Josef Stalin. At the base of almost all the cataclysms which have afflicted the land and its people—war, famine, purge, transfer of populations, forced industrialization and collectivization—was the character of the man who dictated the shape of Soviet life for a generation and shaped the instrument of that dictation, the Communist Party of the Soviet Union. With Stalin's death an era ended, yet for almost two decades since, the new era struggling to be born has been a stillbirth, chiefly because of the legacy Stalin left behind embodied in the personnel and institutions of Soviet life. What happens when an icon is shattered, when an idol worshiped is publicly discovered not only to have feet of clay but to be clay almost altogether?

The death of the despot in 1953 left the Soviet Union in a moral and political dilemma; for more than two decades Stalin had arbitrarily controlled the destinies of the nation and the people with an authoritarian harshness and cruelty that have few equals in history. At the same time he had presided over building the Soviet Union into the second greatest industrial and military power on earth. His death left the nation unprepared; neither Stalin nor the Communist Party he had created had prepared the way for a legitimate and peaceful transfer of power. There were no institutions adequately equipped to dismantle the awesome authority which Stalin had acquired over twenty-five years, no established way of parceling his powers out to various individuals and instrumentalities in Soviet society. Consequently, a struggle to see who would take up Stalin's mantle ensued almost immediately.[1]

After Stalin's death, Georgy Malenkov at first assumed the two most powerful positions in the country, both of which Stalin had previously held, and became Premier of the Soviet Union and First Secretary of the Communist Party. Within two weeks, however, Malenkov had relinquished the Party leadership, presumably under pressure from his colleagues. From March through June of 1953 the secret-police chief, Lavrenty Beria, attempted to establish himself in Stalin's place, but he was thwarted by other members of the Politburo who conspired against him and, probably with the help of the Soviet army, had him executed in June. In September, Nikita Khrushchev was made First Secretary of the Party and within what was described as a "collective leadership," began his struggle for power and pre-eminence with Malenkov. Since Malenkov had announced his support for a policy of shifting to a consumer-goods production emphasis domestically and to "peaceful existence" in foreign policy—a way of popularizing himself with the Soviet people, giving them a higher standard of living and sense of security; he was the "liberal" [2] —Khrushchev allied himself with Vyacheslav Molotov, Lazar Kaganovich, and other old-guard Stalinists who opposed Malenkov's views and power. As a result, early in 1955, Khrushchev was able to oust Malenkov and to appoint Nikolai Bulganin in his place as Premier.

Khrushchev then shifted to and absorbed his rival's policies,[3] publicly favoring "peaceful coexistence" and implementing it by signing the treaty to free Austria from Four-Power occupation, by removing Red Army occupation units from Finland, and, in the middle of the year, by going to Belgrade in an attempt to bring Tito and Yugoslavia back into the Communist fold from which they had been excluded by Stalin's interdiction in 1948. He also made clear that he was going to raise the Soviet standard of living, not only by an improvement in consumer-goods production, but by a great transformation in farm production which would provide more meat, milk, vegetables, and fruit for the deprived ordinary man's market basket.

In order for Khrushchev and those forces associated with him to remain in power and function effectively, they had to cope with new problems—problems due only in part to Stalin's death. The two most important were the ineffectiveness of much of the Soviet economic system, and the political apathy and resistance of the people. What was needed was a "new course," [4] a thorough shake-up of the old centralized, authoritarian (Stalinist) bureaucracy and its methods, and the introduction of new initiative and flexibility into the economic organization in order to cope with the demands of an atomic–electronic–space-age technology. To modernize the Soviet economy, to make it more efficient and productive, required greater cooperation from the Russian people—workers, peasants, technicians, managers, intelligentsia. To elicit such cooperation meant giving people more freedom and security (what the regime called "strengthening socialist legality") and more and better wages and working conditions, consumer goods and housing (what the regime called "material incentives").

People also had to be persuaded that such reforms would not serve merely as temporary lures for temporary regime purposes, that the initiatives required of them would not be deliberately misconstrued and used against them, as had happened so frequently in the past, that their lives would, indeed, be more secure, stable, and prosperous. People had to be convinced that the reforms were there to stay, that there would be no reversion to Stalinist methods; so the government campaign to strengthen "socialist legality" was an attempt to assure the people that their rulers would no longer invoke or tolerate the brutality, coercion, and violence of the past. It was a campaign in which the writers were to be especially useful, or so the leadership imagined.

One startling and effective way of reassuring the people was to inform them of some of the truth about Stalin's tyranny, and in so doing make clear that the new rulers dissociated themselves from Stalin and his methods. This campaign of denigration of Stalin—so-called de-Stalinization—was undertaken the following year at the Twentieth Congress of the Communist Party of the Soviet Union, in February 1956, when Khrushchev made his "secret speech" about Stalin's crimes, though not without opposition by many of the ruling elite. In great measure, de-Stalinization was undertaken for reasons of state, but among the motives was also an almost visceral revulsion against Stalin's terror and personality, a revulsion rooted in the fear and degradation under which even the highest leadership had lived during the Stalin era, as well as, in some measure, a moral recoil from the frightful crimes of the Stalinist dictatorship.

At the Twentieth Congress, Khrushchev asked what subsequently were to become critical post-Stalin questions: "Where were the members of the Political Bureau of the Central Committee? Why did they not assert themselves against the cult of the individual in time? And why is this being done only now?" Khrushchev answered the questions by explaining that Stalin had terrorized them, and that all, even those in the Politburo, feared for their lives. He told how Stalin had arbitrarily barred Klimenty Voroshilov, one of the oldest Party members, from Politburo meetings. "Stalin also toyed with the absurd and ridiculous suspicion that Voroshilov was an English agent. . . . A special tapping device was installed in his home to listen to what was said there." Khrushchev further stated that had Stalin lived much longer, he might also have imprisoned or executed both Vyacheslav Molotov and Anastas Mikoyan, because Stalin was planning "the future annihilation of the old Political Bureau members" in order to cover up his past criminal acts. Khrushchev recounted an incident in which he and Nikolai Bulganin were traveling together in an automobile when Bulganin remarked, "It has happened sometimes that a man goes to Stalin on invitation as a friend. And when he sits with Stalin, he does not know where he will be sent next, home or jail." [5]

A partial version of Khrushchev's five-and-a-half-hour speech was made public in June 1956, four months after it was delivered to the Twentieth Congress, by the American State Department, and its contents rapidly became common knowledge in the West. But the speech was never published inside the Soviet Union, although the gist of it was carefully disseminated to key groups and individuals. At that Congress, Khrushchev cautioned: "We cannot let this matter get out of the Party, especially not to the press. It is for this reason that we are considering it here at a closed Congress session. We should know the limits; we should not give ammunition to the enemy; we should not wash our dirty linen before their eyes." [6] It was a typical and significant caution.

With his "secret speech" Khrushchev set in motion forces—political, social, juridical, cultural—which he could neither measure nor control. The forces continued to broaden and deepen and intensify beyond his intentions or those of the leadership who shared his views, not to speak of those of a more conservative cast of mind. For, once you deposed an icon, where did you stop the iconoclasm? And how? If the people were informed in 1956 that Stalin had been a paranoid monster and an incompetent, and if they could no longer put their trust in him, why should they now put their trust in those who came after him, especially since most of the top men of the Soviet hierarchy had for years been closely associated with both Stalin and his policies?

To accomplish the changes they envisioned, then, the Soviet rulers were faced with a fundamental and perhaps insoluble dilemma: they had to engineer the necessary political, economic, and social reforms without undermining their own power, without disenchanting the people in them or in their purposes. They had no intention of sacrificing the framework of Communist Party rule or of the centralized authoritarian control of Soviet life they had acquired, yet enough de-Stalinizing had to be permitted to persuade the people that the new rulers were going to be different from and better than their predecessors—but not so much de-Stalinizing that the people would blame those in power now for having been connected with Stalin and would consider them equally culpable with him. That was at best a very fine line, and drawing such lines, once de-Stalinization was begun, was exceedingly difficult without employing precisely those (Stalinist) methods which they were trying to convince the people they had eschewed.

The aim of the reforms, then, was modernization and amelioration, not democratization or liberalization, not even the very limited liberalization many Soviet intellectuals hoped for. What the Soviet rulers wanted to do was induce initiative and responsibility at all levels of the economy in order to reshape the economy to meet the needs of the second half of the twentieth century. To accomplish this, the bureaucratic apparatus (of the Party, the state, and industry) had to be kept from relapsing into its old authoritarian habits.[7] Simultaneously, the leadership was greatly exercised that middle- and lower-echelon bureaucrats be prevented from actually encouraging mass initiative of the kind that would make for genuine participatory democracy; in short, people were not to be given enough freedom to contest seriously the decisions and purposes of the "center," only enough to fulfill the center's purposes more effectively.[8]

The first stage of de-Stalinization begun at the Twentieth Party Congress met with stiff resistance from some of the top Party leaders, a resistance that intensified in the late fall of 1956, after it appeared that the Polish upheavals and the Hungarian revolt were direct results of liberalization and de-Stalinization. Until the spring of 1957 a power struggle raged in the Politburo between Khrushchev and his rivals, who, because they lost, soon became known as the "anti-Party group"; in June, Khrushchev's position was imperiled when the majority of the Politburo voted to oust him.[9] Only by convening a plenary session of the Central Committee was Khrushchev able to reverse the Politburo vote and, in turn, to oust his rivals. In doing so, he was abetted by Marshal Georgy Zhukov, commander of the Red Army, who was rewarded for his aid by an appointment to the Politburo. But it was not long thereafter, in the fall of 1957, that Khrushchev removed Zhukov from his post as Minister of Defense and dismissed him from the Politburo for planning to fulfill his "Bonapartist" aspirations, indulging in "adventurism," trying to split the army from the Party, and opposing the army to the Party leadership.[10]

In Khrushchev's efforts to change the shape of Soviet life and to secure his own power by defeating the "anti-Party group," liberalization and de-Stalinization were essential levers. In identifying the anti-Party group with Stalin, Khrushchev had much to gain. Domestically, by tarring that faction with the Stalinist brush, he turned the hatred and revulsion felt by many people, particularly those in the Party and government, against his opponents, thus discrediting them and their policies and destroying or undermining their political influence and support. At the same time, by downgrading Stalin and supporting socialist legality, Khrushchev dissociated himself from Stalin's excesses and brutalities in the public mind, though he had himself been one of Stalin's more assiduous and bloody partisans in the Ukraine.

Khrushchev opened the second stage of de-Stalinization on October 18, 1961, at the Twenty-second Congress of the Communist

Party, in Moscow, where for the first time some of the evidence of Stalin's tyranny was made available to the Soviet people. The speeches detailing Stalin's crimes "produced widespread shock in the country. Not only does this indicate that many Soviet citizens believe the original versions of these events [given by Stalin], but even more important the shock revealed that large numbers of Soviet citizens knew little or nothing about the original [Khrushchev] exposure of Stalin." On the eve of the Congress of 1956, Khrushchev now explained, the issue facing the Party was whether it would condemn Stalin's misrule "and reject the methods of the Party and State leadership which had been a brake on progress, or [whether] forces clinging to the old things, resisting everything that was new and creative, would gain the upper hand in the Party." [11] (This appeal to the new and young, which had been part and parcel of the original de-Stalinization, was to have widespread repercussions.) Khrushchev warned that unless abuses of power and violations of socialist legality were openly condemned, the Party would be divorced from the people and the pace of the nation's economic growth seriously hindered. Grave consequences in the field of foreign policy would also undermine the nation's international position.

Thus, the second stage of de-Stalinization at the Twenty-second Party Congress resulted in a vote ordering the removal of Stalin's embalmed corpse from its place of honor next to Lenin's in the Lenin Mausoleum in Red Square, in a recommendation to erect a monument to Stalin's victims in Moscow, and in a rash of name changes for cities, factories, kolkhozes, and so on, which had previously carried Stalin's name; the most noteworthy change was from Stalingrad to Volgograd.

Undoubtedly, some of the men associated with Stalin and his policies also foresaw some of the inevitable dangers and consequences of the dethronement of Stalin and were, therefore, opposed to de-Stalinization on those grounds as well as on grounds of their personal culpability. And the Hungarian revolt and the Polish October changes gave them more ammunition for their opposition. Khrushchev himself was by no means unaware of the difficulties of reconciling Stalin's crimes and ineptitudes, his cruelty and paranoia, with the Party's infallibility and the "building of socialism." Yet, though Khrushchev himself had shown some caution in de-Stalinizing, he was willing to take the risk that de-Stalinization would boomerang, declaring at the Twenty-second Congress:

The Leninist course expounded by the 20th Congress had to be implemented in the face of fierce resistance from anti-Party elements, zealous champions of the methods and systems in vogue at the time of the personality cult. . . . A fractionist group, consisting of Molotov, Kaganovich, Malenkov, Voroshilov, Pervukhin, Saburov, and later also Shepilov, opposed the Leninist course of the Party. . . . Such a position was not coincidental: they bear *personal responsibility* for many mass repressions against Party, government, economic, military and Komsomol personnel and for other similar incidents which occurred during the period of the personality cult.[12]

The implied threat in the words *personal responsibility* (the italics are mine) indicates that Khrushchev may actually have been holding that culpability over the heads of the anti-Party group members to prevent their trying to coalesce opposition against him once more. At the Twenty-second Congress, Khrushchev reminded the Party that the anti-Party group had continued to attempt to retard his inquiry into Stalinist abuses of power "fearing lest their part as accessories to mass repressions be brought to light"; and although in his speech, Aleksandr Shelepin, head of the security police, declared, "The members of the anti-Party group are political corpses who do not represent any danger now," he had earlier pointed out that they bore "direct responsibility for . . . physical annihilation of" and "illegal mass persecutions against many Party, administrative, Komsomol and military workers." [13] It was a reminder that they could be made more than political corpses.[14]

As in domestic policy, so, too, in foreign policy, Khrushchev was trying to walk that fine line between "liberalization"—or what was sometimes called "revisionism"—on the one hand and neo-Stalinism on the other.[15] De-Stalinization had very important foreign-policy implications. First, and perhaps primarily, it gave support to Khrushchev's peaceful coexistence policy with the West, whose purpose was to provide him with time, money, and energy to devote to the Soviet Union's domestic problems. It also secured the West as one "front," so he could turn to the problem of the Chinese threat on the other Far Eastern front, for by 1957 it was already clear to Soviet leaders that a rift with China was in the offing, and by 1961, at the

Twenty-second Congress, divergences with China were openly acknowledged.[16]

De-Stalinization also brought Khrushchev support from East European Communist parties, some of whose leaders and members had been decimated by Stalin; and it made Khrushchev seem to favor looser Moscow control over the European satellite countries, in spite of the role he had played in crushing the Hungarian revolt of 1956.[17] Khrushchev permitted considerable liberalization of the satellite regimes, but only as much as did not threaten the Soviet Union. For the Soviet rulers the higher standard of living and the higher level of cultural and political sophistication in the East European countries had to be "restrained" so that they would not constitute either a "threat" or a "temptation" to the Soviet Union's people. At the same time, from 1957 onward, in the Far East, the Chinese Communist leadership was involved in its own forced industrialization program of the Stalinist variety—the "Great Leap Forward"—which hoped to "skip" several slower stages of industrial development in order to catch up to the Soviet Union and the United States.

Khrushchev was trying to steer Soviet policy between the liberalizing regimes of such East European countries as Yugoslavia, Hungary, and Poland (in 1956) on the one hand and the neo-Stalinism of the Chinese on the other, between the higher standards of living and political sophistication of Eastern Europe and the lower ones of both in China. Nor was Khrushchev eager to accede to Chinese pressures to equalize Russian and Chinese living conditions at the expense of Russia. Nevertheless, in foreign policy, Khrushchev had been forced to pay a great price for the de-Stalinization campaign, because if Stalin, and through him the Soviet Communist Party, was not the fount of wisdom in the past, then other Communist Parties throughout the world were bound to feel freer to seek their own ways to the promised land in the future. Increasingly, from 1956 onward and more rapidly after the Twenty-second Party Congress in 1961, de-Stalinization had been feeding and reinforcing the centrifugal forces in the Soviet empire which would leave the international Communist movement in considerable disarray and Soviet control over the Communist parties of the world greatly eroded.[18]

2 Engineers of the Soul

> An author is not a piece of machinery.
> *Ilya Ehrenburg*

More than any other art, literature in the Soviet Union is considered an instrument for achieving state purposes, a means of motivating people's behavior, mustering their support, molding their character. The tasks assigned to and imposed on Soviet writers by their rulers, consequently, have changed according to the political and economic plans of the leadership. From 1934 to 1940, writers were called upon to help carry out the State program of heavy industrialization and forced collectivization of agriculture. From 1940 to 1945, they were asked to sound a nationalist note in order to mobilize Russian resistance to the Nazi invasion in what came to be called the "Great Fatherland War." From 1945 to 1954, writers were required to concern themselves with the postwar problems of reconstructing a war-torn nation.

In the new circumstances after Stalin's death the role required of the writer became more subtle, ambiguous, and difficult, yet more important than ever to the ruling elite. If they were to enlist the support and cooperation of the people, if they were to steer a course beween Stalinism and liberalism, the ruling elite needed the writers to walk the political tightrope with them and, in doing so, help them to define the Party line as well as promote and support it. And if the leadership was to persuade writers to cooperate in achieving its purposes, it had to give the writers incentives, though not necessarily material ones. These incentives were, basically, a less stringently regulated art—with writers permitted a wider latitude of subject matter and artistic techniques, and a more personal, truthful, and passionate projection of their feelings and ideas in their work—and guarantees that the rule of law would also apply to them: that writers would no longer be purged, exiled to Siberian concentration camps, imprisoned, or shot as they had been in Stalin's time.

As in politics and economics, it was some time before the boundaries of cultural permissiveness were clearly defined; the Khrushchev leadership, committed to a "middle course," had no intention of permitting writers freedoms which might threaten or subvert its powers and purposes. To enlist writers' cooperation in the de-Stalinization, a *quid pro quo* was forthcoming, however: between 1953 and 1962, when Aleksandr Solzhenitsyn appeared meteorically on the scene, there were two periods of relaxed controls over the cultural and intellectual life of the nation—two "thaws"—but in both instances, when those thaws threatened to flood and inundate what the rulers considered important bastions of control, "freezes" were instituted to stop them.

The first thaw began only six weeks after Stalin's death, in March 1953, with an article by the poet Olga Berggolts in *Literaturnaya gazeta*, defending personal expression in lyrical poetry, insisting on the poet's right to his own individuality and mood and tone.[1] It was followed by articles by the novelist Ilya Ehrenburg and a young literary critic, Vladimir Pomerantsev, both calling for more passion and spontaneity in art, less interference in the artist's creative life, and fewer "made-to-order" works of art. That the discussion was carried on in all the most important Soviet journals—*Pravda, Izvestia, Literaturnaya gazeta, Kommunist, Komsomolskaya pravda, Novy mir, Znamya*, and others—indicates that if the debate was not regime-sponsored, it was, at the least, regime-tolerated. The musicians Aram Khachaturian and Dmitry Shostakovich joined the assault against control of artists and their work by attacking the role of the cultural bureaucracy.[2] But the campaign really hit its stride in October with Ehrenburg's essay, "On the Role of the Writer," in which he wrote, half-rebelliously and half-pleadingly:

An author is not a piece of machinery. An author writes a book not because he knows how to write, not because he is a member of the Union of Soviet Writers and may be asked why he has published nothing for so long. An author writes a book because he must tell people something of himself, because he is "sick" with his book, because he has seen people, things and emotions that he cannot help describing.[3]

In November, Khachaturian declared that "creative problems cannot be solved by bureaucratic methods," and demanded that composers be freed from "the petty tutelage of officials." [4] It was not until December 1953, however, after *Novy mir* published Pomerantsev's essay, "On Sincerity in Literature," that the regime's counterattacks began in earnest.

Calling for a more truthful literature which permitted personal "sincerity" and individual artistic bent, Pomerantsev maintained that "political rightness" according to the Party's canons was not enough to make good books. Pomerantsev wrote from well within the Marxist-Leninist framework and was careful not to attack openly the restrictive Zhdanov decrees on art imposed after the war, or the official support for "socialist realism." Instead, he focused the blame on editors, critics, publishers, and the Union of Writers.[5] "I have heard that Shakespeare wasn't a member of a union at all, yet he did not write badly," Pomerantsev remarked acidly,[6] but because his criticism seemed to attack political orientation and Party control of literature, it could not go unanswered.

The next month, in January 1954, the counterattack began with an article by Vasily Vasilevsky,[7] and the debate between liberal and conservative continued throughout 1954, up to and including the Second All-Union Congress of Soviet Writers, in December. The general line of the official attack on Pomerantsev was revealing; it showed clearly that the authorities feared that Party control of letters and the official view and values of Soviet society were being called into question. A poet and leading literary bureaucrat, Anatoly Surkov, gave it expression:

Pomerantsev's injurious publication is directed, at bottom, against the principles of our literature—against its intimacy with life, against its Communist *ideiinost* [ideological emphasis], against Lenin's principle of *partiinost* [party-mindedness], against the most important canons of socialist realism. Hiding behind an abstractly understood demand for "sincerity in literature," the author, by the whole tone and feeling of his article, turns the reader's attention to consideration chiefly of the dark, unwelcome sides of our reality.[8]

The assault on Pomerantsev and on Ilya Ehrenburg's *The Thaw* for portraying Soviet bureaucrats critically and for displaying "bourgeois vestiges" in various aspects of Soviet life was the major one.

There were also severe official censures of those poets who had stressed the virtues of personal and individual feelings, particularly Olga Berggolts and Margarita Aliger, and a number of other literary works drew their share of fire as well.[9] But it was *Novy mir*, the magazine in which most of the liberal writers appeared, that drew the lightning. Its editor in chief, Aleksandr Tvardovsky, was dismissed and replaced by Konstantin Simonov, but not before both Tvardovsky and his deputy editor, A. Dementyev, had been forced to endure the ritual self-criticism.[10]

At the Second Writers' Congress, though, there was some heated discussion, and it was obvious that there were important difficulties both in the Writers' Union and in Soviet writing in general. Even Mikhail Sholokhov, that eccentric conservative, was impelled to remark on "the dreary torrent of colorless, mediocre literature which in recent years has been gushing from the pages of the journals and flooding our book market." It was equally obvious that neither discussion nor difficulty had moved the authorities to make significant changes in the writers' freedom or in the Writers' Union's restrictions. As had happened before, Aleksandr Fadeyev, novelist and Party spokesman in literature, again delivered the ukase that writers would have to toe the Party line and conform to the canons of "socialist realism." [11]

In 1956, the first wave of de-Stalinization after the Twentieth Party Congress brought with it the second thaw; but the dethronement of Stalin raised far more complex and uncontrollable political problems than had the despot's death. The issues rocked the very foundations of Soviet society, and writers seemed suddenly to be giving voice to all those who for so long had kept silent because they had no public forum for discussing political ideas, for criticizing the institutions of Soviet life, for a radical and searching examination of all the afflictions of Soviet society. Now, through the liberal writers, they might in fact be able to say something about how their lives were to be lived and how the future of their society was to be organized. They might not be able to "do" much, but even speaking out in the Soviet Union was "doing" a good deal. "The year 1956," the Moscow correspondent for the Italian Communist newspaper *L'Unità* wrote, "was the year of passion." [12] A passionate upsurge of socialist idealism and Marxist humanitarianism inspired the liberal writers to give socialism a "human face." [13] "The writers' main theme was the discrepancy between the propaganda image of Soviet society, the ideals on which it is allegedly based, as well as the notions of a 'good society' in general, on the one hand, and Soviet reality on the other." [14] Their urge was for renewal of all aspects of Soviet life: a burning desire to break with the methods of the past by searching out the truths of what Soviet life had become and how it had become that way. They were determined to declare their discoveries and insights openly and without equivocation so that, like Stalin's ghost, the past might be laid to rest; and they were resolved that conditions such as had existed under Stalin should never again be permitted. All seemed to be a reaction to the dogmatic oppressiveness of the "cult of personality":

Where cult is present, scientific thought must give way to blind faith, creativity to dogma, public opinion to caprice. The cult gives birth to a hierarchy of servants of the cult—the deity must have worshippers and obsequiousness. The cult is incompatible with criticism; the healthiest criticism is easily twisted into a heresy. . . . Where the taste of one man becomes incontrovertible, a leveling down and a crude interference in the artistic process . . . are inevitable. . . . Where one man owns the truth uncontrolled, artists are relegated to the modest role of illustrators and singers of odes.[15]

And the writers did not want to be singers of odes and paeans. They wanted to portray the conditions of life which had continued to surface between 1954 and 1956 in an honest and truthful way, revealing their personal and subjective reactions to them. To do so they sought new concessions from the authorities, new ways of extending the limits of freedom. These desires were now reinforced by the Twentieth Party Congress and the resulting de-Stalinization, by a wave of corrosive criticism of the canons of "socialist realism," and, even more important, by a burst of brilliant and incisively truthful judgment of "socialist reality" from East European writers, particularly Poles and Hungarians.[16] Some idea of how Soviet writers felt about their role under Stalin and after can be gleaned from Yevgeny Yevtushenko's portrait of the cynical writer in his poem "Zima Station," written in 1956:

> . . . And what is a writer today?
> He is not a creator, but the guardian of thoughts.
> Yes, change, yes, but behind the speeches
> There's some kind of shady game.
> We talk about what yesterday we kept quiet,
> And keep quiet about what we did yesterday.[17]

The clash between writers' ideals and the reality of their work and possibilities was shocking and many of the liberal writers were determined now to fight for their ideals and for an honest estimate of reality. As Yevtushenko was later to write: "I realized that a struggle lay ahead, a struggle to the death with those who preach communism in theory and discredit it in practice." [18]

The central literary focus of this second thaw was Vladimir Dudintsev's novel *Not by Bread Alone*,[19] though Ehrenburg had published a sequel to his *The Thaw* in 1956. Dudintsev pitted an honest and creative individual against an opportunistic and callous Soviet bureaucrat, just as Ehrenburg had done in the first volume of *The Thaw*, only in Ehrenburg "the artist who conforms to the demands of 'socialist realism' and prostitutes his talent is 'successful'; the one who paints freely lives as a social outcast and close to starvation. Dudintsev . . . registered the hostility of the bureaucracy toward creative work in the technical field." [20] (In Volume II of his memoirs, Ehrenburg was later to say, "In 1955, I made another mistake by writing a sequel [to *The Thaw*], pale and, even more important, artistically superfluous, which I have now dropped from my collected works." [21] Ehrenburg does not mention that this second novel also backtracked from the harsher criticism of Soviet life in the first novel, "lacquering" somewhat the reality of the cynicism and lack of principle he had earlier portrayed in the Soviet bureaucracy.) But Dudintsov was doing much more. Through his major character, Drozdov, he was depicting the most deep-seated and prevalent vices of the Soviet bureaucrat: "materialism, snobbery, servility to authority, arbitrary use of power, habits of intrigue, and above all their [the bureaucrats'] remoteness from the ideals which in theory they exist to serve." [22] Soon Soviet intellectuals would use the name Drozdov as a term of opprobrium for the neo-Stalinists who were still in the bureaucracy, opposing change and progress with their inflexibility, arbitrariness, and simple-minded Philistinism.

In many ways Dudintsev and some of his fellows reminded their admirers of the opposition literature of Tsarist times. It was almost as though they had deliberately revived some of the strongest traditional themes of Russian literature. Here, once again, were the two Russias: official Russia and the Russia of the people—the one oppressive, corrupt, inhuman, the other exploited, innocent, and helpless. Here too was the traditional hatred of the intelligentsia for the Philistine, the *meschane*—identified now with the luxury-loving, complacent, pompous bureaucratic class. For there is no denying the work of the literary opposition is full of hatred and contempt for the false ideals and political emptiness of bureaucrats as a social species, not just of particular bureaucrats.[23]

Consciously or not, the writers were in fact becoming an "opposition," in the sense that they were calling the Party and the government to account, probing the sore points in Soviet life. In their fervor to set the record straight, the liberals by no means confined their attacks to the Drozdovs or the bureaucracy. They refused to accept the simplistic explanation that everything wrong with Soviet society could be conveniently explained away by the "cult of the individual," or even by the person and personality of Stalin himself. They delved deeper, revealing corruption, public and private cowardice, apathy and indifference, economic backwardness.[24] They saw Russia in the throes of what seemed to them a congenital disease for which no one had yet offered an adequate diagnosis, much less a prospective cure. In his surrealist poem "Seven Days of the Week," for example, Semyon Kirsanov was saying that at the root of the whole Soviet system was an essential failure of heart. The poem tells how the poet tried to create a new heart for a friend who needed one badly (by implication for all Soviet men, but particularly for the rulers):

> . . . a completely new heart,
> A heart for the future,
> Able to feel and to love,
> A heart to understand all men.

But the rulers permitted such new hearts to be allocated only to those in the upper echelons of the bureaucracy: "The Double-dealers, the

Turncoats, the Slanderers, the Perjurers, / All had permits for new hearts." Eventually, even the new hearts are rejected, because

> Such hearts are not needed.
> And in general, novelties
> Are not in demand on our market.
> We need useful hearts,
> Like iron locks,
> Uncomplicated, convenient,
> Capable of carrying out any order:
> To malign? To malign!
> To praise? To praise!
> To annihilate? To annihilate! [25]

The writers defended, as part of the overall regeneration of Soviet life, the sincerity and personal integrity of the artist in his work, calling for his freedom of personal and truthful expression. They opposed all dogmas and stereotypes in literature, approved of varied experiment and technical innovation in form. They assaulted "socialist realism" and Party control of the arts, insisting that literature refuse to be the servant of politics, or even its handmaiden. And they refused to accept the Party as the ultimate authority in the arts. Shostakovich, for one example, pointed to the proliferation of lifeless works in music, works awarded prizes precisely because of the Soviet musical milieu and the Secretariat of the Union of Soviet Composers:

The dogmatists often present composers with a naive and ridiculous demand for some kind of arithmetical balance between the "negative" and "positive" in a work. They cannot understand the ideological meaning of a work is not determined by the superficial proportion of "mournful" and "cheerful" passages, but by the power of civic emotions expressed, by its general humanistic trend and its humanity.[26]

The words were as applicable to literature as they were to music. Even Sholokhov admitted that no recent works had won the hearts of Soviet readers, and he criticized the emphasis cultural bureaucrats (of the Writers' Union) placed on quantity:

Is the growth of literature really measured by the number of books published? He should have said that very few good, intelligent books have been published in our country in the past twenty years, but that there have been any number of mediocre ones. In twenty years a thousand authors' pens have produced about ten good books. Not much, is it?

Sholokhov was also interested in attacking the literary canons of the liberal writers and berating them for being "divorced from the masses." Such writers, he said, had lost their contact with life and the people, because "many of our present writers, especially many of the Muscovites, live in a closed triangle: Moscow, the country cottage, the health resort, and again, the health resort, Moscow, the cottage." [27]

Whether the liberal writers thought of themselves as instruments of the Party in implementing the decisions of the Twentieth Congress or imagined themselves an "opposition"—or both—they were, in fact, with their zeal for truth and reform, arrogating to themselves some of the prerogatives the Party claimed as its monopoly, prerogatives the leadership had no intention of surrendering or sharing. The upheavals in Poland and the revolt in Hungary in the fall of 1956 had more than amply demonstrated what influence liberal Hungarian and Polish writers had exerted on those events, so the Soviet rulers moved to impose more severe controls on their own writers lest such occurrences take place in the USSR. Although the Party leadership at first seemed slow to reassert its authority, that was largely because its major energies were involved in the power struggle between the Khrushchev faction and the anti-Party group until the late spring of 1957, but from 1957 to 1959, Khrushchev was to make concerted efforts on three separate fronts to control the writers.

On the first, he attacked and tried to isolate individual liberal writers. They, in turn, united in a "conspiracy of silence" against the Party's accusations and criticisms, refusing to discuss them and refusing to confess their own "errors." Reluctant to use Stalinist coercion, the regime, to begin with, was unable to make the writers engage in the ritual breast-beating and declaim the penitent and self-abasing speeches which had in the past been standard in such circumstances. But at a meeting of the administrative board of the Writers' Union in May 1957, Khrushchev threatened them in a way that demonstrated the seriousness and determination of the regime. He told them personally that he had understood the relevant lessons of the Hungarian revolt and that under no circumstances would he permit Soviet authors the liberties their Hungarian counterparts had enjoyed, and, according to Khrushchev, abused. If the Hungarian leaders had summarily dealt with a dozen of their rebellious writers, Khrushchev declared, the entire "counterrevolution" could have been prevented. Khrushchev warned Soviet writers that, in bringing them into the line, his "hand would not tremble," [28] and he singled out Dudintsev and Margarita Aliger for his most stinging invective. So fierce was his attack on Aliger that she fainted.[29]

The May meeting was the turning point. Khrushchev accomplished what he had set out to. Aliger bowed to the power of the Party; in June she made her first obeisances—not quite demeaning enough to satisfy the Party—and in October her second, at a meeting of the board of the Writers' Union, at which, appropriately, Valentin Katayev's keynote address was entitled "We Are Grateful to the Party." There, also, two of the archconservatives, Leonid Sobolev and Anatoly Sofronov, indulged in an orgy of attacks on *Novy mir*, *Moskva*, and *Literaturnaya Moskva*. To understand what this "self-criticism" must have cost Aliger in integrity and pride, it is instructive to read the published version of her second obeisance:

As a Communist who accepts every Party document as something wholly and unreservedly her very own, something unquestionable, I can now, without any evasion or qualification, without any false fear of losing my sense of personal worth, say frankly and firmly to my comrades that it is all true that I really committed those mistakes about which Comrade Khrushchev speaks. I committed them, I persisted in them, but I have understood and admitted them deliberately and consciously, and you know this. I spoke of this at a similar meeting more than three months ago. However, since that time . . . I have succeeded in understanding more profoundly the causes of those mistakes, and even that some of the causes lie simply in my character as a human being, which perhaps somehow hinders me in my public work.

I am sometimes inclined to substitute moral and ethical categories for political categories. . . .

Obviously, I must now be much more exacting with myself, free myself of an inclination toward abstract thinking, more rigorously verify my views on the phenomena of life by life itself . . . , see with my own eyes those enormous changes which have taken place in the life of the people, especially since the 20th Party Congress—in short, do what Comrade Khrushchev teaches and urges in his speeches.

I think that I shall be able to tell fully of the profound conclusions which I have drawn for my future life only by doing worthy work, by always remembering that any work of a Soviet writer is political work, and that it is possible to perform it with honor only by steadfastly following the Party line and Party discipline.[30]

It was in June (when Aliger made her first "confession") that the resistance of the writers began to break down. One by one they capitulated and performed the requisite ceremonies of self-criticism and self-abasement. Despite his threats, however, Khrushchev did not push for a rollback to Stalinist rigor in the arts, because that was not what he wanted. Instead, he stuck to the "middle course" he had previously outlined, rejecting "embellishing reality" and prohibiting focusing on the "negative phenomena of Soviet life." But he did lay down the law on the writer's hewing to the Party line in the arts:

The question of his [the writer's] approach to the facts of reality is clear. He does not have to force himself to adapt. The truthful representation of life from positions of Communist Party spirit [*partiinost*] is the necessity of his soul. . . . [The writer] will be able to support the positive and to show it faithfully in bright colors. But if the author takes no joy in the achievements of his characters, he will search out only the bad, the negative, digging it out of garbage heaps, and will present it as typical of life.[31]

Khrushchev thundered that he would defend the Party from any writers who tried to divert Soviet literature into the "wrong paths." During that spring and summer of 1957, Khrushchev took time and energy to give three separate speeches to writers, an indication of how much stress the Party leadership gave to the issue. Abridged versions of those speeches were combined and issued in a pamphlet under the title "For a Close Tie between Literature and Art and the Life of the People," [32] which then served as the summation of the Party line in the arts and was widely circulated and publicized through the country.

Yet, in June, just when it seemed that the regime had succeeded in bringing all the rebellious writers to heel, Ilya Ehrenburg's essay on Stendhal appeared. It explicitly points out to Soviet writers the lessons they might now learn from the French novelist's experiences a century earlier. "For me," Ehrenburg wrote, "the lessons of Stendhal lie primarily in his exceptional truthfulness." With a swift dig at Soviet cultural bureaucrats, he reminded them that because Stendhal was not a "professional writer," he would surely have been refused membership in the Soviet Writers' Union on grounds that he was a dilettante. But the major thrust of the essay was against Stalin and Stalinism:

[Stendhal] hated despotism and despised toadyism: "Even if a king is an angel, his government will destroy art—not by forbidding the subject of a picture, but by breaking the artist's spirit. . . ." Distortion of the soul by coercion, hypocrisy, bribery and threats was a major and perhaps the main theme of Stendhal's novels. . . . The crux of the matter is not the tyrant personally but the nature of tyranny. A tyrant can be intelligent or stupid, good or evil, but all the same he is all-powerful and powerless; he is frightened by conspiracies, he is flattered and deceived; the jails fill up; cowardly hypocrites whisper, and a silence settles in that is enough to stop the heart.

This was a description of cultural and intellectual life under Stalin; and it applied equally to cultural and intellectual life under Khrushchev. (There is a strange personal intensity in the essay which indictates that Ehrenburg identified closely with the French novelist, and therefore he may also have been talking about himself when he wrote, "Stendhal played at hide-and-seek all his life. Mérimée says that he learned to do this because of the Empire police and the all-seeing eye of Fouché." [33] Ehrenburg had to cope with a far more powerful political police than Fouché had ever had at his command, and with the "all-seeing" Soviet secret-police chiefs—Yezhov, Yagoda, and Beria—far more cruel and ruthless than Fouché.)

With the anti-Party group for the moment defeated, and with the memory of the Hungarian revolt fresh in his mind, early in 1957 Khrushchev began a cautious retreat from his de-Stalinization campaign. Slowly, he began to refurbish some of Stalin's reputation, so that in literature the Party now took the position that although the "cult of the individual" had been quite detrimental,

the unhealthy distortions which took place . . . should not be mistaken for the main line of our literary development, which remained sound and creative during every stage in the development of Soviet society. The attempts of some writers abroad to declare all Soviet literature of the past two decades "ruined" by the cult of the individual leader constitute part of the broad and slanderous anti-Soviet campaign waged by the enemies of Communism in a vain attempt to weaken the great attraction of the 20th Party Congress decisions and to cast doubt on the world achievements of the socialist camp.[34]

On the second front, the regime attacked *Novy mir* and *Literaturnaya Moskva*, the two publications most responsible for printing the objectionable works of the liberal writers. "The great literary monthly, *Novy Mir*, was particularly passionate in tone [then]," Giuseppe Boffa reported, reflecting both the Communist concern and conclusion, "and was quickly attacked. The Party had good reason to be against such an extreme tone; it was afraid that criticism, desirable in itself, might go so far as to become despairing, indiscriminate and without perspective." [35] What Boffa meant by those three terms was that a truthful picture of Soviet society passionately rendered might challenge the Party's ultimate authority in the life and arts of the nation, and perhaps even lead to such upheavals as had occurred in Hungary.

In the Soviet Union editors in publishing houses and on magazines have always played an especially important role, because they act as both literary appraisers and Party censors. During the Stalin era, most carefully avoided being shot, imprisoned, or exiled; but in the Khrushchev era the penalties had been reduced, and many of the more courageous editors, in order to print new and unorthodox writing, were willing to risk losing a job, being reprimanded, or even being expelled from the Party. For this reason, changes in the ruling elite's literary policies were, logically, almost always represented by shifts in editorial personnel. During 1957 and 1958, for example, the editorial boards of both *Novy mir* and *Literaturnaya Moskva* were purged and the latter almost altogether disbanded, with the attendant obeisances from various members. In November, also, Fyodor Panfyorov regained the editorship of *Oktyabr* and Aleksandr Tvardovsky was restored to the helm of *Novy mir*, after both had been fired in the aftermath of the first thaw for what now, in the light of the Hungarian revolt and the Soviet literary ferment, seemed like mere peccadillos. In replacing the more conservative Konstantin Simonov, Tvardovsky once more had the opportunity to carry forward his own and *Novy mir*'s liberal traditions.

On the third front, the ruling elite began, in 1957, to make changes in the organization of the Writers' Union. Always an instrument of regimentation and coercion, the Union had been a prime target of the liberal writers who had, in 1954, tried to disband it; failing that, they had in general ignored the Union's work and meetings. During 1958, the Party leadership organized a new, higher administrative level, the Writers' Union of the RSFSR (Russian Soviet Federated Socialist Republic) in order to swamp the liberal units of the Union which were concentrated in the big cities, particularly the Moscow section, by recruiting a wave of conservative and more pliable writers from the provinces. The liberal Moscow section would have its ability to influence Union policy weakened, and tighter Party control over the nation's writers would result.[36] To make certain there would be no mistakes, the organization of the RSFSR unit was entrusted to conservative stalwarts: the critic Leonid Sobolev and the novelist and editor Vsevolod Kochetov.

Even apologist Alexander Werth remarks, "The Soviet Writers' Union is one of the world's greatest anomalies. . . . If Stalin set up the writers under one roof in 1934, it was in order to exercise on them the strictest control and to subject them to perpetual pressure of one kind or another: that is why I think the Writers' Union today [in 1967] is a particularly dangerous survival of Stalinism in Russia." Werth also shows how this RSFSR reorganization worked to the advantage of the regime and the conservatives: "The result of this system is altogether lamentable: the small minority of writers of quality are swamped by the great majority of writers of quantity, most of them hacks [*halturshchiki*] of the worst sort. The fearful weight of this overwhelming mass of hacks is bound to have a considerable influence on the bureaucrats of the Writers' Union, and it is the hacks, much more than the good writers, who have an influence on the choice and election of those bureaucrats." [37]

But if Khrushchev had threatened the writers with serious reprisals, if he had brandished the stick in a hand "that would not tremble," he also continued carefully to offer the carrot. In March 1959, two months before the Third All-Union Congress of Writers was scheduled, he removed the conservative Vsevolod Kochetov as editor-in-chief of *Literaturnaya gazeta* and replaced him with the presumably less doctrinaire S. S. Smirnov. At the Third Congress, moreover, he ousted the conservative poet and literary bureaucrat Anatoly Surkov as head of the Soviet Writers' Union and replaced him with the ostensibly more moderate Konstantin Fedin.[38]

The Party's attempts at "unified guidance of writers"—that is simultaneous ideological and literary instruction and control—through the Union had never been very effective, though the Union had carried out the Party's dictates in punishing writers with dispatch and would continue to do so. Now Khrushchev organized matters so that there was a whole series of checks to keep culture on his "middle course." On one hand he appointed Fedin to head the All-Soviet Writers' Union; on the other he had the RSFSR Writers' Union organized with archconservative Sobolev as its head. Moreover, the various administrative levels of the Union throughout were subject to the additional (and dogmatic) controls of the Party organizations inside them as well as of the Party Central Committee's Department of Agitation and Propaganda (Agitprop) above them. Holding editorial positions on the periodicals and in the publishing houses were enough conservatives so that any liberal surge could quickly be spied and scotched.[39] From the Party leadership's viewpoint, therefore, it was a very good time to hold the Third Congress of Soviet Writers.

In May, at the Writers' Congress, the literary scene seemed tranquil, at least on the surface, but many of the leading writers made no public statements, and the root conflicts which had shaken the Soviet literary world were carefully buried from view and not discussed. The Party seemed to be in full control of culture, and Khrushchev went out of his way to remind everyone that no one was going to interfere with the leading role of the Party in the society, least of all the writers. "So listen, dear friends," Khrushchev announced, "if there is anyone who reveals and lays bare shortcomings and vices . . . it is the Party and its Central Committee that do this." The Party had deprived writers not only of the right to write badly but "above all of the right to write wrongly." [40] If the writers were not comforted, at least they knew exactly where they stood.

Two months later, in a public speech, Khrushchev returned to what was evidently for him a galling issue:

Among the writers in our country are individuals who say: How can there be Party guidance of literature? . . . One writer or another may sit at his country house, hatching a sniveling book, yet want it to be recognized as an expression of the sentiments of the people of our times, of all the people. Is that not a real cult of one's own personality, which, you see, does not want to suffer the guidance of the Party, expressing the will of millions? And such a man with his contrived book wants to rise above the Party, above the people.[41]

With that casuistry the second thaw came to its end, but the problems had by no means been laid to rest.

3 The Pasternak Case

> They are always shouting at the poets: "Do this! Do that!" But first of all it is necessary to speak of what the poet himself needs. The times exist for man, not man for the times.
>
> *Boris Pasternak*

Many liberal writers had been censured and criticized, some quite severely, during the years 1957 to 1959, but only one brought down the full wrath of the powers that be: Boris Pasternak, in 1958. Though Khrushchev was at that time striving to establish a more moderate, if not permissive, cultural policy, the Pasternak case showed how small the area of maneuver was for any writer in the Soviet Union.

Pasternak himself was a phenomenon in Soviet literary life, a major Russian poet who had managed to retain his integrity as a writer and as a man through all the vicissitudes of Communist rule. To have done so under Stalin was miraculous, and few, especially those of Pasternak's stature, had managed it. Yet Pasternak, like Anna Akhmatova, who had also miraculously survived, had remained an influence and example for many of the younger generation of writers that the Party was most concerned to indoctrinate.[1]

If Pasternak had survived, he had by no means flourished. Shortly after the end of World War II, when the Zhdanov decrees on the arts had shriveled the souls and the works of Soviet writers, Pasternak (with Akhmatova and Mikhail Zoshchenko) had come under severe attack from the regime and been expelled from the Writers' Union. At that time, Union secretary Fadeyev had criticized Pasternak for having contributed only a few second-rate verses to the Soviet war effort, though in the darker days of battle, the authorities had publicly commended his literary efforts and had, in fact, permitted two books of his poems to be published, in 1943 and 1945. But in the postwar political atmosphere of the restrictive and dogmatic

Zhdanov decrees, Pasternak's mistress, Olga Ivinskaya, was arrested and tortured in an effort to make her confess that she and Pasternak were "Western agents." [2] Ivinskaya's refusal to implicate Pasternak in any such trumped-up charges probably saved the poet from imprisonment, but resulted in Ivinskaya's serving a year in Lubyanka Prison and four years in a Siberian labor camp from which she was released (like Solzhenitsyn) only in the general amnesty after Stalin's death.[3]

By and large, Pasternak had saved himself by devoting his gifts to the translation of foreign works into Russian—the major Shakespearean tragedies, Goethe's *Faust*, the works of the Hungarian national poet, Sandor Petöfi, and a group of Georgian poets; but mostly he had been "writing for the drawer." (Rumor had it that one reason Stalin kept Pasternak alive was because of his translation of the poets of Stalin's native Georgia, with which the dictator was pleased. Other rumors insisted that the Machiavellian Stalin deliberately permitted Pasternak to go on writing and living so that he could use him as an example of a true and gifted artist with which to goad more compliant but less talented hacks.)

The writer Valentin Katayev, who had himself survived the purges and was knowledgeable about the literary and political personalities involved, gave a quite different picture of how Pasternak survived. He told Harrison Salisbury:

Pasternak was not a simple unworldly man as many of you in the West think. . . . He was a man of contradictions. He had his own character. But he wished to be part of the Establishment, to be recognized, to belong. He could have been a courtier of Stalin, if Stalin permitted this. He was not really a rebel at all.

Mandelshtam was outspoken. . . . He was a real opponent of Stalin. I remember once he came to our house, it must have been 1936 or 1937. He was shouting against Stalin—what a terrible man Stalin was. We were terrified, my wife and I. We had two small children. Pasternak was never like that.

Some writers still blame Pasternak for not standing up more strongly to Stalin.[4]

In April 1954, after not publishing in the Soviet Union since the end of the war, Pasternak took advantage of the first thaw to have ten of his poems published. These, later to be included in *Doctor*

Zhivago, appeared in *Znamya* and soon came under official critical attack as pessimistic and decadent,[5] and as examples of applying Pomerantsev's canons of "sincerity" to literature.

Shortly after the end of World War II, Pasternak had begun to write a novel which was eventually to become *Doctor Zhivago*, and by the end of 1955 he had finished his work on it. Taking advantage of the second thaw, in 1956, he circulated the manuscript to several publishing houses and magazines, among them the journal *Novy mir*, whose editorial board collectively sent him a personal letter of rejection which subsequently was to play a significant role in the government's condemnation of Pasternak and the novel.[6] But at the time the authorities seemed to be considering a publication of a censored version of the novel—which Pasternak would have consented to—but no decision was forthcoming.

In the interim Pasternak had sent a copy of the manuscript of *Doctor Zhivago* to Giangiacomo Feltrinelli, a prominent Italian publisher and a member of the Italian Communist Party. Feltrinelli was empowered to arrange for publishing various foreign-language editions, and did so; at the same time, he prepared his own Italian translation of the novel. Then Moscow and Italian Communist leaders asked Feltrinelli to postpone the publication of the book for six months while the Kremlin decided what it was going to do. Subsequently, as the Italian publication date loomed closer, Anatoly Surkov, head of the Soviet Writers' Union, and a leading functionary of the Italian Communist Party combined to attempt to induce Feltrinelli to give up publishing the book altogether. They cajoled and threatened, warning Feltrinelli that if he issued the book he would be endangering Pasternak's life. Finally, a telegram bearing Pasternak's name came to Feltrinelli, and other foreign publishers who had contracted to publish the novel, requesting them to abandon publication. Feltrinelli refused, and *Doctor Zhivago* was published in Italy on November 15, 1957, to a chorus of praise, some notes of reservation and disappointment, and general agreement that the book presented serious criticisms of Soviet life.[7]

But not until almost a year later, when on October 23, 1958, the Swedish Academy announced the award of the Nobel Prize in literature to Pasternak, did the storm break. On October 25, Pasternak cabled his acceptance (in French): "Immensely thankful, touched, proud, astonished, abashed." [8]

On the same day, October 25, an anonymous article in *Literaturnaya gazeta* called down the rage of the Kremlin's rulers on Pasternak, accusing him of scorning the Russian people and the "Great October Revolution": "He says not one good word for our workers, peasants or soldiers," the paper pointed out, then went on to call Pasternak a slanderer, a base, small-minded, faint-hearted, and "malicious literary snob" whose novel had placed a "weapon in the hands of the enemy," for which this literary Judas had just been awarded his thirty pieces of silver, the Nobel Prize.

In the same issue, *Literaturnaya gazeta* printed the September 1956 rejection letter the editorial board of *Novy mir* had sent to Pasternak with a covering letter from the present editorial board saying that Pasternak had "flouted the elementary notions of the honor and conscience of a Soviet writer," and that the publication of the book abroad had raised an "anti-Soviet clamor . . . and is an act of pure politics hostile to our country and directed towards the fomenting of the cold war." (The covering letter of 1958 was signed by the entire editorial board, but only two of the members of that board— Konstantin Fedin and B. A. Lavrenov—were among the five signatories of the original rejection letter of September 1956. The other three were Konstantin Simonov, B. Agapov, and A. Krivitsky. In the obvious disparity between the two sets of signatures, Tvardovsky may deliberately but subtly have been making a point.) The rejection letter was a carefully thought-out and carefully written review of *Doctor Zhivago*. The editors refused to publish it for political reasons and directed their criticisms of the novel mainly to political issues in the manuscript because they believed that Pasternak had "written a political novel-sermon, par excellence." [9] The rejection letter charged that the book depicted the Bolshevik Revolution and its aftermath as a disaster for the common people and the Russian intelligentsia alike and that because this hostility to the "socialist revolution" informed the entire work, it was something that "neither editors nor the author can alter by cuts or changes." [10]

The letter also indicts Zhivago and, by implication, Pasternak for being intellectuals "bloated with a sense of [their] own self-importance," involved only with themselves and their own sufferings, turned against the revolution by physical discomfort and deprivation, feeling in no way a part of the nation or any responsibility to the people at large. "This is almost pathological individualism, a naive grandiloquence of people who cannot and do not want to see anything around them and who therefore attach a comically exaggerated importance to their persons"; "Zhivago sees the old life broken up and transformed around him in a brutal, costly, difficult process, the expediency of which can only be gauged from the standpoint of national interests, from the standpoint of a man who puts the nation above everything else. And this is precisely what Zhivago lacks." [11]

Max Hayward gives an exceedingly subtle and intelligent interpretation of why the Soviet authorities hated *Doctor Zhivago* so much. He believes that Zhivago was one of the "great superfluous men of Russian literature," a man who despite his intelligence and good will could never sufficiently focus his gifts to act positively and effectively. What enraged the Party about the novel, Hayward believes, was that it treats Zhivago's ineffectuality with sympathy and in so doing appeals to "the non-activist people, mainly intellectuals, [and so] destroys the position of moral superiority that [the Communists] have created for the political activists." [12] This is a shrewd insight, but it may be oversubtle and may overlook the main thrust of both the book and its threat to the Soviet regime. True, the Party has always been concerned with the "superfluous men" and "Oblomovist" inertia traditionally endemic among the Russian intelligentsia; but the *Novy mir* criticism is probably more to the point. What horrified the Party stalwarts was an evaluation of their achievement as an unmitigated disaster for everyone concerned. What appalled them was Pasternak's defense of the individual human personality as more important than any "collective": people, nation, state, Party. What defeated them was his refusal, in the novel as in life, to accept the transformation of society by brutal means: Pasternak (and Zhivago) could see such a transformation only as brutalizing. Pasternak has Zhivago say, "I was inclined towards revolution, but now I believe that nothing can be achieved by force." And when Zhivago says to Lara, "This construction of new worlds and transition periods is an end in itself to them [the guiding spirits of the Revolution and the Party]. This is all they know and all they can know. . . . A man is born to live, not to prepare for life," Pasternak is striking at the very taproot of the Party's perpetual (and megalomaniac) claim to direct and control the lives and sacrifices of more than two hundred million people now and for generations to come.

The type of campaign the regime directed against Pasternak would tend to confirm such an interpretation. Directly after the Nobel Prize award to Pasternak, Konstantin Fedin went to Pasternak and, as a friend of long standing as well as a writer and literary bureaucrat, warned, "Do you realize that this is not a question of literature, it is pure politics. You have become a pawn in the game that political intriguers are playing. You are now standing on the brink and if you overstep it you will sunder your connections with Russian literature and the Russian people." [13] It was a warning and a threat that Fedin was to make again, some years later, to Solzhenitsyn, and in almost precisely the same terms.

On October 26, the very next day after Pasternak's cable accepting the award, one of Moscow's specialists in journalistic vituperation, David Zaslavsky, was let loose. In an article entitled "Reactionary Uproar over a Literary Weed," Zaslavsky attacked Pasternak as a writer of miniscule talents, isolated from Soviet life and the people, a man who had always been hostile to Marxist philosophy and to "socialist realism" in literature. He dubbed Zhivago an "infuriated moral freak," and said that the entire novel was "low-grade reactionary hackwork." Pasternak was merely a literary weed in the flowering garden of Soviet letters and if Pasternak had "a spark of Soviet dignity left . . . *he would reject the Nobel Prize.*" [14]

Though *Doctor Zhivago* was widely praised, even called a masterpiece, the acclaim was by no means unanimous, even among presumably objective critics. There were a wide gamut of reactions to the book and many dissenting opinions of its worth.[15] Even the *Novy mir* letter of rejection contained some telling literary, as distinct from political, criticism of the novel: remarks about hasty writing, disjointed impressions, and "lifeless and didactically dry sections especially in the second half of the novel." One of the more interesting evaluations was by the Yugoslav critic Mihajlo Mihajlov, who thought the novel artistically inadequate because the plot and general structure were rickety. Yet Mihajlov also thought the novel "unequaled in its time" in Russia. In judging Zhivago's career and character, Mihajlov singles out the same crucial scene that the *Novy mir* editors had, the scene in which the Bolsheviks shoot down the young boys from the White military academy. Both the critic and the editors saw in that scene the moral and political crux of the book. Mihajlov comments that Zhivago obstinately refused "to come to grips with the fact that there comes a time when not to resist is to be no longer a man." [16]

October 27, 1958, the day following Zaslavsky's attack, the Writers' Union expelled Pasternak for "actions incompatible with the calling of a Soviet writer," and condemned him for aiming "against the traditions of Russian literature, against the people, against peace and socialism." [17]

Two days later, on October 29, at Moscow's Luzhniki Sports Stadium, before an audience of fourteen thousand that included Khrushchev and many top Party leaders, Vladimir Semichastny, First Secretary of the Komsomol (a Stalinist and later head of the political police), descending to the nadir of abuse, compared Pasternak to a pig "who fouled the spot where he ate and cast filth on those by whose labor he lives and breathes." Semichastny then "suggested" that if Pasternak chose to become a real emigrant instead of an "internal emigrant," no obstacles would be put in his way; no one would stop his departure from the Soviet Union for a "capitalist paradise." [18] (Such a threat had special meaning for Pasternak, because his parents, the painter Leonid Pasternak and the concert pianist Rosa Kaufman, and his two sisters had left the Soviet Union in 1921. Pasternak, however, had not considered emigration at that time, nor evidently at any time thereafter.)

The Party pressure had been swift, powerful, and overwhelming. Pasternak capitulated. On that same day, he took Zaslavsky's "advice" and sent a telegram to the Swedish Academy renouncing the Nobel Prize:

Considering the meaning this award has been given in the society to which I belong, I must reject this undeserved prize which has been presented to me. Please do not receive my voluntary rejection with displeasure.

But Pasternak's abasement was not yet complete.

Two days later, on October 31, after showering a torrent of abuse on him as venomous as that of the professional Party hack journalists, the Moscow writers adopted a resolution asking the government to deprive the traitor "B. Pasternak" of his citizenship.[19] Among those who attacked him were such well-known and reputedly liberal writers as Leonid Martynov, who had himself spent several years in one of the Arctic concentration camps and who would introduce himself with the words "Leonid Martynov, enemy of the people"; [20] Boris Slutsky; Boris Polevoi, who called Pasternak a "literary Vlasov"; and K. L. Zelinsky who, in high dudgeon after reading *Doctor Zhivago,* reported: "I felt as though I had literally been spat upon. The whole of my life seemed to be defiled in the novel. Everything I had put my energy into for forty years, my creative energy and aspirations, my hopes, had all been defiled." The novel was execrated as written in mediocre prose and poorly constructed, with impoverished philosophy, but the focus of the attack was: "The novel portrays the whole of our people's struggle in the years of the Revolution and the Civil War, waged in the name of the enlightened ideas of the October Revolution, as a series of brutalities, executions and intrigues among leaders. A series of unjust acts—that is what the whole thing is made out to be." Because of that, *Doctor Zhivago* is simply an "apologia for treachery," and "a godsend for . . . our enemies." [21]

On the next day, November 1, Pasternak wrote directly to Khrushchev, apologizing because he had not realized that he and his book would become the center of a Western political campaign; when he had realized it, he had renounced the Nobel Prize. But, he continued—and here the note of pleading, though dignified, was plain: "I am linked with Russia by my birth, life and work. I cannot imagine my fate separate from and outside Russia. . . . A departure beyond the borders of my country would for me be equivalent to death, and for that reason I request you not to take that extreme." [22]

Still Pasternak had not been made to drink the cup to its very dregs. On November 5, four days later, he made the required public self-criticism (and self-abasement) in *Pravda;* saying that he had never intended to harm either the state or the people, Pasternak confessed, "When I saw the scope of the political campaign around my novel and realized that this award was a political step which has now led to monstrous consequences, I conveyed my voluntary rejection on my own initiative and without any compulsion."

The assault on him now began to abate. In December, at the congress of the Writers' Union of the RSFSR, Surkov described Pasternak as a traitor, an apostate and a "putrid internal émigré." But what really concerned Pasternak were the threats to Olga Ivinskaya and her daughter. Once before, Ivinskaya had been his hostage to fortune, and his misgivings were not now misplaced, although the authorities did not take steps against Ivinskaya until after Pasternak was dead.

On February 11, 1959, the *London Daily Mail*, without the author's permission, published a brief Pasternak poem entitled "The Nobel Prize." Profoundly pessimistic, it lamented:

> But what wicked thing have I done,
> I, the murderer and villain?
> I made the whole world weep
> Over my beautiful land.
>
> Even so, as I near the grave,
> I believe the time will soon come
> When the spirit of good will prevail
> Over malice and evil.[23]

Though appeals in behalf of Pasternak came from all over the world, from such eminent writers and intellectuals as Bertrand Russell, J. B. Priestley, Graham Greene, and even such Communist writers as Jorge Amado, the gifted Brazilian novelist, and Halldor Laxness, the Icelandic Nobel Prize winner in literature, who cabled his objections to Khrushchev directly, none seemed to have any effect.

Years later the conservative novelist Galina Serebryakova was to publish her reminiscences of Pasternak, in which she called *Doctor Zhivago* a boring novel and described Pasternak as a man "of great talent who sincerely loved his country in his own way and wished it to flourish, but was absolutely separated from its everyday labors and life. . . . The world was torn apart, steep icebergs rose and fell and new ones were born in pain, but Pasternak covered his face with his hands and stood aside. Behind compassion he did not see the main thing. Mourning dead friends, he nevertheless did not venture out of his chocolate sphere." [24]

Some critics believe that much of the clamor surrounding Pasternak and the novel was part of a power struggle in the Writers' Union. *Literaturnaya gazeta,* the organ of the Union, which led the attack on Pasternak, was then edited by Vsevolod Kochetov and his deputy editor, V. Druzhin, and both of them were die-hard dogmatists.[25] When subsequently interviewed by Patricia Blake, Kochetov did say that he never wanted to see *Dr. Zhivago* published in the Soviet Union, because it was a badly written book. Even more, he opposed its publication, he said, because of its contents: "What would be your attitude towards a writer like Pasternak who described your countrymen as gangsters?" [26] Therefore, I think the emphasis is misplaced. The Party leadership wanted Pasternak shamed and punished, and the dogmatists in the intra-Union power struggle may have taken advantage of that, but I doubt that it was the other way round. Harold Swayze points out that when *Literaturnaya gazeta* was "reorganized" in March 1959 to fit it into the "middle course" Khrushchev was trying to maintain, both Kochetov and Druzhin lost their jobs.[27] Here, too, I believe that Swayze mistakes the way the regime, in punishing and rewarding people, uses its favors and those done for it. The desire to come to some accommodation with the writers in 1959 meant "appeasing" some of the liberal ones in a public way. Removing Kochetov, a liberal *bête noire,* and his deputy was a good "symbolic" political gesture. The excuse given to Kochetov and Druzhin may have been that they were being reprimanded for their role in the Pasternak affair, but it need not have been, and very likely was not, the essential reason.

In 1967, Werth was to report:

Those who had taken part in the hounding of Pasternak, now a sick and deeply discouraged man, were feeling uneasy about it, too. They blamed not so much Pasternak as the Nobel Prize Committee, for having tried to stage an "anti-Soviet provocation" by awarding the prize to him. As for him, he was a "pigheaded old man" who had rejected even the slightest cuts and changes in the manuscript of *Dr. Zhivago.* "Of course, of course we would have published it"; and some even said, "It was a mistake we didn't print a small edition of even the full text;

there would have been a few nasty notices in the press and that would have been the end of it." And it was said that Khrushchev, "who had never read a line of Pasternak in his life," thought it had all been rather a stupid mistake to make such a fuss.[28]

But this was hindsight and a not unusual rewriting of Soviet history by the Party leadership and its stalwarts.

On May 30, 1960, a little more than a year after the regime had brought Pasternak to his knees and forced him to relinquish the Nobel Prize, he was dead of cancer of the stomach. He was buried in the small country graveyard near his home in Peredelkino. The Soviet press and radio made only the briefest mention of his demise,[29] and though no important officials of the government, the Party, or the Writers' Union attended the funeral, the Politburo had during his final illness sent physicians from the Kremlin hospital to care for the poet. Despite the fact that no public announcements of the funeral services were made, several thousand people came to pay their respects—among them at least a hundred KGB (political police) agents in addition to the ordinary militia.[30] Pasternak was buried in his only suit, the suit his father had given him. The mourners included the concert pianists Svyatoslav Richter and Judina, Konstantin Paustovsky, Vsevolod Ivanov, and Veniamin Kaverin. Ilya Ehrenburg was in Stockholm, and his wife, Lyuba, represented him. (Stockholm is only a short flight from Moscow, and had Ehrenburg been truly intent on a "symbolic" appearance at the obsequies, the three days between Pasternak's death and the funeral services would have given him ample time to travel from Sweden to Peredelkino. Four years later, Ehrenburg would remark sarcastically about poet Andrey Voznesensky, "Andryusha is developing in the shadow of Pasternak. No doubt, it is a nice shadow, but still a shadow. Incidentally, when the clamor against Pasternak was raised Andryusha was bravely silent and did not take a stand in defense of his teacher.") [31] Pasternak's coffin was carried out of the small Church of the Transfiguration by Andrey Sinyavsky and Yuli Daniel.

Paustovsky, who had come to Peredelkino and stayed for several days after Pasternak's death, then went to Moscow, to the Presidium of the Writers' Union, to try to persuade it to restore the dead poet to membership in the Union. The issue was carried all the way to the Politburo where Mikhail Suslov was said to have categorically forbidden the restoration.[32]

Seven weeks later, the KGB arrested Olga Ivinskaya and her daughter, charging both with currency manipulations involving Pasternak's foreign royalties.[33] They were tried on December 7, 1960, found guilty, and sentenced to eight and five years respectively in Siberian penal colonies. Soon, a campaign of gossip, officially instigated and disseminated, created the image of Ivinskaya as an adventuress who had taken advantage of Pasternak in his dotage and unduly influenced him. Not only was it whispered that Ivinskaya was mercenary, having endeavored to usurp Pasternak's royalties to the exclusion of his legitimate heirs, but she was also assigned the responsibility for his "anti-Soviet" views. The latter accusation may very well have been the first step in laying the groundwork for the gradual but ultimate rehabilitation of Pasternak's poetry now that he was no longer inconveniently alive. Seven years later, Kornei Chukovsky told Alexander Werth that during the last two years of his life Pasternak had felt like a hounded animal and would often burst into sobs because of the gratuitous malevolence and viciousness people displayed toward him. The elderly Russian novelist and critic, and friend of Pasternak, had no good words for Ivinskaya:

She *was* a bad woman, she made him sign any old thing to get hold of his foreign royalties, and she went in for currency speculation in a big way. But there was something even worse. Ivinskaya played on his senile eroticism—he was nearly seventy then. Pasternak's wife, Zinaida, would nurse him when he was ill, give him enemas, carry bed pans. But the moment he was better, he would rush off to Ivinskaya. No, Zinaida—she died only a few months ago—was a very wonderful woman, but she got a very, very raw deal. She was a true companion to Boris; but Ivinskaya played a very evil part in the last years of Boris Leonidovich's life.[34]

Yury Krotkov reported that Pasternak's wife, "in the presence of his brother and Nina [Tabidze], asked Pasternak if she should call Olga Ivinskaya to his bedside, but Pasternak refused. Ivinskaya was Pasternak's literary secretary and his mistress. Every day she came to the *dacha* and stood waiting outside the gate. The doctors and nurses went to her, reported to her tersely on Pasternak's condition and sent her away." [35] Krotkov does not make clear what he himself saw and what Nina Tabidze told him. Even if Mrs. Tabidze's reporting is perfectly accurate, one can easily conceive myriad reasons why Pasternak might not have wanted to see Ivinskaya or have her see him under those circumstances, other than the final act of rejection Krotkov implies was the poet's motivation. Whatever the difficulties and unfairness in Pasternak's treatment of his wife and his mistress, such complicated relationships between complicated people are always difficult, if not impossible, to unravel. Chukovsky seems to do Ivinskaya less than justice. Her earlier imprisonment and torture at the hands of the political police while trying to protect Pasternak would seem to indicate that she was interested primarily in Pasternak's welfare rather than his royalties.

4 The Heirs of Stalin

Poetry is not a peaceful chapel,
Poetry is a cruel war.
It contains its own deceptive maneuvers.
When there's war, then war is what poetry must be.

Yevgeny Yevtushenko

In 1961, the second stage of de-Stalinization resulting from the Twenty-second Party Congress had powerful repercussions in the arts.[1] What was happening in literature came to be of immense political import. The picture emerging from the liberal writers' portrayal of Soviet life showed that fundamental changes in Soviet institutions were necessary if conditions were to improve. The institutions of Soviet life remained essentially Stalinist; Stalin was dead, but his heirs remained in power, and those of his cohorts who had been accomplices in his crimes had neither been brought to account nor punished. It was from this contradictory reality in the theory of de-Stalinization that most of the difficulties for the ruling elite were to flow.

Though none of the liberal writers had drawn up a specifically political program, it was no more possible to keep the literary *social* criticism from overflowing into politics than to keep the political *social* criticism from overflowing into literature. If de-Stalinization involved the most serious criticisms of Stalin for his failures as a wartime leader, for the purges of the Party, the military, and the government, for the imprisonment and death of millions in the camps, this could not be kept out of literature. And because in a country where there is no other public forum for the discussion of political questions discussion will flow into whatever channels are available, in the Soviet Union they poured into literature. The Party leadership, locked in a struggle for power, might attempt to use the liberal writers calculatedly for its own purposes; but the writers in their ways were bound to attempt to turn the regime's purposes to their own account. As anti-Stalinism gave Khrushchev the lever with which to pry the "men of the old order"—Malenkov, Molotov, Kaganovich—from power, so, too, it gave the literary liberals their means of discomfiting the literary Stalinists—Vsevolod Kochetov, Nikolai Gribachev, Anatoly Sofronov, Leonid Sobolev, D. Starikov, Vladimir Yermilov, Georgy Markov, to name only some of the more doctrinaire.

Because coexistence between Stalinist institutions and an anti-Stalinist literature was impossible, literary and political criticisms coalesced and reinforced one another until the literary "opposition" was in some measure politicalized and began to evolve, as much as was possible in Soviet circumstances, into a kind of political opposition.[2] Through literature, at least, people might conceive of themselves as thinking freely and, in some measure, expressing themselves freely—if only by buying and reading a book or attending a poetry recital. Not self-consciously organized and with neither a thought-out political program nor any profound roots in or influence on the masses of the Russian people, the writers strove first for a literature unshackled by "socialist realism" and Party control and censorship. But that struggle was given added impetus by de-Stalinization and liberalization and moved them toward the most serious and fundamental criticisms of Soviet society

As the fear of physical liquidation and repression was reduced, the literary intellectuals became braver and freer in carrying out the Khushchevian de-Stalinization and liberalization; but in their thirst for "truth" and "sincerity," for writing candidly about the world they saw around them, they were bound to come into basic conflict with the aims of the Party and the government. The writers, in writing truthfully, were bound, either explicitly or by implication, to ask questions which cut to the core of Soviet life. How, for instance, did a maniac and monster like Stalin achieve and retain power in "socialist" conditions? Why had not the Party and its "leading representatives" unseated the dictator the moment his "distortions" become apparent? How could such horrible means—Stalinism—produce a halcyon end—socialism? One question inevitably led to another and finally to that unwritten and unspoken question: Was it perhaps precisely *because* of the Soviet institutions they had built that Stalin came to leadership?

These questions were by no means abstract, for they had immediate political consequences.[3] Two of those consequences became problems which afflicted and continue to afflict Soviet society: one, known as the problems of the "heirs of Stalin," after the Yevtushenko poem, was concerned with the present fate and power of those who had carried out Stalin's policies and shared his guilt; the second, the issue of "fathers and sons," after the Turgenev novel, was concerned with the differences in viewpoint between generations. The two problems were indissolubly connected by the single issue of "clean hands," for the younger generation, which had not shared in the depravities of power under Stalin, were by virtue of their age in a position to criticize their elders with impunity, and to ask them to justify themselves.

In de-Stalinization, therefore, Khrushchev had loosed the whirlwind, and though the government would attempt to provide its own answers to some of these problems—it would explain, for instance, that the people and the Party had gone on "building socialism" and winning the war in spite of Stalin and his "distortions"—the answers were not credible. Moreover, those in the ruling elite who had been compromised by Stalinism, as most of them had been in one way or another, were bound to balk, terrified not only of the erosion of Party control and bureaucratic discipline which de-Stalinization had provoked, but ultimately fearing that they might lose their necks. If Stalin is disavowed, those associated with him must be purged. If society is liberalized, they lose their jobs, their *dachas*, perhaps their lives. In short, effective de-Stalinization can come "only with a revolutionary purge of personnel that would shake Soviet society to its foundations." This situation applies in the Party, the government, the police, the armed forces as it applies in the universities, the Academy of Sciences, in law, in the Writers' Union and in the magazines, newspapers, and publishing houses.[4]

Those who had been Stalin's accomplices were therefore put into the position of having to defend the late dictator to defend themselves, for their own pasts were called into question every time the Stalinist past was called into question. The Stalinists and neo-Stalinists resisted, demanding discipline and orthodoxy in literature and, in general, stressing the positive aspects of the Stalinist past, the constructive role of the Party, the government, and the political police.

The atmosphere had begun to change in 1959, not long after the Third Writers' Congress, as the continuing pressure for liberalization was reinforced by the legal reforms of 1958. In the summer of 1959, Ilya Ehrenburg provoked another literary controversy in an essay, "The Laws of Art," which took much the same position he and Pomerantsev had taken in 1953, favoring authentic and "sincere" art, art which faced and told the truth and struck out in new directions.[5] The following summer, in August 1960, *Novy mir* began to print Ehrenburg's memoirs, *People, Years—Life*, which was in time to raise once more some of the major questions concerning Stalinism. Peter Benno astutely remarked that the "success of Ehrenburg's memoirs is to be explained largely by the fact that they made available to the younger Soviet generation, for the first time, a version of the history of Russian literature in the twentieth century which, however fragmentary and even at times not quite honest, reasonably approximates the full story. . . . *Ehrenburg's memoirs constitute for Soviet cultural history the same revelation that Khrushchev's attacks on Stalin were for political history.*"[6] In January 1961, *Novy mir* followed with Viktor Nekrasov's *Kira Georghievna*, a novel about a man returning from a Soviet concentration camp, but it was not until the autumn of that year, when Yevtushenko exposed the painful sore of Soviet anti-Semitism in a poem called "Babi Yar," that de-Stalinization seemed once more in vogue. Named for a gully in Kiev where the Nazis had murdered more than thirty thousand Jews during World War II, the poem focused on Soviet, not Nazi, anti-Semitism; and Soviet anti-Semitism was one of the characteristics associated with Stalin and the neo-Stalinists. Anti-Semitism recalled the Doctors' Plot under Stalin, and it was a liberal benchmark for identifying dogmatists, because anti-Semites were most numerous among the bureaucrats and the common people who would tend to be the strongest supporters of the heirs of Stalin. When he was First Secretary of the Ukrainian Communist Party, Khrushchev had publicly promised to build a monument to the victims of Babi Yar, but "the place remains to this day a desolate garbage dump." [7] Khrushchev himself is commonly thought to have been an anti-Semite, and Andrey Sinyavsky remarked, "One cannot help but recall in this connection Khrushchev's *cri de coeur* against the Jews: 'They are all individualists and all intellectuals. They want to talk about everything, they want to discuss everything, they want to debate everything—and they come to totally different conclusions!' " [8] Such Jewish emphasis on free discussion and democratic multifariousness was not calculated to help either in imposing the monolithic Party line or in keeping intellectuals hewing to it. The day after Yevtushenko read "Babi Yar" for the first time at a public lecture at the Moscow Polytechnical Institute, it was published.[9] In the poem, Yevtushenko denounced the "pogrom thugs" who roared, "Beat the Yids, and save Russia":

> O my Russian people!
> You are really international at heart.
> But the unclean
> Have often loudly taken in vain
> Your most pure name. . . .
>
> Let the *Internationale* ring out
> When the last anti-Semite on earth is buried.
> There is no Jewish blood in mine
> But I am hated by every anti-Semite as a Jew.
> And for this reason
> I am a true Russian.[10]

A hail of abuse descended on Yevtushenko, including an attack from conservative critic Alexey Markov, who called him a "pigmy who had forgotten the people he belonged to." In speaking openly and strongly of Soviet anti-Semitism and its connection with Soviet alcoholism, Yevtushenko had contradicted the official contention that there was no anti-Semitism in the Soviet Union and had, of course, called forth an unseemly outburst of anti-Semitic invective. Though Yevtushenko later testified that, of the more than twenty thousand letters he received about the poem, only thirty or forty were abusive, the regime's continuing use of anti-Semitism as an instrument of policy would seem to indicate its broad-scale effectiveness. When, after the poem was published, Yevtushenko was assigned a couple of husky Komsomol guards because of threats of physical violence, he was embarrassed and remarked, a bit prematurely, "In our country, it is the bastards who are in danger." [11] (This kind of "revolutionary romanticism"—seeing what one would like to see or hope for, rather than what is—is often as characteristic of the liberal writers as it is of the dogmatists. Yevtushenko's account of how "Babi Yar" came to be printed gives the same kind of romanticized version of the fear and tension involved in the Soviet editorial-censorship process.) [12]

The year 1961 also saw the publication of an anthology of liberal writers entitled *Pages from Tarussa*, which included such men as Paustovsky and Bulat Okhudzhava, and such older modernists as Marina Tsvetayeva and Nikolay Zabolotsky. The anthology was issued in an edition of seventy-five thousand copies but withdrawn from public sale by the authorities after only a fraction had been sold.[13] Copies continued to be on sale in the special bookstores reserved for members of the Writers' Union, and eventually, in 1962, Khrushchev himself lifted the ban on the collection. Earlier, in 1959 and 1960, three issues of an underground journal, *Syntax*, had been circulated; and in spring 1961 it was followed by *Phoenix 61*. Their views were politically liberal and literarily modernist, and they and their successors—*Phoenix 66, Tetradi, Russkoye slovo, Kolokol*, and most important of all, the *Chronicle of Current Events*—gradually became the publications around which literary and then political liberal resistance to neo-Stalinism coalesced. Why the government "permitted"—if it did permit—them to circulate remains one of the essential questions in gauging both the strength and the persistence of what Andrei Amalrik was to call the Democratic Movement in the USSR and the intentions of the Kremlin.

The conservatives were by no means routed. At the Twenty-second Party Congress, in October 1961, they not only pressed their own views, but also assailed Ehrenburg and Yevtushenko, while Tvardovsky endeavored to defend the liberal outlook. Yet, in the atmosphere of the Congress, a subtle shift of opinion favoring the liberals was apparent; one evidence was Tvardovsky's election to the Central Committee of the Party as a candidate member. Khrushchev's continuing attacks on his opponents, his pressing de-Stalinization, were effective enough to cause Stalin's embalmed

corpse to be removed from the Lenin Mausoleum but not sufficiently effective to rout his opponents altogether. (Harry Schwartz
believes that there was widespread shock in the USSR after the
Twenty-second Congress because many Soviet citizens simply knew
nothing of the Khrushchev "secret speech" exposing Stalin at the
1956 Twentieth Party Congress.[14] But Yevtushenko reported that
the 1956 text of the secret speech was read at Party meetings
throughout the country, and afterward Party members "went away,
their eyes on the ground. Probably many among the older people
tortured themselves with the question: had they lived their lives in
vain?") [15]

Conservatives in literature retained many of their strongholds, but
some changes in literary life seemed to favor the liberals. Kochetov,
an object of particular abhorrence to the liberals, succeeded to the
editorship of the journal *Oktyabr* in 1961, after Panfyorov's death.
On the other hand, the reactionary *Literatura i zhizn* was reorganized, and four of its major editors, all dogmatists—D. Starikov,
Aleksandr Dymshits, Yefim Permitin, and Semyon Babayevsky—
were dismissed. (In a sensitive though brief interview with Kochetov, Patricia Blake gives some indication of the man's personality
and point of view. Kochetov told her: "Some of our writers are
trying to do as you say, following the Western idea that life must
be described as it is. But this is not art. It's the destruction of art.
Art should certainly express truth, but only by certain means. The
aim of Soviet art today must be to form the consciousness of the
people while the material basis of communism is being established.
. . . Only great art that educates and uplifts is genuinely loved by
the great mass of people.") [16]

Two leading liberal writers, novelist Aksyonov and poet Yevtushenko, were added to the editorial board of the youth magazine
Yunost; in April, Voznesensky and Boris Slutsky were named to the
board of the RSFSR Writers' Union after five conservatives in that
dogmatist stronghold had been either blackballed—Sobolev and N.
Abalkin, *Pravda*'s literary editor—or not nominated—Kochetov,
Gribachev, and Sofronov. Aksyonov, a member of the younger generation and one of the dogmatists' chief targets, had only a little
while earlier declared: "[Today's] youth was being formed in the
past few years when the Party and people were involved in the

decisive battle against remnants of the personality cult. . . . Young people rejected the soul-destroying routine of those times, but, unfortunately, they still meet this routine fairly frequently." [17] On a poetry-reading and lecture tour in England, Yevtushenko was continuing to declare:

The very fact that in my poems I attack bureaucracy, dogmatism, chauvinism, means precisely that I am a Communist in my convictions. For me Communism and bureaucracy by no means go together but are simply incompatible.

This applies not only to me but to the whole younger generation of Russians, who are increasingly beginning to feel themselves master of their own country.[18]

This stress on the younger generation as opposed to the older was something which the conservatives could not condone, and ultimately something which none of the ruling elite was willing to accept publicly, for if they admitted the alienation and the opposition of the young, then all they had fought for would have been for nought: they would have alienated the very generation they had groomed to carry on in their place.

In published writings de-Stalinization led to more and more searing criticisms of every aspect of Soviet life: the farms and factories, the Party and military, the alienated youth and the increasingly bourgeois bureaucrats. *Yunost* printed Aksyonov's "A Ticket to the Stars" and Viktor Rozov's "A B C D E," both of which showed youth alienated from the Party and its policies, and youth's rebellion against the advice and standards of the older generation.[19] So violent was the conservative reaction to these two works that the editor of *Yunost*, the gifted novelist Valentin Katayev, was forced out of his post and replaced by Boris Polevoi. In the spring, excerpts from Konstantin Simonov's war-novel-in-progress, *Soldiers Are Not Born*, containing devastating criticisms of Stalin's wartime military judgment, were published in *Izvestia*. In one scene of the novel, for example, two high-ranking Soviet officers—one a general—who have fought in the Stalingrad battle are reliving the campaign, and one remarks: "And you don't always understand right off where will-power ends and unfathomable obstinacy begins, sometimes costing hundreds of thousands of lives and whole cemeteries of wrecked equipment. . . . Yes, Stalin is Stalin." [20]

Also in the spring, *Novy mir* published Yury Bondarev's *Silence*, a novel in which the whole of postwar Stalinist life between 1945 and 1949 is assailed as corrupt, ugly, and vicious. The hypocrisy, arbitrariness, and injustice of the Party and the political police are especially denounced.[21] Bondarev had chosen the title of his novel advisedly, and it can "be interpreted in various ways: at first, *Silence* (*tishina*) is merely the name of a market in the Zamoskvorechie [a Moscow district]. Then it acquires the meaning of a period of peace following the war [the silence of the guns]; finally, it is the silence born of fear, full of suffering, the silence of solitude, where no one can help and where the individual is powerless [against the depredations of an arbitrary and indifferent government]." [22] The novel tells how a young combat veteran is persecuted by the manipulations of Party comrades and how his father is unjustly imprisoned by an indifferent and vicious political police. Its tone of outrage at the intrigues, greed, and shoddiness of postwar Soviet life was long to remain a subject of contention in more doctrinaire literature and Party circles.

The continued attacks on Bondarev's *Silence* called the novel disappointing because of the way it dealt with young people's adjustment in the postwar world to the moral conflicts that arose between their aspirations and the Stalin cult; and Bondarev was reprimanded for having tried to deal with a large and complex theme without sufficient "ideological vigilance and maturity, clarity of vision and depth of psychological analysis." [23]

Konstantin Paustovsky defended both the book and its author in what was a defense of all the new liberal writers against the denunciations of the conservatives:

If only this book did not exist at all, if only it would go away! Then we wouldn't have to discuss it. It is so much easier to follow the axioms, "It's no affair of mine. Let well enough alone. Don't wash dirty linen in public." These base, allegedly popular truths are the rule for cowards. . . .

If you are an unprejudiced person you will realize immediately how honest and frank this book is. With sharp and bitter power it reminds us about what we must not forget. About the times of the cult of the individual, about the years of terrible misfortune for all the people, which cost the country so many human victims and moral losses. . . .

There were still people who attempted to give an innocent appearance to the things that occurred during the "cult" and almost to show that they had been for the best. Every attempt to justify the "cult" —in the face of those who perished, in the face of the most elementary human conscience—is in itself monstrous.[24]

The attack on Bondarev was to continue, nonetheless, combined with attacks on other writers such as Bulat Okhudzhava [25] and Grigory Baklanov,[26] both of whom had written of the "Great Fatherland War" in more realistic and "pacifistic" terms.

During 1962 liberal sentiment began to assume the proportions of outright dissidence, though, in the main, the liberal criticism remained within the bounds of "socialist humanism," putting a "human face" on Soviet "socialism," trying to prompt the regime to live up to the promises it had made as part of de-Stalinization. But more began to be involved. In January young poets read poems in the Moscow squares which *Molodoi Kommunist* said fulminated against Party policy. Among them were a former Moscow University student, Yury Galanskov, whom the paper described as "a young man who stuffed the diminutive minds of his friends with his doggerel and provoked them to make scandalous speeches"; and a nineteen-year-old named Vladimir Bukovsky, who "composed a treatise in which he proved that the Komsomol does not really exist" [27]—by which Bukovsky obviously meant that the membership and activities of the Young Communist League were largely a government fiction.

Then, in October, two writers went considerably further: Viktor **Nekrasov**, in his travel commentary, *Both Sides of the Ocean*,[28] and Yevtushenko, in "The Heirs of Stalin," his powerful assault on the persistence of neo-Stalinism and the possible revival of a full-fledged Stalinism. As Stalin's coffin is, by decision of the Twenty-second Party Congress, removed from the Lenin Mausoleum, Yevtushenko cries out:

> . . . I appeal to our government
>   With the request
> To double
>   To triple
>   The guard at this slab
> So that Stalin may not rise,

And with Stalin
    The past. . . .

I mean by the past
The ignoring of the people's welfare,
    The calumnies,
        The arrests of the innocent.
We sowed honestly.
    We poured steel honestly
And we marched honestly
    Lining up in soldiers' ranks.
But he feared us.
    Believing in a great goal, he did not believe
That the means
    Should be worthy of the great goal.

He was farsighted.
    Skilled in the laws of battle,
He left many heirs on the face of the globe.
I dream
    That a telephone has been placed in the coffin:
Stalin sends instructions
    To Enver Hoxha.
Where else does the line from the coffin run?
No—Stalin has not given up.
    He considers death remediable.
We rooted him
    Out of the Mausoleum.
But how to root Stalin
    Out of Stalin's heirs?
Some of the heirs snip roses in retirement
And secretly consider
    The retirement temporary.
Others
    Even condemn Stalin from the platform,
But themselves
    At night
        Pine for the old days.
Evidently not for nothing do Stalin's heirs today
    Suffer heart attacks.
They, once his lieutenants,

Do not like these times
When the camps are empty
    And the halls where people listen to poetry
    Are crowded.
The Party
    Ordered me
        Not to be quiet.
Let some repeat over and over:
    "Relax!"—I cannot be
        Calm.
As long as Stalin's heirs exist on earth
It will seem to me
    That Stalin is still in the Mausoleum.[29]

Yevtushenko had written the poem almost a year before, after the Twenty-second Party Congress, and had even read it before a number of small audiences, but "someone had spread the rumor that it was anti-Soviet," [30] so it was not published until he sent it to Khrushchev, who, for his own purposes in combating his rivals in the Politburo, approved it. (Michel Tatu believes that the reference to the man in temporary retirement is to Nikolay Bulganin, but Alexander Werth says that it is to Aleksandr Poskrebyshev,[31] Stalin's personal secretary, who was later—at least in name—to play a role in an attack against Ehrenburg and the liberals. Priscilla Johnson comments: "It is unlikely that the poet [Yevtushenko] had anyone in the Kremlin in mind. If he was thinking of someone in particular, perhaps it was some elderly crustacean in the literary bureaucracy. Those who decided to publish the poem [i.e., Khrushchev and his cohorts], however, may have had something more pointed in view. For Kozlov had had a heart attack in 1960, and Molotov in 1962.") [32] On the very same day that "The Heirs of Stalin" appeared, October 21, 1962, another anti-Stalinist poem by Yevtushenko, "Fears," was published in the Communist youth league paper, *Komsomolskaya pravda*.

Yevtushenko's "Heirs of Stalin" was the clearest attack on "Stalinist vestiges" in the Soviet system, and it pointed out that the threat of a revival of Stalinism was by no means over, that some of Stalin's heirs and accomplices were still in power and others waiting in the wings. Shrewdly, too, the poem associated Stalinism with the concentration camps and with oppression in literature. In perfect consonance with Khrushchev's policies, it declared that the Party was insisting that Yevtushenko speak out truthfully and fearlessly. It was, and is, this continuing consonance of Yevtushenko's verse with leadership policy that has made many skeptical of Yevtushenko, or at least gingerly. Peter Benno remarks, "Many of Yevtushenko's contemporaries, suspicious of his somewhat too facile success, consider him a *podkhalim* (toady) almost an agent of the regime." [33]

Nekrasov's *Both Sides of the Ocean* is a book of travel notes noteworthy not so much for their insight or originality as for their attempt at a balanced objectivity about trips the writer had made to Italy and the United States. Although the brunt of the attack soon to be directed against him was on his "fifty-fifty" treatment of capitalist countries as compared with the Soviet Union, the main cause of pique was his depiction of domestic Soviet flaws: the arrest of the Italian publisher Einaudi in Kiev for taking some innocent photographs; the use of KGB "collars" or supervisors during all trips abroad by Soviet citizens and these supervisors' fears of letting their charges do anything individually or independently; the regime policy of cultural isolation which kept Soviet authors from being informed about major Western writers, painters, and film makers.[34]

A month later, Khrushchev's son-in-law, Aleksey Adzhubei, printed another vitriolic anti-Stalinist poem in the government newspaper, *Izvestia*, which he was then editing. It was Boris Slutsky's "The Boss":

> My boss had no love for me—
> Did not know me, hear or see me,
> And yet he had a deathly fear of me,
> And gloomily, sullenly hated me.
> Whenever he made me weep
> He thought that I was acting;
> When I bowed my head to him
> He thought I was hiding a sneer.
> I worked my whole life for him,
> Late to bed, and early rising.
> Loved him. For him was wounded.
> But all to no avail.

> I carried his picture around with me,
> Hung it in dugout and tent,
> Kept it constantly in view,
> Never tired of the sight of it.
> But less and less as the years went by
> Did his dislike distress me.
> Now it upsets me not a bit to recognize
> The patent fact that from the start of time
> Bosses bore no love for such as me.[35]

Having first written it in 1954, not long after Stalin's demise, Slutsky had prudently kept it in the drawer. And now he read it at the Moscow Sports Palace on November 30, 1962, to a mixed reception from his audience, which both cheered and jeered.[36] (Yevtushenko has stated that Slutsky had managed to have only one poem published, in 1940, and at the age of thirty-five had still not been allowed membership in the Writers' Union, so that he was barred from such material advantages as the Union conferred on its members. "His desk drawers were stuffed with sad, bitter, grim poems, sometimes frighteningly like Baudelaire's," Yevtushenko recalled. "They were typed and ready, but it would have been absurd to offer them to a publisher." Yevtushenko commented that Slutsky was nonetheless hopeful and serene. "I fought in the war," Slutsky told him. "I'm riddled with bulletholes. And I didn't fight in order to keep those poems in my desk. But everything will change. Our day will come. All we have to do is wait for that day and have something ready for it in our desks and in our hearts." [37]

Also late in November, Slutsky published a bitterly anti-Stalinist poem he had written in 1955, simply entitled "God":

> We all lived near to god,
> Right next to god, in fact.
> He dwelt not in a distant heaven—
> It came our way to see him
> Alive. On the mausoleum.
> A wiser and angrier god he was
> Than the one—the other one
> Who bears the name Jehovah,
> And tormented, roasted on hot coals,
> And then plucked from the abyss
> And gave him room and board.
> We all lived near to god,

Right next to god, in fact.
One day I was walking down Arbat Street,
And god drove by in five motor cars.
The guards in their mouse-colored greatcoats,
Line up, stood all a-tremble,
Hunched nearly humpbacked with fear
The hour was both late and early—
The sky was graying, day breaking.
He threw a look that was cruel and wise
With his all-seeing eye
—An all-piercing glance.
We all lived near to god,
Almost next door to god.[38]

The political situation that autumn had grown abruptly more difficult for Khrushchev. His position in the Politburo had been gravely weakened by the Cuban crisis and the Penkovsky spy case. (Greville Wynne, Penkovsky's British Intelligence contact, believes that the Penkovsky case seriously undermined Khrushchev. One of the reasons was the obvious security breach at the top levels of the Soviet government. More important, Wynne maintains, was the fact that Penkovsky had photographed reports Khrushchev had given to the Politburo which purported to be reports of meetings of Khrushchev with President Kennedy and the Italian Foreign Minister and which gave a false account of what had, in fact, taken place. With the Penkovsky copies at hand, accurate versions of those meetings were made available to the Politburo, and these, Wynne thinks, ultimately contributed to the Politburo's loss of confidence in, and ouster of, Khrushchev.) [39] The increasingly difficult relations with China, the Chinese invasion of northern India, and important domestic issues concerning the modernizing of the economy and the restructuring of Party control of the country added to Khrushchev's burdens. Moreover, the harvest that year was poor, and he was forced either to buy grain abroad or let his people starve. Khrushchev tried to turn that situation to account by reminding his people that in similar circumstances in 1947, Stalin preferred to let his people go hungry rather than import wheat, and Khrushchev also blamed the crop failures, not on his agricultural policies, but on the drought and bad weather which had added to the farm fiasco.[40]

5 *Denisovich's Day*

Tell me what your attitude is toward Ivan Denisovich, and I
will tell you who you are.

Anonymous Russian

In this context, in November 1962, Aleksandr Solzhenitsyn's literary career was launched. More than a year and a half earlier
Solzhenitsyn had completed the manuscript of a short novel, *One
Day in the Life of Ivan Denisovich*, submitted it to various magazines, and received only rejections. And then, "an editorial associate
put the manuscript of *One Day* in with a portfolio of others for
the editor-in-chief of the literary magazine *Novy Mir*, the adept
establishment liberal, Aleksandr Tvardovsky. He took the manuscripts home to read in bed, tossed them one by one aside. Then
he picked up Solzhenitsyn's novel and read ten lines. As he later
told a friend, 'Suddenly I felt I couldn't read it like this. I had to
do something appropriate to the occasion. So I got up. I put on my
best black suit, a white shirt with a starched collar, a tie, and my
good shoes. Then I sat down at my desk and read a new classic.' " [1]

Tvardovsky sent the manuscript to the Central Committee for approval and finally to Khrushchev himself, at a singularly opportune
moment for Khrushchev.[2] His program of reform and de-Stalinization had been virtually stalled since the Twenty-second Congress,
and not until that fall had he been able to mount a renewal of de-
Stalinization as an attack on his rivals for power in the Politburo.
Khrushchev had the Solzhenitsyn manuscript copied and distributed
to members of the Presidium, for now, ready to hand, he had a book
exposing one of the most vicious Stalinist institutions, the concentration camp, a horror personally experienced by millions of ordinary Russians from all levels of society.[3] The Central Committee

was deeply divided about releasing *Ivan Denisovich*, and so was the Politburo, where Frol Kozlov and Mikhail Suslov raised objections; but "Khrushchev overrode them, shouting, 'There's a Stalinist in each of you, there's even some Stalinist in me. We must root out this evil.' "[4] Khrushchev then personally authorized the uncensored publication of the novel, because "no one has the right to alter the author's version."[5] It was finally permitted to appear in the November number of Tvardovsky's *Novy mir*, the same number with Nekrasov's *Both Sides of the Ocean*.[6]

The magazine issue was soon sold out. A hundred thousand copies of *Ivan Denisovich* appeared in book form, and those too were swiftly bought up. "At the same time, government publications launched a coordinated campaign to give the novel maximum publicity: *Soviet Literature* translated it into English; *Moscow News*, a weekly newspaper for foreign consumptions, was authorized to run a serialized version; and *Izvestia* and other non-literary newspapers published highly favorable reviews of the book."[7] *Pravda*, for example, compared Solzhenitsyn favorably to Tolstoy.

In the foreword that editor Tvardovsky wrote especially for the publication of *Ivan Denisovich* as a book, Khrushchev's political purposes as well as those of the liberal intellectuals were revealed, though they were by no means the same. Tvardovsky wrote:

The raw material of life which serves as a basis for A. Solzhenitsyn's story is unusual in Soviet literature. It carries within itself an echo of the painful features in our development related to the cult of personality that has been debunked and repudiated by the Party, features that, although they are not so far away from us in time, nevertheless seem to us to be in the distant past. But the past, no matter what it was like, never becomes a matter of indifference to the present. The assurance of a complete and irrevocable break with everything which beclouds the past lies in a true and courageous comprehension of its full consequences.

Shorn of doctrinal euphemism, Tvardovsky's statement sought to assure the Soviet people, and particularly the intellectuals, that the past, even the recent past, was over and far behind, and that Khrushchev would no longer consider employing the repressive methods of Stalinism. But the truth of the past must nonetheless be taken into account and exposed so that *in the present* the people's confidence in the words and intentions of the Khrushchev leadership will be reinforced and, *in the future*, make them more amenable to the new policies. Tvardovsky then both makes the mandatory obeisance to the Party and shows the power of his connections (and therefore the reliability of what he has written) by quoting the First Secretary himself:

It was about this that N. S. Khrushchev spoke in his concluding words at the 22nd Congress of the Communist Party of the Soviet Union, words so memorable for all of us: "It is our duty to gain a thorough and comprehensive understanding of the nature of the matters related to the abuse of power. Time will pass and we shall die, we are all mortal, but so long as we work, we can and must clear up many points and tell the truth to the Party and to the people. . . . This we must do so that such things never happen again." [8]

Tvardovsky was not only genuinely concerned with striking the shackles off political prisoners, with eliminating the cruelty, arbitrariness, and lawlessness inflicted on the people by Stalin's secret police and Gulag,[9] the instruments of which were still available to the government, he was also committed to freeing Russian literature from its Stalinist shackles. So, almost in passing, Tvardovsky noted, "This is a grim story—still another example of the fact that there are no areas or facts of reality that can be excluded from the sphere of the Soviet artist in our days or that are beyond truthful portrayal." [10] Increased freedom from fear of the KGB is also increased freedom from fear for writers and their writing.

Politically, *One Day in the Life of Ivan Denisovich* was the most explosive of all the anti-Stalinist literary works which had been permitted to appear as part of Khrushchev's de-Stalinization. The concentration camps had touched almost every family in the Soviet Union: from 1934 to 1953, they had been the prisons and sometimes the tombs of peasants, workers, Party leaders, generals, bureaucrats. Not only did *Denisovich* portray the camps as evidence of a systematic and mass mania, but it put them beyond the scope of mere "distortions" or "excesses." It gave the temperature of the whole Stalinist climate and showed how it affected naval captains and Baptists, moving-picture writers and students of literature, Russians, Latvians, Estonians, and gypsies. And it demonstrated beyond rebuttal the simple facts of Soviet injustice, Party injustice, KGB injustice, Gulag injustice: Captain Buinovsky sentenced to twenty-five years because a British admiral on whose cruiser he had served during World War II had sent him a gift as a token of gratitude for his work as a liaison officer; Senka, who had three times escaped from Buchenwald and three times been recaptured, who had worked with the Communist underground there, sentenced for having been captured; Ivan Denisovich Shukhov, who had been surrounded by the Nazis in the war, been captured, and escaped, returning to his own lines, sentenced for high treason; representatives of every "wave" of repression, of the kulak purge in the early 1930s, the Kirov purges of 1935, the military purges of 1937–1938. Innocence meant nothing; nationality meant nothing; Party membership meant nothing: justice was denied to all.

No sooner had the book been published than it was greeted by a general accolade. All the press but Kochetov's *Oktyabr* reviewed the novel favorably—how often, after all, did a novel appear with such powerful sponsorship? (It was reported that Aleksandr Dymshits, the deputy editor of *Oktyabr*, had left the magazine's editorial board in December because he wanted to review *Ivan Denisovich* favorably and Kochetov refused to allow it. Only in 1963, when the atmosphere had grown much more conservative, did *Oktyabr* comment on Solzhenitsyn's work—and then very critically. *Oktyabr*'s position was presumably supported in the Presidium by Kozlov because "in Moscow literary circles, Kozlov was spoken of as Kochetov's protector," [11] and also because Kozlov's position committed him to maintaining the efficiency and morale of the bureaucracy.) On November 22, 1962, *Literaturnaya gazeta* carried Grigory Baklanov's review in praise of *Ivan Denisovich*, "That This May Never Happen Again." Baklanov wrote that now was the time to try to understand what had happened under Stalinism and to make sure that the past would not be repeated.

But must we reopen old wounds? Is that necessary now? Old healed wounds don't hurt. But a wound that still bleeds must be healed and not hidden cravenly from view. And there is only one cure—truth. The Party summons us along this path of truth.

Among other notions that helped Stalin to remain beyond censure while committing unlawful acts was the fact that we ourselves believed, persuaded ourselves to believe, not the self-evident facts, not ourselves, but him. He knew; he was wise; if he did it, there must be the highest reason for it. This blind faith not only was supported, it was elevated into a virtue. To make such blindness impossible in the future, to eradicate from the soul the traces engraved on it by the cult of the individual is neither an easy task nor one quickly accomplished. In this, our literature, a literature telling the people the truth, has an enormous role to perform.

Four days earlier, Konstantin Simonov had welcomed the novel as written "by the confident hand of a mature, original master," a work about the "black days of the Stalin cult." "The Party," Simonov reminded his readers, "has called writers its assistants. It appears that Solzhenitsyn in his story has shown himself to be a true assistant to the Party in the sacred and necessary cause of combating the cult of the individual and its consequences." [12]

6 The Turning Point

What are we, gambling chips or great human beings?
Andrey Voznesensky

The publication of Yevtushenko's "The Heirs of Stalin" in October and of Nekrasov's *Both Sides of the Ocean* and Solzhenitsyn's *One Day* in November was at once the high point and the turning point of de-Stalinization and liberalization in the arts. The political and cultural forces of conservatism now rallied, fed by a series of setbacks for Khrushchev. In foreign policy, the Cuban missile crisis with the United States in October and the worsening relations with China worked against Khrushchev. Domestically, price rises had caused considerable dissatisfaction and even violent outbreaks in various parts of the country. The government had decreed rises on June 1, 1962: butter prices rose 25 percent; meat prices, 30 percent. In Novocherkassk there were riots in which the police shot down unarmed demonstrators, and there were upheavals in Leningrad, Odessa, Krivoi Rog, and a number of other industrial cities.[1] The liberalization in literature had resulted in Soviet magazines and publishing houses being flooded with manuscripts describing prisons, labor camps, and other unsavory aspects of Soviet life. Because all these phenomena threatened the political leaders and literary bureaucrats, a reversal of policy was abruptly engineered to divert the flood into more acceptable channels, and Khrushchev's conservative rivals in the Presidium and the Party were able to halt both his de-Stalinization and liberalization.

On December 1, Khrushchev and four Presidium members were visiting an exhibition of "Thirty Years of Moscow Art" at the Manezh gallery, into which a small collection of abstract art had mysteriously been introduced some days earlier from the studio of

Eli Belyutin. Khrushchev's outbursts against these abstract paintings and the artists who painted them "proved to be the signal for the most far-reaching crackdown on the creative arts . . . since the Zhdanov purge of 1946–1948." Khrushchev's attacks were full of menace and characteristically coarse:

As long as I am president of the Council of Ministers, we are going to support a genuine art. We aren't going to give a kopeck for pictures painted by jackasses. History can be our judge. For the time being history has put us at the head of this state, and we have to answer for everything that goes on in it. Therefore we are going to maintain a strict policy in art. . . .

Gentlemen, we are declaring war on you.

Throughout the tour of the gallery Khrushchev's vulgarity and philistinism were rampant. In describing a modernist canvas, he said, "It consisted of some messy lines which looked, if you will excuse me, as though some child had done his business on the canvas when his mother was away and then spread it around with his hands." In front of some formalist paintings Khrushchev raged at the artists who had done them: "Are you pederasts or normal people? I'll be perfectly straightforward with you; we won't spend a kopeck on your art. Just give me a list of those of you who want to go abroad, to the so-called 'free world.' We'll give you foreign passports tomorrow, and you can get out. Your prospects here are nil. What is hung here is simply anti-Soviet. It's amoral. Art should ennoble the individual and arouse him to action. . . . What's the good of pictures like this? To cover urinals with?" And the Premier threatened, "We aren't going to spend a kopeck on this dog shit. We have the right to send you out to cut trees until you've paid back the money the state has spent on you [for education]." [2]

The conservatives followed this declaration of war with actions so swift and sharp that it seemed as if both the Khrushchev explosion at the Manezh and the subsequent antiliberal campaign had been planned in advance.[3] Editorials were written calling for a single unified union of creative artists, in order to oust the liberals from control of some branches of various creative unions—such as, for example, the Moscow branch of the Writers' Union—though the conservative thrust was not at first directed at literature. The liberals fought back with a letter from seventeen distinguished artists and scientists calling on Khrushchev not to prohibit new and experimental methods in arts. Among those who signed the letter were two Nobel Prize–winning scientists, Igor Tamm and Nikolay Semyonov; writers Konstantin Simonov, Ilya Ehrenburg, Kornei Chukovsky; composer Dmitry Shostakovich; and cinema director Mikhail Romm. The "letter of the seventeen" was symptomatic of what was to become increasing cooperation among the leaders of the scientific and artistic communities in the Soviet Union to forward liberalization in the country.[4]

On December 17, the Party leaders called four hundred writers, artists, and intellectuals together at the Pioneer Palace on Lenin Hills, where Khrushchev introduced the then virtually unknown Aleksandr Solzhenitsyn to the assemblage.[5] Khrushchev was to have delivered the major speech, but instead, Leonid Ilyichev, chairman of the newly organized Ideological Commission of the Party Central Committee, spoke, reportedly for ten hours.[6] Ilyichev's purpose was to set boundaries to what was permissible, and he asked if, "since an end has been put to arbitrariness in our country and people are not arrested for political dissent, this means that everything is allowed and there are no restrictions on what one wishes." He answered his own question with a resounding no. Art's Party nature (*partiinost*), its ideological militance (*ideiinost*), and its roots in the life of the people (*narodnost*) remained the bases of a socialist realist art. On the one hand, writers must give up the idea that they can create without restrictions or prescriptions from the Party: such freedom is mere "anarchy." However unfashionable it seemed to defend Party positions for fear that one might be accused of "dogmatism, sectarianism, narrowness, backwardness, Stalinism, etc.," Party positions must be defended. On the other hand, "the prettifying of reality, the smoothing over of contradictions, the rosy complacency, philistine smugness" would also not be tolerated. The Party itself had exposed the cult of the individual and was still encouraging "artistically and politically powerful works that truthfully and boldly expose the arbitrariness that prevailed [then, such as] A. Solzhenitsyn's tale, *One Day in the Life of Ivan Denisovich*." In no uncertain terms, Ilyichev made clear that Soviet society, "socialist" ideology, and "socialist" culture must not be "shaken and weakened under the pretext of the struggle against the cult of the individual. The exposure of the cult and overcoming its consequences should not weaken but strengthen our forces." [7]

Ilyichev kept one eye on Western influences on Soviet art and ideology, cautioning his audience that "peaceful coexistence" in ideology would not be accepted and bourgeois influences disorienting and subverting Soviet life would be combated. As always when Soviet leaders refer publicly to the West, there was a curious mixture of political ploys, feelings of inferiority, and uncontrollable paranoia which was difficult to weigh and separate into components.

In an unaccustomed give-and-take at the meeting, Yevtushenko bravely spoke in defense of the abstract painters and sculptors, especially the gifted sculptor Ernst Neizvestny. "We must have great patience with this abstract trend in our art and not rush to suppress it," Yevtushenko advised. "I know the artists. I am convinced that formalist tendencies in their work will be straightened out in time."

Khrushchev's reply was blunt and threatening: "As they say, only the grave straightens out the hunchbacked." Swiftly, Yevtushenko admonished him: "I hope, Comrade Khrushchev, we have outlived the time when the grave was used as a means of correction." The stunned audience burst into applause in which Khrushchev himself sheepishly joined. [8]

The confrontation between liberals and conservatives at the meeting grew increasingly heated when Galina Serebryakova accused Ilya Ehrenburg of having betrayed his colleagues on the Jewish Anti-Fascist Committee between 1948 and 1952. Similar charges had been brought against Ehrenburg before, but Serebryakova, a widow of two of Stalin's purge victims, Grigory Sokolnikov and L. P. Serebryakov, was herself Jewish and a survivor of twenty-one years of Siberian concentration camps under Stalin—facts which gave her charges special force. She added additional impact by saying that she could corroborate her accusations with the testimony of Aleksandr Poskrebyshev, whom she had met in a rest home not long before. Everyone at the meeting knew that Ehrenburg had been one of Stalin's favorite propagandists and a skillful apologist for Stalin's regime. Everyone also was aware that Poskrebyshev had been Stalin's personal secretary and as informed, or more informed, about the purges than anyone else. In asking what Ehrenburg had been doing under Stalin, Serebryakova was skillfully turning the whole de-Stalinization campaign back on some of its leading advocates, and in so doing, deflecting it from the conservatives. Many observers believed that Serebryakova's charges against Ehrenburg were not spontaneous, but a planned assault on Khrushchev and the whole de-Stalinization campaign. In attacking Ehrenburg, a particularly vulnerable target, she was reminding Khrushchev and his partisans that the threat of criminal punishment had two edges and could be used to cut both ways.[9]

Ilyichev attacked Shostakovich's *Thirteenth Symphony*, scheduled to have its premiere the following night, because the composer had included a choral interlude of Yevtushenko's poem "Babi Yar." Khrushchev added his voice to this criticism, insisting that there was no anti-Semitism in the Soviet Union but that it was better for Jews *not* to hold high government office because it provoked popular envy and resentment. He also remarked that the 1956 upheavals in Poland and Hungary had been caused by the fact that too many Jews occupied high places in the Polish and Hungarian parties and governments.[10] (Khrushchev's statement was an oversimplification, but not altogether without truth. Some popular anti-Communism in those two countries, both traditionally anti-Semitic, was due to the fact that many top Party and government leaders were Jewish. But that fact was only a small element of the popular hatred for the government and the Party.) [11] Ehrenburg had intended to devote a chapter of his memoirs to his attitude toward the anti-Semitic repressions of 1948–1952, but "that chapter was censored when the rest of the work was published in spring 1963." [12] Later, when things had quieted down, Khrushchev tried to reassure Ehrenburg that none of what he had said was to be taken personally. That Ehrenburg was not reassured was revealed in an interview some years later, when he remarked:

Khrushchev wasn't really a bad man, and he will always have to his credit the fact that he (though not only he) had a good deal to do with throwing open Stalin's labor camps. But God only knows why our so-called statesmen have to stick their necks out and lay down the law on what kind of books we are to write and what kind of pictures we are to paint. In this respect, Khrushchev was particularly absurd, and he behaved with the greatest arrogance too, pretending he knew what he was talking about. Also, he had lived for too long in my—though not his—native Ukraine and had been infected by the kind of visceral anti-Semitism that is still very far from having been stamped out there. It has practically disappeared in a place like Moscow, but you still get a lot of it in Kiev. As for Ilyichev, he was a typical old-regime *zhidomor* [Jew baiter], though a member of our Central Committee and what have you.[13]

Shostakovich and Yevtushenko agreed to make the changes required. The poet deleted two lines and added two others. The new lines were "I am proud of the Russia which stood in the path of the invaders" and "Here, together with Russians and Ukrainians, the Jews" [were slain in the Babi Yar ravine]. Yevtushenko blandly announced publicly that the changes were part of a "natural process which all poems undergo," [14] but obviously he was responding to the criticism that he had failed to show how much the Russians had suffered from the Nazis, while he stressed Jewish suffering at Babi Yar. For the moment the capitulation meant a respite, but Yevtushenko had not yet heard the last of the matter.

The meeting was a turning point in the liberal-conservative struggle in the arts. Although Konstantin Fedin, now head of the Writers' Union, had made a public plea in a New Year's Day address to spare literature another round of repression,[15] the new year saw an increasing assertion of conservative power and Party control over literature. As a result of his having published "Babi Yar," though, officially, the reason given was for rejecting an article attacking abstract art, V. A. Kosolapov was removed as editor-in-chief of *Literaturnaya gazeta* and replaced by the far more conservative Aleksandr Chakovsky. At the same time the entire editorial board was reorganized.[16] The bureaucratic conflict was to continue until the liberals had been driven from most of their strongholds, with the exception of *Novy mir* and the Moscow branch of the Writers' Union.

On January 20, 1963, *Izvestia* attacked the novelist Nekrasov for *Both Sides of the Ocean*. Nekrasov had committed the sin of "bourgeois objectivism" in painting both the dark and bright sides of the United States on a "fifty-fifty" basis, and the government paper took him to task for not seeing "the sharp social contrasts and class contradictions in American life, and the war psychosis fanned by imperialist circles." *Izvestia* also rebuked him for having expressed his irritation at the security services for constantly shepherding and supervising Soviet travelers abroad.

At the end of January, Nikolay Gribachev, the fifty-two-year-old Stalin Prize winner, attacked another leading liberal writer in a parody of Yevtushenko's poem "Go Ahead, Boys" which Gribachev called "No, Boys!" And in the same satire he took sideswipes at the young poets who read their verses in Moscow squares and at Bulat Okhudzhava, the popular guitar-playing singer and writer:

> The foot is free to slip and the tongue to chatter
> But there is that terrible moment on the border,
> Where you make one step and become rootless
> And no longer stand under the Red banner. . . .
>
> No, boys, we didn't raise you
> Almost falling from exhaustion
> To let you be seized, abducted, seduced
> By rootless traffickers and dodgers.
> We didn't stand up under the weapons' roar
> Or march to building sites in padded jackets
> To let you show off in market places
> Or play guitar for languishing girls.[17]

Early in February another leading reactionary, Vladimir Yermilov, attacked another leading liberal, Ilya Ehrenburg. Yermilov had been an NKVD informer in the 1930s and had served the regime then as part of a slander campaign against the poet Vladimir Mayakovsky. Now Yermilov picked up the charges Galina Serebryakova had made against Ehrenburg at the December 17 meeting and elaborated them. In reviewing Ehrenburg's memoirs, running serially in *Novy mir*, Yermilov turned the de-Stalinization campaign against its initiators still further. The memoirs themselves, Yermilov wrote, were equivocal, full of omissions and untruths, and written in a sleazy self-defensive way which gives force to the comment (made subsequently by Western scholar and critic Peter Benno): "Such accomplished old weather vanes as Ehrenburg or cinema director Romm are suspected by many of capitalizing from the safe sanctuary of old age and of long-established celebrity, on still another good thing in order to finish out their careers in glory—at the price of a few only minor inconveniences." [18] In the memoirs, Ehrenburg said, "Yes, I knew about many crimes, but stopping them was not in my power. Yet what can I say? People who were more influential and better informed than I could not stop the crimes." At first he had thought, like some others, that Stalin did not know about the crimes being committed in his name, but he kept his mouth shut even when he realized that "the orders for annihilation of the Old Bolsheviks and of the leading Red Army commanders whom I had met in Spain could only have come from Stalin himself." Moreover, Ehrenburg believed that many of those who perished were altogether innocent: "Among those who perished were my close friends and no one will ever persuade me that Vsevolod Meyerhold, Semyon Chlenov, Isaak Babel or Nikolai Bukharin was a traitor." [19] In remarking that many people knew that large numbers of Stalin's victims during the terror were innocent and had, out of fear and impotence, held their tongues, Ehrenburg was touching on one of the most explosive issues in Soviet society. Ehrenburg's assertions exacerbated both the "fathers and sons" and "the heirs of Stalin" problems, calling into question the behavior of all the top leaders, who, if Ehrenburg knew, must also have known. And if they knew, they were implicated in Stalin's crimes for having neither resisted nor exposed Stalin's wrongdoing or for having remained silent.

The truth was, according to writers who had examined the situation, that Ehrenburg himself escaped arrest and execution by the narrowest of margins. In March, 1949, he sat at home waiting the knock of the police. Unlike the purge days of 1937–1938 when, like many other Muscovites, he kept a packed bag beside his door to take along if the police came, Ehrenburg did not bother this time. He just sat and waited. His telephone occasionally rang. He would answer, but all he would hear on the line was heavy breathing. A friend, afraid to speak, had called to see whether Ehrenburg still answered, to see whether he was still at liberty. Moscow buzzed with rumors that Ehrenburg had been arrested or was about to be arrested.

Finally, he could not stand the suspense. He wrote a letter to Stalin. If he was going to be arrested, let them arrest him. If not, end the suspense. The next day his telephone rang. It was Georgi M. Malenkov,

Stalin's close associate, expressing surprise. Why hadn't Ehrenburg reported this before? Ehrenburg responded that he had but had got no response. Hardly had Ehrenburg replaced the telephone receiver when his telephone began to ring. Every editor in town wanted him to write an article.

Trapped in this situation, could Ehrenburg have saved the lives of Itzik Fefer, Peretz Markish, and the other Yiddish writers? Not in the opinion of Konstantin Simonov. The guilt lies elsewhere, he believed. "We were all guilty," he says. "All of us bear part of the blame." [20]

It is typical of his memoirs that Ehrenburg never mentions this incident of waiting to be arrested in *People, Years—Life.*

Yermilov declared that those in responsible positions were under no moral compulsion to speak out, because they really did *not* know about Stalin's crimes. He accused Ehrenburg of "insulting a whole generation of Soviet people in trying to protect himself"; [21] the implied threat in the accusation was, of course, that unless Ehrenburg gave ground, he might in time find himself in the dock as one of Stalin's accomplices.[22] But the truth was that Ehrenburg had known and had kept silent: "I made myself keep quiet about a lot of things: those were the years of the swastika, the Spanish war, of the life-and-death struggle, that period which we now call 'the cult of personality'; and, therefore, voluntary silence was added to the enforced silence." This self-censorship and deliberate lying in defense of the regime, for whatever motives, kept Ehrenburg from exposing Soviet and Stalinist crimes at home and abroad. For example, when he returned to Barcelona from Moscow in 1937, he told no one about the purges sweeping the Soviet Union. In his subtle way, he tries to lay the blame for Stalin, not on Soviet institutions or on the people of the USSR, but on "capitalist fanatics, businessmen who thought of themselves as crusaders, and trigger-happy militarists, whether they wanted to or not, helped to consolidate the Stalin cult." Ehrenburg thought of Stalin as an Italian Renaissance politician, one of the Medici or Borgias, and his references to Stalin, even in the memoirs, reverberate with a naked fear and a naked relief at having been able to survive that the reader can still feel. He wrote:

During the years of tyranny, they could have arrested me as they arrested so many of my friends. I do not know what thoughts Babel had in his mind when he died; he was one of those whose silence was not merely a matter of circumspection but one of faith. I could have died in the postwar years, up to the Twentieth Congress, like Tairov, Suritz, and Tuwim. They also suffered torment over the crimes committed, allegedly in defense of ideas which they shared and for which they felt themselves responsible. I was fortunate to live to the day when they called me to the Writers' Union and gave me Khrushchev's report on the cult of the individual to read.[23]

Ehrenburg's defense was published as a letter to the editor of *Izvestia*, a tremulous, almost frightened letter which tried to clarify his position during the Stalin era. In defending himself against what he said was an attempt "by insinuations to insult me as a man and a Soviet citizen," [24] Ehrenburg might very well have been aware of the possibility that he would actually be charged with complicity in Stalin's crimes. During the purges, Yermilov had often enough served in denouncing writers to the NKVD (the secret police). Nonetheless, Ehrenburg insisted in the letter that people had gritted their teeth and remained silent during the Stalin period: "I was not present at a single meeting at which people took the floor to protest the arbitrary persecution of comrades whose innocence they never doubted; not once did I read an article protesting against a 'case' or 'occurrence.'" In a reply published in the same issue, Yermilov reiterated his accusation that Ehrenburg was "a man who was well aware that senseless persecution was taking place, that evil was being done, and . . . decided to 'keep silent' about it."

In his memoirs Ehrenburg remarked that Soviet writers, journalists, and military men, in Moscow and Madrid, during the 1936–1939 Great Purges and the Spanish Civil War, often knew of many individuals who were innocent, yet were arrested and executed. Though they talked about these things among themselves, none of them found it possible to protest publicly. The basic weakness of Ehrenburg's moral position, as distinct from his political posture and his understandable desire to survive, is probed by the obvious question, implied by Yermilov but asked quite explicitly by many others, "Why not?" Ehrenburg, who continued to travel relatively freely outside the Soviet Union, could easily have denounced Stalin's crimes in Paris or Barcelona or Vienna, but he *chose* to remain silent.

It is easy enough for someone "outside" to ask such a question, but Tatu recounts a story which circulated in Moscow after the Twentieth Congress which perhaps goes a long way toward explaining why many remained silent. "According to the story, Khru·shchev was reading his famous Secret Report when the following anonymous note was handed to him: 'Why didn't the Politburo and you do anything to prevent these awful things?' Khrushchev allegedly broke off, read the note aloud, and then asked, 'Will the writer identify himself?' When no one in the audience stood up, Khrushchev went on: 'There, comrades, is the answer to the question.' In other words, he then espoused 'Ehrenburg's thesis' about gritting one's teeth and keeping silent." [25]

There were also conservative censures of Tvardovsky and Boris Polevoi for publishing liberal writings in their magazines. In January and February the attacks were against Polevoi particularly for having published two "commonplace and banal" Voznesensky poems, "Two Italian Melodies," in the January 1963 *Yunost*, and against Tvardovsky for an Aleksandr Yashin short story, "Vologda Wedding," which had appeared in the December 1962 *Novy mir*. Yashin's story was denounced for lacking positive characterizations and for being filled with crooks, drunkards, skirt chasers, wife beaters, and altogether repulsive and reprehensible characters. "I do not dispute that there are still drunkards and swindlers among us," one such criticism ran, "but they are exceptions. Everywhere around us there are honest good people." Moreover, the critic refused to believe that the miserable rural village Yashin described, in which there was no electricity, radio, library, or club, and in which traveling cinema had not been seen for the past two years, could exist. If such villages did exist, they were rare indeed, but Yashin had made his village seem typical.[26]

Early in January, Solzhenitsyn's immunity from attack also began to erode. Lydia Fomenko took him to task for having failed to "rise to a philosophical perception" of the Stalinist period in *Ivan Denisovich*, and for having failed to understand that the people and the Party had gone right on building socialism *in spite of* Stalin.[27] It was the opening criticism in a campaign against Solzhenitsyn, and such criticism was increasingly to become the regime's means of handling the problem of the heirs of Stalin. "Socialism," whatever that was, had been built "by the people" and, by extension, by the Party, even while Stalin was making his "errors" and "distortions." Apologists pointed to the achievements of Soviet industrialization and the victory over Nazi Germany in the war as proofs positive of what *they*—the Party and the people, the Party leading the people—had accomplished as distinct from what *he*—Stalin—had thwarted or twisted. Once committed to such an apologia, however, the Party leaders had to rehabilitate Stalin, at least in part, so that their logic and history, however faulty and warped, would not appear altogether absurd.

(Even Ehrenburg was ultimately forced to conclude that ends and means are indissolubly connected. In the memoirs, he wrote: "The old debate about whether the ends justify the means seems to me too abstract. The end is not merely a signpost on the road but something real in and of itself; the means is a reality now, not a vision of tomorrow, but today's action. The end must define not only political strategy, but also moral strategy. One cannot establish justice by consciously committing unjust actions. One cannot fight for equality by turning people into 'cogs' and 'screws' and oneself into a mythical godhead. The means always affect the end; either they ennoble it or they corrupt it." [28] If those are the final conclusions of Ehrenburg's maturity, then no more damning indictment of the regime he served and of his own behavior could have been written.)

7 Ebb Tide

Time for winding up the verses.
Time to bring the ballads to a close.
No need to make a start on any new ones.
Boris Slutsky

Two months after Lydia Fomenko's attack on Solzhenitsyn, at a meeting March 7–8, 1963, of six hundred writers, artists, and intellectuals in the Kremlin's Sverdlov Hall, the leadership called a halt to de-Stalinization and liberalization. At this third meeting in three months—a previous one took place on December 17, 1962, and was followed that month by an All-Union Conference of Young Writers—Khrushchev and Ilyichev spoke, stressing that the Party would not give up its control of artists and their art. Coupled with warnings that no more deviations from "socialist realism" would be tolerated were attacks on liberal writers, particularly Ehrenburg, Yevtushenko, and Nekrasov. Ehrenburg was singled out as the Pied Piper who was leading the young astray, and Ilyichev attacked him for his "theory of silence" in the Stalinist era, quoting some of Ehrenburg's earlier panegyrics to Stalin and asking whether Ehrenburg had been insincere then or was lying now. Ilyichev also damned an early Ehrenburg novel, *The Life of Lazik Roitshvants,* as anti-Soviet, remarking intimidatingly that the novel was "still being used widely in anti-Communist propaganda. Somehow, though, we have not heard that the author has expressed his attitude toward this." [1] This same method of holding a writer responsible for how "enemies" of the Soviet Union use his work was subsequently invoked against other writers—Sinyavsky, Daniel, Aleksandr Yesenin-Volpin, and Solzhenitsyn, to mention only a few. This standard weapon in the Stalinist arsenal of abuse and intimidation has never been relinquished by the regime. It is a component of the continuing assessment of behavior as useful or harmful to the regime, irrespective of the "subjective" or "objective" intention of the works or of their authors.

Youth and the problem of influencing it were factors in the battle of the generations and consequently important elements of the struggle between conservative and liberal, both of whom wanted the soul and allegiance of the young in support of the values they espoused. Because the youth were in general less doctrinaire, more receptive to new ideas and methods, the Party accused the liberal writers of sowing distrust in their minds about Party positions and trying to "pass themselves off as spiritual 'mentors,' the spiritual 'leaders' of our young people." [2] Only the Communist Party would serve as spiritual leader of the people and particularly of youth, Ilyichev declared, and he was especially concerned to deny the existence of any generation gap between fathers and sons.

The enemy was also preaching "fables" about Marxist-Leninist ideology being incompatible with freedom, was saying "that if you wish to preserve socialist realism in art, then you cannot escape a 'return' to the methods of 'the Stalinist epoch.' " [3] Ilyichev denied that this was true, but he faced one of the central problems that arose from loosening restrictions on literature. As one abandons the notion of Party spirit in literature and Party control over literature, one also begins to abandon the idea of the Party's control over life. For if the Party is incapable of dictating the spirit and content of literature, how can it be the most reliable and skillful means for dictating the spirit and content of the society? Part of the Party's megalomaniacal commitment to total control over the life of the society (which is what totalitarian governments strive for and, however successful, never achieve) would thus be compromised; moreover, art in Soviet society must be subjugated to politics or else the entire notion of the relationship between the "base" and the "superstructure" collapses.

The following day, Khrushchev took up the same matters in an unremitting attack on all who deviated from the Party's purposes, though he was gentler with some than with others. His main targets were Ehrenburg and Yevtushenko, but a number of other writers came in for their share of castigation. Khrushchev met the "fathers and sons" issue head on, denying that any conflicts existed between Soviet generations. In this regard, he commented adversely on a film written and directed by Marlen Khutsiyev, "Ilyich's Gate," [4] and on Viktor Nekrasov's laudatory remarks about it in *Both Sides of the Ocean*. Nekrasov had commended the preview of the movie he had seen because it asked the right questions, the questions Soviet youth were asking: What is the right way to live? What can I make of my life?

I am endlessly grateful to Khutsiyev and Shpalikov for not dragging in the old worker by his greying moustache, the one who understands everything and always has exactly the right answer for anything you ask him. If he had come by with his instructive sayings, it would have ruined the picture. Instead, they tried something else, something much more difficult. Sergey takes the question to his father, his father who died at the front: he asks his father how he should live. This is one of the most powerful scenes in the movie. A meeting of father and son. Is it a dream, a fantasy, a hallucination, I don't know. But the son meets his father. His father is wearing his army cap and poncho, and he is carrying a machine-gun across his chest. Suddenly the room is transformed into a dugout. Soldiers are lying asleep where they have fallen. On the table there is a lamp made out of a shell case. Father and son have a drink together.

The son tells the father, "I wish I'd been with you in the attack when you were killed."

"Why?" says the father. "You must live."

And the son asks, "But how?"

And the father only asks a question in return:

"How old are you now?"

"Twenty-three."

"And I am only twenty-one."

These last words make the shivers run up and down your spine.

The father leaves without answering the question. His comrades are waiting for him. And they set off, three soldiers in ponchos, three comrades with machine-guns across their chests, marching through the Moscow of today. . . . They march on, just as at the beginning of the picture, three other soldiers marched along the streets of another Moscow, a Moscow of 1917, three soldiers of the Revolution. And the even staccato of their footsteps is drowned out by other footsteps: Red Square, the changing of the guard, the Mausoleum, and the inscription: Lenin.[5]

This powerful scene portraying the generation gap clearly showed that the older generation had no satisfactory answers to offer the younger generation; the fathers could not tell the sons how to live *now.* Consciously or unconsciously, it also implied that perhaps the answers contained in the Mausoleum, the repository of Lenin and Stalin's embalmed corpses, were also not adequate. There was, there had to be, a *changing of the guard;* the young would soon have to take up the burden the older generation had heretofore borne, and they would have to exercise the power which would shape not only their individual futures but the collective future of Soviet society.

That such a film and Nekrasov's encomium should offend Khrushchev and the Party leadership is not surprising. The First Secretary declared that the movie's purpose was "to impress upon the sons that their fathers cannot teach them in life, that there was no point in asking them [the fathers] for advice." This was absolute rubbish, he averred, and he counseled the young: "Learn from the Revolution in which your fathers and mothers took part and sacredly revere the memory of those who are not with us any longer, treat respectfully those who live on," and learn from them in order to be "worthy inheritors of their cause." Khrushchev categorically rejected the film, because its most moving scenes "cover up the real meaning . . . which is to assert ideas and standards of public and private life which Soviet people find alien and unacceptable." Khrushchev made no bones about the fact that "our Soviet youth has been brought up by our Party, it follows our Party, and sees in it its educator and leader." [6]

In high dudgeon Khrushchev also castigated Nekrasov for his sarcastic comments on the old worker with "his greying moustache," the stereotyped know-it-all figure of Soviet films and letters, who always has the right—and Party—answer to all questions; Khrushchev declared: "And that was written by a Soviet author in a Soviet magazine! It is impossible to read such things, in a tone so haughty and contemptuous about an old worker, without indignation." [7] Thus began a campaign of vilification against Nekrasov that was to continue for months.

To regain the confidence of the young, Party leaders had to meet the major issue of the complicity of the older generation in the Stalinist crimes that the young could neither forget nor admire.

This Khrushchev endeavored to do by contradicting Ehrenburg's "theory of silence" in two ways: first, by insisting that most of the leadership knew nothing of Stalin's crimes against the innocent; second, by remarking that when some of the leaders learned of specific injustices, unlike Ehrenburg, they spoke up against them—even to Stalin himself. "At Stalin's funeral," Khrushchev reminisced, "many, including myself, were in tears. These were sincere tears, Although we knew about some of Stalin's personal shortcomings, we believed in him." They believed in him so much that they could not conceive that "repression could be used against honest people devoted to our cause." Khrushchev claimed that he himself had averted purges both in Moscow and the Ukraine, and that Mikhail Sholokhov—the novelist to whom he sharply and adversely compared Ehrenburg— "as a real Bolshevik writer [had] refused to accept crying injustice: he rose against the lawlessness which was rampant at the time [during the forced collectivization in the Don district in 1933], but Stalin remained deaf to these warnings from Sholokhov, just as he did to many similar warnings from other courageous Communists." [8] This comparison between Ehrenburg, a leader of the liberal writers, and Sholokhov, one of the leaders of the conservatives, cuttingly stressed Sholokhov's involvement with the Revolution and its problems while Ehrenburg stood aside. Suffering by the comparison, Ehrenburg seemed an indecisive and inadequate Bolshevik to begin with, but also a collaborator with Stalin who wrote paeans of praise to the dictator yet kept his mouth shut about Stalin's crimes. Sholokhov, on the other hand, was shown to have stood his ground—even against Stalin. Khrushchev was recommending to the young: If you must choose a model, Sholokhov, not Ehrenburg, is the man to imitate.

It was, of course, a recommendation that cut both ways, for if one recommended resistance to Stalin's "excesses," by implication one also recommended similar opposition to Khrushchev's "excesses." Priscilla Johnson sees a logical contradiction in Khrushchev's lumping the crimes of collectivization (1933–1935) with those of the great purges (1937–1938), yet declaring that Sholokhov was aware of them while Khrushchev, a high Party official, was not. [9] Yet Khrushchev's lumping both types of Stalinist crimes together is quite logical. Moreover, Khrushchev had already tried to clear himself by implying that he had stood against Stalinist purges in Moscow and in the Ukraine in the 1930s.

So sharp was Khrushchev's attack on Ehrenburg that the writer was reported to have lamented that although he would never see the flowering of Soviet arts in his lifetime, in twenty years others might. (Tatu remarked that "it was difficult to tell whether this prophecy erred on the side of optimism or pessimism." [10]) Thereafter, without recanting or indulging in self-criticism, Ehrenburg quietly isolated himself in his dacha outside Moscow. Years later, he was to tell Alexander Werth: "I shall not live to see it, but I firmly believe that in twenty years' time our country will start producing a great literature, yes, something of the Tolstoy-Dostoyevsky class. Here we have on the one hand the immense genius of the Russian people and, on the other, a hideous bureaucratic machine which continues to encourage the mediocrities by printing them in our 'best' magazines. . . . But it can't go on forever." [11] Later that summer of 1963, however, after Kozlov had had a second heart attack, Khrushchev talked to Ehrenburg and personally encouraged him to finish editing his memoirs.[12]

Khrushchev then took the next, and inevitable step, the partial rehabilitation of Stalin, explaining that though the Party denounced and continued to denounce "the arbitrary acts and abuse of power committed by Stalin which damaged seriously the cause of Communism [the Party] nevertheless . . . pays credit to Stalin's services to the Party and to the Communist movement. We continued to maintain that Stalin was devoted to Communism. He was a Marxist, and this cannot and should not be denied." [13] Khrushchev had always carefully hedged his bet on Stalin in his de-Stalinization program. After each of his major de-Stalinization speeches, he had managed to insert some small but important escape clause: after his speech to the Twentieth Party Congress in 1956, he had given Stalin some of his due in 1957, saying, "The term Stalinist, like Stalin himself, is inseparable from the high title of Communist"; [14] and after his de-Stalinization speech to the Twenty-second Congress in 1961, he had added the following accolade: "Stalin was dedicated to Communism with his whole being. Everything he did was for Communism." [15] If Khrushchev had underestimated how far and how swiftly the liberals would take his policy of de-Stalinizing, he was now ready to stop them, rein them in, and even, if necessary, roll back the boundaries of what he himself had made permissible. Now, Khrushchev said, the Stalinist period was all over, and "today all people in our country breathe freely, regard one another trustfully, without suspicion, and are confident of their present and their future, which is guaranteed them by the entire system of life." [16] In short, de-Stalinization had gone far enough and would have to be terminated. With Ilyichev he was endeavoring to drive liberals back to the "middle course" he had set earlier, and if doing so required refurbishing Stalin's reputation somewhat and even employing some neo-Stalinist personnel and methods, he was prepared to accept that price.[17] (One of the rumors then rife in Moscow was that Khrushchev's rivals in the Presidium had brought pressure to bear on him to relinquish either his leadership of the government or of the Party, to surrender either the Premiership or the First Secretaryship. Kozlov was presumed to be behind this continuing effort of his colleagues, the so-called collective leadership, to prevent Khrushchev from achieving his own "cult of personality." [18] Kozlov was thus pressuring Khrushchev to stop the de-Stalinization which threatened other members of the Presidium with being accused of complicity in Stalin's crimes.)

In this "re-Stalinization" Khrushchev warned: "Magazines and publishing houses are said to be flooded with manuscripts about the life of people in exile, in prisons, and in camps. I repeat once again that this is a very dangerous theme." [19] According to Peter Benno, "Floods of literature poured in and many of these authors knew they had no chance of being published but the editing houses are 'required to review every manuscript submitted'; some six to ten readers get the material, often show it to friends who in turn copy it and circulate it farther afield. In effect, submitting a story or poem for publication constitutes quasi-publication or crypto-publication." [20] There had been four million people in the camps at the time of Stalin's death, so such a flood of "recollections" was justifiable. There had been hints and mentions of the concentration camps in Yury Bondarev's *Silence*, in Nekrasov's *Kira Georghievna*, and in Galina Nikolayeva's *The Running Battle;* and two stories had been written and published in Hungary about the camps themselves,

Gyula Oszko's *The Twelfth Sunday* and Jozsef Lengyel's *From the Beginning to the End* (Lengyel had spent seven years in Soviet penal camps during the 1950s, before Stalin's death),[21] but only *Ivan Denisovich* had depicted the camps in all their murderous detail and been published in the USSR. Khrushchev's warning made it plain that the concentration camp theme was, in the future, to be avoided, because de-Stalinization had for the moment been halted, and because such works were thought to give aid and comfort to foreign foes of the Soviet Union. This spelled the end of the possibilities for publication of Solzhenitsyn's other writings on the labor camps.

It was now Yevtushenko's turn to be rebuked, and Khrushchev belabored him for wavering and instability, cautioning: "If the enemies of our cause start to praise you for works which please them, the people will justly criticize you. So choose what suits you best." Khrushchev then returned to the theme of anti-Semitism and "Babi Yar," accusing Yevtushenko of political immaturity and ignorance of the facts, because in the poem the poet "represents things as if only Jews were the victims of fascist atrocities." [22]

After sideswipes at Nekrasov, Konstantin Paustovsky, Voznesensky, and Valentin Katayev, as well as at Yevtushenko, for currying favor with the "bourgeois public" abroad, and for speaking carelessly and irresponsibly to Western newspapermen, Khrushchev reiterated his basic point: the reins of the Party and the government were going to be tightened. "The press, radio, literature, painting, music, the cinema, and the theater are a sharp ideological weapon of our Party. And it sees to it that this weapon is always in fighting trim and hits the enemy without fail. The Party will not allow anyone to blunt this weapon or weaken its effect." [23]

Why Khrushchev had decided to reverse de-Stalinization and had begun a campaign of repression of the arts in December, and now, three months later, had stepped up its intensity was not easily explained. Doubtless, he wished to turn the "heirs of Stalin" question away from himself and his government. "The campaign against the cult of personality did more than unmask a dictator," one Soviet student said; "it unmasked a whole generation." [24] Also, Khrushchev was facing opposition in the Politburo because his policies, including de-Stalinization, had produced untoward consequences. The lifting of fear of physical terrorizing by the KGB had encouraged ferment, so that some Soviet intellectuals and even ordinary citizens were for the first time speaking their minds openly. Others acted out their resistance to Stalinist restraints. There was widespread "labor indiscipline," and in many parts of Siberia great construction projects came to a halt because workers simply quit. There were "minor disorders in the country on a scale substantially larger than the handful of such disturbances reported . . . in the Lower Volga regions last summer," [25] this last a reference to the riots that had taken place in Novocherkassk and other cities. Housewives and others protested consumer-goods shortages. The bureaucracy, target of much of the "heirs of Stalin" criticisms, grew increasingly demoralized. Top-level leadership conflicts about whether to increase the production of consumer goods, farm machinery, and fertilizer, or to continue to give priority and a major portion of the funds to the "metal eaters" of heavy industry wracked all levels of the bureaucracy. Khrushchev remained in a vulnerable position because his Cuban policy had failed and the rupture with China was about to become public. Among the dogmatists there were many, like secret-police chief Semichastny, who called for tightening the reins throughout the country, for extending the death penalty against economic crimes (earlier decreed by Khrushchev) to other types of civil indiscipline as well as for bringing the liberal writers to heel. [26]

Following the climax of the March meetings with Khrushchev, the conservatives tried to force the liberal writers to the wall. The possibility that the Party might use police coercion to force compliance with its wishes was by no means ruled out, and Kochetov, only days after the March meetings, was calling for "actions not words" against the recalcitrant writers; [27] in brief, he demanded police reprisals, which, under Stalin, had euphemistically been called "administrative measures," against the liberal writers. The sculptor Yevgeny Vuchetich proposed that all the unions of writers, painters, musicians, and other cultural workers be unified into a single artists' organization—a proposal seconded by Aleksandr Chakovsky—as a means of imposing greater discipline on creative artists. [28] The conservatives also recaptured control of the liberal stronghold in the Moscow section of the Writers' Union, replacing the sixty-four-year-old liberal Stepan Shchipachev, a poet of the older generation who had encouraged and defended the young liberal writers, with

Georgy Markov, a hard-line conservative. Kochetov publicly exulted. The conservatives were able to effect similar changes in the fine-arts and cinema organizations, thus consolidating their control of the cultural unions, and engineered the dismissal of two of the liberals from the editorial board of *Literaturnaya rossiya*, Oleg Mikhailov and Aleksandr Borshchagovsky, so that the magazine, intended as a liberal successor to the dogmatist *Literatura i zhizn*, also came under conservative control. Moreover, Moscow was rife with rumors that Tvardovsky had been dismissed as editor of *Novy mir* and replaced by Vladimir Yermilov,[29] but the rumors were formally denied by both men.[30]

This time, moreover, the conservatives were determined, not only to bring the liberal writers into line, but to force them to their knees. The liberal writers, especially the younger ones, were going to have to recant publicly and endure the whole ritual of self-criticism. They were not going to be permitted to engage in a "conspiracy of silence," refusing to write or recant, as they had during the earlier freeze in 1957–1958.

The attacks against Voznesensky, Aksyonov, Bondarev, Okhudzhava, Yashin, Yury Kazakov, and Baklanov were all scathing, but two writers bore the brunt of the assault: Yevtushenko and Nekrasov. Because Yevtushenko was considered the "poet laureate of the Khrushchev regime"[31] and the Party spokesman to the youth, he came in for especially rough handling. Conservatives called for his expulsion from the Writers' Union,[32] and others demanded his removal from the editorial board of *Yunost*.[33] The authorities found it particularly offensive that Yevtushenko had published *A Precocious Autobiography* in *L'Express*, in Paris, without first submitting the book to Party censorship or asking Party permission. At a meeting of the Writers' Union, March 25–28, 1963, Yevtushenko and Voznesensky recanted, but not to the satisfaction of the leadership. Three days later, *Komsomolskaya pravda* took Yevtushenko to task for having come "to regard himself as the herald of a new generation," a martyr who had surrounded himself with "romantically dramatic props including the crown of thorns of a sufferer and the staff of a wandering prophet." And the Young Communist League's paper went on to excoriate him for seeking dubious applause from bourgeois newspapers and indulging in pious stupidities and confessionals. Ominously, it warned, "He must realize that one cannot fall down endlessly and then get up, shake oneself off and pretend that nothing has happened." [34] Earlier, the head of the Komsomol, Sergey Pavlov, had vented his rage against those who crawl "on their bellies before the foreigner, begging him for foreign rags or chewing gum." [35] Yet, two weeks later, in an interview, Pavlov remarked about Yevtushenko, "Everything is open to him. Nobody is closing any doors," and told how he had received a thousand letters about the *Komsomolskaya pravda* attacks on Yevtushenko, of which only fifteen defended the young poet.[36]

The attacks continued, because the conservatives were seriously concerned about the allegiance of youth, and well they might be. A year earlier Boris Polevoi had warned that the young people speak to the older, ruling generations in these terms: "You want to measure youth by old yardsticks. . . . You impoverish the image, you wish to depersonalize individuality." [37] The persistence of the "fathers and sons" problem was a thorn in the conservatives' sides; Aleksandr Korneichuk, the playwright and friend of Khrushchev from the Ukraine days, in attacking Yevtushenko (and Voznesensky), exclaimed: "Don't you realize that it is for you [the young and the young writers] that we are fighting? We want you to be our comrades in the struggle for a Communist culture, and want to feel your shoulders next to ours as we march forward together." [38]

What Yevtushenko must have felt during that time is brilliantly conveyed by Priscilla Johnson, who interviewed him at that time in Moscow.

Facing Yevtushenko across a luncheon table in Moscow is like watching a politician on TV. There is the same split second of hesitation, the same nearly reflexive choice among alternative answers. The only spontaneous reaction is calculation. Clearly, this young man has repressed his high spirits at heartrending cost. His rebelliousness rarely breaks into the open. Frequently his remarks are so loaded with ambiguity that it is difficult to guess whether he means what he appears to be saying or the opposite.[39]

Some years later she speculated that the regime had not permitted the conservatives to destroy Yevtushenko because "partly by virtue of his compromises, of the split between poet and politician in his personality, the Party had been able [through him] to keep the entire youth movement under control. Some may have felt that, grown too big for his breeches, it was time for Yevtushenko to go. Others must have asked: Will the next idol be controlled so easily?" [40]

Under the severe Party pressure and threat of reprisal, one writer after another recanted during the spring, but none of the recantations and self-criticisms, ambiguous and reserved as they were, satisfied the dogmatists. The one writer who did not at first perform the litany of self-abasement was Nekrasov, and on him the Party leadership brought all its weight to bear. In Kiev, Nekrasov's home city, Nikolay Podgorny asked: "For what truth do you, Comrade Nekrasov, stand? Your speech and the ideas you continue to maintain carry a strong flavor of petty-bourgeois anarchy. The Party, the people, cannot and will not tolerate this." [41] Two months later, though Nekrasov had finally written a letter of self-criticism to the Central Committee of the Ukrainian Communist Party, Khrushchev attacked him once more for having lost his sense of Communist partisanship and recommended that he be expelled from the Party. Though Nekrasov had been a Party member for just a little less than twenty years, Khrushchev told the Central Committee plenary session on ideology, June 21: "The Party should get rid of such people, who set their personal delusions above the decision of the Party." In a menacing, if literary comparison, the First Secretary warned: "He who shifts from our camp of builders of Communism to the other camp will sooner or later have to answer to his people. Nikolay Vasilyevich Gogol showed well how Taras Bulba killed his son for having gone over to the enemy's side. Such is the logic of combat." [42]

In spite of the harsh words, the peak of the campaign had been reached. Nekrasov was not, in the final analysis, expelled from the Party, nor were the younger writers, although they were shipped off to various parts of the country to re-establish their "connections with the people," and Khrushchev rejected the dogmatist suggestion to combine the various artists' unions into one big union. And though there had been consistent and powerful attacks on the liberal magazines, their editorial boards remained intact, and the two chief dogmatist targets, Tvardovsky and Polevoi, retained their editorial positions. Already, in June, there was evidence that another, abrupt, shift in policy was in process.

8 Matryona's House

Open all the doors,
It is stuffy in the house.
Oh, land of the Soviets, you are generous,
You are freedom itself,
Then open your doors,
Remove the barriers,
And accept from us with your kind hands
A complaint against those
Whose hearts are hard as stones.

Semyon Kirsanov

In spite of the curbs Khrushchev and Ilyichev had placed on the liberal writers at the December 1962 meetings, Tvardovsky published two stories by Solzhenitsyn in the January 1963 issue of *Novy mir:* "The Incident at Krechetovka Station" and "Matryona's House." Solzhenitsyn's immunity from criticism had already begun to fade, for that same month Lydia Fomenko denigrated *One Day in the Life of Ivan Denisovich* as lacking a broad and comprehensive view of the Stalin epoch,[1] and the publication of the two new stories brought intense criticism down on Solzhenitsyn and on his work.

"The Incident at Krechetovka Station"[2] depicts one day in the life of Zotov, an assistant transport officer of a small railway terminal in Russia during the critical days of World War II. On that day a straggler named Tveritinov arrives at the station without his papers, asking to be shipped ahead so that he can overtake his unit. Tveritinov, an actor older than Zotov, is something of a Bohemian intellectual. Zotov is charmed because he is able to unburden himself to the older man as he cannot to those ordinarily around him. But Zotov's suspicion that Tveritinov is a spy—the actor has lost his papers and can't remember the name Stalingrad—causes him to turn the man over to the political police.

Very few dramatic events occur in the story, but the exploration of Zotov, an essentially decent man, something of a prig, intelligent and idealistic but provincial and narrow-minded, who eventually commits a profoundly evil act of betrayal, is adroit. Solzhenitsyn portrays Zotov as a boyish, even childish man who is offended by the untidiness of life, a man of schedules and charts, planned arrivals and departures. All about him he sees human weakness and inefficiency, slovenliness and corruption, yet he remains hard-working, honest, efficient. Zotov is a product of the Soviet system, a bureaucrat who, the moment he acts officially—Solzhenitsyn symbolizes the contradictory aspects of his character by having Zotov don his uniform hat when acting as a bureaucrat and take it off when acting as a human being—betrays all the vices of the system: paranoid suspicion, hatred of individuality, absence of initiative, blind stupidity.

In contrasting Zotov with those around him, Solzhenitsyn portrays the USSR of 1941 so that it reflects the basic nature of Soviet society—a society constantly in a state of war, and repellent with its cries for vigilance and militancy and its paranoid quest for spies and traitors. He also shows the kindness of ordinary people, their willingness to help one another, the continuing necessity of exercising individual initiative if one is to survive, sometimes to the point of looking out only for oneself. Everywhere there are stealing, foraging, bartering, trading, *blat*, which humanize the harshness of the system and make it endurable—perhaps even make it work. At the same time, Solzhenitsyn conveys the common people's pervasive hatred of injustice, their consciousness of class division and class bias in Soviet life, their anti-intellectual prejudices.

In anatomizing Zotov's "high-minded" puritanism, Solzhenitsyn describes the transport officer's inflexible dogmatism, the way a good man betrays another man because he has neither understanding of, nor sympathy for, human irregularity and difference. Among other things, Solzhenitsyn was saying to the Soviet audience of 1963 that there are always enough people to carry out a terror, some of them perfectly decent individuals who will be accomplices of injustice for "perfectly reputable" reasons. Artistically, Solzhenitsyn embodies something of Hannah Arendt's "banality of evil" in his story. At the same time he represents Soviet society as perpetually—then, in 1941, as now, in 1963—in a state of war, a state of siege, in which personal feelings and personal decency must always "officially" be suppressed. Yet when they are, there is a grievous price to be paid. After Zotov betrays Tveritinov, he is never able to find out what happened to the actor, and although he inquires of an NKVD officer, he is brutally disregarded, in effect told to mind his own business, and is then afraid to ask further. As a consequence, "he was never the same man again." Solzhenitsyn is cautioning that once individuals become police informers, accomplices of terror, they can never be the same again—they are forever corrupted. If the story was a thrust against the heirs of Stalin even before Stalin's actual death, it was also a blow against the gap between fathers and sons, for Zotov and Tveritinov are of different generations, a point Solzhenitsyn also subtly stresses.

"Matryona's House" is set in 1956,[3] and, whatever the implications of "The Incident at Krechetovka Station" for post-Stalin Russia, is closer in time and circumstance to the present—hence far more threatening to the heirs of Stalin. The story surveys the countryside with an unrelenting eye and judges the whole kolkhoz system to be bankrupt. But because that bankruptcy is set in 1956, three years after Stalin's death, during Khrushchev's tenure and in the year of the Twentieth Party Congress, and touches on the situation in farming, an area of the Soviet economy where Khrushchev had sought to use his new policies as part of his drive for power, it is a direct criticism of the dogmatists still in power. The story was published simultaneously with a number of others delineating rural greed, poverty, ignorance, and ineptitude, mainly Aleksandr Yashin's "Vologda Wedding"[4] and Fyodor Abramov's "Round and About."[5] Solzhenitsyn's story dispelled the myth of happy, cooperative kolkhozniks and their devotion to the system, describing how deeply the problem of fathers and sons afflicted the countryside and how the heirs of Stalin still ruled the farm roost arbitrarily.

"Matryona's House" takes a central character like Ivan Denisovich, a "simple heart" in the Russian literary tradition, a poor countrywoman whose life has been one of unrelenting misery and hardship, and delineates her moral and personal worth. A sick widow, who has been discharged from the kolkhoz without a pension, she is always on the verge of starvation. Her attempts to get her pension are fobbed off from one bureaucrat to another, and although in 1956 "Party officials were no longer sitting behind dark, leather-upholstered doors, but behind glassy partitions, as in a pharmacy," [6] no one helps her or gives her her due. The only time Matryona is happy is when she is working, digging potatoes or peat, picking berries, trying to find fodder for her one white goat.

The story is told by a mathematics teacher just released from a concentration camp who has come to the village to live because he "wanted to cut . . . loose and get lost in the innermost heart of Russia—if there was any such thing—and live there." [7] Ultimately, he finds shelter in Matryona's home and learns the story of her life, its deprivation and exploitation. Abruptly, the kolkhoz, perennially short of labor, drafts her for work without pay, but that winter her pension at long last begins to arrive, the mathematics teacher begins to pay rent for his room and board, and Matryona is able to buy felt boots and a quilted jacket and to set aside enough money for her burial.

Now her only surviving daughter returns and wants Matryona's house and land. They dismantle the house and put the logs on a makeshift sledge, which pulls away from the tractor hauling it and lands on the railway tracks, where it is struck by two locomotives traveling without lights. In the accident, Matryona is killed.

Then Matryona's relatives quarrel about what she has left behind —the shed, the goat, the garden plot, all the meager property of the widow—with a voracious, heartless, evil greed that is staggering. In their disagreements, they convey to the mathematics teacher the scorn and contempt they had for Matryona. They tell him that her husband had had a mistress in the city and betrayed her. They laugh at her because she worked for others without pay and "never tried to acquire things for herself. She wouldn't struggle to buy things which would then mean more to her than life itself." Matryona, made a misfit by her moral standards, was misunderstood and abandoned by everyone.

We all lived beside her and never understood that she was that righteous one without whom, according to the proverb, no village can stand.

Nor any city.

Nor our whole land.[8]

This is the conclusion of the mathematics teacher who had hoped to lose himself in the inmost heart of Russia—if there was any such thing. Matryona Vasilyevna, the ethical soul of the village, and by implication of Russia, is killed by two locomotives hurtling through the dark without lights—the Party's forced industrialization and collectivization?—but even when her hard work and honesty, her cooperativeness and kindness are gone, the living have only contempt for them and for her.

Open criticism of Solzhenitsyn was, at first, relatively mild, for the novelist still was protected by the power of Khrushchev's public approval. Early in 1963, in a review of the fiction of 1962, Lydia Fomenko had taken the line about *One Day in the Life of Ivan Denisovich* which the Party was increasingly to take about Stalin and Stalinism: in censuring the novel, she said that Solzhenitsyn had neglected to show that in spite of Stalin, the Party and the people had continued to build socialism, their lives filled with heroic effect and faithfulness to Communist ideals.

Solzhenitsyn's tale, with all its artistic refinement and its cruel and bitter truth, nevertheless does not reveal the entire dialectic of that time. In it a passionate "No!" is said to the Stalin order. . . . But the tale does not rise to a philosophical perception of that time, to a broad generalization capable of embracing within itself the conflicting phenomena of that epoch.

One must not see in the past only monstrous evil-doings. The fortunate fact is that the cult was not as all-powerful as Stalin himself thought, as almost everybody thought then. The mighty power of the people was ascribed to one man, but that inexhaustible creative force carried on its great historical task.[9]

In February, moreover, the Soviet government announced that it had canceled its contract with the E. P. Dutton publishing firm for an American edition of *One Day in the Life of Ivan Denisovich* [10]—another straw in the wind that indicated official policy toward Solzhenitsyn was shifting. Then, early in March, just before Khrushchev's March 8 speech to the writers which lumped Solzhenitsyn with the other liberal authors as an acceptable target, a playwright and editor of *Znamya*, Vadim Kozhevnikov, wrote an essay highly critical of "Matryona's House," applying to it the very same standard Lydia Fomenko had applied to *Ivan Denisovich*—in essence, that Solzhenitsyn did not really understand the "dialectic of the time."

The science of joy is inseparable from our literature, an evincing of its deepest optimism. . . . It appears to me that "Martryona's Home" was written when its author was still in a state of mind in which he could not comprehend the life of the people, the movement and real perspectives of that life, with any profundity. . . . Solzhenitsyn's story convinces one over and over again: without a vision of historical truth, of its essence, there can be no complete truth, no matter how great the talent.[11]

In the turmoil after the March meetings, the dogmatists pressed their advantage against the liberals with a vengeance, and in the new dispensation Solzhenitsyn became fair game. Criticism centered on "Matryona's House," but not even *Ivan Denisovich* was spared. Other pressures on Solzhenitsyn were also made public. On March 25, it was reported that his play *The Love-Girl and the Innocent*, accepted for the stage in 1962 by the Moscow Sovremennik ("Contemporary") Theater,[12] had now been delayed in production and would not be performed at all unless Solzhenitsyn rewrote it—which he had agreed to do.[13]

At the end of the month, in an article entitled "Matryona's House and Its Environs," conservative critic Viktor Poltoratsky expanded the point of view developed earlier by Fomenko and Kozhevnikov. Poltoratsky agreed that Solzhenitsyn was an "honest artist," filled with sadness, pain, and indignation at the fate of Matryona Vasilyevna, but he had failed to see the forest for the trees. Solzhenitsyn had "selected such a viewpoint as limited his horizon to the old fence of Matryona's house. . . . If he had looked beyond that fence, he would have seen the Bolshevik Collective Farm a mere twenty kilometers from Talnovo, and he might have shown us the righteous men of the new age—people enthusiastically transforming the land and establishing new Communist relations in public life." In censuring the story, Poltoratsky was shrewd; he demonstrated that the events were rooted in Solzhenitsyn's own experience, set in an actual place "near Palishchi, and it was he, appointed teacher of the secondary school [there] who rented an apartment at Talnovo and later wrote the story 'Matryona's House.' "[14] So the failure of the story might be laid to Solzhenitsyn's partial and perhaps even distorted vision of the reality. By implication, then, "Matryona's House" presented only a subjective and imperfect perception of Soviet reality and failed to grasp the basic revolutionary elements which were in fact transforming the Soviet countryside and Soviet man. In portraying Matryona Vasilyevna and her fate, Solzhenitsyn had seized, not on the *typical* aspects of events, but on the deviant, the exceptional case.

The emphasis on the *typical* was what the conservative critics counterposed to any adverse portrayal of Soviet reality by the liberal writers. Yes, the conservatives admitted, there might be run-down kolkhozes, arbitrary arrests and unjust imprisonment, cheats, liars, cowardly soldiers, wily and unscrupulous bureaucrats, but these were not *typical;* they were exceptions to the rule. The proper role of Soviet writers was not to focus on such *deviants* but to set them in perspective against what was *generally* true, depicting those honorable, hard-working, and optimistic Soviet men and women who were "building Communism" and who had accomplished great things. Optimism, or the "science of joy," arose from perceiving the general revolutionary development of society, noting the positive and progressive movement of events, and was communicated by the writer to the reader. Subsumed under this view, of course, is the notion that even if the *typical* is *not* general, it should be; and the role of Soviet writers should be to educate and uplift the spirits of the Soviet people, to strive toward the goal of actually making the typical general.

The crucial difficulty for the Soviet leadership was embodied in *One Day in the Life of Ivan Denisovich*, however. What was rumbling under the surface of Soviet political and cultural attitudes toward that book could have been extrapolated from what was happening in Hungary during that winter and spring of 1963. There, not only Solzhenitsyn's novel on the concentration camps had been published, but also another on the same theme by a Hungarian writer, Jozsef Lengyel. He was a Kossuth Prize winner and had written a short novel, *From the Beginning to the End*, which gave his account of the seven years he had spent in Soviet concentration camps. Though *Ivan Denisovich* was published in installments in the magazine *Nagyvilag* and thus given wide publicity, and in a ten-thousand-copy edition by the Europe Publishing House in book form, Lengyel's work appeared only in the literary journal *Uj Iras*, with a circulation of six to eight thousand.

A young Hungarian writer and critic, Lajos Galambos, attacked the "unhealthy interest" many Hungarians were displaying in *Ivan Denisovich*. In an article entitled "I Protest," Galambos maintained that everywhere he went he saw people who never read anything before but the sports pages now reading the latest issue of *Nagyvilag*. Galambos is outraged because "the great interest is unfortunately not literary. It is an interest in things which smell foul, which smell of scandal. I am sorry but my whole being protests such a hysterical mood. Yes, it is true that such a mood has developed and it is expanding and swelling and growing until it obliterates all other topics in daily meetings. A shiver goes through people, accompanied by cynical nods of the head and by sidelong glances, as if some racy bedroom story had been told among good friends who heard it from a well-informed person." Even in the countryside, Galambos finds the "county president, the Party secretary, a tractor driver, an electrician, a teacher, a journalist, and an engineer" all reading *Ivan Denisovich*. Their opinions and reactions to the novel also displease him, because they are either "thoughtfully in agreement, cynical, malicious, skeptical, pseudo-objective, passionately protesting or the opposite, [containing] unmistakable hints about the similarities between Fascist camps and the forced labor camps described in [*Ivan Denisovich*]." [15] Galambos neither attacks the novel's literary merit nor defends the Stalinist crimes committed, but he is profoundly concerned about the vast amount of attention the press has devoted to Solzhenitsyn's book and to the political and social reverberations it is having among the people.

Lengyel's *From the Beginning to the End* provoked another but related problem: Could a foreigner understand what had happened during the Stalinist era simply by virtue of his presence in Russia then? A leading political commentator, Tamas Zala, attacked Lengyel because he had not given a "psychologically and historically authentic analysis" of the Soviet camps.

Are personal experiences and a writer's talent for portraying them sufficient to enable someone to tell the truth about the consequences of the cult of personality? Isn't something more required, something which only those people possess whose life and mentality are rooted in Soviet soil? Is a life transplanted there capable of absorbing and reflecting all those historical traditions, this complexity of society and the mysteries of another people's soul, which taken together provide an explanation for the extremely complicated symptoms of the personality cult and for the fact that it could influence Soviet life for such a comparatively long time? I think Togliatti was right when he said that the ultimate truth in the Stalin question had to be reached in the Soviet Union. This does not mean that it is forbidden to discuss it everywhere else; after all, arbitrariness did not spare the international workers' movement either. I do not believe, however, that we can expect a historically and psychologically valid analysis from any other country except the Soviet Union itself—and this is equally valid for works of art and history.

Zala attacked Lengyel's book not only because of its "distortion," but more important, because "no good could come of it." There, it is obvious, he came to the crux of the issue: *"In the Stalin issue justice must be administered in such a way that in people's minds socialism is not identified with violations of the law."* [16] He was also perturbed by the political implications of the novel's hero finding "a camp outside" when he is released from the labor camp, and meeting former prison mates who wish to return to the hell behind the wire from the hell outside, because at least they had bread in the camps.

Six days after Zala's article appeared, Sandor Tatay, a prominent writer and a member of the Hungarian Party's Central Committee, took it upon himself to defend Lengyel; [17] the defense was followed by an even sharper rebuke to Zala from Gyula Hevesi, a Kossuth Prize winner, a vice-president of the Hungarian Academy of Sciences, and also a member of the Central Committee. Hevesi compared Zala's criticism to the kind of literary slander which passed for criticism in the "heyday of the personality cult, in which by means of all kinds of irrelevant talk or wandering thought, totally unjustified insinuations were attributed to the writer, by which the writer rather than the writing was vilified." Hevesi approved the excellent descriptions of the "moon area" given by Solzhenitsyn and Lengyel and reminded Zalas that the locale was "unfortunately, . . . not on the moon but . . . an area of the earth." [18]

Hevesi then attacked the notion that criticism of Soviet reality was reserved to Soviet citizens:

There are people obsessed by the notion . . . that the roots of the Stalinist personality cult have to be sought for in the mind of the Soviet people, in the historical traditions of the Soviet peoples, and in the wealth of Soviet society, and there still exists a printing press with printer's ink that does not blush when it turns out such a text in several thousand copies. I often had a chance to debate with people of various political stances who, lacking personal experience and remote from the events, tried to find some explanation for how the cult of personality could have gained ground and had such persistent consequences. I encountered several incorrect interpretations, but this is the first time that I have heard the explanation of the origin of the cult lies in the "mysteries of the Soviet people's mind" and—at least in part —in Soviet historical traditions. At the time of our own personality cult, Zala's abortive article could easily have resulted in the author's being given a direct "briefing"—not only seen with his eyes but perhaps felt by other parts of his body as well—and this would demonstrate clearly that the roots of the Rakosi brand of personality cult are as little to be sought in the mysteries of the Hungarian heart as the roots of the Stalinist cult can be found in the mind of the Russian people and their historical tradition.[19]

The intensity of Hevesi's rebuke only demonstrated that Zala had touched on an especially sore—and especially relevant—point, that both Soviet institutions and the mentality of the Russian people had been important factors in permitting the cult of personality to be imposed and prolonged in the USSR.

That spring of 1963 there were three organizational meetings— the Fourth Plenum of the Board of USSR Writers, March 25–28; the Eighth Plenum of the RSFSR Writers' Union, April 2–3; and the All-Union Conference of Young Soviet Writers, May 7–10—whose major purpose was to bring young writers back into line. The regime therefore indicted them for their cynicism, nihilism, and corruption by bourgeois influences, and for rejecting the Soviet revolutionary past. The dogmatist position was plainly stated: "We must glorify, sing, inculcate heroism!" [20] The meetings led the younger writers to recant, and dogmatist control of the writers' organizations was strengthened and publicly confirmed. "It is impossible," the conservatives declared, "to agree with those who claim we have had a period of disorder, of ideological hesitation." Mikhail Suslov himself declared: "We went where the Party called us. There were private mistakes, but these mistakes were made by living people. And it is time to inquire about those people, time to bring order into our writers' organization." The conservatives were doing just that, attacking the "private mistakes" of leading liberals—Ehrenburg, Yevtushenko, Voznesensky, Nekrasov, and others—and denouncing the magazines which published them, mainly *Novy mir* and *Yunost:* "Obviously, all is not well with Party guidance in the magazines and newspapers." And Suslov was sharp in noting, "Why, for example, is it precisely in the pages of *Novy mir* that there appears now one, now another, then a third work, upon reading which one can only shrug one's shoulders—Ehrenburg's memoirs, Nekrasov's notes, Solzhenitsyn's stories, and others?" [21]

The conservatives used the organizational powers of the writers' unions to ship writers out of Moscow to the provinces to renew their "ties with the people," and cut off foreign trips and the huge public readings some of the liberal writers had enjoyed. Sergey Pavlov, First Secretary of the Komsomol, denounced the works of the liberal writers for spreading "such pessimism, obscurity and hopelessness that any uninitiated person who did not know our life might think he had totally lost his mind." Pavlov echoed Suslov's criticism of *Novy mir*, remarking, "Incidentally, *Novy mir* prints such works with inexplicable consistency." Pavlov also took *Yunost* to task for exerting a pernicious influence through its editorial board's choice of works characterized by "their tough *stilyaga* [the equivalent of the British "teddy boy" or sharpie; in regime terms, hoodlum or juvenile delinquent] slang, their predilection for calvados, which is the word they use for Chechen-Ingush cognac, and their cowboy bravado when it comes to sexual questions." [22]

Dogmatists continued to try to provide viable answers to the questions raised by the issues of the "heirs of Stalin" and "fathers and sons." Aleksandr Chakovsky made some basic points in his speech to the USSR Writers' Union Fourth Plenary Session, recognizing that the regime's problems arose from "incorrect conclusions [drawn] from the criticism of the cult of the individual, an inaccurate interpretation of this period as a time marked by nothing but mistakes and crimes, and . . . by wilful or involuntary acceptance of bourgeois attitudes hostile to us." [23] Leonid Sobolev declared that ideological enemies were trying to poison "our young people with the subtle venom of false revolutionary boldness, instill an idea about a split between generations through literature, theater and film, and shake the faith in the great cause of the construction of Communism, and infect young people with the cynical psychology of the beatniks and 'Broadway boys.' " [24] Speaker after speaker at the meetings stressed that they "were continuing the cause of our fathers," and exhortation followed exhortation—none altogether free of a tinge of threat—reminding writers, "We should all feel that we are soldiers of the Party." [25] Young Communist League leader Pavlov summed it all up cogently: "Ideological content, civil responsibility, patriotism have always been and must remain the chief, the definitive features of youthful literature." [26]

In April, Solzhenitsyn continued to garner his share of the criticism. On April 2, Vladimir Sokolov, another conservative critic, in a sweeping rejection of Solzhenitsyns' writings, remarked that "they deserved no more than a shrug." [27] This was followed by an attack on *Ivan Denisovich* by dogmatist critic N. Sergovantsev, who found that the novel's "hero is absolutely without the characteristics of modern Soviet man," because he makes no internal (or external) protest against his plight and is concerned only with surviving. What sort of courage does Ivan Denisovich have "when [his] circle of interests does not stretch beyond an extra bowl of gruel, earning some extra money illegally, and a desire for warmth." [28] It was the nub of a criticism which was soon to blossom into a full-fledged controversy. Building on the Fomenko "dialectic of the time" argument, dogmatist critics would soon deny that Ivan Denisovich was *typical* of the prisoners in the camps. Precisely because Ivan Denisovich, like Matryona, was a "simple heart," an ordinary man who could symbolize all of Russia—*typical* in the sense in which the dogmatist critics used the term as well as in the traditional connotations of the term in Russian literature—the novel was bound to become a major target of dogmatist attack. Perhaps the novel had been published in the first place because "its hero was a peasant, a simple man of the people, who would appeal not only to Khrushchev, himself a son of the soil, but to the person by whom the story had to be approved first, Aleksandr Tvardovsky." [29] Early in April, too, the Sovremennik Theater dropped the production of Solzhenitsyn's play *The Love-Girl and the Innocent* altogether.[30]

In the last days of April, Khrushchev told industrial workers:

Some creative intellectuals have drawn the wrong conclusions from the Party's efforts to overcome the injurious consequences of the Stalin cult. They failed to understand that struggle against the cult does not mean weakening leadership, denying authority. Some have even begun to assert that the time has come when everyone can determine his own conduct and direction of work, without considering the interests of society and the state. This is nothing but an anarchist idea, hostile to Marxist-Leninism.[31]

In the following two months the indications seemed confused, sometimes even chaotic. On May 12, an interview Tvardovsky had given to UPI correspondent Henry Shapiro in the last days of April was printed in *Pravda* in which the much attacked editor of *Novy mir* admitted that the March meetings had been justified because there were "certain tendencies in present-day art and literature . . . that the Central Committee . . . rightly found it necessary to criticize." Tvardovsky accepted that literature had to go hand in hand with revolution, but it also had to "reveal and unmask everything old and stagnant" that might impede progress—the classical liberal argument for truthful exposure of the realities of Soviet life. Tvardovsky's forecast of what would be published in *Novy mir* during the rest of the year seemed to indicate a fence straddle: works characterized by "serious knowledge of reality, by truth, by a Party approach to the events of life, and a profound sense of the artist's responsibility to the people." [32]

Obliquely, however, Tvardovsky defended most of the writers who had been under attack during the winter and spring, but he defended Solzhenitsyn openly, declaring that *Ivan Denisovich* was particularly important, "not only because it is based on specific materials and shows the antipopular character of the phenomena associated with the consequences of the cult of the individual, but also because its whole aesthetic structure confirms the unchanging meaning of the tradition of truth in art and decisively counters false innovationism of the formalist, modernist sort." He was simultaneously taking the opportunity to express continued approval of de-Stalinization and to slap the modernists and their mode, both of which were inimical to him. Reminding everyone that Khrushchev himself had liked and approved *Ivan Denisovich* and had himself introduced Solzhenitsyn to the authors assembled at the Palace of Meetings in December, Tvardovsky adduced the conclusion that "this once again irrefutably proves the complete baselessness of the hostile talk of the 'restrictions' and 'regimentation' that, according to certain people, characterize Soviet literature." [33] It was as if Tvardovsky hoped that by declaring that there was freedom in Soviet literature, of which *Ivan Denisovich* was an example, he could defend the liberalized extension of the boundaries of publishing in the Soviet Union as though it was an actual fact.

As the authorities were trying to salvage the political and economic contributions of the Party and the people from the errors and manias of Stalin and Stalinism, so, too, Tvardovsky tried to prevent the literature produced in the 1930s and 1940s from being considered "inaccurate, unoriginal and falsely ceremonious." "Just as the historic creativity of the masses aroused by the Great October Revolution could not be halted in the economic and social fields," Tvardovsky explained, "so did it continue to make itself felt in the field of the development of the new culture, art and literature." [34]

Tvardovsky also denied that any conflict between "fathers and sons" existed:

This expression comes from Turgenev's noted novel *Fathers and Sons*. It deals with the conflict between the "fathers"—the liberal nobels—and the generation of "new people," representatives of the revolutionary democratic intelligentsia of the middle of the last century, who were then appearing on the scene. It is quite clear that the relationships between Turgenev's "fathers and sons" bears not the remotest resemblance to the relations between different generations of our revolution, who had always stood shoulder to shoulder in the struggle for the common cause.

There was something equivocal in that comparison, for clearly the "fathers and sons" issue in the Soviet Union was not a conflict between "liberal" forebears and "revolutionary" sons; it was between repressive Stalinist fathers and liberal offspring. So, too, there was something equivocal, even tongue-in-cheek, in Tvardovsky's additional denial that there was any division of Soviet writers into opposing "liberal" and "conservative" camps. Disputes and differences of opinion, normal in literary life, the editor of *Novy mir* was willing to admit, but "the totality of our Soviet socialist literature" was harmonious, and the so-called divisions between liberals and conservatives, fathers and sons, were created "by the bourgeois press from some broken-down collection of concepts which are inapplicable to our literary relations." [35]

A week later, *Pravda* seemed to be confirming a more moderate line regarding culture, in an editorial which said:

Although the Party directs the development of art and literature in accordance with Leninist principles, it sees no need to control our intelligentsia at every step, to explain to it in detail how to write a book, stage a performance, produce a film, or compose music. . . . The creators of art must not be the sort of people who are accustomed to having all their food chewed for them.[36]

Yet only two days later, Khrushchev's son-in-law, Aleksey Adzhubei, was inveighing against the peaceful coexistence of ideologies in the arts and in the press, and warning Soviet writers and journalists not to fall into the grievous trap of global humanism and universal ideals.[37]

Early in June, writers who were Party members were ordered to register with Party units in such places as factories, institutes, and schools—an order evidently designed to force writers into closer association with workingmen rather than with one another, presumably on the assumption that "restoring their links with the masses" would make them more amenable to Party direction. The order did not apply, however, to non-Party writers.[38] Later that month, in a plenary session on ideology, held by the Central Committee, Khrushchev made clear that although all Communists might express their opinions, once the Party had set the line, everyone must carry out what the "collective thought and will of the Party" had decreed. "Democratic centralism" had never been abandoned, and those who did not bow to the Party decree ceased to be Communists.[39]

Party discipline applied in literature. The Party did not want writers to prettify reality, but to "write truthfully from a life-affirming position" instead of taking the "themes for their works from the rubbish heaps [in order to] pour dirt over everything the Soviet people have been through, won and suffered." [40] The "dialectic of the time" was once more being invoked: there were rubbish heaps, of course, but they were not within the proper purview of the Soviet writer, nor could de-Stalinization be used as an excuse for focusing on them.

Khrushchev showed himself indifferent to the conservative proposal to unify all the creative unions into a single union; he called for a tighter control of the publishing industry so that fewer "negative" books might slip through the censorship and review net. Once again, he warned the writers that neither they nor any other group in Soviet society would be permitted to usurp the leading role of the Party:

We are in favor of self-administration in the arts and for creative unions, if this helps the arts in the right direction. But if some people are thinking of making use of the unions for a struggle against the Party line, they are profoundly mistaken. To these people we say: we recognize a leading role in society for no unions whatever, except for one single union—our Communist Party.

As usual, Khrushchev's speech was full of the language of warfare, one example of which will suffice: "Semyon Mikhailovich Budenny, who is participating in our plenary sessions, knows well that the blade with which the soldier battles the enemy must be clean. If the blade rusts, the soldier throws it away and replaces it. So it is with our ideological weapon. Even less can it stand the least rust, and it must always be ideologically clean." [41]

Among those singled out for Khrushchev's disapproval were Viktor Nekrasov and Mikhail Romm; the latter was censured for having "incorrect views about the role of films"—views which the First Secretary thought Romm had better reconsider. Six months earlier, in the fall of 1962, Romm had told a group of film and theatrical workers: "Some people argue like this; in the long run no one today is arrested, and as long as Khrushchev lives, no one will be arrested. This is perfectly clear. No one will be imprisoned, no one will be forbidden to work, no one will be exiled from Moscow, and no one will be deprived of his wages. And in general there will be no such unpleasantnesses as in those days. Let Kochetov and company behave like hooligans. The leadership will decide." But Romm warned that such an attitude was an abdication of responsibility and a survival of the psychology of Stalinist times. He insisted that instead of relying on leaders, people begin to look into such matters themselves. "So let us look into what is happening," Romm advised. "We have been silent long enough!" [42]

Khrushchev then turned his attention to dissociating himself from the heirs of Stalin, denying Ehrenburg's claim that everyone had lived in silence and with "clenched teeth" during Stalin's reign of terror.

You remember the film *Kuban Cossacks*. As soon as it was shown, we told Stalin that the life of the collective farmers was portrayed untruthfully in this film. In it there was full abundance. Stalin was pleased when the screen showed every collective farmer sitting at a festive table dining on a turkey. At the time I told Stalin that those turkeys had been bought by the Minister of Cinematography, Bolshakov, and that it wasn't farmers eating them but actors. This wasn't what was happening in real life—the countryside was then experiencing great hardships.

You recall that it was not only into films that hoodwinking penetrated. Malenkov's report to the 19th Party Congress, in which he said that the grain problem had been solved, that there was an abundance of bread—this was deception of the Party and the people.

The 19th Congress ended and thousands of letters poured in from all over the country. People wrote to the effect that if the grain problem had been solved, why was there no bread? . . .

Then, in a discussion in the Central Committee, I said, "Comrade Stalin, the Ukrainians are very dissatisfied that they are not given white bread. At the Party Congress it was said that the grain problem has been solved, but the Ukrainians who have always eaten white bread do not have any now." Stalin said: "The Ukrainians must be given white bread." This was almost like the French queen who, when told that the people had no bread, said, "If there is no bread, let them eat cake." [43]

Khrushchev then told how the leaders had clashed about whether to unmask Stalin's crimes at the Twentieth Congress. "Some people," Khrushchev said, "who felt much guilt for the crimes they had committed with Stalin, feared the truth; they feared their own unmasking." Since Khrushchev was in favor of de-Stalinization, was indeed its prime architect, then presumably he had nothing to fear. Though many opposed the "stirring up" of Stalin's crimes, since Stalin and many of his victims were dead, Khrushchev reported that he had insisted on revealing those crimes—and immediately, at the first post-Stalin congress—or the people might never have believed them; and the truth had to be told *"not for personal reasons,* but to defend the purity of the Party." [44] It was a naked confession of how badly the Party needed to restore the people's confidence in its leadership.[45]

It was apparent, then, that Khrushchev had not yet altogether abandoned de-Stalinization, and in July, he was to add, in no uncertain terms:

Anyone who wants to raise Stalin to a pedestal and affix him there does not want what our Party, our people want. Those who do so obviously like Stalin's methods. However, we must view those methods as bad. Respect for the Party and its leadership must not be inculcated by fear; the respect and love of the people, their support, must be won by a vital tie with the people.[46]

Yet in that same month, the reorganization of the publishing houses, the purge of liberals in the Moscow branch of the Writers' Union, and a new State Committee for the Press to supervise the publication of books, under the former head of Glavlit (the official censorship organization), Pavel Romanov, demonstrated that orthodoxy was triumphant organizationally; earlier that spring, however, two dissident writers, Valeriy Tarsis and Aleksandr Yesenin-Volpin, were released from confinement in mental institutions, despite a vicious attack on the latter by Leonid Ilyichev during the December meetings of Party leaders and artists and intellectuals.

9 For the Good of the Cause

A Communist is a man who puts the people's interests above his own, but who, at the same time, would never wantonly squander human lives in the name of those interests.

Yevgeny Yevtushenko

During the summer of 1963 it seemed as if Khrushchev had once more begun a new program of de-Stalinization. In July and August, there was a resumption of the publication of Ehrenburg's memoirs; Tvardovsky's poem "Tyorkin in the Other World" and Solzhenitsyn's novelette *For the Good of the Cause*, both of which were not only severe attacks on Stalinism but on the heirs of Stalin, were printed. At a time of important political changes such as the agreement with the West on banning nuclear tests in the atmosphere, the open rupture in Sino-Soviet relations, and the disastrous harvest of 1963, which was going to necessitate extensive grain purchases in the West if Soviet citizens were not to go hungry, perhaps starve, Khrushchev seems to have permitted or encouraged such publication. The crackdown on the liberal writers had drawn criticism from East European and Western Communist Parties, so Khrushchev may have reversed his course in order to gain their support against China. Frol Kozlov's heart attack in April had removed him from the political scene, so "the main point was that the tough men in cultural matters had lost their most powerful protector." [1]

The summer had been further remarkable for two major clashes between foreign artists and intellectuals and Soviet intelligentsia. The first had taken place in mid-July at the Third International Film Festival in Moscow where, in order not to compromise the impartiality of the festival in foreign eyes, the award had been given to Federico Fellini's *8 1/2*, arousing the fury of Khrushchev and the frustration of the cultural dogmatists. [2] The second major clash took place at the August 5–8 meetings of the European Community of

Writers in Leningrad. The Community, jointly organized by Italian intellectuals friendly to the Soviet Union and Soviet writers, was sponsoring a symposium on modern fiction.[3] There, the speeches by Konstantin Fedin, Leonid Leonov, and Konstantin Simonov, among others, enraged the Western writers by their provincialism and doctrinaire arrogance. Only Ilya Ehrenburg, flown in on the second day of the meetings, presumably having been sent by Khrushchev, was able to compose some of the ruffled feathers.[4] A group of writers from this conference, both Western and Soviet, were invited to Khrushchev's villa at Gagra, on the Black Sea, where the Premier treated them to a harangue, full of ambiguities and contradictions, defending his program of refusing "peaceful co-existence of ideologies," vindicating his crushing of the Hungarian revolt of 1956, praising and also criticizing Stalin—and then asked Tvardovsky to recite his poem "Tyorkin in the Other World" to the assembled writers.

The poem had long been circulating clandestinely in Moscow, and six months earlier the original version—Tvardovsky read a revised version to Khrushchev's guests at Gagra—had been published in an émigré magazine, *Mosty*, in Munich.[5] It was a slashing attack on Stalinist bureaucracy and, by implication, on the heirs of Stalin. Tyorkin, the "ordinary Russian soldier" Tvardovsky had made famous in a series of World War II poems, is now shown in "the other world," which, somewhat to his surprise and chagrin, he finds just the same as the Stalinist world he has left behind. ("The other world" can be understood to mean the post-Stalinist world as well as heaven or hell.) He must go through all of the bureaucratic procedures—fingerprinting, filling out autobiographies, medical checking—and endure all of the bureaucratic rudeness and indifference of the Stalinist world. There is a shortage of essential goods, no hot water or any water for baths, no bedding and no beds; there are corps of fawning bureaucrats, and when he asks for a complaint book to register his complaints, the response is unequivocal:

> But the answer was firm
> To this seditious request:
> In this world there are no complaints,
> Everyone here is contented.

This "other world" is also divided into Soviet and capitalist sections, walled off from each other, and in the Soviet section there is the ubiquitous secret police,

> Subordinate to neither civilian
> Nor military authorities here. . . .

> There—row on row according to the years
> Kolyma, Magadan
> Vorkuta and Narym
> Marched in invisible columns

> The region of eternal frost
> Wrote men off into eternity,
> Moved them from the category of "living"
> To that of "dead" (little difference between them)—

> Behind that barbed wire,
> White and grizzled—
> With that Special Article of the law code
> Clipped to their case files.

> Who and what for and by whose will—
> Figure it out, History.
> No bands played, no speeches;
> Utter silence here.

> Notch it, though it bitter be,
> Forever in the memory.[6]

Six weeks later the dogmatist critic D. Starikov attacked the poem for mocking the regime and for being politically wrong and without literary merit. Harshly, Starikov claimed that Tvardovsky had tried, "as Gogol once tried in *The Inspector General*, to collect in one heap all the bad there is in Russia . . . all the injustice that was practiced in those places and in those situations in which more than anything justice is demanded of men, and to ridicule everything in one breath." The poem, Starikov explained, "does not rise to political categories" and does not "go beyond purely practical acuity." [7] Speaking so plainly of Soviet bureaucracy and concentration camps, the poem had touched some of the rawest spots in the past—and in the present—yet it had obviously been published with Khrushchev's personal approval and in his son-in-law Adzhubei's *Izvestia.*

Tvardovsky not only did his share against the bureaucracy and the heirs of Stalin as a poet in August; in July he had done his share as an editor by publishing Solzhenitsyn's novelette *For the Good of the Cause* in *Novy mir*, which brought a storm of criticism on both the author and the magazine. If *Ivan Denisovich* was a shock to the old-line dogmatists because it showed cruelty and injustice to be a matter not of accident but of state policy, the novel after all was set in the early 1950s, in Stalin's era, at a distance in time so great that events could be "handled" by consigning them to a past that was over and would never return. *For the Good of the Cause*, however, was an explicit attack on the Stalinist "remnants" still present in the Soviet system, an assault on all the arbitrary, petty bureaucrats, portraying them as hard-hearted, greedy, and authoritarian careerists; and the time *was the present*. That Khrushchev had permitted its publication could only be attributed to his need to revitalize the sluggish economy, which he hoped might be accomplished by eliminating the dogmatic inflexibility of Stalinist bureaucrats.

For the Good of the Cause tells the story of how a group of young people help to construct a new school building for themselves because the old one is inadequate, and how when the building is completed, they lose it to the bureaucrats and the careerists. The people dig all the ditches, unload all the bricks, stack them, clear the earth, and remove the trash, so that the contractor has to assign only skilled men to the construction; in fact, the boys and girls train two teams of plasterers and painters from among themselves. When a new teacher of engineering, Anatoli Germanovich, arrives and is told of this achievement, he is skeptical, but a woman explains: "There's nothing to be skeptical about. We are just tired of living badly. We want to live well! Isn't that why people did voluntary work on Sundays in Lenin's time?" [8] Anatoli Germanovich's skepticism and the careful avoidance of allusions to Stalin's time indicate the disenchantment with Stalinist "voluntary labor."

The moving spirit of the students' work is one of the teachers, Lidia Georgievna, in charge of the Komsomol. She is beloved by all the students, and though married herself and with a two-year-old daughter, she manages to come to the building site in working clothes to do more than her share, never ordering anyone about but inspiring them all.

When the school is completed, the nine hundred students want to move equipment from the old school to the new building by hand, instead of waiting for the trucks to come, which might take a week or more; but the school principal, Fyodor Mikheyevich, arrives and informs them that they cannot move into the new quarters because of a variety of bureaucratic red-tape complications. A limousine drives up after the students leave; in it are a group of bureaucrats, among them Vsevolod Khabalygin, the local manager of a relay factory and hence nominally the "proprietor" of the new structure. The principal goes to meet them, hoping that they are going to expedite matters so that the students can move, because the semester begins the next day. Instead, the bureaucrats inspect the new building and tell him how well off he is in the old one, adding, "The Department have decided that a research institute of national importance should be set up in this town and accommodated in the buildings originally intended for your school." Khabalygin promises that in three or four years an even better school will be built for the students, and consoles Fyodor Mikheyevich: "That's how things go, my friend, so don't let it get you down. It can't be helped. It's all for the good of the cause!" [9]

Fyodor and Lidia are stunned. They feel cheated, they are ashamed, and they don't know what to tell the students. Fyodor realizes that in order to make the new building suitable for an institute, much of what has already been constructed will have to be torn out, because the building has been designed for a school. Enraged, he calls the head of the Town Party Committee—an old war comrade, Ivan Grachikov—and tells him that the conversion of the school to the institute would cost between a million and a half and two million rubles, while the building of the school cost four million altogether. This is both stupid and unfair. Grachikov replies that he would like to help but that the decision will be made "at the top," with very little concern for what the local people want, and he doubts that the principal will be able to get the building.[10] Grachikov does try to help, however, going with the principal to the District Party Committee, whose head, Viktor Vavilovich Knorozov, already knows about the transfer of the electronics school to the research institute.

It was Knorozov's boast that he never went back on his word. As it had once been in Moscow with Stalin's word, so it was still today with Knorozov's word: It was never changed and never taken back. And although Stalin was long dead, Knorozov was still here. He was a leading proponent of the "strong-willed school of leadership" and he saw in this his greatest virtue. He could not imagine any other way of running things.[11]

Knorozov sees Grachikov but refuses to admit the principal into his office to participate in the discussion. Knorozov tells Grachikov that in fact there is to be no more discussion; the decision is final: the institute will get the building. Furious, Grachikov says harshly:

We are not medieval barons, vying with each other over the grandness of our coats of arms. What we should be proud of in this town is that these kids built something and took pleasure in doing it. And it's our job to back them up. But if we take the building from them, they'll never forget what it means to be cheated. They'll think: If it can happen once, it can happen again! . . .

"Communism has to be built with people, not with bricks, Viktor Vavilovich!" he shouted, quite carried away. "That's the hard way, and it takes longer. And even if we finished building Communism tomorrow, but only in bricks, we'd still have a long way to go." [12]

This reference to the professed though unrealized ideals of Communism is a trenchant comment on the reality of Khrushchev's Russia in 1963.

Another evidence of the generation gap is contained in a touching scene in which Grachikov tells the principal how much more the young people know than he did in his own youth:

I sat there and I felt sorry for myself. After all, I thought, I've been around for fifty years, and what's *my* specialty? That I once knew how to work a lathe? But the sort of lathe I operated is a thing of the past. That I know the history of the Party and Marxist dialectics? But that's something everybody ought to know. There's nothing special about it. It's high time that every Party official should have some special knowledge or skill.[13]

Such a confession was bound to be anathema to the neo-Stalinist bureaucrats, but Solzhenitsyn was touching on a real political and economic problem which was to dog the footsteps of the leadership. If the Kremlin was to modernize the Russian economy, then its bureaucrats were going to have to be skilled technicians, particularly knowledgeable about the latest advances in computer science and management techniques. Neo-Stalinist bureaucrats like Knorozov were bound to find such a prospect threatening in the most intimate way; few of them had technical skills—in physics, chemistry, engineering, economics, computer mathematics, or management—and without such expertise they would lose their powers and privileges if there was any such modernization.

Dogmatist response to *For the Good of the Cause* was fierce. The very next issue of *Literaturnaya gazeta* carried an article by the deputy editor of the paper, Yuri Barabash, entitled "What Is 'Right'?" in which Barabash flays Solzhenitsyn for writing a story untrue to life, built on a situation which could not possibly have existed in contemporary Soviet society. Moreover, he finds a "sarcastic undertone" in the story which questions the good will of the Soviet authorities, and notes that Solzhenitsyn depicts the champions of justice as both weak-willed and helpless in "the face of some indifferent unfeeling force which can be sensed behind the faceless, nameless representatives of unnamed institutions." Barabash remarks on Solzhenitsyn's special emphasis on the terms "right" and "wrong," and on how the terms are repeated throughout the story in such a way that the "right" and "wrong" clearly express the author's own view of the essence of the conflict.

The scene in Knorozov's office is the culminating point of the story. At this juncture, the conflict over the new building becomes more than just a private misunderstanding; it is transplanted from the moral into the political sphere and is interpreted by Solzhenitsyn as a conflict between two styles of Party work, between two political lines: Lenin's and the one that was decisively condemned at the 20th Congress.

But Barabash maintains that Solzhenitsyn has created a caricature in Knorozov, an unreal symbol of the era of the cult of personality, whose voice is "metallic" and whose words fall "like steel girders," whose "face seemed cast forever in one mold, never betraying any trivial or momentary emotions. . . . He was truly made of steel and all of a piece." Moreover, though the day of the Knorozovs is past, Solzhenitsyn has failed to show those who are taking their places. In portraying Knorozov's ambitions and Khabalygin's careerism, Solzhenitsyn has obscured the basic questions about the significance of the new institute: Is its immediate opening dictated by pressing necessity? Isn't it just possible that the school's interests will be safeguarded? And so forth. Solzhenitsyn's failure in this story lies in "his attempts to resolve the most complex intellectual and moral problems, to pass judgments on people and their actions, without reference to actual, living relationships; he operates in abstract categories which are not invested with concrete social content. In 'Matryona's Home' it was the 'righteous woman' without whom neither the village nor the town nor 'our whole land' was supposed to be worth anything. In this story it is the 'little' people who have racked their brains in fruitless efforts to answer a scholastic question, posed without reference to space or time: What is 'right'?" Nonetheless, Barabash feels impelled to point out: "And yet we are undoubtedly in the presence of a writer of great and honest quality who is uniquely sensitive to any manifestation of evil or untruth or injustice." [14]

Six weeks later Daniil Granin countered in an article in *Literaturnaya gazeta* called "Is the Critic Right?" in which he defended Solzhenitsyn against Barabash's charges of not having been true to life in the story, declaring: "Seriously and courageously, he [Solzhenitsyn] poses a moral and social problem: What does 'for the good of the cause' mean? . . . He exposes those who, while using the interest of the state as a cover, look after their own petty interests at the expense of the state. He demands justice." Granin approves and accepts Barabash's criticism that it is necessary to have specific information about how urgent the need for the institute was, and so on, but "the trouble is that no one familiarizes Fyodor Mikheyevich with all the circumstances, no one cares about his participation and cooperation. They leave him out of account, merely telling him that it is necessary 'for the good of the cause.'" Had the principal been informed of the circumstances honestly and straightforwardly, so that he could judge whether the decision was for the good of the cause or not, then the reader might also accept it. "And here," Granin says, "I have in mind the national cause, the cause for which one can readily sacrifice one's own interest." What is at stake is not genuine national urgency but local and selfish interests, the petty ambitions and careerism of Knorozov and Khabalygin. Granin praises the story for being "sharply contemporary" and sees it as dealing with the problem of the democratization of Soviet life "in recent years," in which "participation of the entire public in administration and control in the most diverse areas of Party and Soviet life" is being encouraged. But "there are people who find that this democratization gets in their way. Why does it get in their way? How do they think? What are their methods? What is their philosophy? This is what Solzhenitsyn is investigating." [15]

Four days later, *Literaturnaya gazeta* published an article by the local Party functionary N. Seliverstov which called *For the Good of the Cause* "behind the times" and asked "Can that atmosphere of passivity and helplessness described by Solzhenitsyn exist in any community today?" He answered the question by saying No, declared that the story was contrived and artificial, and went on to deny that the "little Stalins" were still everywhere in control of Soviet life:

Yes, anything can happen in life. I myself know of a case when a technicum was "moved out" of the accommodations that belonged to it. But then all the "springs" of what happened, which was actually unjust, were clear. The incident took place in a neighboring province, yet word of it instantly reached Leningrad, and this is understandable: In our day such things immediately come to the surface; you can't hide them from the people. All the efforts and potentials of our democratic system are quickly set in motion, people insistently knock on all doors seeking the truth. . . . Therefore, it is difficult to detect this "recognition of our own lives," the lives of today, in A. Solzhenitsyn's story. A sense of yesterday's life comes sooner.[16]

The argument was shrewd: such things do happen now, but they are swiftly resisted and the injustices rectified. What Solzhenitsyn is depicting, he maintains, is not *contemporary* reality with neo-Stalinists still in control, but "yesterday's life" when Stalinists were truly in control.

The editors of *Literaturnaya gazeta* took this opportunity to support Barabash (their deputy editor) and Seliverstov against Granin, and quoted one of its readers, an engineer named Dunayevsky, who had written that Solzhenitsyn had enough "ability to instill in people not hopelessness but confidence in the strength of the truth, confidence that although there are still many Knorozovs and Khabalygins, they are no longer omnipotent; that the struggle against them is governed by natural law." The editors considered this to be good advice that Solzhenitsyn should, in the future, follow. They were also careful to note that they were not objecting to the choice of subject, because Soviet artists were not in any way circumscribed in selecting subjects for representation, that even negative aspects of Soviet life were acceptable for literary portrayal, but that "a sharp ideological struggle is going on in the modern world, and not for a moment can we lower the ideological criteria in evaluating literary works." [17]

Solzhenitsyn had also become a target for Kochetov's *Oktyabr*, and that month the conservative literary magazine published two articles pertaining to Solzhenitsyn and his work. The first, " 'Saints' and 'Devils,' " by V. Chalmayev, was a critique of all Solzhenitsyn's published work to date for having reduced the complex living world to "two ideological and moral poles and two sets of characters corresponding to these poles. . . . In one of them the writer invariably concentrates humility and meekness, righteousness that as a rule is impotent in practice, and in the other he concentrates all-powerful evil, overbearing cruelty, and blind obedience." Chalmayev was still gingerly in attacking *Ivan Denisovich*, where this "abstract, non-social, timeless" rendering was in some measure countered by "a vitally active, inspired attitude towards work"; but in "Matryona's House" this rigid, abstract quality has grown worse, Dostoyevskian in fact, because though "it was work which exalted Ivan Denisovich . . . Matryona is 'great' . . . for no other reason than her suffering." *For the Good of the Cause* is even worse, according to Chalmayev, because, like "The Incident at Krechetovka Station," the incident in itself "is isolated from all the rest of the life of our country and is, moreover, placed in opposition to it as the sole truth. It is as if the author did not know that the state is building scores of schools and institutes every year, yet this is far weightier than the ardent altruism that he passes off as the sole 'condition' for achieving happiness." Chalmayev denounces Solzhenitsyn's division of characters into positive and negative, good and evil, not because such didacticism is in itself bad, but because Solzhenitsyn does not include "the dynamics of social movement," and therefore deforms his characters. This "idealistic conception of good and evil" cannot be taken seriously, and as a result *For the Good of the Cause* fails in its effects: "Everything in it is toylike, stage setting, borrowed. The naive counter-posing of 'bureaucratic' designs to the dictates of personal kindness, of the official to the human, all these contrived constructions crumble to dust upon comparison with modern life, which is filled with a different complexity, rich in other conflicts, and bountiful in true human beauty and courage." Chalmayev concludes that Solzhenitsyn should discard the "archaic" notion of an eternal battle between good and evil in human life, the conception of righteousness as "a form of moral feat, of the elevating of man through suffering and tears," and should refuse to accept either the failure of the "saints" or the triumph of the "devils." [18]

In the same issue of *Oktyabr*, N. Sergovantsev, in a review of a documentary short story, *Endured*, which had appeared in *Zvezda* earlier in the year, took the opportunity to attack *Ivan Denisovich* by comparison. The short story, by Boris Dyakov, concerned "those Soviet people whose destinies took on a tragic form during the years of the Stalin cult, . . . their unusual fortitude and spiritual strength, which the brutal conditions of Beria's camps could not break." Dyakov made the point in his introduction that "true Communists, no matter what terrible tribulations befell them, always remained Communists." The review noted that there were two approaches to this "highly complicated ideological and creative task"—i.e., the portrayal of the innocent victims of Stalin confined in concentration camps: one (presumably Solzhenitsyn's) shows the camps as an arena of suffering and torture, and in so doing "oversimplifies [the theme and] reduces the entire tragedy exclusively to a description of suffering." The other (presumably Dyakov's) offers an opportunity to show how Soviet people transcend the difficulties of being victims of Stalinism. Dyakov does not "oversimplify" the concentration camp by emphasizing the suffering of prisoners and the bestial malice of the authorities; instead, he shows the Communists retaining their faith in "Communist ideals, in the durability of Soviet power, in the triumph of justice, and warm love of homeland." [19]

The essence of the objection to "oversimplification" was defined in an article significantly entitled "We Remained Human," in *Kazakhstanskaya pravda*, by Aleksandr Afanasyevich Gudzenko, who had himself been sentenced to twenty years' imprisonment under Stalin. Essentially, Gudzenko took the same tack about *Ivan*

Denisovich explicitly that Dyakov had implicitly, noting that Sol-zhenitsyn had failed to show that camp inmates had "strength of conviction, faith in the people and the Party, and . . . passion for creative activity in any situation," that he had portrayed all camp inmates as primarily concerned with staying alive by any means and at all costs. Solzhenitsyn "depicted the sufficiently unpleasant conditions of a special-regimen camp with the precision of a camera, but when it came to portraying people he failed. His hero's highest goal . . . was to lap up a bowl of stew. . . . His animal side was overemphasized. He is prepared to toady to anybody for a piece of sausage or a pinch of makhorka tobacco." But, Gudzenko insisted, the special camps did not destroy all the inmates or reduce them to mere stomachs intent on survival; in spite of the power of the instinct for self-preservation, the inmates did not survive

by playing the lackey but by hard work or services that did not demean human dignity. Human feelings and comradeship did not die out even there, but on the contrary grew stronger. . . . We shared our bread and a bit of precious garlic and a drag of makhorka tobacco.

Among us, too, there were some Ivan Denisoviches who smoked secretly under the covers, but they were exceptions and not the rule.

What Gudzenko was trying to demonstrate was that camps did not reduce men to animality, to survivalism, but that the prisoners retained their sense of the "collective," their commitment to the Party, to the people, and to "building socialism." Moreover, the men even went on with political and cultural life—painting pictures, growing flowers, organizing a chorus of prisoners, and even refusing to perform a cantata about Stalin (in 1951)! Gudzenko also denied the verisimilitude of Solzhenitsyn's depiction of all the guards as beasts, saying that "very many, at risk to themselves, showed a humaneness forbidden by the rules." Many overseers and convoy guards, he testified, had slipped the prisoners bread, cigarettes, or bowls of porridge, and he himself had been kept alive during sixty-seven days in solitary confinement only because a guard had now and then managed to sneak him some barley coffee, bread, or kasha with salt pork. "In my heart," wrote Gudzenko, "I shall always preserve a deep gratitude not only to the Party and Nikita Sergeyevich Khrushchev, who smashed the Stalin cult, but also to many known and unknown persons who kept me and many others like me alive." [20] This defense of the prison guards may very well have resulted from considerable pressure by various liberals to see that former camp personnel were tried for their crimes during the Stalin era.[21] And Gudzenko's bow to Khrushchev is accompanied by a gratuitous though logical slap at Mao Tse-tung because an even more terrible cult is now being fabricated around him in China.

The next month, in its October issue (published in November), *Novy mir* set off a literary controversy with *Literaturnaya gazeta* by publishing three letters to the editor, one of them signed by three "Old Bolsheviks," [22] which defended Solzhenitsyn's *For the Good of the Cause* against Barabash's criticisms. One of the letters spoke of the story as "intensely gripping, tragic . . . evidence of the growth of our social consciousness, which is making it harder and harder for all kinds of degenerates, careerists, dogmatists and demagogues to remain 'right side up.'" The letter from the three "Old Bolsheviks" declared that "some bureaucrats (we still have them) cover their bureaucratic designs and actions with the artificial 'state' consideration that these are 'for the good of the cause,'" and declared further, "We are against Knorozov's 'iron' style, which reeks of the style of the time of the Stalin cult." The last letter defends *For the Good of the Cause* as a story which shows how things should *not* be done, a story which "defends our Soviet Communist justice, the ethical norms of the moral code, the democratic foundations of our life." [23]

Literaturnaya gazeta replied the next month, upbraiding *Novy mir*'s editors for printing only letters which "praise the story unreservedly and unanimously attack the authors of the critical articles in *Literaturnaya gazeta*," for losing their objectivity and sense of proportion in doing so, and moreover for giving a false impression of the popular response to the story by suppressing readers' responses which were critical of it. "It is difficult to assume," the editors of *Literaturnaya gazeta* said, "that *Novy mir* has received only letters extolling the story (and *Literaturnaya gazeta*'s mail confirms this)." [24] *Novy mir*'s editors replied swiftly, in a letter to the editors of *Literaturnaya gazeta*, rebuking them for having accused the editors of *Novy mir* of falsifying the opinions of their readers. The facts were that they had received 58 letters about the Solzhenitsyn story, 55 of which were emphatically in favor of it. Moreover, they noted that 12 of those were copies of letters that had been sent to *Literaturnaya gazeta,* so it was *Literaturnaya gazeta* that had suppressed readers' mail in forwarding its own point of view.[25]

The reply by the editors of *Literaturnaya gazeta* in the same issue was unconvincing; it said that *Novy mir's* editors would "undoubtedly agree [that] a judgment [of a work of art] cannot be reached by using statistical computations. An 'arithmetical' approach to the complex of literature never benefited readers, artists, or art as a whole." "We remain convinced," they wrote, "that the editors of *Novy mir,* knowing of the existence of differing viewpoints on this work, would have acted more correctly had they opened the pages of their journal to opinions not corresponding with their editorial position." [26] That was, of course, precisely what *Novy mir* had done, and *Literaturnaya gazeta* had failed to do; but there, for the moment, the matter rested.

10 The Lenin Prize

> One must never stop praying. If you have real faith you tell
> a mountain to move and it will move.
>
> *Aleksandr Solzhenitsyn*

The denigration of Stalin and the renunciation of elements of the
Stalinist legacy had caused the Stalin Prize in literature to fall into
disuse after the dictator's death, but in 1956 it had been revived as
the Lenin Prize, refurbished, and made the most important and the
richest (75,000 rubles) award for a book in the Soviet Union. All
during the fall of 1963 and into 1964, discussion in Soviet intellectual
and literary circles centered on whether or not Solzhenitsyn should
be awarded the coveted Lenin Prize. Giving him the prize, of course,
would be of more than mere literary significance, for everything
Solzhenitsyn had written arose out of the climate of de-Stalinization
and liberalization, and the award would, inevitably, be construed as
symbolizing the intention of the regime to continue and perhaps
intensify those campaigns. Even *Literaturnaya gazeta,* under the
editorship of Chakovsky, no friend of Solzhenitsyn's, felt called
upon to publish a letter from a reader recommending that *Ivan
Denisovich* be awarded the prize, although the journal carefully
bracketed it with another letter which maintained that, except for
the "virginity" of the theme, *Ivan Denisovich* said "almost nothing
about those who held out, who preserved all human feelings and
whose loyalty to lofty ideals was not destroyed." [1] The following
week, the paper again returned to the subject to remind its readers
that the novel should not be singled out, because of the controversial nature of the character of Ivan Shukhov, whose "humility
and submissiveness" it found distasteful.[2] *Pravda* also soon took a
hand in the polemics, praising the laconic understatement of the

novel, defending the action and the characterization, and calling Solzhenitsyn "a master of that true folk language whose riches have by no means been exhausted by our literature." [3] The author of the article, the noted writer Samuil Marshak, also insisted that many of the camp inmates retained their dignity and their "civic feeling."

Literaturnaya rossiya also greeted the new year with a debate about "Matryona's House." In an article entitled "Co-Author Wanted!" the critic Leonid Zhukovitsky gave criticism a new twist by remarking that the story had a meaning quite different from Solzhenitsyn's "intent" or from that of the critics who had analyzed the tale in terms of his "intent." What Zhukovitsky believed Solzhenitsyn meant, he stated thus:

Regardless of the original intent of the author, the story showed, that despite Matryona's splendid personal, spiritual qualities, the ethic of the righteous is senseless, self-destructive, and even immoral. And the magnificently drawn picture of the old peasant woman evokes not a desire to emulate her not quite gloomy reflections: How much evil is perpetrated on this planet by the obedient hands of just such righteous people! How many crooks and scoundrels are used to counting on such people's humble submissiveness and indiscriminate kindness! How many careerists climb over their backs, which are conveniently bent over not for selfish reasons, but out of an utterly sincere desire to help their fellow men!

For this reason, Zhukhovitsky insisted that he accepted the story, "which is true to life," while disagreeing with Solzhenitsyn's "original intent." The critic, of course, was turning the argument against the heirs of Stalin back against the people. It was an argument about the cooperation of the good people, the decent "little" people in Stalinism that was hard to gainsay. In thus involving the good people who did not resist, Zhukhovitsky weakened the argument against the Stalinist holdovers as well as those who had used those men during the Stalinist era. [4]

In the same issue of *Literaturnaya rossiya*, G. Brovman replied with an article, "Is It Necessary to Be a Co-Author?" taking Zhukhovitsky to task for making evil goodness and goodness evil, for trying and failing to reconcile opposites, and most of all for ignoring the "new moral traits . . . being formed that differ from bigoted, martyrlike righteousness. Perhaps it is precisely these new human spiritual qualities that constitute the real moral support of the village and the city and our whole Soviet world." [5]

The debate continued, and Zhukhovitsky's view was defended by V. Bushin, who agreed, Solzhenitsyn's intentions notwithstanding, that Matryona may be the salt of the earth, but she lacks savor; "we also see some [qualities of character] that we cannot accept at all: meekness, submissiveness, uncomplaining patience and humility in a situation where protest, if not a struggle, is called for. The author does not separate the good from the weak in his heroine; everything within her is equally valuable to him." [6] Here, of course, Communist activism had better materials than in Ivan Denisovich, for the implication was that struggle and resistance "for the good of the cause" outside a concentration camp was at least in the realm of the conceivable.

In January, also, an energetic *Izvestia* reporter went far toward discrediting those who had criticized Ivan Denisovich for being "atypical" of prisoners in the camps.[7] V. Pallon interviewed Boris Burkovsky, Chief of the Central Naval Museum's branch on the cruiser "Aurora" moored in the Neva off Leningrad, who turned out to be the model for the character of Commander Buinovsky in Solzhenitsyn's novel. Burkovsky, it turned out, had at the time of the Yalta Conference been appointed a liaison officer to some American warships which arrived in Sevastopol, because he spoke English. He had fought bravely during the war in the Soviet navy, had been a loyal Party member and brave commander, and after his stint as a liaison officer with the American officers and admiral of the visiting flotilla, he was returned to his regular duties with a commendation from his superiors.

Four years later, though he had continued to serve ably as a naval officer, Burkovsky was sentenced to twenty-five years for those contacts with Americans. Though Burkovsky testified that some of the characters in the novel bore a close resemblance to actual prisoners—particularly Buinovsky, the brigade leader Tiurin, the film director Tsezar Markovich, and the Baptist Alyosha—he could "not remember the convict who served as the prototype of Ivan Denisovich . . . because there were many such people." He defended the fidelity of Solzhenitsyn's portrayal both of the camp conditions and of the inmates, saying that the detailed and overall picture of the camp in the novel showed it closely resembled the reality; and of the prisoners, he remarked: "While doing time in the camp many fell out of the habit of speculating on the future, probably because they didn't expect anything good. They thought only of the next day—what kind of work there would be, how to get some tobacco, how to mend torn mittens." Delighted that the book had been nominated for the Lenin Prize for 1964, because the "story is also a day from my life," Burkovsky concluded that "with rare exceptions" the prisoners had "never identified the evil done to them with the Party, with our system." [8] No more crushing refutation of the many charges brought against Solzhenitsyn's novel by his critics could have been imagined, for not only was Burkovsky a loyal Party member who had for four years lived in the same barracks with Solzhenitsyn in the camp, but his prototype Buinovsky was one of the characters in the novel whom the critics had considered "positive."

Some weeks earlier, the same paper had printed a letter to the editors from Viktor Ivanov, a worker, who affirmed that Solzhenitsyn had given a truthful picture of the past in a work of striking artistry. The truthfulness of the material, the documentary character of the story could not be called in question, yet Ivanov nonetheless refused to accept the "undemandingness" of Ivan Denisovich Shukhov as a virtue. Because he saw in Solzhenitsyn's portrait of Shukhov the ascription of certain qualities of the Russian people in general —undemandingness, patience, the desire to survive physically— Ivanov thought it inadequate. The Russian people have "proved that they know not only and not so much how to be patient [but] the chief thing about them [is] that they are above all a fighting people, a revolutionary people." [9] To just such charges of inadequate portrayal Burkovsky had given the lie.

At the end of January, in a continuation of the debate it had begun at the beginning of the year, *Literaturnaya rossiya* printed a full page of (seven) letters about Solzhenitsyn and his work, the most intelligent of which remarked that "Matryona [was] an extension of the image of Ivan Denisovich," and that both were typical of the unselfish, kind, hardworking farmers who had loyally served the country during the worst Stalinist hardships "for 'matchsticks.' " The writer went on to say that "the truth is all on Solzhenitsyn's side! The story contains no exaggerations." Perhaps its would be right to search out the new moral traits which are beginning to be formed, but let some other writer do that, "and let Solzhenitsyn with his keen sense of the wrongs done to the people, write in his own way." [10]

The major defense of Solzhenitsyn and of his recommendation for the Lenin Prize came, not surprisingly, from *Novy mir*, in an article by its deputy editor, V. Lakshin, who not only defended *Ivan Denisovich* for the "harshness and directness of its truth," but also noted that its appearance in print "was that rare instance in literature when the publication of an artistic work rapidly became a social and political event." Lakshin thus clearly connected defending Solzhenitsyn's work and supporting him for the Lenin Prize with far greater issues: "The very fact of the story's appearance was interpreted by people as the affirmation of the Party's will to be done forever with the arbitrariness and lawlessness that clouded our recent past." [11] Lakshin attempted to deal with each of the negative criticisms brought against Solzhenitsyn's work. To the charge (Fomenko's) that the novelist had failed to present "the whole truth about those times," he took the position: "How is it possible to capture in one day of a convict's life the dialectic of all relations, struggles, and contradictions of an era!" [12] What should be appreciated is how much Solzhenitsyn *has* managed to include in that brief novel. "Instead of marveling at his talent and civic courage, at how deep and truthful everything is in the picture he has drawn—in which . . . you cannot find a dot or a line that is contrived or false—the author is reproached for leaving outside the frame of his picture many subjects and characters that are worthy of portrayal." [13]

Calling Sergovantsev's article a "prosecutor's monologue," Lakshin attacked the critic for rejecting Ivan Denisovich as "not typical" of Soviet people who are fighters, "active, searching and vigorous," and for a contemptuous attitude toward ordinary people. The appearance of Ivan Denisoviches and Aunt Matryonas in Soviet literature, Lakshin believed, was evidence of further "democratization of literature following the 20th Party Congress, evidence that it [literature] is actually getting closer to the people's life, not just claiming to." He thought that the appearance of commonplace heroes in literature made the critics uncomfortable, accustomed as they were to having leaders, organizers, and inspirers as heroes of their books. Why, Lakshin asked, should Ivan Denisovich be an "ideal hero," free of faults? Why indict Shukhov for becoming what he became instead of indicting the system which forced the man into such a state in order to survive? "The entire system of imprisonment in the camps through which Ivan Denisovich passed was calculated to suppress mercilessly, to kill, all feelings of right and legality in man, demonstrating in matters large and small an impunity for arbitrariness against which any outburst of noble indignation was powerless." Lakshin pointed out that Solzhenitsyn had deliberately remarked that Commander Buinovsky would have to learn to "become a sluggish, wary convict in order to survive the twenty-five-year sentence meted out to him." [14]

Lakshin then thrust to the heart of the political as well as the artistic question, and the most dangerous part of the novel and the debate: "In order to struggle one must know for what and against what the struggle is being waged." Since Ivan Denisovich was aware that his fate was not exceptional, that all around him were innocent people, that no attempts to restore justice were effective, the question arose: *Who was responsible for all this?* Lakshin passed over this question, but in posing it he was menacing all those heirs of Stalin who had been accomplices of Stalin: the political police, Gulag, and even those, like Ehrenburg, who had gritted their teeth and held their tongues.

Early in February 1964, Moscow writers met to discuss the nominees for the Lenin Prize. Those favoring Solzhenitsyn included Veniamin Kaverin, Kornei Chukovsky, and Ilya Ehrenburg; his opponents were led by Dmitry Yeremin, and there were attacks both on Solzhenitsyn and on Lakshin for his defense of the novelist.[15] At a combined meeting of the board secretariats of the RSFSR Writers' Union and the Moscow writers' organization at the end of February, the controversy continued, with increasing hostility toward Solzhenitsyn and his work.[16]

Not until April did the Party leadership hand down its edict that the award would not go to Solzhenitsyn. In a *Pravda* editorial it was concluded that though *Ivan Denisovich* deserved "a positive assessment . . . it cannot be classed among the outstanding works worthy of the Lenin Prize." Solzhenitsyn had made much use too of prison jargon and slang, thus failing to elevate Soviet taste; the novel lacked the requisite ideological militance; and most of all, it was filled with too much "goody-goody compassionate and equalizing humanism." [17]

The conflict had not by any means been resolved by the leadership's decision not to give Solzhenitsyn the award, nor had the partisans of both liberals and conservatives been reconciled. Feelings had, instead, been exacerbated, divisiveness intensified, and fundamental differences more sharply defined by the controversy. The heirs of Stalin question could be answered only if the Stalinist holdovers were removed from office and punished for their complicity in Stalin's crimes. With an extraordinarily difficult year just ended, in which the Soviet Union had been ravaged by a disastrous wheat-crop failure, in which the government had had to buy foreign grain to give its people bread, in which a sharp cutback (of 17 percent) in housing construction, a postponement of a rise in the minimum wage, and a continuation of high prices had combined to increase domestic dissatisfaction, and in which an open and serious breach with the Chinese Communists had widened,[18] the Party leadership was by no means disposed to disrupt the unity and order of domestic events even further by more de-Stalinization or even by awarding the Lenin Prize to a controversial book which pointed in that direction.

Part II ARTISTIC DISSIDENCE

11 The Brodsky Case

> . . . we learned to warm ourselves
> By the hidden sun
> And to reach the shore
> Without pilots and sailing directions;
> But—most important of all—
> We learned not to repeat ourselves.
>
> *Josif Brodsky*

In the winter of 1964 the permissible boundaries of literary free-dom began to be restricted. Though controversy still racked liberal and conservative intellectuals, increasingly the dogmatists began to manifest their power in the kinds of "actions" Vsevolod Kochetov had earlier called for to take the place of polemics. One such action came on February 18, when Josif Brodsky, a twenty-four-year-old poet, was tried in Dzerzhinsky District court in Leningrad on charges of "parasitism." [1] The trial, divided into two hearings a month apart, was a portent of things to come, and its conduct was much like what would two years later characterize the Sinyavsky-Daniel trial. Brodsky had left school at fifteen and worked at thir-teen different jobs in seven years while he continued to write poetry and study languages in order to qualify as a translator. He had earlier received the attention of the authorities when, in 1962, the police searched his flat and confiscated his diary, letters, and private papers.[2] This invasion of privacy and the use of private papers arbi-trarily confiscated by the political police as material evidence in a trial were identical with the techniques to be employed against Sinyavsky and Daniel, and though they were somewhat different, resembled those used against Solzhenitsyn in prosecuting the charges brought against him by the Writers' Union. On the earlier occasion Brodsky had been subject to a special hearing under the new ukase of February 4, 1961, on "parasitism"—an edict ostensibly intended to clear "idlers" from the cities. Both the political police and the militia had warned Brodsky then that he had better get a permanent job, but Brodsky had instead continued to write and read his "decadent poems at evening gatherings" and to do translations, taking whatever temporary employment was required to tide him over. Now, two years later, he was being brought to trial under that very same parasitism ukase, but the facts were probably closer to Soviet defector Yury Krotkov's estimate of them:

I do not have an altogether clear picture of the ideals of Brodsky and his friends, but in general I am convinced that many young people have their doubts about the doctrines of Marx. . . . These young people do not organize explosions, or threaten their country's leaders; they don't even publish revolutionary pamphlets. They merely think. . . . They resist the incubator system which in the U.S.S.R. is considered constitutionally indispensable for a young person. . . . They seek other, sometimes untravelled paths.[3]

By Western standards the trial was a farce. Brodsky had already been publicly vilified and in effect tried by the newspaper *Evening Leningrad* under the headline "The Near-Literary Drone," and at his trial the sign outside the courtroom read: "The Hearing of the Parasite Brodsky." The issue of Brodsky's "guilt" had evidently been decided beforehand. Yet Brodsky's defense attorneys did try, sincerely if cautiously, to defend him, though without much effect.

The judge, Mme Saveleva, was clearly hostile to the defendant, had a "no-nonsense" attitude toward poets and poetry in general, and made no bones about siding with the prosecution against Brodsky during the proceedings. When she asked Brodsky, "And what good have you done for your country?" she would not accept his reply: "I write poems. That's my work." Instead, she upbraided him and asked him to explain "how we are to evaluate your participation in our great progressive movement toward Communism." [4] The conflict between "fathers and sons," the inability of the older Stalinist generation to understand or speak the language of the younger post-Stalin generation, was never more clearly expressed. Moreover, the anti-intellectual and anti-Semitic overtones of the trial were everywhere in evidence.

Though Brodsky was considered by Anna Akhmatova to be one of Russia's most gifted young poets, and though such outstanding Soviet artists as Kornei Chukovsky, Samuil Marshak, Konstantin

Paustovsky, and Dmitry Shostakovich came to his defense, writing letters to Khrushchev, praising Brodsky's translations and gifts, none of that was enough to establish his *bona fides* as a poet or translator, or to assure him a more objective and fairer trial. In fact, Krotkov remarks that such letters of protest were tragicomically ineffective: "Khrushchev's assistant Lebedev stuck the letters in a file, each with an appropriate number, and thus ended this epistolary, ideological commotion." Yet even the relatively cynical Krotkov admitted that "this was new, for no such petitions were sent to Stalin." [5]

When a number of defense witnesses—a literary historian, a linguist, a translator—who knew Brodsky personally testified that the young poet was assiduous and hardworking, helped to support his parents, who encouraged his writing and approved of it, and had devoted himself to perfecting his skills as a poet and translator, denying himself all but the most meager creature comforts, both judge and prosecution ignored and denigrated their testimony. One such witness, a teacher and anthologist of poetry, remarked: "There is a joke to the effect that the difference between a parasite and a young poet is that a parasite eats and does not work, whereas a young poet works and does not eat." Mme Saveleva thought this a frivolous comment and rebuked the witness: "In our country every person receives according to his effort, and therefore it cannot be that he has worked a great deal and received little for it." She went on to explain that the government devoted great sums to the welfare of young poets.[6]

The prosecution accused Brodsky of being a parasite, a cad, a rogue, a morally depraved individual, a draft dodger, and a writer of "anti-Soviet" verses. Not a single one of the prosecution witnesses knew Brodsky personally or had received his poems from his own hand. Instead, the secret police had provided them not only with some of Brodsky's poems (and some attributed to him which were not his at all), but also with letters and a diary which he had written in 1956, when he was sixteen years old, and which Brodsky asked to have excluded from the trial, a request peremptorily denied. The police had, of course, supplied the witnesses with the diary, letters, and poems without either Brodsky's knowledge or consent.[7]

A sample from the testimony of one prosecution witness gives some feeling of the tone of the trial:

Smirnov: I don't know Brodsky personally, but I want to say that if all the citizens of this country reacted toward the production of material wealth as Brodsky does, then it would take us a long time to build Communism. The mind is a dangerous weapon for its owner. Everyone has said that he is a smart fellow and practically a genius. But no one has said what sort of person he is. . . . Why doesn't anyone say that he's all muddled up in his head? And what about anti-Soviet verses?

Brodsky: That's not true!

Smirnov: He needs to change a lot of his thoughts. I am suspicious about that certificate that Brodsky was given in the "nerve" clinic concerning his nervous illness. This is nothing but his fancy friends ringing all the bells and demanding: "Save the young man!" But he should be treated with forced labor, and no one will help him, no fancy friends. I do not know him personally, I know about him from the newspapers. And I am acquainted with the certificates. I'm suspicious about the certificate which deferred him from service in the army. I'm not a doctor, but I'm suspicious about it.[8]

When Brodsky insisted that specific lines of his verse be read to prove what was "anti-Soviet," the judge refused to allow any such "quotation."

From December 1963 to January 1964, Brodsky had undergone psychiatric treatment at the Kashchenko Hospital in Moscow. His defense counsel tried to show that Brodsky was therefore unfit for regular work, but the judge sent Brodsky for an "official psychiatric examination" to determine "whether this illness will prevent Brodsky from being sent to a distant locality for forced labor." The official psychiatric report declared that Brodsky had "psychopathic character traits" but "is capable of working. Therefore, administrative measures can be taken."[9] Increasingly, the Soviet regime would use psychiatrists and psychiatric testimony, as well as mental hospitals, to punish dissidents.

Another prosecution witness, a Writers' Union member, one Voevodin by name, gave a more important clue to why the regime had chosen to make an example of Brodsky. "Brodsky tears the youth away from work, from the world and life," Voevodin testified. "This is Brodsky's great anti-social role."[10] Private life, personal dedication to professions or causes not specifically approved of or considered socially useful were "impermissible," for in effect they contested the Party and the government's total control over the individual. The court declared Brodsky guilty and sentenced him to five years in an Archangel forced-labor camp, where he was assigned to carting manure.[11]

After a series of fraudulent reports intended to take the edge off domestic and foreign protests about Brodsky's trial and confinement, rumors that Brodsky had been freed and that Soviet authorities had approved publication of a book of his poems were circulated. Patricia Blake showed these rumors to be deliberate plants and reported that as of January 1965, Brodsky was ill and still in a concentration camp in the Arctic.[12] A book of Brodsky's poetry was published—but in English, not in the Soviet Union—in 1967 when Longmans issued a collection under the title *Elegy to John Donne and Other Poems*.[13] Not until some time in 1967 was Brodsky in fact freed and permitted to return to Leningrad.[14] Alexander Werth visited him there that year and found him "childishly and Jewishly arrogant . . . and he did bellow his poetry—some of it a little mystical, mildly religious, obscure in spots, but enormously effective in its rhythms, images and rhetorical sweep." [15] As usual, the pro-Soviet apologist Werth tries to pass off Brodsky's conviction and imprisonment as "one of those things": he reports that Aleksandr Prokofiev, one of the bosses of the Leningrad branch of the Writers' Union and a leading dogmatist, had taken a violent dislike to Brodsky, and also that "what annoyed some of the pundits of the Writers' Union was that he [Brodsky] threw his weight about too much, fancied himself the Leningrad version of Voznesensky and Yevtushenko, loved to bellow his poems at all kinds of meetings; so they decided to teach him a lesson." [16] Yet even Werth is uncomfortable with this example (and explanation) of Soviet "justice" and maintains that the efforts of Chukovsky and Shostakovich did result in Brodsky's being brought back from his Archangel dung heap "within a fairly short term" (although more than two years in the Arctic carrying manure can seem a short term only to someone reporting another's anguish).[17] Nonetheless, it does seem likely that the group of artists and intellectuals who petitioned the authorities in Brodsky's behalf were responsible for shortening the young poet's five-year term.

The real reasons for the trial of Brodsky transcended mere personal vendetta, whatever role spite and pique played. Patricia Blake believes that the trial was an attempt on the part of the regime to discredit the liberal intelligentsia; [18] and it seems likely also that the authorities were beginning to explore some old and new methods for coping with dissidents and nonconformists as part of a renewed effort to impose orthodoxy on the intelligentsia—methods that were to include harassment, dismissal from jobs, expulsion from professional unions, psychiatric examinations and confinement to mental institutions, trials and exile to concentration camps for forced labor. Such treatment was considerably better than what Stalin had given the writers, but the trial and treatment of Brodsky had far to go before it could lay claim to being "socialist," "legal," or "just," even in the very special way in which those terms are used in the Soviet Union. The Brodsky trial and sentencing, and the confinement of Aleksandr Yesenin-Volpin and Valeriy Tarsis to psychiatric hospitals, as well as the powerful administrative pressures brought to bear against Boris Pasternak, were symptomatic of what was increasingly to become the regime's practice in dealing with dissidence and nonconformism.

The trial against Brodsky took place at almost the same time as a number of other trials "held in Moscow and other Soviet cities where Jews were convicted as the chief culprits—the scapegoats—in 'economic crimes.'" [19] There was further evidence of anti-Semitism at the Brodsky trial in the way in which Judge Saveleva said she could not pronounce the names of Jewish defense witnesses, such as Efim Grigorevich Etkind, and asked to see their domestic passports, in which "Jew" is inscribed for those of Jewish origin. The judge asked: "Let me have your passport inasmuch as your last name is pronounced somewhat unclearly. (She takes passport.) Etkind . . . Efim Gershevich [sic!]." This procedure was repeated with Professor Admoni of the Herzen Institute; Mme Saveleva called, "Witness Admoni! Please give me your passport, since your last name is unusual." [20]

The trial was also a warning to the young nonconformists of the literary underground, those who read their poetry in the city squares. "The Leningrad trial was not aimed at established, if rebellious, poets like Yevtushenko or Voznesensky. They belong to the Writers' Union where the Party can still exercise a restraining influence on them." [21] Soon, however, the trials would be aimed at members of the Writers' Union, and neither Party nor Union would demonstrably be interested in anything beyond promoting the prosecution and the persecution.

The persistence of the heirs of Stalin in the legal system, as in the bureaucracy of other Soviet institutions, was clearly revealed in Mme Saveleva's method of exercising her role as judge: she was ignorant, dogmatic, arbitrary, anti-Semitic, and appealed to all those qualities in the courtroom audience. It was also manifest in the willingness, even the readiness, of apparently ordinary Soviet citizens to attack nonconformists—poets and other intellectuals—evidence of the persistence of neo-Stalinism among the people.

12 Changeover

> The fact is, however, that Sinyavsky's writings do have a political meaning. To portray [Soviet] people in the guise of witches, thieves, graphomaniacs and drunkards is tantamount to active rejection of our form of government.
>
> *Zoya Kedrina*

Though the Brodsky case was symptomatic, most leadership time and effort during the first nine months of 1964 was devoted to more pressing domestic and foreign issues, most important the now open break with China. In cultural affairs, the regime hewed closely to Khrushchev's "middle course": in April, the Lenin Prize was carefully awarded to a noncontroversial candidate, Oles Gonchar, an obscure Ukrainian writer, but if the prize had not gone to Solzhenitsyn or Daniil Granin, neither had it gone to Aleksandr Chakovsky or Galina Serebryakova.[1] In March, V. Ozerov, editor-in-chief of *Voprosy literatury*, celebrated the anniversary of the March 1963 meetings between Khrushchev and the intellectuals by approving the general course of literary developments in the year since. There had been, Ozerov said, strict but solicitous criticism of writers who had erred, but no "head chopping." Yet he noted, "The dogmatists are straining mightily at slandering the positive work done by Soviet art since the 20th Party Congress. . . . The revisionists do not like the Party spirit in literature, they are trying to shake and destroy the methodology of Marxist-Leninist aesthetics." [2]

In April, at a meeting of a dozen of the young writers, among them some who had been severely criticized in 1963, the deputy editor of *Molodaya gvardia*, Aleksandr Rekemchuk, remarked: "A year ago people abroad began to write about 'the return to Stalinist methods of directing literature.' The last year has convincingly demonstrated that we have finished with those methods once and for all." [3] Moreover, nearly all those young writers who had been subjected to criticism were now once again appearing in print.

In May, at a meeting between Party ideologists and Soviet intellectuals, writers and artists were promised greater freedom of expression in return for their cooperation in supporting the government position against the Chinese; in a long article in *Pravda*, Stalin Prize winner Konstantin Simonov delivered a public rebuke to the Chinese Communists who had evidently attempted to solicit the loyalties of some Soviet intellectuals surreptitiously.[4] Also in May all publishing activities were consolidated under the control of the USSR Council of Ministers State Committee for the Press, and the number of publishing houses was reduced from sixty-two to forty-four; centralized control was thereby considerably strengthened.[5]

On the anniversary of the June 1963 ideological Plenum of the Central Committee, in an article significantly (if awkwardly) titled "Service to the People the High Calling of the Art of Socialist Realism," *Literaturnaya gazeta* announced that things on the literary front were steadily improving.[6] Eight days later Boris Polevoi exulted that young writers had learned at last to "distinguish the main stream from the swampy channels." [7] There were other symptoms of leniency in cultural policy when the May edition of *Moskva* appeared with excerpts from a Boris Pilnyak novel, *The Salt Storehouse*, written just before Pilnyak was purged by Stalin in 1937, and when *Literaturnaya gazeta* honored Anna Akhmatova on her seventy-fifth birthday by reviewing her life and work sympathetically.[8]

Public controversy about the conflict between generations seemed for the time under wraps and de-Stalinization relatively dormant, but the "heirs of Stalin" debate continued. General A. S. Gorbatov's memoirs, published that May in *Novy mir*, were replete with the horrors of purge, prison, and the political police, and strongly anti-Stalinist in tone.[9] Almost simultaneously, *Izvestia* printed two human-interest stories of Stalinist "excesses" during the period of the cult.[10] By autumn the paper was printing quite different stories, the personal reminiscences of a purge victim titled "This Must Not Be Forgotten," admonishing one and all to remember the kindnesses of the political police, the "good Chekists." The woman told how her husband was innocently imprisoned and executed, how she was innocently convicted and exiled to the labor camps and her small son taken away from her. For years she remained in the camps, but wherever she was sent individual Chekists treated her with humane consideration; finally restored to her son and "rehabilitated," she was able to explain to him, "Evil people were to blame for our misfortune. Neither the Party nor Soviet rule is at fault." [11] Her son's reply is not recorded. These contrasting articles revealed that the clash between those who wanted reprisals against informers, prison guards, political police, and those very same informers, prison guards, political police, and their accomplices in the terror had not yet been resolved.

In April, Khrushchev's seventieth birthday was celebrated with all the fanfare due Stalin's heir. He was awarded the Order of Hero of the Soviet Union; the press coverage, public recognition, and official tribute had all the qualities of another cult of personality,[12] so when, abruptly, six months later, on October 16, it was announced that Khrushchev had resigned because of advanced age and deteriorating health, the world was taken by surprise. The very next day, the new collective leadership led by Leonid Brezhnev and Alexey Kosygin vigorously attacked their predecessor for "harebrained schemes, half-baked ideas and hasty decisions and actions divorced from reality, boasting and empty rhetoric, attraction to rule by fiat, the refusal to take into account all the achievements of science and practical experience." [13] Such accusations and many others more dire might with justice have been leveled against Khrushchev, but whether these were the reasons for his being unseated remains unknown, nor are the precise reasons for his being overturned likely to be established until the Soviets make their archives available to historians. Yet some general ideas of the whys and wherefores of his ouster can be conceived.

Whether Khrushchev sought to expand his powers in order to impose his policies or to impose his policies in order to expand his powers will probably never be fully ascertained, but both the expansion and the imposition offended powerful forces and personalities in Soviet institutions, among them members of the Presidium who, ostensibly, shared "collective leadership" with him. Some took the hostility of the other members of the Presidium to be the major reason for Khrushchev's downfall. It was reported that Khrushchev had been preparing a November Plenum of the Central Committee in which he was going to "divest members of the collective leadership of true responsibilities." [14] In short, Khrushchev was going to purge some of his colleagues with the intention of elevating himself to one-man leadership. This prospect of a Khrushchev "cult," of Khrushchev's being discontent with being *primus inter pares*, probably precipitated his ouster.

There were other, and important, reasons as well. Domestically, Khrushchev's de-Stalinization had threatened strong and implacable forces in the bureaucracy, undermined the Party's authority, and provoked, or at least permitted, uncertainty, ferment, and even resistance to the Party and the leadership. Khrushchev's splitting of the Party machinery into industrial and agricultural divisions had offended both the Party apparatus and the government bureaucracy. He had also offended the "metal eaters," the heavy industrial bureaucrats and planners, by stressing consumer-goods production and endeavoring to shift power, funds, and emphasis away from them. He had simultaneously irritated farm bureaucrats by his frequent interference in and risky projects for agriculture, including cultivation of the virgin lands in Central Asia, corn planting, schemes for fertilizer production, cutting down on the private plots and privately owned animals of kolkhozniks, the most productive sector of farming.[15] Moreover, in 1964, the effects of the catastrophic drought of 1963 were still evident, as was the expenditure of scarce foreign exchange to purchase grain from abroad. The recollections of disorders in Novocherkassk, Krivoi Rog, Ryazan, Omsk, Odessa, and other places were still fresh in their minds.[16] In addition, Khrushchev had antagonized the military by cutting expenditures for armaments and by exaggerating his own role during World War II.

In foreign policy Khrushchev's de-Stalinization had also undermined Soviet authority abroad, particularly in the satellite countries and in foreign Communist parties. Reluctantly, the Communist Party of the Soviet Union's leaders were forced to the conclusion that they could no longer dictate "the road to socialism" to be taken by their allies and client states. Other "socialist" states would be able to follow "many roads to socialism," their own roads, though which such paths could be trodden without Kremlin anathema—or invasion of their countries—still remained problematical, as Albanians, Chinese, Czechs, Hungarians, Poles, and Romanians—not to speak of Yugoslavs—were dramatically to discover. Khrushchev had compromised Soviet prestige and credibility in the Cuban missile confrontation with the United States, thus offending his own military, and later justifying charges by the Chinese of both "adventurism" —in installing the missiles—and "capitulationism"—in "giving in to" the American ultimatum. Moreover, Khrushchev's tentative moves for rapprochement with West Germany outraged the professional diplomats of the Foreign Ministry, and Gromyko, when asked about Khrushchev's ouster, growled, "Why was Khrushchev overthrown? Because he sent Adzhubey to Bonn, of course." [17]

Khrushchev's fall was by no means as earth-shaking as Stalin's demise had been, but it too had important and wide-reaching consequences. Milovan Djilas, former Yugoslav Vice-President, who had the dubious pleasure of conducting personal negotiations with Stalin, was many years later moved to comment: "The structure of Russia is still such that reforms are realized by the personal power of the despot-reformer. Even in Khrushchev's case reformism was unseparable [sic] from personal power." Djilas, whose own experience with Communist power and its "new class" is almost unique, saw clearly how Khrushchev threatened the heirs of Stalin and how de-Stalinization as he had carried it out could only lead to a purge:

With the overthrow of Khrushchev . . . the Soviet Party bureaucracy finally freed itself from the nightmare of a purge, in this case an "anti-Stalinist" purge, that could have resulted in the hazardous loss of the bureaucracy's preponderance of power.

Thus, the party bureaucracy attained peace and security, but it lost the creativity and vision which from the revolution onward had been accompanied by purges in the ruling ranks and the weeding out of social forces "condemned by history." It sounds horrifying and absurd, and it is: in a totalitarian system such as the Soviet new forms of social existence are unrealizable without a cleansing within the ruling stratum and mass repressions.[18]

With the assumption of power by Brezhnev and Kosygin, the tide of Solzhenitsyn's fortunes began to ebb still further. He had already finished another novel, *The First Circle*, but the manuscript was confiscated by the KGB, as were a number of his other literary, personal, and private papers. A government campaign against him was begun which was to continue and mount; it used all those finely honed techniques developed by the Soviet authorities to break a man's spirit and resolve—if not his neck. Solzhenitsyn was kept under regular surveillance by the secret police; his friends and visitors were interrogated and intimidated; he was denied payment of the royalties on his books from Western publishers;[19] a campaign of character defamation was officially sponsored and slanderous accusations and innuendoes disseminated. And, except for the underground circulation of typewritten copies of his manuscripts through *samizdat*,[20] he was denied an audience.

But *samizdat*, in which typescripts are circulated chain-letter fashion among presumably close, trusted, and like-minded friends, each recopying a typed copy or carbon of the manuscript, is a most precarious kind of distribution for both author and audience. Retyping and otherwise copying manuscripts are bound to lead to errors, omissions, and even outright distortions in the text. *Samizdat* copies also have a not-so-strange way of being sent abroad, sometimes with the author's connivance, often without it. It was not long, therefore, before Solzhenitsyn's banned manuscripts began to find their way out of the Soviet Union to publishers in West Germany, Italy, France, Britain, and the United States. Publication abroad may, as in the Sinyavsky-Daniel case, send the author to prison; it deprives the writer of financial and literary control of his book; and in the Soviet Union, it can also endanger a reader, for possession of an "illegal book" may be adjudged a crime.

In 1965, Solzhenitsyn began to protest against confiscation of the manuscript of *The First Circle* and his other papers. Aware that with or without his connivance, his books would be published abroad, he warned officials that Western publication might be impending. Aside from the problems of the integrity of his texts and the possible loss of his copyright and royalties, Solzhenitsyn had to be concerned with what might happen to him at home as a consequence of foreign publication of his works. He may very well have recalled Khrushchev's warning to Yevtushenko in similar circumstances, "If the enemies of our cause start to praise you, our people will justly criticize you; so choose which suits you best." Against just such a dilemma Solzhenitsyn hoped to guard himself by protesting against the KGB confiscation of his papers—but to no avail.

The new rulers of the Soviet Union tried to ingratiate themselves with various strata of the population. To the peasants they gave expanded private plots; to the consumers they distributed flour, which had not been available for some months. The scientists were appeased by the swift denigration of T. D. Lysenko;[21] the writers and artists were promised that no new restrictions would be imposed on them. The attack on Lysenko was led by Zhores Medvedev, but was a concerted effort by biologists to overthrow Lysenkoist-Michurinist theories in biology and agriculture and to replace Lysenko and his cohorts (scientific heirs of Stalin) in the various bureaucratic and academic posts they held. In this struggle, similar to that of the liberals against the dogmatists in literature and the arts, the biologists were to have some signal successes after Khrushchev's ouster, but the attack had begun a few months earlier, while Khrushchev was still in power, after Medvedev circulated his first memorandum on Lysenko and Lysenkoism. Medvedev's paper, among other things, had moved Khrushchev to begin withdrawing his support from Lysenkoism and Lysenko early in 1964. The new spirit of accommodation and liberalism engendered by the Brezhnev-Kosygin regime was relatively short-lived; it was soon obvious that the Kosygin-Brezhnev regime was even less inclined than its predecessor to tolerate extending the limits of freedom.

For the moment, however, it seemed that the balance had swung in favor of the liberals, and the October (1964) Plenum, which was what the unseating of Khrushchev came to be called, seemed to portend greater liberalization. In January 1965, *Novy mir's* Tvardovsky, celebrating the magazine's fortieth anniversary issue, continued to plead "for works giving a truthful and accurate reflection of reality. . . . The author should study life honestly and boldly below the surface, and he can be of real help if he reveals something new and important which has perhaps never yet been mentioned in the daily press, or in any official documents or decrees." Remarking on the endeavors to silence Solzhenitsyn, Tvardovsky called on the Party to permit the novelist to go on writing and to give writers in general "the greatest possible freedom."

In January, in an almost despairing poem, "The Ballad of the Poacher," Yevtushenko once more protested against the regime's literary rigidities, especially with regard to the young writers.

> Are the rules of honest fishing
> > really unknown to you?
> In the nets, you've drawn in the meshes:
> > these nets of yours are illegal!
> And if it is really impossible
> > to live without nets in the world,
> At any rate try to ensure
> > that they are legitimate nets.
> The old fish have got entangled:
> > they cannot get free again;
> But the young ones are caught in it too;
> > why do you go after them?
> Make the meshes wider,
> > as it is they're impossibly fine!
> Through these devilish meshes,
> > hungering for their freedom,
> They will get through just the same,
> > tearing their gills on the way.
> But after they've been in these nets,
> > the young are no longer young.[22]

Organizational changes also showed that the liberals were contesting once more the conservative hold on the administrative posts in the Writers' Union. After tumultuous sessions in January at the Moscow and Leningrad Writers' Union meetings, the Moscow organization removed four of the most doctrinaire dogmatists from the secretariat: Kochetov, Gribachev, Sofronov, and Vasily Smirnov.[23] The archreactionary Georgy Markov was also replaced as First Secretary by Sergey Mikhalkov.[24] In Leningrad, the neo-Stalinist First Secretary, Aleksandr Prokofiev, was replaced by M. Dudin, and Daniil Granin, the author of the much criticized *A Personal Opinion*, was elected deputy to the First Secretary.[25] In addition, at the election meeting of the Moscow section on January 20, Konstantin Fedin spoke out sharply against Markov's reactionary remarks, singling out a specific sentence in Markov's *rapporteur* speech to the meeting: "How the writer feels, his time and his attitude toward his creative work constitute invaluable national capital which must not be squandered at anyone's whim or by anyone's arbitrary action." Fedin wanted to know "what whims, what arbitrary actions" Markov was talking about; and then angrily he declared, for the first time in his seven-year tenure as First Secretary of the Union, that administrative measures might have to be taken against Stalin's heirs: "If these whims and arbitrary actions are not specters of the past, then we must put an end to them, *if necessary by administrative action.* But if they are specters, who are they supposed to intimidate?" [26] Such a threat of force against the dogmatists was altogether out of keeping with Fedin's previous and later tone.

As a result of the elections, the board of the Moscow section of the Writers' Union was expanded to more than ninety members, to include ten additional writers, most of them liberals. Among them were Yevtushenko, Voznesensky, and Aksyonov, all of whom had been expelled in 1963 during the Khrushchev campaign against the liberal writers. [27] Among the two hundred delegates appointed to the Second Congress of the RSFSR Writers' Union was a virtual roster of the liberal writers, including Aksyonov, Aliger, Bella Akhmadulina, Bondarev, Voznesensky, Yevtushenko, Vera Inber, Kaverin, Yury Kazakov, Semyon Kirsanov, Yury Nagibin, Paustovsky, Polevoi, Viktor Rozov, Tvardovsky, Ehrenburg, and Yashin. [28]

In February, even stronger efforts were brought to bear to change the cultural atmosphere by the new editor in chief of *Pravda,* Alexey Rumyantsev, who denounced Khrushchev's anti-intellectualism and condemned "attempts to impose one's subjective evaluation and personal taste as yardsticks of artistic creation, especially when they are expressed in the name of the Party." Rumyantsev asserted that genuine "creativity is possible only through search, experimentation, free expression and the collision of differing viewpoints." Rumyantsev also invoked a 1925 policy statement on literature, which said: "Communist criticism must rid itself of the tone of literary command. The Party must in every way eradicate attempts at homebred and incompetent administrative interference in literary affairs." He tried to establish a "general criterion" for works of literature to bring them into accord with the Party's interests in "all-round free development of the personality of every member of society."

Everything that promotes the flowering of the human personality, broadens its outlook, inspires high ideals, elevates it morally and intellectually, improves the aesthetic perception of the surroundings, helps more acutely to distinguish good and evil in the world and to react more pointedly to them, in short, everything that elevates the genuinely human in man, falls into the stream of genuine art and constitutes its real value.

He called for various and competing styles, for a broad spectrum of literary schools and trends in the arts, and then attacked the general anti-intellectualism which often relegated intellectuals to the place of "second-class citizens." Rumyantsev even attacked Khrushchev as a "one-man boss" who considered himself the supreme arbiter in all fields of human endeavor and "regarded with suspicion and impatience intellectuals who, without justification from his point of view, pretended to be the authority in any specific sphere of knowledge." [29]

On the day Rumyantsev's article appeared in Moscow, Soviet intellectuals were busy discussing the jubilee number of *Novy mir*, which not only carried Tvardovsky's eloquent appeal for truthtelling in the arts, but also contained the first Pasternak prose to appear in print in several years, the first installment of Ilya Ehrenburg's memoirs since 1963, and the first Viktor Nekrasov story since Khrushchev had tried to expel the writer from the Party.

Late in March, Leonid Ilyichev, Khrushchev's ideological expert, was removed from his position as head of the Central Committee's Ideological Commission and replaced by Pyotr Demichev.[30] Two days later, *Pravda* launched an attack on the conservative bastion, *Oktyabr*, accusing it of living in the past and of "tendentious and subjective" assessments of current Soviet literature. The article was written by Suren Gaisaryan, deputy editor of *Voprosy literatury*, who remarked that the reader of *Oktyabr* "gains the impression that the journal, having got hold of the past, wants to hold on to that position." [31] In East Berlin, at a meeting of Communist writers from seven Communist countries including the USSR, Soviet literature was criticized for "provincial narrowness, isolation, lopsided information and a lack of modern style." Stefan Heym, a former American citizen now resident in East Germany and an uninvited guest at the conference, was applauded when he called for an end to hypocrisy, fear, and silence. "What we need," Heym announced, "is to clear out the dirt swept under the carpet, clean the carpet itself and disinfect the room that Stalin has moved out of." [32]

In April, a group of young poets and students, the so-called Smogisti, marched from Mayakovsky Square in Moscow to the Writers' Club on Herzen Street, blocking traffic and reading their poetry aloud.[33] Such unsponsored youth demonstrations did not please the regime.

In that spring of 1965, Ilya Ehrenburg gave an address to the Moscow Foreign Literature Library calling for writers to stop examining how they had suffered under Stalinism and to devote themselves instead to "how Stalinism could have happened." [34] Ehrenburg's advice followed a public speech by Party leader Brezhnev on the twentieth anniversary of V-E Day, in which he made some positive statements on Stalin's role as a wartime leader.[35] Though Brezhnev's remarks at first seemed only an endeavor to restore some balance to the judgments of Stalin's contribution to the war, they were, in fact, the opening step of a new campaign of what, for the sake of a better term, may be called re-Stalinization.

Not until summer, however, was the Brezhnev-Kosygin policy clearly defined. In August there was a flurry of critical articles in the press about authors who tended to stress the negative aspects of Soviet life, and a simultaneous attack on the two publications judged to be their sponsors and forums: *Novy mir* and *Yunost*.[36] The orthodox strictures about tightening Party discipline and about the need for better indoctrination of youth were reiterated. At first, the tone of the criticism was restrained, but that tone soon changed. In the last week of August, in a major article in *Pravda*, Komsomol leader Sergey Pavlov charged that books, magazines, plays, and movies were imbued with "unhealthy criticism, a restricted outlook on life, concern with petty occurrences, a glorification of suffering, [and] preaching hopelessness." Pavlov wrote: "It cannot be a matter of indifference to us in which direction the force of literary expression is headed—toward stimulating revolutionary-creative energy or toward promoting in young people a skepticism about all that is pure, advanced and progressive, and constitutes the essence of our society." That the "fathers and sons" problem was still alive was evident from Pavlov's continued emphasis on how the regime faced the task of "combating evidences of nihilism, thoughtless and presumptuous rejection of authority and scornful or ignorant attitudes toward the historical experience of the older generation of Soviet people." [37] Pavlov also said that youth remained ignorant of "what a high price and great sacrifice" were endured to achieve the "benefits of a Socialist society."

Pavlov's article was the sixth in a little more than two weeks expressing the Kremlin's dissatisfaction with the writers' viewpoint. The leadership emphasized the writers' failure to create works of uplift which would reinforce youth's idealism and striving "to build Communism" rather than stressing material affluence as, by implication, Khrushchev had. During the summer, the same writers remained the targets: Aksyonov, Yevtushenko, Voznesensky, and, of course, Solzhenitsyn. In early spring the change in official attitude toward Solzhenitsyn was clearly apparent when the Party theoretical journal described *Ivan Denisovich* as "an undoubtedly controversial work both ideologically and artistically," charging that "it tended to disorient youth about the Soviet past." These charges, growing out of the "heirs of Stalin" and "fathers and sons" controversies, were announced as among the reasons why the regime was denying the Lenin Prize to the novel and to its author.[38]

At the beginning of September, Rumyantsev was still writing editorials in *Pravda* calling for more freedom for intellectuals and for more trust by the regime in its writers and artists,[39] but it was now evident that the Brezhnev-Kosygin government was on a quite different course. In August there had been a swift tightening of controls in the Ukraine, and now, on September 8, the writers Andrey Sinyavsky and Yuli Daniel were arrested, accused of having smuggled their literary works out of the country in order to have them published in the West under the pseudonyms Abram Tertz and Nikolai Arshak respectively. Thirteen days later, Rumyantsev was removed as editor in chief of *Pravda* and replaced by the dogmatist Mikhail Zimianin.[40] The campaign of repression in the Ukraine which had led to the jailing of seventy Ukrainian intellectuals had not been widely publicized, but the Sinyavsky-Daniel arrest and trial were to receive worldwide attention. They were to prove the watershed in the struggle between those intellectuals attempting to broaden the narrow bounds of Soviet freedom and justice and the political powers striving to contain and divert "reform" into the channels of their own purposes and interests. The arrest was to give the conservatives the upper hand in the recurrent literary battles, not only because Sinyavsky was closely identified with *Novy mir*, but more important, because the regime now had swung its support to the conservatives.

Though the Sinyavsky-Daniel trial was to become the *cause célèbre* of those resisting a return to Stalinist repression, at the time the two Russian writers were arrested, an ominous wave of intimidation, arrest, and trial was already rolling across the Ukraine, a portent of things to come nationwide. During the summer and fall of 1965 and well into the spring of 1966, a sweeping regime campaign against intellectuals saw twenty leading Ukrainian writers, artists, scientists, and academicians tried and sentenced for "anti-Soviet agitation and propaganda." Among the best known were painter Mihailo Masiutko, linguist Sviatoslav Karavansky, historian Valentyn Moroz, psychologist Mihailo Horyn, and his art-critic brother Bogdan Horyn. The regime campaign and the intellectual dissidence in the Ukraine defined the positions and methods of both antagonists. The regime, using the catch-all Article 62 of the Ukrainian Criminal Code which covered "malicious defamation of the Soviet system," was determined to crush any further de-Stalinization or liberalization. As a result, most of the accused Ukrainian intellectuals were tried and convicted under Article 62 for "anti-Soviet slander" in their writings and ideas, and for possessing proscribed literature, but not for what ordinarily would have been considered active opposition.

It was some time before these trials came to public attention, and then chiefly through the courageous efforts of a young Ukrainian journalist, Vyacheslav Chornovil. Assigned to cover some of the trials, Chornovil was so outraged by the blatant violations of "socialist legality" that he petitioned the public prosecutor and the head of the KGB in the Ukraine; and subsequently, in May 1966, the First Party Secretary of the Ukraine, Pyotr Shelest, as well, in behalf of the accused. Chornovil noted that the regime was persecuting these intellectuals for their beliefs, and he denied that, according to Marxism, even ideas and books that were hostile could determine individuals' actions or take root in a soil that was not socially, economically, and politically ripe for them. In this regard, he quoted

Lenin and reminded them that Lenin had chosen to indulge in polemics with his opponents rather than imprisoning them.

Chornovil showed that Article 62 of the Criminal Code was as elastic as an accordion, so that anyone could interpret its "anti-Soviet slander" provisions in any way he chose; it was, Chornovil maintained, like the Ukrainian folk-saying: "The law is like a draft-bar, it goes in the direction in which it is pointed." Chornovil also denounced KGB surveillance, harassment, censorship, provocation, persecution, arbitrary arrest, and cruel interrogation of the accused. Citing chapter and verse and giving individual examples, Chornovil documented the facts that the trials were arbitrary and secret, the courts packed, the witnesses intimidated, the defense attorneys impotent or suborned, the sentences cruel and unfair, the accusations absurd. He appealed to Soviet law and "Leninist norms," to the guarantees of the Soviet Constitution and to the United Nations' Universal Declaration of Human Rights, to which the Ukraine was a signatory.

Although there was an obvious nationalist discontent in the intellectuals' protests—the Ukrainian intelligentsia opposed Great Russian chauvinism, Russification of the Ukraine, the destruction of Ukrainian culture and language, bias in the assignment of jobs and university admissions which favored Great Russians, and so on—the major issue was the failure to "liquidate the cult of Stalin" and to "implement the resolutions of the 20th Congress"; i.e., they were opposed to repression and a regression to Stalinism.

In September 1965, the same month that Sinyavsky and Daniel were arrested, Chornovil was dismissed from his job. In May 1966 he was convicted and sentenced to eighteen months of hard labor in the Mordvinian concentration camps. In the last months of 1967, Chornovil's petition defending the intellectuals, and a collection he had made of their letters, petitions, and diaries under the title *The Misfortune of Intellect*, were smuggled to the West a few pages at a time and published in Paris in Ukrainian. (The petition and *The Misfortune of Intellect* subsequently were published in English under the title *The Chornovil Papers*.)

Before Sinyavsky and Daniel were tried, but after the news of their arrest was circulated, Aleksandr Yesenin-Volpin, a mathematician, philosopher, and poet, and son of the famous Soviet poet Sergey

Yesenin who had committed suicide in 1925, was one of the leaders of a demonstration on Soviet Constitution Day, December 25, 1965. The demonstration of more than two hundred students from the Gorki Institute of Literature (where Sinyavsky was employed) took place in Moscow's Pushkin Square; the demonstrators carried banners protesting the arrest of Sinyavsky and Daniel and demanding an open and public trial for them. After the students had made a few speeches, the KGB broke up the demonstration and detained many of the protesters for questioning. Among them was Yesenin-Volpin, who had carried a banner which read, "Respect the Soviet Constitution!" When police asked him if the motto was addressed to the Soviet leaders, Volpin replied, "If you feel they need the advice, let them have it!" [41] Within a few hours all of the demonstrators were released, including Yesenin-Volpin—but not before he had been assured that the Sinyavsky-Daniel trial would be fair and open, nor before he had been personally threatened by the KGB for continuing his course of opposition to the regime.

The natural son of Yesenin and the translator Nadezhda Volpin, Aleksandr Yesenin-Volpin had been arrested in the summer of 1949 and put into the Lubyanka Prison because of two of his poems, "I Never Put My Hand to Plowing" and "The Raven." [42] Though he had only weeks earlier successfully defended his Ph.D candidacy at Moscow University, Volpin was declared "irresponsible" and confined in Leningrad Psychiatric Prison. In autumn 1950 he was sentenced to five years of exile in Karaganda and was freed only in the general amnesty following Stalin's death in 1953.

In 1961 a book of his poetry that also included a philosophical essay was published in the United States under the title *A Leaf of Spring*, and Volpin was arrested shortly thereafter for having sent the book abroad. None of his poems had been published in the USSR —their point of view was anathema to the Soviet authorities—but they had been circulated in *samizdat*. For a most striking example of why they would not be published, one can read what Volpin writes of Communism in "I Never Put My Hand to Plowing":

> . . . And when they thrust on me, as sacred law,
> "The dream of all the ages," the dream
> Requiring no vindication,
> And add moreover, "You must love,"

> Then, even if being sent to prison
> Is no mere penalty, but spells my doom,
> I answer back: "I just can't stand that crap!" [43]

In the meetings organized by Khrushchev and Ilyichev in December 1962, Ilyichev attacked Volpin as deranged and *A Leaf of Spring* for containing "a pretentious and illiterate 'philosophical treatise' as well as a misanthropic anti-Soviet doggerel, the ravings of a mental case." The book, he said, was "imbued with savage hatred of Soviet society and Soviet people." [44] Ilyichev's attack was then reinforced by a letter to *Pravda* from Volpin's two aunts, Aleksandra and Yekaterina, who condemned Volpin in almost the same terms, saying that his book contained "misanthropic anti-Soviet doggerel, the ravings of a mental case." [45] They were, they said, revolted by those across the seas who use the ravings of a sick man "for [their] own foul anti-Soviet purposes." The two aunts publicly apologized for Volpin by explaining that he had repeatedly been treated in psychiatric hospitals. Early in 1963, *Ogonyok* said Volpin was quite sane and charged him with spying for the United States,[46] so it seemed that the authorities had decided to bring him to trial on much more serious charges. He was, however, sent to a mental institution instead, and released only when many of Moscow's scientific elite petitioned the authorities in his behalf.

Yesenin-Volpin was no mean opponent; intelligent and brave, he had an international reputation as a philosopher and academician and many friends among the Soviet intelligentsia, and was one of the few Soviet intellectuals who straddled the "two cultures" of the literati and the scientists. Around him a dissidence of artists and scientists combined began to coalesce.

Unlike most other dissidents, Volpin did not make a fetish of proclaiming his pro-Soviet loyalties. Instead, his most profound and public commitment was to freedom, a freedom the authorities and the neo-Stalinists saw only as anarchy.

For A. Yesenin-Volpin, "only one objective is clear, an unreasonable objective—freedom!" which he interprets as "the possibility of choice, certainly not because it pleases us to choose (the necessity is sometimes frightening and almost always unpleasant!), but because we want to choose without compulsion." Quite consistently he takes arms against all monisms and all faiths—Christian, Communist, even a faith in reason

—as inescapably bound up with compulsion. But for Yesenin-Volpin the denial of faith in reason does not mean anti-intellectualism. "It is not necessary *to believe* in reason. For a thinking person it is sufficient to be reasonable," he writes. He is against faith and for free thought; yet nowhere does he show any inclination to join the hearty, sporty liberalism which views everything as a "competition of ideas" and proclaims "let the strongest win." He sees the social trend toward monism as inexorable, "with the exception, perhaps, of the latest Western and also Indian culture"; consequently, he perceives a permanent, tragic contradiction between freedom of thought and the demands of life. Not denying to others the right to side up with practical life, which "consists in the search for the useful," Yesenin-Volpin resolutely dedicates himself to "thinking which consists in the search for truth." [47]

Of Soviet "advances" toward freedom, of Soviet "progress," Yesenin-Volpin was skeptical, perhaps contemptuous:

Even the relative freedom which we have gained (a level of freedom which would seem to a person from another country to be the most shameful slavery) was not won by our society itself, but was granted to it . . . as a sort of cat-and-mouse game with the people, rather than for the sake of more civilized rule, and only because Stalin's successors have lacked the imagination and courage to follow in the footsteps of their leader.[48]

Though this may have been Volpin's philosophical and intellectual perspective, it did not keep him from continuing his own struggle to broaden the areas of freedom in the Soviet Union—and bravely to suffer the consequences.

13 The Sinyavsky-Daniel Case

> Experts, what a distance
> You are from life! Formalin!
> You stink of it, and incense.
>
> They've got their virgin lands I know,
> Where not one pearl of grain can grow.
> *Andrey Voznesensky*

In the five months between the time Sinyavsky and Daniel were taken into custody, on September 8, 1965, and the time they were brought to trial, on February 10, 1966, a number of Western (including some Communist) inquiries about them elicited little information. Not until January 13, 1966, when a 1952 Stalin Prize winner, Dmitry Yeremin, one of the most savage conservative partisans, attacked Sinyavsky and Daniel in *Izvestia*, were the Soviet people publicly informed that the two writers had been arrested and were in custody. Yeremin's article, "The Turncoats," set the tone for the pretrial campaign against the two, and for the trial itself, accusing Sinyavsky and Daniel of anti-state activities, dirty satires against the Soviet Union and the Communist Party, hatred of the Soviet system, moral perversion, and "high treason."[1] Sinyavsky and Daniel, Yeremin wrote, "like nothing in our country, nothing is holy for them either in its past or its present. They wish to slander and curse everything that is dear to Soviet man."[2]

Ten days later the second major article in the campaign, "The Heirs of Smerdyakov," by Zoya Kedrina, went considerably further than Yeremin in attacking the two writers and anatomizing their work.[3] (Smerdyakov is the name of a fictional character in Dostoyevsky's *The Brothers Karamazov*. The depraved illegitimate son of the elder Karamazov, he finally kills his own father. "The name is derived from the Russian word for 'stink,' and . . . is commonly used by Russians to describe someone who is evil beyond redemption.") Kedrina inundated Sinyavsky and Daniel with invective, calling them writers without talent, boring, crude, boorish, their work a veritable "waste land of rhetoric." Daniel was damned for "straight fascism," and Sinyavsky was charged with plagiarism and anti-Semitism. After censuring both writers for "dismal malevolence, such slimy filth and utter cynicism," [4] Kedrina moved on to what the government considered the real crime: disfiguring, defiling, and besmirching everything Soviet.

A month after they were arrested, Sinyavsky's introduction to a new collection of Pasternak's poetry which he had edited was severely criticized.[5] (Pasternak had been a friend and mentor of Sinyavsky's, and Sinyavsky had been one of the pallbearers with Yuli Daniel at the older poet's funeral in Peredelkino. In March 1962, Sinyavsky had written a severely critical review of an earlier collection of Pasternak's poetry published in *Novy mir*.) In November 1965, two months after they were arrested, Mikhail Sholokhov, on the occasion of being awarded the Nobel Prize for literature, had denounced them, though without mentioning their names. "I stand for those writers," he said, "who look honestly into the eyes of Soviet power and publish their works here and not abroad." [6]

At first it seemed that the Soviet authorities planned to try Sinyavsky and Daniel for having published their works abroad under pen names, but Western protests that the Soviet penal code did not make such pseudonymous publication a punishable offense seem to have changed their minds and judicial strategy. Instead, the two writers were tried under the catch-all Article 70 of the Criminal Code, which reads:

Agitation or propaganda carried out with the purpose of subverting or weakening the Soviet regime or in order to commit particularly dangerous crimes against the state, the dissemination for the said purposes of slanderous inventions defamatory to the Soviet political and social system, as well as the dissemination or production or harboring for the said purpose of literature of similar content, are punishable by imprisonment for a period of from six months to seven years and with exile from two to five years, or without exile, or by exile from two to five years.

The prosecution asked for the maximum sentence and made clear just what the political leadership was intent on quashing: "Imperialist reaction is on the watch for means of ideological subversion to discredit the Soviet people, their government, the Communist Party of the U.S.S.R. and its policies. For this purpose, use is being made of anti-Soviet works of underground writers that are passed off by hostile propaganda as truthful accounts about the Soviet Union." [7] The prosecution concerned itself not only with the fact that Sinyavsky and Daniel's works had been published abroad, but also with the fact that their works were then broadcast back to the Soviet Union by Radio Liberty.

The trial opened in Moscow district court on February 10 and lasted for four days. The prosecution's case was directed primarily against the political content of Sinyavsky's and Daniel's writings; although the chief judge of the court, L. N. Smirnov, insisted that they were being tried not for their literary works but for acts punishable by law, Sinyavsky and Daniel were attacked for having taken positions in their writings which the authorities considered inimical to Soviet interests. According to Max Hayward, it was the first time in Soviet history that writers were tried for what they had written: "Many Soviet writers have been imprisoned, banished, executed or driven into silence, but never before after a trial in which the principal evidence against them was their literary work." [8] Under the guise of criticism of the personality cult, Sinyavsky's *The Trial Begins* was said to mock the Soviet system and Marxist-Leninist principles, and Sinyavsky's essay "On Socialist Realism" was seen as an invidious assault on the leading role of the Party in Soviet culture. Sinyavsky was also sharply rebuked for having dismissed the achievements of all Soviet literature and for having slandered all aspects of Soviet society. Sinyavsky's "anti-Soviet" attitude was in great measure deduced from a manuscript, "An Essay in Self-Analysis," taken by the KGB in a search of his home. Judge Smirnov cautioned, "This manuscript does not figure in the charge against Sinyavsky," because Sinyavsky had neither circulated it nor sent it abroad to be published. But in precisely the same way that the regime had used Josif Brodsky's private papers and manuscripts in the trial against him, and as they were subsequently to use the manuscript of Solzhenitsyn's play "Feast of the Conquerors" against him, so they used this manuscript against Sinyavsky. [9] Daniel was censured for sharing and propagating the same "anti-Soviet views," for depicting Soviet life as morally and politically decadent, and for suggesting in the short story "Atonement" that all the Soviet people were responsible for the cult of personality.[10] Though a number of distinguished writers and critics, among them Paustovsky, Vsevolod Ivanov, and Lev Kopelev, gave written testimonials about the works of the two writers, Judge Smirnov refused to admit them as evidence.

According to Tass, Sinyavsky and Daniel had confessed their guilt in pretrial examinations but in court had withdrawn their earlier confessions. The two men did admit that they had sent their works abroad and shown them to their friends at home, but they denied the anti-Soviet character of their writings and refused "either in full or in part" to plead guilty. Both behaved bravely and with great consideration for one another, but their approaches were quite different. Sinyavsky's defense was cooler and more controlled, intellectual and detached. Daniel's was a bit more uncertain and uneven, but given with greater warmth and vigor. Sinyavsky maintained that he was eccentric but not anti-Soviet, that literary and juridical standards were not the same nor comparable; nor could literal-minded interpretations of literary works in terms of their so-called political content be accepted either in a literary or juridical sense.

The interrogation of Sinyavsky was much sharper, and very close attention was paid to the "intention" of his texts, for under Article 70, the state had to prove the defendant's *intent* to defame or slander the Soviet system (not that what was defamatory or slanderous was clearly definable). Sinyavsky himself, interestingly, was by no means willing to discard completely the cult of the individual or all the achievements of Stalin and Stalinism, and in this, at least, he was a rarity among the liberal intellectuals. In court, he testified:

I regard Communism as the only goal that can be put forward by the modern mind; the West has been unable to put forward anything like it. . . . I talk about our difficulties and contradictions in the last few years under Stalin; I say that brutalities and inhuman methods were used. But the Stalinist period has its legitimate place in history and I don't reject it. I reject the accusations of the Western world about the brutalities; they resulted from action against inertia. The Western ideas about the renunciation of force have no appeal to me. My reply to liberal critics is: And what have all your humane old dodderers achieved? [11]

Daniel's final plea was moving. Though he had at first considered waiving his right to such a plea, he "then realized that it is not only my last word at this trial, but perhaps the last word I shall be able to say to people in my life. . . . In the final plea of my comrade Sinyavsky there was a note of despair about the impossibility of breaking through a blank wall of incomprehension and unwillingness to listen. I am not so pessimistic." [12]

Earlier, Daniel had explained how he came to write "This Is Moscow Calling":

In 1960–1961, when I was writing this story, I—and not only I, but any person who thought seriously about the situation in our country— was convinced that the country was on the eve of a restoration of the cult of personality. We all remembered well what were called "violations of socialist legality." And I saw again all the symptoms: there was again one man who knew everything, again one person was being exalted, again one person was dictating his will to agricultural experts, artists, diplomats, writers. We saw again how one single name appeared in the pages of newspapers and on posters, how the most banal and crude statement of this person was being held up to us as a revelation, as the quintessence of wisdom.

Daniel stressed not only that Khrushchev was building a new cult of personality but that there had been silence concerning those heirs of Stalin responsible for the murders and brutalities of the Stalinist era: "Every member of society is responsible for what happens in society. . . . Nobody has ever publicly stated who was to blame for those crimes and I will never believe that three men—Stalin, Beria and Ryumin—could alone do such terrible things to the whole country." [13] In raising this question, Daniel was running against the whole current of the Brezhnev-Kosygin regime's slow refurbishing of Stalin's reputation. The regime was carefully avoiding the question of punishing the heirs of Stalin, so that the bureaucracy's stability would be preserved.

Daniel defended his writings against the charge of being "anti-Soviet," maintaining that the prosecution had foolishly attributed the characters' ideas and feelings to the authors because the prosecution simply did not understand the nature of literary creation and technique. Moreover, the prosecution was quoting him out of context, without awareness that his stories were set in the 1950s, *not* the 1960s. After 1963, he said, when he saw how his works were being construed in foreign countries, he stopped writing and sending works abroad. Finally, Daniel pleaded, "We are guilty, not for what we have written, but for sending our works abroad. There are many political indiscretions, exaggerations and insults in our books. But isn't twelve years of Sinyavsky's life and nine years of mine a rather excessive payment for our frivolity, thoughtlessness, and misjudgment?" [14]

The court was unmoved. Judge Smirnov sentenced Sinyavsky to seven years and Daniel to five, failing only to add the additional terms of exile which the prosecution had asked for. They were condemned to hard labor for having put into print ideas and beliefs that "could be used profitably by enemies of Communism." The verdict of the court stated that the writings of the two men "attracted the attention of bourgeois propaganda organs by their anti-Soviet content and they were exploited in the ideological struggle against the Soviet Union." [15]

The actual sentences were evidently influenced by two other factors. The longer sentence of Sinyavsky indicated that the prosecution saw him as the "elder" of the two and the tougher. Moreover, he was a well-known critic associated with the liberals of *Novy mir*. It was also implied that Daniel's term was reduced because of his outstanding war record. Daniel had gone directly from school into the front lines to fight on the Ukrainian and Byelorussian fronts and had been severely wounded and pensioned as a war invalid. In contrast, Sinyavsky was accused by Judge Smirnov of having had an "easy war." Sinyavsky's relative assurance and his position as senior staff member at the Gorki Institute of World Literature were bound to play roles as well, but perhaps the most important consideration was the actual nature of Sinyavsky's work—writing which struck with savage irony and fantastic imagination at some of the favorite shibboleths of the Soviet regime. Sinyavsky's character is more difficult to understand than Daniel's, more subtle, hidden, devious, and complex; in the same measure those qualities differentiate his writing from Daniel's. Though the arrest of Sinyavsky's father in 1951 might have given him an intense personal cause for antiregime sentiments, his distaste for many aspects of Soviet life seems to be the result of a

perceptive and rigorously intelligent nature, of great independence
of mind. A not altogether convincing portrait of Sinyavsky emerges
from a description given by Hélène Peltier-Zamoyska, a French specialist in Russian literature, who studied at Moscow University with
Sinyavsky and through whom he sent his manuscripts to the West.

Son of a militant revolutionary, he could not imagine his country with
any other structure than the one created by 1917. The very word
revolution . . . had an emotional quality for him, the ring of something sacred which foretold the coming of a juster social system, a
new humanism which would regenerate the world. . . . Was he
shocked by the cruelty used to establish that new order? Certainly less
than I. . . . He would tell me that the law of historical progress regrettably demanded human sacrifices. Nonetheless, his conscience was
uneasy with such facile argument. . . .
. . . Then the shock of Stalin's death came. The famous "secret"
speech by Khrushchev to the 20th Congress was incalculably important
to the whole U.S.S.R., particularly for the generation of my [Moscow
University] friends. "A world has collapsed," Pasternak told me, "a
new one will be born." I saw a complete change of values. My old university friends, for example, had suddenly become aware of the tragedy
endured by millions of innocent people in concentration camps, and
they felt personally responsible for and accomplices in those crimes
because they had permitted them to occur in the name of a patriotism
identical with conformism. This feeling of shame gave rise to a determination not to be passive or indifferent to the slightest injustice. People
who had the rare courage not to permit their consciences to bow before
the slogans of the day became heroes.

This was Sinyavsky and Daniel's reaction, and what impelled them to
write. In 1956, the year of the 20th Congress, Sinyavsky wrote his essay,
"On Socialist Realism," and his first short novel, *The Trial Begins*.
Manuscripts began to circulate all over the country, which was gripped
by the necessity to tell of those years which had gone by in tears, blood
and terror. The abscess had to be lanced, not only by the leadership
but by ordinary men as well, a right that was granted to them only
very reluctantly. The brutal attacks on *Dr. Zhivago* (1958) arrived
shortly as a reminder that the burning questions of the day were still,
in practice, forbidden, and that one was unable to deal with them in
any way different from the spirit imposed by official dogma.[16]

On February 19, five days after the court passed sentence on Sinyavsky and Daniel, Yesenin-Volpin publicly challenged the legality

of the verdict. In an interview with the *New York Times*'s Moscow correspondent Peter Grose, Volpin declared that the guilt of the two writers "was merely asserted by the prosecution and others. This is not proof, and I personally believe they were not guilty of deliberate anti-Soviet activity." Only a few "selected" Soviet citizens were permitted into the courtroom, but no foreigners; Volpin noted that although the trial was therefore not "open," it was "public," and therefore was a "significant advance" over the secret trials of the Stalin era. "It is a tragedy that Sinyavsky and Daniel have been convicted," he said. "They are lucky, for their case has been taken up by the whole civilized world. There were so many others about whom the civilized world knew nothing—knew as little as people know of a rabbit eaten by the wolves in a forest." [17]

The civilized world had, indeed, heard. There were protests from intellectuals and writers in the West, and perhaps most helpful for the liberal Soviet intellectuals, from the Western Communist parties, almost all of which dissociated themselves from the trial. In a front-page editorial, the Italian Communist paper, *L'Unità*, announced its refusal to support the trial or the sentence.[18] John Gollan, Secretary-General of the British Communist Party, criticized the conduct of the trial in the *Daily Worker*.[19] The famous French poet and member of the French Communist Party's Central Committee, Louis Aragon, attacked the Soviet Communist Party in the pages of *L'Humanité*, declaring that the trial had established the "criminality of an opinion" and created a precedent "more damaging to socialism" than anything that Sinyavsky and Daniel could write. Even the American *Daily Worker* appealed for clemency for the two writers.[20] But none of the furor had any effect on either the conviction or the sentence.

During the first weeks of March, in the preparations for the Twenty-third Party Congress, it became increasingly apparent that the political implications of dissent, and of the Sinyavsky-Daniel trial, had gone beyond the problems of freedom of literary expression and violation of "socialist legality," though both of those remained germane issues. The literary conflict between liberals and conservatives broke into the open once again at a two-day meeting of the Writers' Union on March 4 and 5 in Moscow, where the deliberations concerned themselves with the "ideological and artistic correction of *Yunost*'s course." [21] In a review of two years of Boris Polevoi's youth magazine, one conservative critic reproached it for printing stories full of "infantile heroes locked in their own private worlds and standing aloof from the main problems that trouble Soviet youth." A representative of the Central Committee of the Komsomol challenged some *Yunost* authors for their "lack of a clear-cut moral position," and called for heroes in literature who would have "human significance." Viktor Rozov, a member of the *Yunost* editorial board, defended the magazine and maintained that "young people need no artificial models for emulation and do not accept them." He reinforced his assertion by revealing that *Yunost*'s circulation had in two years doubled and was then two million copies per month.[22]

As a prelude to the Party Congress, three petitions were sent to the Soviet leadership, two from writers in Moscow and Leningrad, protesting the conviction of Sinyavsky and Daniel. Solzhenitsyn was one of those who signed the Moscow petition, and with him was a virtual roll call of liberal writers, including Yevtushenko, Voznesensky, Aksyonov, and Akhmadulina. The petition asked that the convicted writers' sentences be reduced, and simultaneously pointed out the great harm that the trial and conviction had done to the Soviet Union in intellectual circles abroad.[23]

Many of the Russian intellectuals were now profoundly concerned with the possible revival of "neo-Stalinism." A month before the March 29, 1966, opening of the Twenty-third Congress, the third petition was sent directly to Brezhnev by a group of scientists, artists, writers, and other intellectuals, who stressed the dangers of rehabilitating Stalin. Among those who signed were some of the most eminent representatives of Soviet art and science: physicists Igor Tamm, Pyotr Kapitsa, and Andrei Sakharov, writers Konstantin Paustovsky and Viktor Nekrasov, dancer Maya Plisestskaya, film maker Mikhail Romm, former diplomat Ivan Maisky. They warned that the Soviet people would neither understand nor accept a retreat from the condemnation of Stalin, nor would Western Communist parties, which would believe that re-Stalinization was only capitulation to the Chinese.[24] The ideological poles were Chinese "Stalinism" on the one hand, and "Czechoslovak revisionism" on the other, neither of which was acceptable to the Soviet leadership.

When, in the second week of March, Lev Smirnov, the chief judge of the court that had convicted Daniel and Sinyavsky, appeared before the Writers' Union to deliver a lecture, he was put in the dock himself and forced to defend the role he had played at the trial.[25] The writers assaulted Smirnov with angry questions the judge was unable to answer to their satisfaction. The writers did learn from the judge that a "prominent writer" had been refused a request to be allowed to defend the two prisoners in court. It was soon discovered that the man involved was the venerable and respected Konstantin Paustovsky, who had volunteered his services in Sinyavsky's and Daniel's behalf.

No sooner had the Twenty-third Congress opened than it became evident that *Novy mir* and *Yunost* were to be prime targets of the regime. Tvardovsky, *Novy mir*'s editor, who had been a delegate to the two previous Party congresses, was not elected a delegate to this one, nor was *Yunost* editor Boris Polevoi; consequently, both magazines were subjected to a barrage of criticism without having their editors present to defend the publications' policies. *Yunost* and *Novy mir* were denounced roundly for publishing fiction that portrayed "nihilism" as rife among Soviet youth, for showing shortcomings in Soviet life, and for printing memoirs, particularly Ehrenburg's literary, Maisky's diplomatic, and Gorbatov's military reminiscences, that called former Soviet policies into question, and by implication cast aspersions on those in the leadership who had initiated and carried those policies out.

At the Congress itself, Brezhnev not only signaled the return to orthodoxy in the arts by calling on writers to serve the Party; he also indicated that there would be a return to more doctrinaire policies in other sectors of Soviet life. The automatic rotation of Party officials, for example, was canceled. The Party Presidium would once again be called the Politburo, and the First Secretary would once again take on (Stalin's) title of Secretary-General of the Party. Though Brezhnev declared his opposition to "administration by mere injunction and against arbitrary decisions in art or literature," he also warned that those intellectuals whose creative work did not contribute to "building Communism" would be cut off, and he lashed out at those "very few hack artists who specialize in smearing our regime . . . renegades to whom nothing is holy. . . . It is fully understood that the Soviet people cannot let pass unnoticed their shameful activities. They get what they deserve." [26]

Brezhnev and Kosygin proceeded with a circumspection and practicality that belied the grandiosity of Khrushchev's Party congresses. They made no speeches about a twenty-year plan "to build Communism," as Khrushchev had done in 1961, nor about overtaking and surpassing American industrial achievements. Instead, they set out a Five-Year Plan for 1966–1970 which undertook to provide modest increases in consumer-goods production, in food supply, and in the construction of new houses—all things which would make the new regime popular with the people. (In 1966, the USSR was blessed with the best harvest in its history, so Brezhnev and Kosygin were freed of the chronic agricultural shortages that had plagued Khrushchev, and for the first time in three years, the government was not forced to buy grain abroad.)

The new regime's emphasis was conservative, on order and stability, and in addition Brezhnev and Kosygin made a reactionary effort to develop its ties with the Stalinist past. Refurbishing the image of Stalin was an essential element in this effort, and in the spring of 1965, Marshals Ivan Konev and Ivan Bagramian called for a "just historical evaluation" of Stalin's wartime role.[27] Khrushchev had supported serious criticisms of Stalin's negligence and ineptitude in preparing for World War II and had encouraged historians to show Stalin responsible for some of the disastrous defeats and enormous destruction suffered by Soviet armies early in the war. Khrushchev's supporters among the young historians included Aleksandr Nekrich, who had dissected Stalin's prewar errors in his book *22 June 1941*, published in the spring of 1965, and Pyotr Yakir, who defended Nekrich's thesis, as well as the older General A. S. Gorbatov. Moreover, both Nekrich and Gorbatov had especially stressed the deleterious role the Stalinist purges—particularly of the officer corps of the Red Army—had played in the military preparations for World War II, and the conduct of the early part of the war. The viewpoint was intended to force a showdown with the heirs of Stalin, as one more way to denigrate the Stalinist heritage.

This debate, an aspect of de-Stalinization, had been fostered and continued until 1966, when the new leadership openly identified itself with the dogmatists. Then, at the beginning of the year, three neo-Stalinist historians accused the liberal historians of a subjectivity inimical to Marxism and of coining the "un-Marxist phrase, the period of the personality cult." [28] Not long afterward, Nekrich was expelled from the Party, and by summer the official and prevailing view had changed almost 360 degrees. In 1965, the de-Stalinized view of Stalin's prewar preparations was that Stalin had been inept and trusting, had unwisely relied on Hitler's word to rule out the possibility of a Nazi invasion, and had refused to heed the advice both of foreign diplomats and his own intelligence services that Germany was preparing war against the Soviet Union. "The information which it [the Soviet intelligence service] gathered was ample enough, but it could not persuade Stalin that Germany had really decided to abrogate the mutual non-aggression pact and begin a war against the Soviet Union," the major journal of history had maintained then.[29] A year later the Party line was that Stalin and the Party leadership had been fully cognizant of the dangers of invasion and had taken the necessary precautions to meet them.[30]

The only writer given the platform at the Twenty-third Congress was Sholokhov, and his speech carried ominous echoes of Stalinist times. He regretted the leniency the court had shown to Sinyavsky and Daniel, calling them traitors to their country who, in other times, would very likely have been shot: "Had these rascals with black consciences been caught in the memorable 1920s, when judgment was not by strictly defined articles of the Criminal Code but was guided by a revolutionary sense of justice, the punishment meted out to those turncoats would have been quite different." After that call for the swift and arbitrary firing squad of the Civil War period, Sholokhov attacked the writers who had rallied to Sinyavsky's and Daniel's defense: "I feel ashamed not for those who slandered our homeland and flung mud at everything most sacred to us. They are immoral. I am ashamed of those who tried and are trying to defend them, no matter how this defense is explained. I feel doubly ashamed of those who offered their services, who vouch for the condemned outcasts." [31] This was a thrust at Paustovsky for his offer to defend the writers in court, and at the sixty-three intellectuals who had rallied to their cause and had sent a letter to the Party Presidium and the Supreme Soviets of the USSR and RSFSR, offering "to stand surety" for Sinyavsky and Daniel. Those sixty-three included some of the most gifted people in Soviet society, and they had reminded the government that "condemnation of writers for the writing of satirical works creates an extremely dangerous precedent and could impede the progress of Soviet culture. . . . We need more, not less freedom for intellectual and artistic experiment. From this standpoint, the trial of Sinyavsky and Daniel has already caused us more harm than did any of their mistakes." [32]

A searing response to Sholokhov came in an open letter from Lydia Chukovskaya—over sixty, in poor health, half-blind—whose husband had been shot as an "enemy of the people" during the Stalinist terror.[33] The daughter of the eminent literary critic, historian, and writer of children's books, Kornei Chukovsky, and a novelist of brilliance herself, she addressed the letter to the Rostov-on-Don section of the Writers' Union to which Sholokhov belongs (considered among the most conservative branches in the Union), and also to the editors of *Pravda, Izvestia, Literaturnaya gazeta,* and *Literaturnaya rossiya,* as well as to the boards of the USSR and RSFSR writers' unions. "In the whole history of Russian culture," Chukovskaya wrote, "I know of no other case of a writer publicly expressing regret, as you have done, not at the harshness of a sentence but at its leniency." Berating him for his desire to see harsh and summary justice inflicted on Sinyavsky and Daniel, Chukovskaya reminded Sholokhov: "Stalin's contempt for the law cost our people millions of innocent victims. Persistent attempts to return to the rule of law, to strict observance of the spirit and the letter of Soviet law and the progress made in this direction, constitute the most precious achievement of our country during the last ten years." Sholokhov had cut himself off from the great traditions of Russian letters which "always taught and still teach us that we must never oversimplify, but must try with all the resources of social and psychological insight to understand as deeply as possible the complex causes of human error, misconduct, crime and delinquency. The humanizing message of Russian literature is indeed to be found mainly in this quality of understanding." [34]

How insignificant the "return to the law" may seem to a detached

Western eye is one thing; but to a Russian it made and makes a crucial difference. As Ehrenburg was to remark to Alexander Werth almost two years later:

We're told that there's a more liberal atmosphere in Moscow today. I'm not at all sure. This month it may be more liberal, next month it may be less liberal. We've had all sorts of beastly things happening in the literary field in the last few years; and the Sinyavsky-Daniel affair is not the worst. After all, they had a trial of sorts, they were sentenced under some article of the Criminal Code. They could even plead not guilty. There is here a difference between a trial, even of sorts, and the Stalin method Sholokhov advocated in the case of Sinyavsky and Daniel—standing them up against the wall and just bumping them off.[35]

In all the dissidence—cultural, political and scientific—this constant emphasis on the rule of law is evident.

Chukovskaya indicted the Sinyavsky-Daniel trial as illegal "because a book, a piece of fiction, a story, novel—in brief, a work of literature—whether good or bad, talented or untalented, truthful or untruthful, cannot be tried in any court, criminal, military or civil. It can only be tried in the court of literature. . . . Literature does not come under the jurisdiction of a criminal court. Ideas should be fought with ideas, not with camps and prisons." [36] Chukovskaya's letter was never published anywhere in the Soviet Union, but "everybody somehow read it or came to hear it. *It was like the voice of the old Russian intelligentsia speaking to the Party inquisitor.*" [37]

Chukovskaya also scathingly and skillfully asserted that Sholokhov's own best work, *And Quiet Flows the Don,* had just such an understanding of the complexity of human motive that he now demonstrably lacked. She also declared that he had for a long time written and talked publicly about Soviet writers with "crude mockery and scorn," but this time he had surpassed even himself. The flick of the bastinado was in the reminder that Sholokhov had not written or published anything of consequence in more than thirty years; Chukovskaya wrote: "Literature will take its own vengeance, as it always takes vengeance on those who betray the duty imposed by it. It has condemned you to the worst sentence to which an artist can be condemned—creative sterility. And neither honors, nor money, nor prizes, given at home or abroad, can save you from this judgment." [38]

Among the others who attacked Sholokhov's stance was the still relatively unknown Yury Galanskov, who made the accusation that the elderly novelist was unable to "envision the Soviet government as anything other than a military encampment and would like to picture Sinyavsky and Daniel, in their turn, as spies who have suddenly made their way into one of the barracks, namely the Union of Soviet Writers." Galanskov defended Sinyavsky's and Daniel's desire for creative freedom and for publishing their works abroad because there was neither freedom to create nor to publish available to them in the USSR. Although the Soviet Union guaranteed those freedoms verbally, "all that is guaranteed is the mockery of freedom by police and bureaucrats." Galanskov maintained that the absolute majority of the Russian literary intelligentsia favored creative freedom yet only minor protest had been evoked from them in behalf of Sinyavsky and Daniel, and that "still the protest of slaves, but . . . a protest nevertheless." He summed up by stating that "in today's Russia, there are no free organizations, no free press, no free court. In contemporary Russia, everything is left to the power of the state." [39] What Galanskov meant was that so long as the Party controlled reform, monopolized its possibilities, it could at its own pleasure and for its own purposes advance or revoke liberalization at will. Unless the people had *genuine rights* embodied in *adequate institutions* which were protected by legal and political guarantees, the Party could suppress or ignore any freedoms which seemed to threaten its power or interests. The regime would tolerate only such criticisms as it considered "officially acceptable," but the moment the designated bounds were overstepped, the authorities fell back on semi-Stalinist methods of coercion to enforce their will. The Sinyavsky-Daniel trial was just such a reversion.

Another rebuke to Sholokhov came from veteran Communist, former concentration-camp victim, and leading dissident, Aleksey Kosterin. Kosterin applauded Solzhenitsyn's letter for having publicly revealed that no free press existed in the Soviet Union, and for having openly castigated the mockery made of creative people and their rights. Kosterin went a step beyond Solzhenitsyn; remarking on the novelist's naïveté in believing that mere elimination of the KGB and Glavlit would bring about freedom of publication, he invoked Lenin's dictum that a free press could exist only when citizens, all citizens and any citizens, could freely express their opinion. Kosterin's attack on and judgment of Sholokhov was as harsh as Chukovskaya's. He accused Sholokhov of having refused to confront the accusations Solzhenitsyn had made of the "path of suffering" trod by Soviet artists; and he rebuked him for failing openly and honestly to debate Solzhenitsyn's letter, Chukovskaya's, and his own. Such behavior was abysmal failure of literary integrity and simple intellectual cowardice: all Sholokhov could do these days was to circumvent issues and the realities of regime repression by taking refuge behind the walls of his estate, well guarded by police, and by mouthing the propaganda clichés of the regime.

With the prospect of the fiftieth anniversary of the Bolshevik Revolution in the offing, Party leaders were in a dilemma that winter of 1966. How could they point with pride to the past in such "jubilee" celebrations if twenty years of Stalin's tenure and ten of Khrushchev's had been denounced as periods of misrule riddled with crime and error? Where had the Party been and what had it been doing during that time? Part of the purpose of the Twenty-third Party Congress, consequently, was to defend the Party's monopoly of wisdom, to reassert the notion of Party infallibility. In doing so, the new Party leaders had to keep themselves from being portrayed either as Stalin's heirs or as his dupes. They had to stress their accomplishments in order to inspire their friends and allies around the world, and to reinforce the pride and purpose of their own citizens at home. To achieve these purposes, portions of Stalin's career had to be rehabilitated, and the Party leadership set about the task. The history of the Soviet Union, the largest part of which was the history of Stalin's reign, had therefore to be depicted as positive and basically constructive; such works as *Ivan Denisovich*, which portrayed the crimes and cruelties of the Stalinist era, had to be suppressed, not only to keep the knowledge from embittering the young, but to keep from reminding their elders and opening their wounds. The new line, already pioneered by Khrushchev, gave the Party credit for having industrialized the country, though not the blame for waste and duplication; for having collectivized the countryside, though not the responsibility for the violence and brutality of the methods employed; for having built up the armed forces so that the USSR could defeat Hitler, though not the onus of Stalin's purges of the officer corps or his ineptitude as a wartime leader. In short, enough of Stalin's reputation was rehabilitated to allow the Party to continue to assert its infallibility without appearing altogether ridiculous.

But haunting questions remained. If the Party is infallible, if it is the source of everything positive in Soviet society, why had the Party *not* spoken the truth about the leaders—Stalin, Malenkov, Molotov, Khrushchev—*while* they were still in office? Why hadn't the Party stepped in to rectify their errors before havoc was wrought, stopped the crimes and terror before millions had perished and "the revolution devoured its children"? The leadership chose to avoid those questions, for answering them would have led to opening to scrutiny the basic organic flaws in the Soviet system, the Communist Party and its leadership.

14 The Aftermath

> Heine considered that history must eventually become the history of minds rather than the history of brigands. . . . But today history is still made by brigands.
>
> *Valeriy Tarsis*

During the same week Sinyavsky and Daniel were tried, another dissident Soviet writer, Valeriy Tarsis, was abruptly given a visa for a lecture tour in England. Why the KGB had given him the visa precisely at that juncture was not disclosed,[1] but some thought it a diversionary measure, others a gesture to liberal intellectuals at home and in the Western Communist parties where the Sinyavsky-Daniel trial had raised the specter of Stalinism once more. Two other reasons were also forwarded: first, the Kremlin hoped Tarsis would not return to the Soviet Union, thus giving the authorities another opportunity to portray dissident writers as anti-Soviet traitors; second, the KGB hoped Tarsis would denounce Daniel and Sinyavsky, thus making it seem that the liberal writers did not completely support the condemned writers. When asked if he could account for the Soviet authorities' permitting his friend Tarsis to go abroad, Aleksandr Yesenin-Volpin could only reply that when he himself had expressed a desire to leave the Soviet Union, he had been thrown into an insane asylum. Volpin, labeled insane and three times confined to mental institutions, had just then returned from six weeks in a sanitarium to cure a nervous skin ailment. Traditional Russian and Soviet Communist use of mental institutions as means of political punishment and political isolation, as "ameliorated" versions of the labor camp, has raised serious questions about who and what are truly insane, as well as about the general political role of psychiatry in the USSR. Some individuals have remarked that anyone who expects even the minimal essentials of freedom—personal, political, or intellectual—under a totalitarian government has no hold on reality and *is* insane; therefore, he should be confined to a mental institution. Others note that the pressures generated by the Soviet state and security police are enough to drive even the most balanced individuals beyond the borders of "normalcy." Still others see the present Soviet regime's use of the term "insanity" as simply another label to be pinned on opponents in order to discredit them or what they stand for. All these interpretations Valeriy Tarsis was to take up in his *Ward* 7, an only slightly fictionalized account of his own incarceration in the infamous Kaschenko Psychiatric Hospital in Moscow.

To begin with, Tarsis seemed ready to fulfill the KGB expectation that he would denounce Sinyavsky and Daniel. In Moscow, on February 6, 1966, on the eve of his departure, he called them "cowards, hypocrites, liars." [2] On February 8, having arrived in London, he changed his mind, though he had with him the KGB's watchdog, the mysterious and imperturbable Victor Louis. (To reporters who interviewed Tarsis, Louis appeared to be handling the public relations and other details of Tarsis' trip, and Tarsis was reported to declare that he "could do nothing without Louis.") [3] Tarsis explained two days later that his unflattering remarks about Sinyavsky and Daniel were due to his hot temper and an alleged personal insult the imprisoned writers had offered him which, upon investigation, turned out to be a malicious (KGB?) fabrication. Tarsis said he *did* disapprove of Sinyavsky's and Daniel's use of pseudonyms on the works they had published in the West; but, he added, "Sinyavsky and Daniel struggle against the common enemy and I wish them all the best." [4]

Born in 1906, Tarsis was a writer of the older generation and had from his youth been a Communist. As a result of his father's death in the Stalin purges of the 1930s and of his own travels, he had evidently become disenchanted with the Soviet system. During World War II he had been a combat correspondent with the Red Army and a captain. Wounded twice at Stalingrad, he had for a long time been confined to a hospital in a cast. In the hospital he met the niece of General Alksnis, the former commander of the Soviet Air Force who had been executed in 1937; Tarsis later married her. The war also apparently turned Tarsis to religion.

Since 1961, Tarsis had striven to get a visa to leave the Soviet

Union for Italy, and had consistently been refused. In 1962 he sent the manuscripts of two books, *The Tale of the Bluebottle* and *The Red and the Black*, to England for publication, but his publishers, afraid of endangering his position at home, brought the works out under the pseudonym Ivan Valery, though Tarsis had neither asked them to nor made any effort to conceal his authorship or identity.

That same year, in August, he was arrested and committed to the Kaschenko Psychiatric Hospital for having written a letter to Khrushchev saying that the Soviet Union was an unbearable place to live. The candor cost him seven months in the mental hospital, but he made Kaschenko famous by his fictionalized memoir, *Ward* 7, published in London in 1965. Though the book appeared with his name, and though excerpts were reprinted in the *London Observer* which resulted in considerable publicity, Tarsis continued to live unmolested in his three-room Moscow flat. The Soviet press was already beginning to refer to him as a paranoid and megalomaniac who slandered the Soviet people in his writings, but Tarsis spoke out even more sharply against the government. "The authorities know very well that I detest Communism, that I hate the Soviet regime," he said. "I believe in God and I cannot live in a land where one cannot be an honest man. This is not a democratic country; this is fascism." [5] In another interview, Tarsis reported that a KGB colonel had warned him that if *The Tale of the Bluebottle* was published abroad, he would be shot, yet when the book was issued, nothing happened. [6] In Britain, Tarsis openly proclaimed that all the Soviet peoples were eagerly awaiting the downfall of the regime.

On February 21, 1966, in an almost unprecedented move, the Presidium stripped Tarsis of his Soviet citizenship, announcing that he was both a sick man and a traitor, though if he was mentally unbalanced, taking his Soviet citizenship from him while he was in London did not make much human or logical sense. [7]

Tarsis had been granted a three-month visa only, and shortly thereafter he asked for political asylum. He said he would request Greek citizenship because his father was of Greek origin, and hoped that he could live in Italy, especially in Sorrento. In late July, Tarsis was scheduled to appear at a PEN club congress in New York, and when this information was made public the Soviet Writers' Union denounced PEN and withdrew the Soviet delegation to the congress. [8]

Increasingly there was evidence of mounting dissent and correspondingly mounting repression. In January a secret organization of some two hundred chemistry students at Leningrad University was discovered to have been involved in the clandestine publication and distribution of a magazine, *Kolokol* ("The Bell"), named after Aleksandr Herzen's nineteenth-century anti-Czarist magazine. *Kolokol* denounced the neo-Stalinism in Soviet life and called for freedom of thought and expression.[9] The KGB broke up the group, suppressed the magazine, and brought the leaders to trial. The organizer of the periodical was said to have been sentenced to seven years' imprisonment, and eight of his associates were given terms of up to five years, although only two issues of the publication had been circulated.[10]

Only a few days after the close of the Twenty-third Congress, news reached London that two Ukrainian literary critics, Ivan Svetlichny and Ivan Dzyuba, had a few weeks earlier in March been arrested for "smuggling nationalist and anti-Soviet" verses and a young poet's "bitter diary" to the West.[11] The author of the diary was presumed to be Vasyl Symonenko, a poet who had died of natural causes in 1965 and who was said to be a passionate defender of Ukrainian national and cultural values. His verses, highly critical of the living conditions of Ukrainian peasants, had been published in the Ukrainian émigré magazine *Suchanost* in Munich,[12] and excerpts from his diary dealing with the political repression of Ukrainian writers had been published in the United States.[13]

The regime's intention to stop Ukrainian writers who violated the official Party line had been announced to the Ukrainian Party Congress by playwright Aleksandr Korneichuk, who warned young writers: "Come to your senses, because otherwise we shall stand you up before the entire nation and . . . take away your Soviet passport [i.e., send you to prison]."[14] Both Svetlichny and Dzyuba had for some time been identified with the young Ukrainian poets' resistance to the Soviet literary and political bureaucracy's attempt to impose conformity on them. The two were now tried secretly. Svetlichny was sentenced to a Siberian labor camp, but Dzyuba was released.

As a consequence of having been criticized at the Twenty-third Congress, the editors of both *Novy mir* and *Yunost* were required to perform their self-criticisms. How they did so is, in some degree, the measure of the different men, Tvardovsky and Polevoi. After Stalin's death Tvardovsky's poem "Horizon beyond Horizon," with its attack on literary regimentation, had been one of the germinal works of the first "thaw." In the "freeze" that followed, Tvardovsky was removed from the *Novy mir* editorial board, but some years later was able to regain his post. Now, because in addition to his other sins, he had printed Sinyavsky's and Daniel's works in the magazine, he was dropped from the Party Central Committee, of which he had until then been an alternate member. Yet Tvardovsky stood his ground. In tribute to the poetess Anna Akhmatova, who died on March 5, and who had been one of the victims of Stalinist policies in culture, especially during the Zhdanov period, Tvardovsky reminded his readers that her audience "could not be impeded by the extremely crude and unjust attacks against her in a certain well-known era." [15] In an editorial in that same issue of *Novy mir*, Tvardovsky continued to insist that only truthful writing is in the highest and best interests of Communism—literature that sees "reality as it is, in all its complexity, in its real contradictions and movements. When this reality is simplified or schematized, then art ceases to be art." [16] Tvardovsky's play *Tyorkin in the Other World*, based on the poem Tvardovsky had written and published three years earlier and recited at Gagra to Khrushchev and his guests, was removed from the stage while the Twenty-third Party Congress was in session, then restored to the Theater of Satire's boards after the Congress was ended. The play gives "strong support to those who resist hard-line ideologists." [17] Despite the Congress' criticism of *Novy mir* and Tvardovsky for writings that give a dark picture of Soviet life and a "distorted" view of recent Soviet history, *Tyorkin* continued to be performed as an outspoken mockery of ideological humbug and official cant. (Two other anti-Stalinist plays were taken off the boards on the eve of the Congress, Konstantin Simonov's *The Quick and the Dead* and Leonid Sorin's *Dion*. For two weeks they were replaced by more orthodox plays, but all reappeared after the Congress was over and the vast majority of delegates had left Moscow for the provinces.)

Yunost's reaction to the Party criticism was different in tone and content. In an unsigned and presumably collectively written editorial, the editors admitted that "some authors have not always asked enough of their heroes' morals. . . . The social life of youth has been inadequately reflected, particularly that of the Komsomol; the problems of developing the world-view of our youth have been neglected; we have published too few works on rural life and not paid enough attention to the national literatures." They promised to improve the magazine as the Party had directed, because the Party's criticism "mobilizes all of us for a profound and thorough examination of the complex problems of contemporary life, for an increase in our personal civic responsibility as writers. . . . It is precisely in this way that Soviet writers have always accepted, and still accept, Bolshevik criticism." [18] Among the members of the editorial board were such prominent liberals as Yevtushenko, Aksyonov, and Viktor Rozov. The self-criticism was doubly important because *Yunost* had in four years, from 1962 to 1966, quadrupled its circulation, from 550,000 to more than 2,000,000. Usually consisting of about a hundred pages, the journal sells at a price of forty kopecks. That the dogmatist *Oktyabr* had declined in readership during that time only made for more bad blood and envy between liberal and dogmatist factions.[19]

Tvardovsky, on the other hand, continued to publish stories which "exposed economic and social ills and blunders by past political and military leaders." [20] Among them were Valery Bykov's novel *The Dead Feel No Pain*, which portrays brutal Stalinist officers executing their own men on the battlefield during World War II rather than allow them to be captured; [21] A. Makharov's short story "At Home," in which a soldier on leave drinks, brawls, rapes, and in general behaves like a savage; and B. Mozhayev's "From the Life of Fedor Kuzkin," a story portraying kolkhoz poverty and bureaucracy in the early days of Khrushchev's reign. Since the Red Army and its leaders are sacred cows, stern rebuttals soon came from *Pravda* [22] and the Defense Ministry paper *Krasnaya zvezda* ("Red Star").[23] *Pravda* excoriated Bykov for false and humiliating depictions of military officers, and "Red Star" accused *Novy mir* of having lost its "moral base" and also called attention to the fact that *Novy mir*'s editors had not yet made the self-criticism called for by the Twenty-third Party Congress.

When Tvardovsky's *Tyorkin in the Other World* was restored to the stage after the Congress, it contained some changes. In the pre-Congress version, Tyorkin had held up a copy of his autobiography, saying, "Why ask? You know it is all there." [24] In the post-Congress version, Tyorkin shows the audience the earlier volume of Tvardovsky's Tyorkin poems, proclaiming that it was cleared by the authorities, and what is more, that its creator is a member of the Union of Soviet Writers! His inquisitors are not much impressed, however, and chant in reply:

> This doesn't mean too much.
> We use other measures.
> Just wait a bit and the author
> Himself will be under investigation.[25]

They then turn to the audience, holding up copies of the latest issue of *Novy mir* with its familiar blue cover.

When Tyorkin learns that the other world contains the very same institutions which plagued him in this world—political police and forced-labor camps, for example—he asks who is responsible for such things even beyond the grave, and is told:

> He who sent you and me
> To this place,
> He whose name you cried, soldier,
> As you fell on the field of battle.[26]

In short, Stalin.

Like the poem, the play concludes with the discovery that Tyorkin is not dead, only seriously wounded, and he is therefore dispatched back to this world. Tvardovsky is, thus, apparently suggesting that Tyorkin, that symbol of the ordinary Russian citizen, will in time win through to a "new life" in spite of Stalinist repressions.

The pleasure of having the play restored to the boards was to last Tvardovsky only a very short time, for in October it was once more removed from the stage.

In May, a young writer named Andrei Amalrik was sentenced to two and a half years of exile on a bleak collective farm in the Siberian village of Guryevka, about a hundred miles south of Tomsk, under the same law concerning "parasites" used against Josif

Brodsky. Amalrik, arrested in 1965 for being without regular employment, was in fact being tried for his nonconformist artistic intellectual tastes and opinions, and for entertaining foreign guests, among them a *Newsweek* correspondent and an American Embassy official. Though Amalrik was, in fact, busily employed as a freelance writer and assiduously caring for his paralyzed father, the court refused him the right to introduce evidence of those facts at the trial. Amalrik, a man with a certified heart condition, was sentenced to hard physical labor on a kolkhoz in the freezing Siberian climate, and was later to remark that what had happened to him was "nothing surprising or exceptional in my country. But that is just why it is interesting." Tough-minded, recalcitrant, and independent, Amalrik wrote that though he could not find any job he really wanted, it would probably have been prudent to find some sort of steady employment as the KGB had "suggested" he should, but, he said, "even prudence must have its limits. One must insist on one's rights to an independent existence. Why should I go and work as a handyman or a night watchman when I believe that my proper work is to write plays and poems, or to do research on history and art?" [27] Such assertions of private bent and personal fulfillment are not officially countenanced.

Amalrik also recalled how prisoners cursed Khrushchev for having issued the "parasite" ukase; they called the First Secretary a "bald pig" and sang a song that Amalrik was subsequently to hear sung by the peasants on the kolkhoz to which he was exiled:

> Once there were three bandits,
> Hitler, Stalin and Nikita.
> Hitler hanged us, Stalin beat us,
> Nikita made us starve.[28]

More evidence of the regime's neo-Stalinist intentions came in the late fall of 1966, when, quietly and without fanfare, the Presidium of the Supreme Soviet of the RSFSR added three new articles to the Soviet Criminal Code, two of which, Articles 190/1 and 190/3, made spreading "slanderous inventions about the Soviet state and social system, and disturbances of public order punishable offenses." Article 190/1, in particular, was important. It read: "The systematic dissemination by word of mouth of deliberately false statements derogatory to the Soviet state and social system, as also the preparation or dissemination of such statements in written, printed or any other form, is punishable by three years of detention, one year of corrective labor, or a fine of up to one hundred rubles." Published in the *Bulletin of the Supreme Soviet of the RSFSR*, the decrees were not mentioned anywhere else in the Soviet press, though the questions they raised were of immense social, political, and juridical import. What, for instance, was "systematic dissemination"? How did one distinguish what was deliberately false from what was unwitting, not to mention defining what was true and false? Who was to judge what was derogatory to the Soviet state, and how? Though the decrees were published virtually secretly, the news of their inclusion in the Criminal Code spread swiftly; shortly thereafter a group of some of the nation's most eminent intellectuals—including Igor Tamm, Andrei Sakharov, Dmitry Shostakovich, Veniamin Kaverin, Viktor Nekrasov, and Mikhail Romm—addressed a letter to the top echelons of the government protesting against the decrees because they opened the way to "subjective and arbitrary interpretation of any statement as deliberately false and derogatory to the Soviet state and social system." [29] Their letter was never given a public reply. The new decrees were a clear endeavor by the authorities to broaden the already catch-all Article 70 of the Criminal Code, also promulgated against "anti-Soviet agitation and propaganda," in order to deal with dissidents "legally" but more easily.[30]

Though the "Letter of the 63," planned by Ehrenburg and Chukovsky, had also failed to effect the release of Sinyavsky and Daniel, had even failed to lighten their sentences, the liberals still nurtured hopes that the impending fiftieth anniversary of the Revolution might include a general amnesty which would free the imprisoned writers. The liberals were soon to realize that the new articles of the Criminal Code, confirmed by the Supreme Soviet at the end of December 1966, were shortly to be employed in imprisoning more writers and liberals.

In the interim, on November 17, at a meeting of the Moscow section of the Writers' Union, there was an extended discussion of the first half of Aleksandr Solzhenitsyn's new novel, *Cancer Ward*. Some of the conservatives there, like Zoya Kedrina and N. Asanov, were reserved in their praise, but most of those present spoke of the book and the writer in glowing terms, comparing Solzhenitsyn's gifts to those of Leo Tolstoy, Chekhov, and Saltykov-Shchedrin. At the close of the meeting, Solzhenitsyn announced that he was very grateful for the criticisms and for the high opinion of his talents, which he would try to justify in completing *Cancer Ward*. The fact that his books were not published had prevented him from receiving that necessary professional criticism of his work which he had gotten there. He concluded by reporting that *Novy mir* had rejected the first half of *Cancer Ward*, and that he had just sent the manuscript off to two other literary magazines, *Zvezda* and *Prostor*.

The end of 1966 also saw the first punishments of *Novy mir*'s editors for their daring. Two members of the editorial board, A. Dementyev, deputy editor-in-chief, and B. G. Zaks, managing editor, were dropped from the masthead. At the turn of the year the magazine was under severe and consistent Party criticism which was to continue all through the winter and spring preceding the Writers' Congress. (In an interesting critique of *Novy mir*, Vittorio Strada, the Italian Communist specialist on Soviet literature and friend of Solzhenitsyn, though admiring the magazine's role in Soviet life, remarked:

From Dudintsev to Nekrasov, from Solzhenitsyn to Tendryakov, from Ehrenburg to Dombrovsky, from Tvardovsky to Zabolotsky, these and others are the names which have given the world the authentic sensation of a new and positive period in Soviet literary work. And it is on their pages, more than on those of the politicians, journalists, and sociologists, that history will find printed the living outline of Soviet man of these difficult years.

Despite his Communist affiliations, Strada was objective enough to point out that such permissiveness as the authorities did allow to *Novy mir* and such editorial daring as Tvardovsky ventured applied *only to fiction*. "Is it not strange," Strada asked, "for example, that while they have published the strong narrative work, *One Day in the Life of Ivan Denisovich* by Solzhenitsyn, *Novy mir*, exactly like the other organs of the Soviet press, has not published a single article of an historical character on the same theme, on a national tragedy . . . the deportation of so many and so many Soviet citizens?") [31] Despite the criticism of *Novy mir*, Tvardovsky's editorial plans for the year seemed liberal and independent.[32] In the first issue of 1967, he printed a long Pasternak essay, "People and Situations," [33] which originally appeared in 1957—the first Pasternak prose published in the Soviet Union in eight years. A vigorous condemnation of Stalinist literary practice and bureaucracy, it included a searing portrait of the novelist and long-time Secretary-General of the Writers' Union under Stalin, Aleksandr Fadeyev, who soon after Khrushchev's "secret speech" at the Twentieth Congress revealed Stalin's evil-doing, committed suicide.

Fadeyev's tragedy is revealing. Under Soviet rule, murders and suicides among writers have been a veritable plague, and there is a Russian saying which declares that "Russian literature began with two murders [those of Pushkin and Lermontov] and ended with two suicides [those of Yesenin and Mayakovsky]." Pasternak's condemnation of Fadeyev takes on greater significance and irony when it is recalled that Fadeyev interceded with Stalin to save Pasternak's life and was, presumably, a friend of Pasternak. Yury Krotkov tells how Fadeyev, when drunk, would unburden himself to Pasternak and make many indiscreet political remarks. The next morning Pasternak would telephone him to reassure him that he had said nothing and that what he had said was forgotten. Krotkov also reports that Fadeyev sent a letter to the Party Central Committee before he committed suicide, but the contents were never divulged. Popular speculation had it that the letter contained only a single sentence which Fadeyev wrote to the government organ of which he had for thirty-eight years been a member: "The bullet I fired was meant for Stalin's policies, for Zhdanov's aesthetics, for Lysenko's genetics." [34]

Ehrenburg devotes a chapter of his memoirs to Fadeyev, in which he attempts to explore and explain the dilemma of the man's suicide.[35] Ehrenburg notes that Fadeyev was an exceedingly complex man with a literary gift that was both inborn and trained, "but [with regard to Fadeyev] the word 'gifted' meant more than his native gifts; it also meant the ability to make hundreds of corrections on a page of manuscript, it meant inner anguish, a quality of spirit not always suited to the public activities in which he was so diligently and passionately engaged." But such political activity depleted his creative energies, for after thirty-five years as a writer there were only two completed novels, a few short stories, some hundreds of articles. "They won't let me write," Fadeyev complained. "It's always the Writers' Union, the struggle for peace, conferences, meetings, congresses." [36] Although some suggested that Fadeyev's alcoholism kept him from being productive, Ehrenburg shrewdly notes that William Faulkner also drank a good deal yet managed to write dozens of books.

Fadeyev published his most famous novel, *The Young Guard*, in 1945, but after an initially favorable reception, the rulers attacked it violently two years later for having ignored the role of the Party in the wartime events Fadeyev was portraying. Fadeyev dutifully spent the next four years rewriting the novel; when, in 1951, the second edition appeared, he had deleted all the panic, chaos, and confusion of the early wartime retreat before the Nazi panzers, and had added new sections which showed how the Party had organized partisan resistance to the Germans. Of these changes, Ehrenburg writes:

The fate of *The Young Guard* is intimately connected with what we call the "cult of personality." The novel was written, published. It had great success and was awarded a Stalin Prize. One of Aleksandr Aleksandrovich's [Fadeyev's] friends, S. A. Gerasimov, made it into a moving picture. And that's when the storm erupted. Stalin had not read the book, but the moving picture made his blood boil. Young people were portrayed left to their doom in a town captured by the Nazis. Where was the Young Communist League? Where was the Party's leadership? Stalin was told that the director had stuck to the text of the novel. Harsh criticism of *The Young Guard* appeared in the press, followed by Fadeyev's letter to *Pravda* accepting the censure as just and promising that the novel would be rewritten. When I met him, Aleksandr Aleksandrovich said that he was not revising the text but adding new chapters— about the old Bolsheviks, about the role of the Party leadership. After a brief pause, he added, "Of course, even if I should succeed, the novel will no longer be the same. Perhaps I'm carried away too easily by enthusiasm for partisan enterprise. These are hard times and *Stalin knows better than we do.*"

Fadeyev's profound faith in Stalin's wisdom and foresight was at war with his own conviction of the innocence of many of those who had been destroyed in the Stalinist terror and purges—Vsevolod

Meyerhold, Iona Yakir, Isaak Babel, Mikhail Zoshchenko—but his faith was "mixed with fear. Once he [Fadeyev] said only half-jokingly, 'I am afraid of two people—my mother and Stalin. I fear [them]—and I love [them].' " [37]

At the Twentieth Party Congress, Sholokhov had criticized Fadeyev severely for being a Stalinist cultural bureaucrat and had then gone on to criticize everyone else for having taken fifteen of the best and most creative years of Fadeyev's life as a writer. Sholokhov maintained that Fadeyev should have quit being Secretary-General of the Writers' Union and returned to his creative work. [38] Three months later, after Fadeyev had killed himself, many blamed Sholokhov for having—albeit unwittingly—contributed the straw that broke the camel's back. But there is evidence that a strong streak of self-destructiveness was deeply imbedded in Fadeyev's character. A. Gaev has recounted a story of Fadeyev's youth which seems a dramatic foreshadowing of his eventual suicide:

One night in 1918, while still a schoolboy, Fadeyev, then living with his parents in the Far East, fired a Nagant revolver at a portrait of the Tsar and then at his own reflection in a mirror. It was the period of the fighting between the White Army and Red Partisan detachments: that same night, Fadeyev left his parents' house and joined a Partisan detachment in which he received the nickname of Bulyga. [39]

In Soviet literary circles, Fadeyev was known as "the marshal," yet Krotkov asks if, despite being a member of the Central Committee, a deputy to the Supreme Soviet, the winner of several Stalin Prizes, Fadeyev really believed in Stalin or simply hid behind the dictator's skirts. His conclusion is that "the Stalinist regime was *his* [Fadeyev's] regime," that Fadeyev was not simply another run-of-the-mill time-server but a man who was Stalin's personal counselor out of conviction. Yet he also recounts the story of how Fadeyev, drunk, once telephoned Pasternak from the Aragvi restaurant to say to him, "Borinka, you're the only one among us, the only one, who tells no lies." [40]

Fadeyev himself had evidently signed the orders for the arrest of many of his friends and colleagues among the writers, "in fact, for the arrest of 20 writers in Peredelkino alone." For the last three months of his life, Fadeyev seemed quite sober and went to see friends and places as if bidding them farewell; Krotkov believes that the final precipitating factor in Fadeyev's suicide was the return of a writer whose initial he gives as M., who had been "arrested and deported on Fadeyev's orders [and who] returned to Moscow after Stalin's death. He publicly denounced Fadeyev as a scoundrel and hanged himself." [41]

Fadeyev's story is instructive, for it shows what compliance can do to a man of genuine creative talent.

Early in the new year, *Yunost* printed an interview with the distinguished physicist Kapitsa in which he called for broadening and intensifying public debate so that "young people . . . learn skillful polemics from their grandfathers who made the revolution. . . . [They] must develop frank exchanges of opinion to the full and not be afraid of conflict." [42] Without honest controversy and the clash of different opinions, Kapitsa insisted, neither science nor art could fruitfully develop.

In January 1967, *Pravda* took both liberal and conservative factions among the writers to task, indicting both *Novy mir* and *Oktyabr* for having fallen behind the times. *Novy mir* was upbraided for being preoccupied with the dark side of Soviet life, for printing novels, poems, and memoirs which exposed the evils and blunders of political and military leaders, for speaking jeeringly and with disdain of the works printed in other publications: "Unfortunately, what attracts *Novy mir*'s attention in our heterogeneous reality are not instances and phenomena showing that our Party and people emerged from all trials still stronger and more hardened, with unflagging revolutionary optimism, but in most cases only phenomena of one sort, connected with the seamy sides, with various kinds of abnormality, with the afflictions of tempestuous growth." [43] *Novy mir*, *Pravda* concluded, had failed to show the *new* Soviet man in the fiftieth year of Soviet life.

Pravda also criticized *Oktyabr* for being out of step with the times and failing to understand the liberalization of events, for underestimating "the restoration of Leninist norms" and portraying them in a distorted fashion. The Party paper told both magazines that the public was as distressed by *Oktyabr*'s characteristic oversimplification of complex problems as by *Novy mir*'s ideological instability, and censured the *Oktyabr* editors for imperious judgment and unjustified vehemence: "Thus, without excessive modesty, the editors of *Oktyabr* continually lecture all and sundry, evidently claiming that the magazine is nearly the only champion of the principles of socialist realism and is some kind of legislator on those questions. But the works it publishes are colorless and superficial." *Pravda* called for "works that skillfully recreate the heroic past, today's creative activity and the spiritual world of our contemporary—the toiler and the fighter—[which] can educate people correctly in the Marxist-Leninist spirit." Only more party-mindedness and a socialist realism that "is the literature of social certitude" can accomplish such a mission.[44]

In March, the Secretariat of the Writers' Union discussed *Novy mir*'s work still another time and "unanimously pointed out substantial ideological and artistic errors, omissions and shortcomings. . . . Many of the works [published] . . . are lacking in the qualities of the lofty art of socialist realism and do not provide a really truthful, optimistic representation of the many-faceted life and heroic creative labor of the Soviet people. A number of works give a one-sided interpretation of our reality and impoverish the image of Soviet man." The Secretariat also remarked that the magazine's editors "reacted poorly to the public's criticisms of shortcomings in the work of the magazine." [45]

In April, the Secretariat of the RSFSR Writers' Union met to consider *Oktyabr*'s work and found that "hastily written and poor works" appeared in the magazine which revealed "oversimplified treatment of certain topical questions of aesthetics and quickness of temper in appraising individual works of art." [46]

These various considerations were the calculated preparation for the Fourth Congress of Soviet Writers scheduled for spring, 1967, an endeavor to mark out a Party "middle course" between *Novy mir* and *Oktyabr;* but the battering had begun to tell on Tvardovsky, and when Alexander Werth was in Moscow in June of that year, he heard that "there wasn't much fight left in him [Tvardovsky]; he was tired and exhausted. Another blow to him, shortly before, had been Glavlit's refusal to pass for publication . . . Konstantin Simonov's 1941 *War Diaries;* Glavlit proposed an expurgated version, but this Simonov himself rejected." [47]

15 The Alliluyeva Case

Now you can be tried for a metaphor, sent to a camp for figures of speech!

Svetlana Alliluyeva

In January 1967, a group of young dissident poets and writers—Aleksandr Ginzburg, Yury Galanskov, Aleksey Dobrovolsky, Vera Lashkova, and Peter Radzievsky—were arrested for compiling a "White Book" on the Sinyavsky-Daniel proceedings, including the trial transcript and Soviet and foreign reactions to the trial. Ginzburg sent copies of the typewritten volume to Premier Kosygin, to the KGB, and to several members of the Supreme Soviet. As a result four of the dissidents were arrested between January 17 and 19. A few days later, on January 22, at a demonstration on Pushkin Square demanding freedom for those already in custody, Ginzburg too was arrested. These protests were not simply literary but overtly political, defending the public right of protest as well as denouncing government censorship. Amalrik remarks, "This movement was directed not against the political regime as such but only against the culture, which the regime regarded as a component part of itself."[1] That somewhat underestimates the political goals of the cultural dissidents and the enormous threat the regime sees in any alternative to allegiance to the Party and its viewpoint. Nonetheless, his skepticism is proper *cum grano salis* for those observers who see in every act of nonconformism or dissidence the growth of a significant and effective political opposition.

The regime reacted by charging Ginzburg's group with disturbing the peace; with publishing an underground journal, *Phoenix;*[2] with belonging to a literary group called Smog;[3] and with being in contact with the NTS, "the Narodno-Trudovoi Soyuz, an anti-

Soviet organization with headquarters in West Germany and close links to the CIA." [4] All were to be tried under the two new articles of the Criminal Code, 190/1 and 190/3. The NTS, or National Labor Federation, is an organization of Russian émigrés based in Frankfort, West Germany, which publishes the magazine *Grani* and owns the publishing house Possev. It was to be one of the organizations to which the KGB would endeavor to link those writers and dissidents it wished either to compromise or to prosecute. An article on the organization's activities was published by Viv Broughton, which alleged that the funds for NTS were supplied by British intelligence and the CIA and that its purpose was to overthrow the Soviet system and replace it with a parliamentary democracy.[5]

Three important issues were at stake, all of them political: Soviet censorship; the right of peaceful assembly and protest; and the introduction of the new clauses into the Soviet Criminal Code. Though relatively innocuous and only mildly nonconformist, Smog and *Phoenix* were treated by the authorities as meaningful political threats. The Smogisti had recited poetry in the Moscow squares and demonstrations near the Writers' Club, brandishing such slogans as "Socialist Realism Must Lose Its Virginity." This group also "regarded Pasternak, Mandelshtam, and Tsvetayeva as their teachers and took up the cause of artistic freedom—freedom of form as well as of content—" as one of their major concerns.[6]

Further demonstrations protesting these arbitrary arrests were met by the regime with further arrests. The next month, February 1967, Viktor Khaustov and Ilya Gabay were tried and charged under Article 190/3, and Vladimir Bukovsky, Vadim Delaunay, and Yevgeny Kushev were also arrested in February, though not brought to trial until September. The Ginzburg-Galanskov trial was delayed a whole year while the group was kept in custody, although such delays are specifically forbidden by Article 97 of the Soviet Criminal Code. During the February 16 trial of Khaustov and Gabay in Moscow Criminal Court, the prosecution attempted to prove that Khaustov was insane, alleging that he had been diagnosed a schizophrenic in 1964 and that his mother had disclosed that several of his relatives also suffered from mental disorders. Khaustov maintained throughout that he was quite sane, but he was judged to be guilty and sentenced to three years of hard labor in a camp with a "severe" regimen. Although the trial had a KGB-selected audience and Gabay's wife complained she was excluded from the court, her complaint was dismissed as groundless. Moscow University students began to collect signatures to protest the arrest of the demonstrators, but the student who had the text of the protest letter was arrested by the KGB and the letter taken from him. In June Gabay was released, and in August his case dismissed for lack of evidence; though he had taken no part in the demonstration nor resisted arrest, he had been kept in prison for four months.

As early as 1964, the All-Russian Social-Christian Union for the Liberation of the People had been founded in Leningrad, its program a curious mixture of theocracy, democracy, and socialism. The group went about recruiting members in the time-honored conspiratorial fashion of nineteenth-century Russian revolutionary parties, by keeping members in groups of three, so that if one were caught, he could not easily betray more than a few members. Early on, the KGB infiltrated the organization, permitting it to develop and proliferate for almost two years before beginning to arrest members in February and March 1967. Sixty members were arrested, not only from Leningrad, but from as far afield as Tomsk, Irkutsk, and Petrozavodsk. Among them were engineers, scientists, technicians, literary men, and artists. In November 1967, four leaders of the Union were tried in Leningrad for treason, for anti-Soviet agitation, and for participating in anti-Soviet organizations; Vladimir Ogurtsov, a Japanese-Russian translator, Mikhail Sado, an orientalist, Yevgeny Vagin, a literary critic, and a jurist named Averochkina were sentenced to fifteen, thirteen, ten, and eight years of imprisonment respectively. All the men were relatively young, in their twenties and thirties, members of the new generation, as were the seventeen other members of the organization subsequently tried in March and April 1968, who were also given harsh sentences.[7] What they had done that most outraged the regime, apparently, was to distribute such forbidden literature as Djilas' *The New Class*, Tibor Meray's *Thirteen Days That Shook the Kremlin* (about the Hungarian Revolution of 1956), Evgenia Ginzburg's *Journey into the Whirlwind* (a revealing autobiography by the novelist Aksyonov's mother, who had spent eighteen years in Stalin's camps), and such traditional Russian writings as works by Nikolai Berdyaev and Vladimir Solovyev. A letter from fifty prominent French intellectuals addressed to Kosygin, protesting the arrest and trial of "28 university figures in Leningrad," and signed by such prominent men as François Mauriac, Jean Rostand, and André François-Poncet, was dispatched in December 1967, but elicited no response.[8]

Winter brought the Kremlin an even ruder awakening; Svetlana Alliluyeva, the daughter of Stalin, defected to the West. Her husband, Brijesh Singh, an Indian Communist who worked as a translator in Moscow, died on October 31, 1966, and on December 20, Mrs. Alliluyeva was issued a forty-five-day visa to accompany his ashes to New Delhi and to visit his relatives there. Secretly, she approached Indian authorities for political asylum and was refused. Then, on March 6, 1967, after having retrieved her passport from the Soviet Embassy in New Delhi as if planning to return to the USSR, she went to the American Embassy for political asylum. With her she brought the manuscript of an autobiography written three years earlier, in 1963, which was to become a literary and political *cause célèbre*.[9] Despite Soviet protestations to the Indian government, Mrs. Alliluyeva was flown out of the country, temporarily quartered in Switzerland, then brought to the United States. In New York, at a press conference, she placed another burning brand on the fire of the "heirs of Stalin" problem by saying, "Many other people who are still in our Central Committee and Politburo should be responsible for the same things for which he [Stalin] was accused." [10]

Two liberal Soviet writers, Viktor Rozov and Daniil Granin, were at that time on a trip in the United States; when they were interviewed about Alliluyeva, both condemned her. Rozov saw "a certain element of treason" in her defection, and Granin stated, "For us writers she is something of a mystery. We have no knowledge of anything she tried to publish. Certainly at the age of 42 she has had some time to show evidence of literary talent." About her forthcoming recollections of her father, Granin remarked, "It seems to me she could have done that in the Soviet Union." [11] Official Soviet reaction was far fiercer and not long in coming. In June the entire Soviet propaganda machine—all the official and unofficial means at the Soviet government's disposal—was brought to bear to discredit and discomfit Svetlana Alliluyeva, damning her as a traitor, a psychotic, a woman of loose morals, a Judas who had become a turncoat out of greed for American money. *Za rubeshom* set the tone:

American propaganda and the Central Intelligence Agency, in attempting to defame the Soviet system and the achievements of the Soviet state, have raised a propaganda ballyhoo over S. Alliluyeva, the defector who abandoned her country and her children. Playing upon greed (she is promised millions of dollars) and moral instability in Alliluyeva, who is prepared to slander even her own father (J. V. Stalin), certain U.S. circles are using her as a tool for an anti-Soviet campaign.

In an endeavor to discredit both the book and her authorship, the paper said Alliluyeva's memoirs had actually been written by the CIA's Soviet-affairs specialists during the interval Mrs. Alliluyeva had stayed in Switzerland; [12] and the Soviet propagandists maintained that publication of the book was part of an American plot to spoil the fiftieth-anniversary celebrations of the Bolshevik Revolution scheduled that fall.

American officials reported Soviet efforts to delay the publication of the Alliluyeva memoirs until after the anniversary of the Revolution. Arthur Schlesinger, Jr., visiting Moscow that summer, was asked by Yury Zhukov, a leading Soviet journalist and government spokesman, to carry a plea for postponement back to Washington, but though Schlesinger did so, the memoirs were not delayed.[13] (Though Mrs. Alliluyeva's political comments seemed naïve and even fitted into the Kremlin policy of blaming the terror and the crimes not only on Stalin but also on such of his subordinates as the now dead Beria, they made such an intense and vivid claim for the right to a personal and private life, and demonstrated such unconscionable government interference in that life, that the Soviet leadership could scarcely tolerate their publication in the USSR or be unperturbed about their publication elsewhere. Mrs. Alliluyeva's second book, *Only One Year*, is far more sophisticated politically, but politics is not her metier, nor does she claim that it is.)

Soviet embarrassment at her defection was evident from the very violence of the attack on her, which attributed the whole affair to a plot deliberately hatched by the U.S. State Department as early as

1966 to spoil the fiftieth anniversary festivities. "Kerensky has been taken out of mothballs," *Pravda* fulminated; "the 'complete collected works' of the psychologically deranged renegade Tarsis are being prepared for publication; and Soviet citizen S. Alliluyeva . . . is being used for the same ignominious purpose." [14] The onslaught of the Soviet press and of left-wing and Communist publications elsewhere in the world, and that curious word-of-mouth character assassination the Soviet propaganda machine seems able to muster so swiftly all combined to portray Stalin's daughter as a miserable captive of capitalist intrigue, surrounded by "gorillas," and overwhelmed by dollars.[15] At a press conference at the United Nations in New York in June, Premier Kosygin himself attacked her, saying, "Alliluyeva is a morally unstable person and she's a sick person, and we can only pity those who wish to use her for any political aim of discrediting the Soviet motherland." That theme was shortly echoed by Mrs. Alliluyeva's son, still in Moscow, who subsequently (he probably had no other choice) cut himself off from her with a public renunciation.[16]

Soviet hostility was exacerbated by the publication in June of an emotional essay Mrs. Alliluyeva had written in Switzerland in March, an essay dedicated to Boris Pasternak and dealing with *Doctor Zhivago,* a copy of which she had been given in Italy on her way from India and had read for the first time. She found the novel a "revelation about my own life and about the life of the Russia I knew." Sharing some of the same kind of love of Russia, of nature, and of a fatalistic Christianity, Mrs. Alliluyeva identified many events and characters in the Pasternak novel with events and people in her own life. "My beloved, long-suffering, baffled Russia, where I have left my children and my friends to live our unbearable Soviet life, a life so unlike anything else that it can never be imagined by Russians abroad, whether friendly or hostile to it, my beloved children, the indelible memory of my husband and the pain . . . of his death." Like Pasternak, she saw Russia everywhere crucified, the regime everywhere violating peace and love and truth, and had a vision of Andrey Sinyavsky, a former colleague at the Gorki Institute of Literature:

Why do I see you, Andrusha, my poor suffering friend, standing barefoot with buckets of cold water in your hands, your hair unkempt, and your clothes in rags? . . . I have never seen you with buckets in your hands, but perhaps you have to carry water, in the place where you are now, and that is how I picture you in my mind's eye. . . . You never did have much to say for yourself, Andrusha, and you were not the most handsome man in the world, but you had the stubborn courage to be true to yourself and honest before your conscience! Because wasn't that why you wrote your stories and novels: to speak out, although in secret from others, what you thought, and to be honest with yourself, and with God?

Remembering Sinyavsky brings Alliluyeva to consider how the fate of Russian writers is worse under the Soviets than it was even under the Czars.

O martyrs of Russian literature! Nothing has changed since the days of Radishchev and the Decembrists. . . . As before, it is given to gendarmes and policemen to be the first critics of a writer's work. Except that in Russia under the Czars neither Gogol nor Shchedrin was ever brought to trial for the sharpness of his satirical fantasies, and they were not punished for laughing at the absurdities of Russian life. But now you can be tried for a metaphor, sent to a camp for figures of speech! [17]

In a touching recollection of her love for Brijesh Singh, she echoes the plaint of many Soviet writers and ordinary citizens about the continuing intrusions of the government and Party into personal and private life:

. . . What did we care about politics, systems of government, ideologies, parties, and organizations of one sort or another!

How they immediately rose up in arms against us, the Party hypocrites and Pharisees! What deadly danger they saw to themselves in a human attachment and love that took no account of their usual rules! What could they know about us, how could they understand us, these miserable compilers of dossiers and denunciations? All they could see was that you were a foreigner, and it horrified them. [18]

Alliluyeva's defection also had practical consequences: in May, the head of the Soviet secret police, Vladimir Semichastny, was discharged and replaced by Yury Andropov; [19] and during the summer, very likely as a consequence of that change, a carefully thought-out scheme to frustrate the effects of the forthcoming publication of Alliluyeva's book was revealed. It involved the man who had played a role in Tarsis' defection, the man who was subsequently to play a role of considerable ambiguity in Solzhenitsyn's career, a man who is one of the more dubious characters in Soviet public life.

On the surface the Moscow correspondent of the *London Evening News*, Victor Louis, is a Soviet citizen who is frequently the source of news leaks to Western correspondents in Moscow. He was the first to report Khrushchev's ouster; he had been Tarsis's "watchdog" in Britain; and he was the man instrumental in filming the NBC telecast "Khrushchev in Exile." No ordinary journalist, Louis had connections with, or was in the employ of, someone quite powerful in the KGB and the Soviet government. Louis now suddenly appeared in Western Europe offering for sale articles he had ostensibly written himself based on the Svetlana memoirs and also offering to arrange publication of pirated editions of the book from two copies of the manuscript obtained from friends in Moscow and Leningrad with whom Mrs. Alliluyeva had left them. Louis also had more than two hundred pictures of Stalin, his family, and entourage—a number obviously chosen because they showed Svetlana in unflattering poses or with former police chief Lavrenti Beria. The pictures, too, were for sale. Louis also brought "specified pornographic material and other material defamatory of" Mrs. Alliluyeva.[20] Stalin's daughter was later to write bitterly (and quite justifiably):

During the next month I learned from the press many new things about myself. It transpired that all my life I had been under the care of psychiatrists; that I was unusually oversexed; that I wore the diamonds of the Romanovs, ate from their gold plates, and lived in the Kremlin in a former Romanov palace. . . . That my father consulted me on every move, I ran his house, and without me not a single decision had been taken.

All this, Alliluyeva pointed out, revealed the Kremlin intention to buttress through Louis the chief points of their slander campaign against her, to make her seem "a crazy nymphomaniac and her father's closest assistant." [21]

Soviet machinations seemed to be directed toward capturing the copyright of the book by having a first English-language edition published and copyrighted through the Flegon Press in London. Although its Russian-born owner, Alex Flegon, refused to disclose how he had obtained the manuscript, it is probable that Victor Louis was his source. Further evidence indicated that Louis had tried to sell a Soviet-translated English version to other potential English publishers before Flegon entered the picture, and Louis's paper, the *London Evening News*, publicly stated that it had rejected such a manuscript.[22] Had Louis been able to bring the Flegon edition out first, the Soviets would have been able to dispose of the publication rights and income. The American edition of the memoirs was due on October 16, but the British publisher, Hutchinson, was forced by the Flegon maneuver to publish an advance edition of the book on August 4 to protect its copyright. Aside from pre-empting the legal ownership of the copyright, the Soviets may have been trying to make the book's contents public prematurely in order to take the sting out of its revelations when it did appear, or trying to force publication early and as far from the celebrations of the fiftieth anniversary of the Revolution as they could. Some Soviet officials in Moscow let it be known that their purpose was to "keep the CIA honest," that is, keep the American intelligence agency from doctoring Mrs. Alliluyeva's manuscript.[23] There were probably subsidiary motives as well: to deny some of the income to Mrs. Alliluyeva, to complicate her new life, to sow confusion in the West about the authenticity of the manuscript, and so on. In accomplishing some of these purposes, the Soviets, aided and abetted by Mr. Louis, were successful; but the Hutchinson edition did succeed in heading off the threat to the copyright.

16 *Solzhenitsyn and Glavlit*

> Even the simple act of giving a manuscript away for "reading and copying" has now become a criminal act (ancient Russian scribes were permitted to do this five centuries ago).
>
> *Aleksandr Solzhenitsyn*

Against this background of demonstrations, arrests, and trials, Solzhenitsyn chose to speak out at the Fourth Congress of Soviet Writers, several times postponed but at last convened on May 22, 1967. He had originally planned to present his views in a speech to the Congress, but the authorities had no "intention of giving the floor to anyone with such controversial ideas." [1] When the novelist was refused the right to speak, he went from his home in Ryazan to Kornei Chukovsky's dacha in the writers' colony of Peredelkino, "a quiet village of birches, pines and old-fashioned villas on the outskirts of busy Moscow," and there, "about 200 yards from Pasternak's, just beyond Pogodin Street," he wrote a long, carefully but passionately reasoned letter challenging the role of the official censorship department (Glavlit) and the Writers' Union in Soviet literary life.[2] The letter was addressed to the Presidium of the Writers' Union, to the delegates to the Congress, and to all writers and editors; it called for abolishing the censorship of all fictional works and for reshaping the Writers' Union into a defender and promoter of the writers' rights instead of accepting the Union as a repressive arm of the government. Solzhenitsyn had prepared 250 typewritten copies of the letter and distributed them to various literary and political leaders. Copies swiftly made their way out of the Soviet Union and were printed a few days later both in *Le Monde* and the *New York Times*. Solzhenitsyn called on the Congress to discuss openly and in detail

the no longer tolerable oppression, in the form of censorship, that our literature has endured for decades, and that the Union of Writers can no longer accept.

Under the obfuscating label of Glavlit, this censorship—which is not provided for in the Constitution and is therefore illegal, and which is nowhere publicly labeled as such—imposes a yoke on our literature and gives people unversed in literature arbitrary control over writers. A survival of the Middle Ages, this censorship has managed, Methuselah-like, to drag out its existence almost to the twenty-first century. . . .

Our writers are not supposed to have the right, are not endowed with the right, to express their considered judgments about the moral life of man and society, or to explain in their own way the social problems and historical experience that have been so deeply felt in our country.[3]

The essence of the issue, the novelist pointed out, is that "literature cannot develop in between the categories of 'permitted' and 'not permitted,' 'about this you may write' and 'about this you may not.'" Such censorship had reduced Russian letters from the status of the world's leading literature in the nineteenth and early twentieth centuries to its present mediocrity. He lamented, "To the entire world the literary life of our country now appears immeasurably more colorless, trivial, and inferior than it actually is or than it would have been if it were not confined and hemmed in." Not only had outstanding works by young writers been rejected for publication because they could not "pass" the censorship, but many writers had themselves "bowed to the pressures of the censorship and made concessions in the structure and concept of their books—changing chapters, pages, paragraphs, or sentences, giving them innocuous titles—just for the sake of seeing them finally in print even if it meant distorting them irremediably." Consequently, "the best of our literature . . . is published in mutilated form."[4]

Turning to the Writers' Union, Solzhenitsyn excoriated it for failing to protect the rights, freedoms, and very lives of Russian writers. When individual writers were persecuted or their works suppressed, the Union provided them with neither forum nor periodical through which to reply to their attackers; in fact, the Union "through its leadership was always first among the persecutors." He then offered specific cases of Bulgakov, Akhmatova, Marina Tsvetayeva, Pasternak, Zoschenko, Platonov, Aleksandr Grin, and Vasily Grossman as evidence, adding, "The leadership of the Union cravenly abandoned to their distress those for whom persecution ended in exile, labor camps, and death (Pavel Vasilev, Mandelshtam,

Artem Vesely, Pilnyak, Babel, Tabidze, Zabolotsky, and others)." [5]

Solzhenitsyn recounted the persecutions which he had himself endured, accusing the secret police of having taken the manuscript of his novel *The First Circle* two years before, thus preventing him from submitting it for publication. The authorities had then issued it in "an unnatural 'restricted' edition for reading by an unidentified select circle. My novel has thus become available to literary officials but is being concealed from most writers." The security police had also taken some of his literary papers which were fifteen to twenty years old, works he had not intended for publication; "tendentious excerpts from these papers" were covertly published by the police for those same restricted bureaucratic circles. For three years, since 1964, a campaign of slander had been carried on against him, accusing him of having been imprisoned as a criminal, of having surrendered to the Germans during the war; both accusations were offered as false explanations of the eleven years he had spent in camps and in exile. The slander was being deliberately fostered and spread by officials under secret instructions, and though Solzhenitsyn had tried to stop the campaign by appealing to the board of the Writers' Union and to the press, the board had done nothing, nor had a single newspaper printed his rebuttals to the slanders. During 1966 and 1967 the slander campaign had grown more vicious and intense, making ugly use of distorted materials from his confiscated papers. Simultaneously, none of his writing was permitted to be published, and he had been kept from the usual public or radio readings of his work.[6]

Solzhenitsyn formulated two sweeping proposals: first, that the Writers' Union Congress adopt a resolution demanding and insuring "abolition of all censorship, open or hidden, of all fictional writing . . . which would release publishing houses from the obligation to obtain authorization for the publication of every printed page"; second, that guarantees for the defense of Writers' Union members "subjected to slander and unjust persecution be clearly formulated in . . . the Union statutes so that past violations of legality will not be repeated." [7]

After copies of the letter were distributed, about a quarter of the delegates to the Congress asked that it be read publicly and discussed, but the Union officials and the remainder of the delegates were violently opposed, so the proposals were ignored, and the Congress took no action. The Soviet authorities had always used and intended to continue to use the Writers' Union to control writers, as it used Glavlit to control their publications, and they were not about to give up or modify their use. The Writers' Union controls writers' lives in many practical ways. It sees that their works are published and that they are paid; it arranges for special housing, for travel, for many necessities and privileges. Through the manipulation of these concrete advantages, or through withholding them, the regime has a powerful means of controlling and coercing writers. The Union itself is full of literary hacks and timeserving bureaucrats—so much so that even Sholokhov, the "Grand Literary Inquisitor," as Werth called him, thinks it is an anomaly and its "five thousand or six thousand members, all bearing the proud title of 'Soviet author' " ridiculous. Sholokhov's jest about the 2000-percent increase reported in the Tula section of the Writers' Union is most telling: "Superb progress," he remarked sarcastically; "today there are in Tula twenty-three writers; in 1910 there was only one! He was called Lev Tolstoy." [8]

Because Solzhenitsyn's letter was not made a part of the agenda, the formal work of the Congress was on the surface serene. Only the prickly Sholokhov struck a few harsh notes, saying, "The calm business-like atmosphere of the Congress pleases me, but at the same time I have misgivings about our literary leadership's unconcealed desire to steer the Congress through without touching any sharp corner." Sholokhov touched a particularly sharp corner himself, the conflict between the generations of old and young writers. He blamed the young writers for the clash, but also pointed out that the average age at Soviet writers' congresses was rising. At the First Congress, 71 percent of the writers were under forty years of age; at the Second, 20.6 percent; at the Third, 13.9 percent; and now at the Fourth Congress only 12.2 percent were under forty, while the average age of the delegates was sixty. [9] Sholokhov did not draw the obvious conclusions from his own figures that the younger generation of writers was, at the very least, alienated from the Union and its personnel and methods, but he did call for electing more young writers to the Union's executive bodies.

Sholokhov also took the occasion to attack his long-standing enemy, Ilya Ehrenburg, for being absent from the Congress, for "warming his old bones in the Mediterranean sun" instead; by leaving for Italy on the eve of the Congress, Sholokhov maintained, Ehrenburg had expressed his contempt for the "writers' collective" and had offended them. The redoubtable Ehrenburg later commented that Sholokhov had "made an ass of himself; he suggested that I had deliberately gone abroad so as not to be present at the Writers' Congress in May, that I preferred to go to the Stendhal Congress in Italy, 'warming my old bones in the Mediterranean sun,' and that sort of thing. But in fact I had gone to the Stendhal Congress by arrangement with the Writers' Union." He laughed. "The trouble is that we've got only one Party, so everybody gets in, even a fascist like Sholokhov." [10] Though the reason Ehrenburg gave for not having attended the Congress is ambiguous, the remarks about Sholokhov are not; but what Ehrenburg intended by that "we've got only one Party" is deliberately equivocal and open to all sorts of interpretations.

At the end of August, Ehrenburg was dead, and the liberals had lost one of their most skillful and effective leaders. Though he was eulogized in the official press,[11] none of the major political personages of the government attended his funeral, and the burial ceremonies were perfunctory. The Western press's reaction to Ehrenburg was mixed. In an endeavor to clear Ehrenburg of some ugly sins of omission and commission during the Stalinist era, Alexander Werth wrote: "After Stalin's death, he [Ehrenburg] became the greatest and most liberal influence in Russia, even at a time when nobody else yet dared to speak up against Zhdanov or Stalin. . . . He had the courage to defend Pasternak in 1958 and to protest violently against the Sinyavsky-Daniel trial." Werth lamented the absence of important government officials at Ehrenburg's obsequies, quoting admiringly the comment of the Agence France Presse's former Moscow correspondent, Jean Champenois: "Even Stalin once said: 'Ehrenburg, with his propaganda, is worth twenty or thirty divisions to us.' " [12]

With Ehrenburg gone, what the other liberals would have to contend with was summarized in an article, "Always with the Party," by Aleksandr Chakovsky late that year, in which Chakovsky accused "bourgeois ideologists" of trying to dilute the Party nature of Soviet literature because they wished to create a Trojan horse of literary opposition in the country; consequently, "our foreign adversaries aim their heaviest fire at the heart of Soviet literature—its Party adherence." Chakovsky warned that the Party had no intention of relinquishing its tutelage of writers, or of surrendering its rights to define the acceptable shape and content of Soviet letters because it was in the Party's interest—and by implication in the nation's—to develop "the Communist purposefulness of literature." [13]

In the Ukraine there was another trial, of the Ukrainian television journalist Vyacheslav Chornovil, who had been tried and sentenced to eighteen months in a labor camp in May 1966. In March 1967, because his permit to live in Kiev had "expired," Chornovil was forced to move to Lvov. There, on April 20, he completed and began to circulate his *The Misfortune of Intellect*, the collection of letters and petitions and writings of those Ukrainian intellectuals who had been imprisoned in 1965 and 1966. On August 3, the KGB searched his Lvov flat, confiscated some of his manuscripts and books, and that evening arrested him once again. On November 15, 1967, in a secret trial, he was sentenced to three years of hard labor, with eighteen months deducted from the sentence because of the general amnesty in honor of the fiftieth anniversary of Soviet rule.

On August 30, the trial of Bukovsky, Delaunay, and Kushev, all charged under Article 190/3, began in Moscow Criminal Court. During the proceedings it was evident that demands for intellectual freedom were gradually being escalated into demands for greater political freedom; and in the testimony of the accused, as well as in the behavior of those who were prosecuting them, the issues were much more sharply defined. Bukovsky, for instance, declared, "As an opponent of all forms of totalitarianism, I have made it my aim in life to denounce the anti-democratic laws which lead to political inequality in our country." [14] He defended the right to protest and oppose, maintaining: "We do not need freedom 'pro' if there is no freedom 'anti.' We know that protest demonstrations are a powerful weapon in the hands of the workers and they are an inalienable right in all democratic states. Where is this right denied?" In answer to his own question, he held up an issue of *Pravda* in which there was a report that May Day demonstrators in Franco Spain had been tried and sentenced, and commented, "I see a disturbing likeness between Fascist Spain and Soviet legislation." [15] All these comments went far beyond the purview of literary concerns, so it was not surprising that Bukovsky's indictment accused him of being "an opponent of Communist ideology." [16] Bukovsky protested against the way the three had been arrested, describing the arrest as a deliberate KGB "provocation," and he denounced the way they had been interrogated and kept in isolation cells for seven months without being brought to trial.

The judge tried to divert Bukovsky's criticisms of Soviet law and the KGB, attempting among other things to treat him as if he were mentally ill. In this regard the indictment charged that Bukovsky had been convicted in 1962 of circulating anti-Soviet documents which included photostats of Milovan Djilas' *The New Class,* and as a consequence had been sent to a mental hospital until 1964. In moving testimony, Bukovsky's mother reported: "Of the past four years he's spent nearly three locked up: the Leningrad prison mental hospital, the Serbsky clinic, and now he's in Lefortovo. He comes out and they pick him up again. They don't give him a chance even to start to work or to study. But he's not a social parasite and he's not a criminal." Though Aleksandr Yesenin-Volpin testified in Bukovsky's behalf, explaining that the demonstration in Pushkin Square was intended to demand revision of Article 70 and Articles 190/1 and 190/3, the prosecution made clear what was at stake, accusing the three men of staging "a demonstration directed against the KGB. Their impudence is shown by the fact that they criticized existing laws and the activities of the Security Services, *thereby undermining their authority.*" [17]

S. A. Melamed, Delaunay's defense attorney, reminded the court that suppressing intellectual dissent and ferment was unwise:

Some of you have seen wine when it is fermenting. It foams and the foam splashes over the edge of the barrel. What does a good wine-grower do? He doesn't clap the lid on to the barrel, he carefully skims the wine, leaving it to ferment, and the wine is good as a result. But what does the bad winegrower do? He closes the barrel with the foam inside, binds it with iron hoops—and as a rule the wine turns into vinegar. That's what we do with people by our ruthlessness and severity. We turn them away.[18]

Bukovsky's attorney, D. I. Kaminskaya, also pointed out that neither criticism of the law nor criticism of the KGB is a crime under Article 190/3.

Both Delaunay and Kushev apologized for their actions, Delaunay pleading: "I am a writer and I find the conditions at Lefortovo, as I did at the Serbsky Clinic, all the harder to bear. Only with difficulty have I succeeded in keeping up my will to live and to write. Of course, nothing very terrible will happen if I get three years. I don't expect I'll die or commit suicide. But whether the camps will leave me sufficient strength for creative work when I come out, of that I am not sure." Kushev said that he had changed some of his opinions while being interrogated, and thanked his KGB examiner for treating him well. "I ask the Court not to pass too heavy a sentence but to give me a chance to get on my feet. I ask you not to destroy my life and my work." [19] But Bukovsky asked no quarter and gave none. He remained adamant, asserting: "I absolutely do not repent having organized this demonstration. I find that it accomplished what it had to accomplish, and, when I am free again, I shall organize other demonstrations—of course, in complete conformity with the law, as this one has been." [20]

The court found all three defendants guilty and sentenced Bukovsky to three years in a labor camp, while the other two were given suspended sentences of one year each. The only public mention of the trial and sentencing was in a brief announcement in the September 4, 1967, edition of *Evening Moscow*, which falsely reported that the defendants had all pleaded guilty. The next day, both Aleksandr Yesenin-Volpin and Natalya Ilyina wrote letters to the editor denying that Bukovsky and the others had pleaded guilty and declaring that such distortions of fact provoked only cynicism and lack of faith in the government on the part of young Russians. Like those of so many other dissidents, Yesenin-Volpin's letter was careful to dissociate itself from "foreign" and "hostile" propagandists, its last paragraph remarking: "Many of your readers have also heard the case wrongly reported by the Voice of America. This radio station is often accused by the Soviet press of lying, but this does not give it [the Soviet press] any right to compete with other liars." [21]

On September 12, eight days later, Solzhenitsyn, after an unpublicized meeting with the heads of the Writers' Union in June that had produced no results,[22] sent a second letter to the Secretariat of the Union of Soviet Writers complaining that though his letter to the Fourth Writers' Congress had been supported by more than a hundred writers, it had neither been published in the Soviet Union nor elicited by any official response. Instead, the campaign of slander against him had mounted, with new rumors being circulated that he was preparing to defect to the United Arab Republic or to England. His only novel published in the USSR, *One Day in the Life of Ivan Denisovich,* was "now being secretly withdrawn from circulation in public libraries," and people were being warned not to lend it or give it away if they owned a copy. Though *Novy mir* had offered to publish *Cancer Ward,* it had been refused permission to do so, yet officially inspired rumors were still being bruited about that it would soon be printed, and so would a book of his short stories. He knew the rumors to be deliberately misleading and untrue. Solzhenitsyn warned that hundreds of copies of *Cancer Ward* were now in *samizdat* circulation, so unless the book were published swiftly in the Soviet Union, "we cannot prevent its unauthorized appearance in the West." [23]

In response to this letter Solzhenitsyn was invited to a meeting of the board of the Union of Soviet Writers ten days later, on September 22, 1967—a meeting at which the top literary bureaucrats sat in judgment on him. From the first the tone was exasperated on both sides: the bureaucrats were hostile to the novelist, Solzhenitsyn was angry and curt to them, and sharp words were exchanged throughout. The bureaucrats attacked Solzhenitsyn for three basic things: first, he was charged with being used by the West; second, he was unwilling to behave like a "true Soviet writer"; and third, he was personally nonconformist, or, as they put it, "rude." The first charge was far and away the most important; Anatoly Surkov stated it quite succinctly when he asked of Solzhenitsyn: "You should state whether you renounce your role of the leader of the political opposition in our country—the role they ascribe to you in the West." Aleksandr Korneichuk called on the novelist to dissociate himself from the "licentious bourgeois propaganda" which his first letter had evoked in the West. And as the First Secretary of the Union, Konstantin Fedin, summed it up: "You must protest above all against the dirty use of your name by our enemies in the

West"; Solzhenitsyn's works were being used there "for the basest of purposes." The Union officials attacked him for portraying only the black side of Soviet life. Korneichuk excoriated him for failing to understand the role of Soviet writers—"By our writings we protect the interests of our government, our Party, our people"—and then, in a burst of political fury, the playwright adjured Solzhenitsyn: "Do battle against the foes of our nation! Do you realize that thermonuclear weapons exist in the world and that despite all our peaceful efforts the United States may employ them?" [24]

Fedin spoke out against Solzhenitsyn's letter as "an insult to our collective—His letter is like a slap in the face to us, as if we were dullards and not representatives of the creative intelligentsia." [25] Others among them reminded Solzhenitsyn that he had not acted toward them as "brothers in writing and labor." The undercurrents of envy, personal and literary, were clear in the verbal exchanges, as was Solzhenitsyn's prickliness with them and his distaste for their cowardice and conformism. So brusque was he that Tvardovsky was called upon to remind him gently that he was not altogether without friends and supporters.

Solzhenitsyn's rejoinder was angry. He asked how it was that these "brothers in writing and labor have for two and a half years calmly watched me being hounded, persecuted, and slandered" without doing anything in his behalf.[26] He was not being published, his one book was in the process of being withdrawn from the shelves and forbidden, and even his receiving his rightful royalties had laid him open to malicious accusations. If he took his royalties from Western publishers, he was accused of having sold out to the capitalists; if he did not take them, he was actually accused of thereby supporting the capitalists.[27]

To those who accused him of failure as a "Soviet writer," for not doing as Kerbabaev said he himself did—"I always strive to write only about joyful things"—or as Georgy Markov suggested—"When is this man Solzhenitsyn going to stop reviling Soviet literature?"— Solzhenitsyn replied that he was going to defend his honor as a writer by continuing to write the unvarnished truth as he saw it. What he was concerned with was "the destiny of our great literature, which once conquered and captivated the world but which has now lost its standing. In the West they say the Russian novel is dead, and we gesticulate and deliver speeches saying that it is not dead. But rather than make speeches we should publish novels— truly good novels." [28] As for publishing a recantation of his letter, Solzhenitsyn refused outright. How, he asked, could he publish a refutation to a letter of his which had never been made public officially? It made no sense.

Again Surkov put his finger on the dilemma the Soviet literary bureaucrats and their political mentors were confronted with. "Of course, our reader is now so developed and so sophisticated," Surkov reflected, "that no measly little book is going to alienate him from Communism. All the same, the works of Solzhenitsyn are more dangerous to us than those of Pasternak: Pasternak was a man divorced from life, while Solzhenitsyn, with his animated, militant, ideological temperament, is a man of principle." [29] Fedin wanted Solzhenitsyn to cease to be a rallying point for foreign "anti-Soviet" propaganda, but Surkov wanted Solzhenitsyn's works made more tractable for the home audience so that he and they would not become the focus of domestic dissidence and discontent.

Shortly thereafter, in October, the editor in chief of *Pravda*, Mikhail Zimianin, escalated the attack of Solzhenitsyn at a meeting in the Leningrad House of the Press. There, before a group of Soviet journalists, Zimianin accused several writers of having played into the hands of the enemies of the Soviet Union, of contributing to anti-Soviet slander in the Western press, but his major target was Solzhenitsyn:

At the moment, Solzhenitsyn occupies an important place in the propaganda of capitalist governments. He is also a psychologically unbalanced person, a schizophrenic. Formerly, he had been a prisoner and, justly or unjustly, was subsequently subjected to repressions. Now he takes his revenge against the government through his literary works. The only topic he is able to write about is life in a concentration camp. This topic has become an obsession with him. Solzhenitsyn's works are aimed against the Soviet regime, in which he finds only sores and cancerous tumors. He doesn't see anything positive in our society.

It seemed the authorities were beginning to prepare a case declaring Solzhenitsyn mentally unstable so that they could confine him in a mental hospital as they had Tarsis and Yesenin-Volpin. Zimianin made clear, moreover, that only if Solzhenitsyn "writes stories that correspond to the interests of our society . . . will his works be published." [30]

On November 25, the Writers' Union Secretariat sent a brief note to Solzhenitsyn inquiring if, in the two months since his meeting with the Secretariat, Solzhenitsyn had had sufficient time to reconsider his position and if he would now "make a public statement clarifying your position on the anti-Soviet campaign surrounding your name and your letters which has been launched by hostile propaganda." [31]

Five days later, on December 1, instead of giving an answer, Solzhenitsyn replied by asking eight questions of his own. First, would the Secretariat defend him against the campaign of lies and slander which had afflicted him for three years and which Zimianin's speech had worsened? Second, would it take measures to nullify the ban on the use of his books in libraries and the ban which prevented his name from being used in critical articles? Third, would it take steps to publish excerpts from *Cancer Ward* in *Literaturnaya gazeta* and the whole novel in *Novy mir* in order to prevent the uncontrolled publication of the book abroad? Fourth, would the Secretariat appeal to the government to subscribe to the Universal Copyright Convention so that Soviet writers' copyrights would be protected throughout the world? Fifth, would it stop the unauthorized circulation of excerpts from his novels and see to it that those excerpts were destroyed? Sixth, would it see that his papers and the manuscript of *The First Circle*, impounded by KGB, were returned to him? Seventh, would the Secretariat accept Konstantin Simonov's proposal, tendered at the September 22 meeting, that a volume of his, Solzhenitsyn's, stories be published? And, eighth, why had he not received a stenographic report of that September 22 meeting for his perusal? [32]

17 Trials and Transcripts

Bolt by bolt I want a thorough examination made of the entire machine that transformed a person in the prime of life into a cold corpse. I want it to be sentenced. Publicly.

Lydia Chukovskaya

Four days after Solzhenitsyn's confrontation with the Board of the Writers' Union, on September 26, 1967, Pavel Litvinov was called to KGB headquarters in Moscow and warned that if the transcripts of the trials of Khaustov and Gabay, and of Bukovsky, Delaunay, and Kushev, which he had been compiling were to be made public, he would be arrested. Litvinov, the grandson of the former Soviet Minister of Foreign Affairs, Maxim Litvinov, and his British wife, Ivy Low, ignored the warning. A week later, on October 3, Litvinov sent a transcript of his interview with the KGB to various Soviet papers and magazines and to a number of foreign Communist publications as well, the conversations in it reading as if they had been "invented" by Arthur Koestler collaborating with George Orwell. A KGB officer named Gostev said to Litvinov: "What difference does it make what he pleaded? The Court found him guilty, that means he is guilty." And "The account in *Evening Moscow* is perfectly truthful and gives all the information that Soviet citizens *are supposed to have*." [1] Gostev warned Litvinov that no matter who published the compilation of the trial records, Litvinov would be held personally accountable, and that though there was no law against circulating nonsecret documents—in which category the trial transcripts were—the court would nonetheless prove Litvinov guilty and convict him. "Do you think," Gostev asked, "that today, when the Soviet regime is in its fiftieth year, a Soviet court would bring in a wrong verdict?" Gostev also made it perfectly clear that "such a record could be used against us by our ideological enemies, especially on the eve of the fiftieth anniversary of the Soviet regime." [2]

Litvinov's book affords extraordinary insight into the Soviet government's purposes and methods in dealing with dissidents. The flat, careful, documentary—even scientific—tone of the volume contrasts with Bukovsky's blazing courtroom speeches. Anyone concerned with Soviet jurisprudence and with the differences between official constitutional guarantees and their actual implementation in Soviet life will find important insights in it.

Although Litvinov had sent copies of his volume to the editors of *Izvestia, Literaturnaya gazeta, Komsomolskaya pravda,* the French *L'Humanité,* and the Italian *L'Unità,* not a single paper so much as acknowledged the letter's receipt, much less published it. But the material "leaked" and was published in the international edition of the *Herald Tribune* and broadcast by a number of Western radio stations.

In October, Bukovsky's defense attorney appealed to the Soviet Supreme Court to set aside the Moscow City Court's verdict. On November 16, the Supreme Court dismissed the appeal and upheld both the verdict and the sentence. As a result, in December, one of the leading and most courageous of the political dissidents, Major General Pyotr Grigorenko, addressed a petition to both the Supreme Court and the Procurator General calling for the cases to be reviewed, the illegal sentences remitted, and the accused freed. Grigorenko condemned the trials as "political" and insisted that Bukovsky was sentenced only "because he defended himself and because he refused to recognize the right of the organs of the KGB to engage in uncontrolled and illegal interference in the personal lives of citizens." [3]

On January 8, almost a year after they had been arrested, Ginzburg and Galanskov were brought to trial. A petition calling for "airing public testimony, the unprejudiced selection of witnesses and wide coverage of the trial in the press" had been sent to Moscow Municipal Court signed by thirty-one prominent Soviet intellectuals—artists, writers and scientists [4]—but the case was tried in a half-empty courtroom while guards kept the friends of the accused from entering. During the trial Pavel Litvinov and Yuli Daniel's wife Larissa Bogoraz-Daniel, addressed an open letter to "world public opinion" which they distributed to foreign newspapermen. It protested that the trial was "in violation of the most important principles of Soviet law," [5] and no better than the 1930s purge trials "which have involved us in so much shame and so much bloodshed that we still have not recovered from them." They sharply rebuked and condemned Dobrovolsky for his cooperation with the prosecution and for giving false testimony against Ginzburg and Galanskov, and they denounced the packed court, the cowed witnesses, and the open bias of judge and prosecution. After appealing to the Western "progressive press" to publish and broadcast their letter as quickly as possible, Litvinov and Mrs. Daniel added, "We are not sending this request to Soviet newspapers, because that is futile." From America, Svetlana Alliluyeva took up their cause in a rare public statement. Stalin's daughter called for "all possible support to those who remain honest and brave under unbearable conditions and have enough strength to fight." [6] She recalled the trials and sentencing of Sinyavsky and Daniel and Daniel's deteriorating health in concentration camp, remarked on the Bukovsky and Ginzburg trials, then read the entire text of the Litvinov–Mrs. Daniel appeal.

The prosecution's case against Galanskov and Ginzburg was based on their "anti-Soviet" views and, under Article 70, their presumably having slandered the Soviet Union with the specific purpose of weakening or overthrowing it. Under heaviest attack was Ginzburg's "White Book" on the Sinyavsky-Daniel trial. Five of the documents in that collection were held to be "criminal," materials "tendentiously selected" and reproduced with the intention of being sent abroad.[7] In sending such materials abroad, the defendants were cooperating with the émigré NTS, the prosecution charged. The severest state censure was directed against one selection, "A Letter to an Old Friend," by an anonymous author Ginzburg said he could not (or would not) identify. It was an essay which dealt with the trials, purges, and murders of the 1930s with savage honesty:

If this trial had taken place twenty years ago, Sinyavsky and Daniel would have been shot in some MGB cellar or put on the 'conveyor belt' where interrogators were rotated but the accused remained standing for hours and days on end until his will was broken and his mind deranged. Or else drugs would have been injected to suppress the will, another awful technique of the 1930s. Or else there would have been no open trial altogether; the accused would simply have been shot in the corridor. . . . And the cluster of charges would have been quite different: treason, subversion, terror, sabotage. . . .

. . . You and I remember the Stalin era—the concentration camps on an unprecedented, super-Hitlerian scale, Auschwitzes without ovens, where millions perished. We know the corruption, the bloody corruption, of those in power who, having repented, to this day do not want to tell the truth, even about the Kirov case.[8]

On January 12, Ginzburg and Galanskov made their final statements to the court. Ginzburg explained that he had compiled the "White Book" to present an objective picture of the Sinyavsky-Daniel trial and the world's reaction to it in order to have the case reconsidered and the conviction set aside. He maintained that the materials included were "directed not against Soviet rule, but merely against the actions of certain workers of the KGB." He denied any other intentions or having any connection with the NTS, yet he was certain he would be convicted: "I know that you will convict me because not a single person charged under Article 70 has ever been acquitted. I will go to camp calmly to serve my sentence . . . but I am certain that no honest person will condemn me."[9]

Galanskov also refused to acknowledge his guilt, also denied any connections with the NTS, and said that he had conceived his journal *Phoenix* as a pacifist publication, but the Sinyavsky-Daniel trial had made him reshape its character. He reminded the judge that in the West he was "known as a poet and also because of my protest in front of the American Embassy on the occasion of the aggression committed by the U.S.A. in the Dominican Republic." Like Ginzburg, Galanskov insisted that he did *not* have "anti-Soviet" views, that he was truly a good Communist who was trying to "purify the system." And he expressed his confidence that "the Marxist potential of the Party is [now] reasserting itself more strongly than ever before. The October Revolution which . . . has survived a period of dictatorship and has proved strong enough not to be conquered by the dictatorship, has retained its revolutionary-proletarian character."[10]

Galanskov's attorney, D. P. Kaminskaya, skillfully dissected the state's evidence; she also pleaded that Galanskov had painful stomach ulcers and had formerly been diagnosed a schizophrenic. She did a subtle but forceful job of destroying the reliability of Dobrovolsky's testimony as state's evidence. One of the most revealing parts of her summation gave a picture of the audience in that courtroom:

I fail to understand the reason for laughter in this courtroom when the fact that Galanskov has committed good, selfless deeds was mentioned. I do not understand why you [the people in the court] have laughed at the statement that he is a kind man; that he visited an elderly woman, scrubbed her floor and brought her medicine; and that he helped an acquaintance educate her children.[11]

The court's sentence was severe: Galanskov got seven years at hard labor, Ginzburg five. Even Lashkova, who had only typed the copies of the texts in the "White Book," was punished by loss of her right to live and study in Moscow, and was given a year's suspended sentence.

An upsurge of protest against the conduct and outcome of the trial, and against the ensuing official press campaign vilifying the defendants, particularly in *Izvestia, Komsomolskaya pravda,* and *Literaturnaya gazeta,* followed. A series of open letters signed by some of the leading Soviet intellectuals was made public. In one such to the conference of sixty-six Communist parties meeting in February in Budapest to discuss Communist unity (i.e., unity against the Chinese), Pavel Litvinov, Mrs. Daniel, and ten others, including Pyotr Yakir, Aleksey Kosterin, Ilya Gabay, and General Grigorenko, appealed to foreign Communists to bring pressure to bear on the Soviet government to halt the political intimidation, arrests, trials, and imprisonments.[12] In another letter, the chairman of a Latvian collective farm, Ivan Yakhimovich, who had been singled out for praise as an outstanding kolkhoz official in 1964, wrote directly to the Politburo's ideologist, Mikhail Suslov. Yakhimovich, a man of courage and independent mind, and a graduate of the Latvian State University in philology, called for amnestying Sinyavsky, Daniel, and Bukovsky and reviewing all other such cases and convictions. "One cannot achieve legality by violating laws," Yakhimovich wrote.

Such violators [of the law] should be thrown out with a vengeance, for they are doing Soviet power more harm than all your NTSs, BBCs, and Radio Libertys taken together.

Let *Novy Mir* print the works of A. Solzhenitsyn again. Let G. Serebryakova publish her *Sandstorm* in the U.S.S.R. and Ye. Ginzburg her
Journey into the Whirlwind. Anyway, they are known and read. It is
no secret.[13]

As a result of this protest, Yakhimovich was shortly expelled
from the Communist Party.

(Serebryakova, who had so viciously attacked Ilya Ehrenburg at
the December 1963 meetings between Khrushchev and the writers,
had written a novel about her ordeals in the Stalinist concentration
camps. The manuscript had been smuggled abroad and published
without her consent by the Polish émigré publishing house, Kultura,
in Paris. The text of the novel was said to have reached Kultura in
the form of the page proof of a book which had been approved by
Khrushchev for publication after having been serialized in 1964 in
Literaturnaya gazeta. After Khrushchev's ouster, publication of the
book was abruptly shelved. Serebryakova protested the Kultura edition in an article in *Literaturnaya gazeta,*[14] in which she said that she
had herself voluntarily withdrawn the book from publication on the
grounds that it might be misunderstood. In publishing it, she maintained, Kultura had violated her rights, because she had not given
her consent.

Serebryakova had spent twenty years in labor camps. Both her
first and second husbands, Grigory Sokolnikov and Leonid Serebryakov, were killed in the purges during the 1930s. After she herself was released from the camps, she resumed her literary career,
became a biographer of Marx, and one of the leading conservatives
in the Soviet literary controversy.) [15]

Of the various letters of protest, two stood out. Both raised the
haunting specter of a rebirth of Stalinism. The first, signed by Ilya
Gabay, Yuli Kim, and the remarkable Yakir, declared:

The brutish lynching of intellectuals is the logical culmination of the
atmosphere of recent years in public life. Naive hopes for a complete
cleansing of our public life, instilled in us by the decisions of the 20th
and 22nd Congresses, have not borne fruit. Slowly but surely, the
course of Stalinist restoration continues. And in this restoration what is
chiefly being depended upon is our own passivity, our short memory,
and the bitter fact that we are used to an absence of freedom.[16]

Perhaps no other individual sums up in his own person and activities the dissident opposition to the heirs of Stalin and simultaneously the conflict of fathers and sons as does Pyotr Yakir. Son of the General Iona Yakir who was executed with Chief of Staff Marshal Mikhail Tuchachevsky and six other Soviet generals in June 1937 in the Stalinist purges of the Red Army, Pyotr Yakir was arrested at the age of fourteen, after his father's execution, and for seventeen years thereafter was confined to various concentration camps. Yakir's wife and brother were also executed, leaving the young Yakir virtually without a family. Finally released after Stalin's death, Pyotr Yakir, like Solzhenitsyn, remained in exile in Kazakhstan, where, during a Khrushchev visit, he inquired of the First Secretary about his father. Khrushchev had known the elder Yakir when the General was commander of the Kiev military district and Khrushchev a member of the Kiev oblast committee. Khrushchev told of the encounter with the younger Yakir in a speech at the Twenty-second Party Congress:

I was well acquainted with Comrade Yakir. . . . This year during a conference in Alma Ata I was approached by his son who works in Kazakhstan. He asked me about his father. What could I tell him? When we investigated this case in the Presidium of the Central Committee [we] were told that neither Tukhachevsky, Yakir, or Yuborevich had perpetrated any crimes against the Party or state. . . .

. . . It is necessary to say that Yakir once enjoyed great respect with Stalin. One may add that at the moment he was shot Yakir cried out, "Long live the Party! Long Live Stalin!" He believed so much in the Party and in Stalin that he did not even allow the thought than an unlawful action was being consciously perpetrated. He believed that some sort of enemies had penetrated the NKVD. When Stalin was told how Yakir behaved before his death, he cursed.

A few days earlier, at the Twenty-second Congress, Aleksandr Shelepin told how Iona Yakir had died:

. . . at one time, Yakir, the former commander of a military district, wrote a letter to Stalin in which he declared his complete innocence. This is what he wrote: "I am an honest soldier, dedicated to the Party, the state, and the people, as I have been for many years. All my conscious life has passed in selfless and honest work before the Party and its leaders. . . . I shall die with words of love for you, the Party, and the country, and with a boundless faith in the victory of Communism.

On this letter, Stalin wrote: "Scoundrel and prostitute." Voroshilov added. "Absolutely precise definition." Molotov signed his name under it, and Kaganovich wrote in addition: "The death penalty is the only punishment for the traitor, swine, and"—here follows a dirty, unmentionable word.

On the eve of his execution, Yakir sent the following letter to Voroshilov: "To Voroshilov, in consideration of my long record of honest work in the Red Army, I ask you to order that my helpless and quite innocent family be looked after and assisted." [17]

The authorities displayed no such compassion—as Pyotr Yakir's seventeen years in concentration camps attest.

Because of his history, Yakir's appeal against a revived Stalinism carried special moral weight. The letter written with Kim [18] and Gabay specified how Stalinism was being restored.

For several years ominous symptoms of a restoration of Stalinism have been evident in the life of our society. This is manifest most strikingly in the revival of the most terrible acts of that era—through organization of harsh tribunals to judge people who have dared to defend their dignity and inner freedom, who have the audacity to think and to protest.

To be sure, repressions have not reached the proportions of those years, but we have sufficient basis for the fear that among state and Party officials there are more than a few who would like to reverse our public evolution. We have no guarantees that the year 1937, little by little, and with our tacit connivance, will not come upon us again.[19]

Yakir then denounced the trials of Sinyavsky and Daniel, Khaustov and Bukovsky as models of a "cynical lawlessness and perversion of facts" which reminded him of the show trials of the 1930s, and condemned the authorities for treating those who tried to enter the courtroom with "open blackmail and a jeering humiliation of personal dignity. Photographing, ceaseless shadowing, checking of documents, eavesdropping." Moreover, "from the highest platforms the name of J. V. Stalin has been pronounced in an entirely positive context," and the term "cult of personality" has become all but taboo in the press. Books which tell of Stalin's crimes have been banned and those already published held up to opprobrium.[20]

Not a single one of the democratic beginnings has been brought to completion. The literary or artistic taste of the favorite still has the force of law for the writer, the artist, the director, the reader, the viewer. Films are rotting in film libraries which would do great honor to our art. In crowded studios and attics beautiful paintings are aging. In literature a place is found for the low-grade works of Kochetov and Smirnov, which glorify—in particular—J. V. Stalin. And only the lucky few have been able to read Solzhenitsyn's *Cancer Ward*.

Yakir also denounced the police surveillance that was part of the daily life of many Soviet citizens and asserted that the "mute acquiescence with Stalinists and bureaucrats who deceive the people and the leadership, who sit on all trouble signs, all complaints, and all protests leads logically to that which is most to be feared: to lawless punishment of people." Yakir appealed to the creative intelligentsia to raise its voice against the impending dangers of new Stalins and Yezhovs, warning that the tacit acquiescence of the intellectuals could only bring back a revived 1937: "The fate of future Vavilovs and Mandelshtams is a matter for your consciences."

You are the heirs of the great humanistic traditions of the Russian intelligentsia. Before you is the example of courageous behavior on the part of the modern progressive intelligentsia of the West.

We understand that you labor under conditions in which fulfillment of your civic duty is in every instance an act of courage. But there is indeed no choice between courage and cowardly complicity in filthy deeds, between risk or joining forces with the Vasilyevs and the Kedrinas, between committing a few good deeds, or lining up with the yellow pen-pushers of *Izvestia* and *Komsomolskaya Pravda* who have felt it morally possible to take part in public slander of those who have been persecuted.

The most moving letter of protest against the revival of Stalinism was written by Lydia Chukovskaya, who had also suffered the loss of her husband during the great purges, to the editor of *Izvestia*. Written as a lament for those who had perished, her letter had the controlled rage and mournful compassion of a classical threnody; it saw and demonstrated the connections between intellectual and political freedom.

In our day, one trial follows another. Under one pretext or another . . . the spoken and written word is under condemnation. They condemn books written at home and published abroad. They condemn a journal printed in our land but not on a press. They condemn a collection of documents exposing the lawlessness of the courts. They condemn the cry from the Square in defense of those who have been arrested. The word is being persecuted as if to give new truth to the old axiom Leo Tolstoy was wont to use: "The word is deed." Indeed, the word must truly be the deed, if, for the word, people are sentenced to years of confinement in the prisons and camps, if it takes whole years and even decades for the great poetry and great prose . . . so essential to everyone, to break through into the light. I would say that we need them as much as we need bread—because of their penetrating truthfulness, we need them more than bread. And perhaps because the truthful word cannot ring out and become a book, and through the book [reach] the soul of man, or because the truthful word has forcibly been driven inward and forsaken, the artificiality, falseness and awkwardness of other words, the ones that *are* published and *do* reach the reader are so keenly felt.[21]

Chukovskaya called for complete, unvarnished candor in dealing with the Stalinist past, with Stalinist butchery—an approach to the heirs of Stalin most threatening to the authorities. "Bolt by bolt," she wrote, "I want a thoroughgoing examination made of the whole machinery that took a person in the prime of life and turned him into a cold corpse. I want *it* to be sentenced. Publicly." This was the very bone and marrow of the issue: Chukovskaya wanted not only individuals publicly identified as criminals, purged and punished; she wanted the very system and its institutions exposed and reformed.

The thirst for the most essential, elementary justice goes unassuaged. The wives of those who died are issued certificates stating that their husbands were arrested without cause and have been posthumously rehabilitated for lack of any evidence of crime. That is fine. The same certificates are also issued to those prisoners who were fortunate enough to survive. Excellent. They have returned. But what has happened to those who caused all that suffering? Those who fabricated the evidence of crime on the part of millions of people? . . . Who are these people? Where are they and what are they doing today? . . . And what kinds of certificates have ever been issued to *them*, to those criminals—and by whom? [22]

The Brezhnev-Kosygin government had no intention of even listening to Chukovskaya's strictures nor of acting on them. What it wanted was to bury the question of Stalin's heirs with Stalin's victims. All that winter and spring the regime mounted an assault on the dissidents. Litvinov was dismissed from his job as physicist and teacher at the Moscow Institute of Precision Chemical Technology. Yesenin-Volpin was removed from his job at the All-Union Institute of Scientific and Technological Information and confined to the Solboyava Psychiatric Hospital, some seventy kilometers from Moscow. Immediately following the Ginzburg-Galanskov trial, the KGB called in many of those who had protested the trial and threatened them with reprisals should they continue their activities— among them Grigorenko and Yakir and Ginzburg's mother, Lyudmila, and his fiancée, Irina Zhokovskaya, who was threatened with prosecution under Article 190/1 "for spreading false fabrications which defamed the Soviet Union." [23]

In March, Boris Zoltukhin, Ginzburg's defense attorney, was expelled from the Communist Party and removed from his post as chairman of the legal consultative bureau in a Moscow borough.[24] The students and intelligentsia estimated Zoltukhin as a

middle-aged man who was Chairman of one of Moscow's collegia of lawyers. He was a Communist of the humanist, rather than the apparatchik strain. In other words, he was a humane, honorable man, universally respected by his colleagues. He was known never to depart from principle in his defences, never to take under-the-counter payments from his clients, never to betray a subordinate in his collegium when police or prosecution applied pressure for a conviction in a given case—a proud record under the Soviet legal system. And in addition—although it seems almost fulsome to record it—he was called *lyubimets* (the favorite, the darling) of the legal profession in Moscow.

His mistake was to conduct Ginzburg's defense with his usual skill, energy and high principles—protesting bitterly, among other things, against the intimidation of defence witnesses by the prosecution and judge. His concluding speech, which exposed the political and moral evils, as well as the legal absurdity, of the writers' trials, was a courageous and, under the circumstances, brilliantly argued statement, equal to the highest standards of defence advocacy. After circulating underground for two months in Moscow, it was printed in *Le Nouvel Observateur*—and that, according to speculation in Moscow, was his undoing. He was expelled from the Party. (This, for reasons too lengthy to explain here, is tantamount to a criminal sentence: an expelled Communist is in many ways like an ex-convict.) This meant, of course, loss of his chairmanship of the collegium. Then, for good measure, Zoltukhin was expelled from the collegium entirely—which meant that he was deprived of his right to appear in court. He now works as a legal consultant to an enterprise in Moscow—earning enough to live on (perhaps a quarter of his former salary), but in other ways a ruined man.[25]

Investigations, administrative pressures, and reprisals were invoked against many of those who had signed any of the petitions or open letters.[26] Scholars and academicians came under fire—Novosibirsk mathematicians, chemists, and physicists as well as Moscow historians, linguists, and philologists. The president of the Soviet Academy of Sciences, Mstislav V. Keldysh, warned the scientists that Soviet science could get along without them and that their technical gifts would not protect them from prosecution. His words were "reportedly followed by the expulsion of several distinguished scientists—including persons working on military and space programs—from the Communist Party." [27] The scientists, heretofore less publicly and politically active, had now joined with the other members of the Soviet intelligentsia in a common front against repression, against provincial isolation, against the possibilities of re-Stalinization. It was an auspicious step, one which the Soviet government was not only to regard with a jaundiced eye, but which, despite Keldysh's threat, posed more complex problems for the Soviet leadership. The government needed the services of scientists and the technical intelligentsia in a way in which it did not need the work of the literary and artistic intelligentsia; and, Keldysh notwithstanding, it could not so easily afford to dispense with the scientific community.

At a session of the Secretariat of the Moscow branch of the Writers' Union, the writers were also warned to toe the line. Those who had signed statements in defense of Galanskov and Ginzburg were sharply rebuked for "inadmissible political dereliction and lack of principle" in lending their names to "arm . . . ideological adversaries. The antisocial actions of these writers were aggravated by the fact that their letters were published in various bourgeois newspapers and broadcast over foreign radio." [28] The Secretariat reminded the writers, one and all, that "anyone who does not fully understand his responsibility to the people in a period of uncompromising conflict between the ideologies of socialism and capitalism cannot call himself a Soviet writer." [29]

Neo-Stalinism had returned with a vengeance. Some, like General Grigorenko, claimed that it was the result of a policy long planned and slowly implemented. In fact, Grigorenko claimed he had documents which showed that re-Stalinization had been decided on as early as the October 1964 Plenum of the Party Central Committee at which Khrushchev was unseated,[30] although Brezhnev and Kosygin had not made the decision public. Now, four years later, in meetings on April 9 and 10, 1968, the Central Committee endorsed an intensified ideological campaign against "the entire huge apparatus of anti-Communist propaganda . . . directed at weakening the unity of socialist countries [and] at undermining socialist society from within." It also adopted a resolution calling for tightened control over Soviet literature, urging the Party to stand firm "against attempts to drag views alien to the socialist ideology of Soviet society into individual works of literature," [31] and simultaneously expressed its misgivings about the unrest in Poland, the political reforms and intellectual ferment in Czechoslovakia, and the continued dissidence in the Soviet Union proper. On April 3, a regime spokesman announced:

International imperialism spares neither forces nor funds in its subversion against countries of the socialist camp. It resorts to all possible means: bribery, blackmail, slander and ideological subversion. . . . As you know, this has been graphically demonstrated in Poland where the Party Central Committee and the working class succeeded in disclosing in time the secret machinery of provocational antipopular subversion aimed against all the gains of socialist People's Poland. Unfortunately, a segment among Polish writers played quite an ignoble role in reaction's political adventure.[32]

Comment on the Czech and Slovak writers was to be far more vindictive.

The Central Committee of the Party now declared that the "consequences of the cult of personality" were officially liquidated, thus attempting to put a quietus on any further discussion of righting the wrongs of the Stalinist era, exposing or prosecuting those who were responsible for them, or questioning how Soviet institutions could have permitted such "violations of Socialist legality." On April 16, the Supreme Court of the RSFSR made plain that no legal leniency was to be granted. It rejected the appeals of Ginzburg, Galanskov, Dobrovolsky, and Lashkova. All were declared properly tried and convicted—even Dobrovolsky, who, despite his having turned state's evidence and cooperated with the prosecution, was still sentenced to two years.

18 Solzhenitsyn's Ordeal

> . . . I must have strength again
> To see, to know,
> How all that I have loved will torture me again,
> What ugly ghosts will suddenly appear,
> What friend will readily betray me
> And how another will repudiate me.
> They'll try to tempt me
> And they'll order—"Recant!"—
> And all my soul will shrink
> From the dread and the anguish.
> But I will have the strength
> To answer and insist:
> —"I won't recant! This is my life, my faith!
> No, never. . . ."
>
> *Olga Berggolts*

In a letter dated January 7–15, 1968, Aleksandr Tvardovsky wrote to Konstantin Fedin, the First Secretary of the Writers' Union, to take up the cudgels in Solzhenitsyn's behalf.[1] It was a long, carefully thought-out letter, subtle, shrewd, and with the flexible toughness that characterized Tvardovsky's long and continuing effort to forward the freedom of Russian literature and Russian writers. Tvardovsky's letter was devoted to "the still undecided question of Solzhenitsyn," because he believed a proper answer to that question essential to the health of Soviet letters and the Writers' Union. "Whether we like it or not, [Solzhenitsyn has] acquired a worldwide reputation as one of the greatest writers of the present day," Tvardovsky wrote. Solzhenitsyn had also greatly complicated contemporary Soviet literary life: "He stands at the crossroads of two opposing tendencies in the social consciousness of our literature, one which strives to go backward, the other which strives to progress in accordance with the irreversibility of the historical process." Tvardovsky then agreed that the form of Solzhenitsyn's letter to the Writers' Congress deserved condemnation, but, he added, "I do not recall that there have even been any attempts to refute a single one of the points contained in it, nor to declare them false, fabricated, selfish or harmful to the whole of Soviet literature. Why is this? The simple reason is that in the main the arguments are irrefutable." The silence and secrecy with which the Writers' Union leadership treated the issues Solzhenitsyn raised reveal that the leadership is afraid to speak out, because "it cannot, in the last analysis, count on the support or sympathies of either its readers or its writers."

Tvardovsky then accused Fedin of refusing to protect Solzhenitsyn, a Writers' Union member, from the "widespread fabrications concerning his biography," and of permitting Solzhenitsyn to "be handed over to political ostracism." He pleaded with Fedin not to associate himself with Sholokhov, whose harsh dictum had been "Don't let Solzhenitsyn write!"

To Solzhenitsyn as an artist, Tvardovsky maintained "the literary temptations of the West are completely alien, and he can in no way be reproached with the desire to 'please' the West." Moreover, in insisting that the novelist should denounce the West, Fedin and the Union leadership were moving dangerously toward the confessions and self-critical abasements of the past, which "do us immense harm by giving rise to the concept of writers who are morally and ethically undiscriminating, deprived of a sense of their own dignity or wholly dependent upon 'instructions' or 'demands' which, incidentally, are the same thing." Such confessions and self-criticisms, Tvardovsky stressed, are not to the advantage of the Writers' Union, nor do they strengthen its authority.

Tvardovsky then reminded Fedin that *Cancer Ward* had been accepted for publication in *Novy mir* in the fall of 1967 and scheduled for the January 1968 issue, but its publication had been shelved on orders from "above," though the novel would now shortly be issued abroad. Tvardovsky called for three concrete steps to remedy the situation: after extracts were published in *Literaturnaya gazeta*, publish the novel in full in *Novy mir;* instruct the publisher Soviet Writer to prepare an anthology of Solzhenitsyn's writings with a foreword which will include an accurate biography of the author; print that foreword either in *Literaturnaya gazeta* or in *Literaturnaya rossiya.* Tvardovsky entreated Fedin to act in accord with his conscience and intelligence:

But I cannot assume that you will bear the burden of the external influences and compulsions. Thank God the times are past when it only needed a "wagging finger" to decide the specific problems of art and science, ignoring the opinions of the people who work in these specific fields. Whether we are good or bad, it is up to us and to nobody else to decide the problems of literature.

Tvardovsky then took the occasion to thank Fedin for the way in which Fedin had used his good offices "at the highest levels" in his behalf when Tvardovsky was in difficulties with the regime in 1954, and he reminded Fedin that Solzhenitsyn was

a man and a writer who has paid for every page and every line as have none of us who are now judging him and bargaining about how to deal with him. He has endured the supreme trials of the human soul—war, imprisonment and a lethal illness. And, now, after such a successful debut in the literary world, no less a trial, perhaps, has befallen him, including non-literary influences, secret political literary ostracism, direct slander, the banning of any mention of his name in the press, etc. Speaking in good conscience, what is the point in using for the indictment the papers which were taken from him by "special methods" including his manuscript of a play written more than twenty years ago in the hell of a forced labor camp by Prisoner SHCH-232, a man without a name, not by A. Solzhenitsyn, a member of the Writers' Union of the USSR?

Tvardovsky concluded that he saw no need for Fedin to send him a written reply; what he hoped was that Fedin would hand down a favorable decision, for which they had all waited so long.

The play Tvardovsky referred to was "Feast of the Conquerors," which Solzhenitsyn had long since repudiated. He had also destroyed all copies of the manuscript except one which the KGB had confiscated in 1965 with his other manuscripts and private papers. The KGB had reproduced the play in its "special edition" of Solzhenitsyn's works for circulating to the leadership and the Writers' Union functionaries in order to discredit the novelist. In his September 22 meeting with the Union Secretariat, Solzhenitsyn had been attacked again and again because of that play, although he had explained that it was written "in those distant years when there was no return to freedom for political prisoners, and at a time when no one in the community, including the writers' community, either in word or deed spoke out against repression." Solzhenitsyn claimed as little responsibility for the play "as many other authors bear for speeches and books they wrote in 1949 but would not write again today"—a thrust against those who had indulged in the orgy of pro-Stalin panegyric—and maintained that the play bore no relationship to his present work, though he was still angry about how his manuscripts had been "seized . . . from a private apartment." [2]

Critics of Solzhenitsyn were again and again to return to that play, primarily because "it implies that there was little choice between Stalin and Hitler, and that those Russians who fought on the German side under the renegade General Vlasov may have had a point." [3] Solzhenitsyn rebuked the Writers' Union leaders for not understanding that a man changes in twenty years, especially "in the face of a complete change in all our circumstances," and he bitterly admonished the KGB for its role in circulating the play:

If *Feast of the Conquerors* is being widely circulated or printed, I solemnly declare that the full responsibility lies with the organization [the KGB] which had the only remaining copy—one not read by anyone—and used it for "publication" of the play during my lifetime and against my will; it is this organization that is disseminating the play! For a year and a half I have repeatedly warned that this is very dangerous. I imagine that there is no reading room there, that one is handed the play and takes it home. But at home there are sons and daughters, and desk drawers are not always locked. I had already issued a warning before, and I am issuing it today! [4]

The following June, when an intense assault was mounted against Solzhenitsyn and all his work, *Literaturnaya gazeta* was to write of "Feast of the Conquerors" that it "sacrilegiously mocked" the Red Army and showed sympathy for the army of Soviet defectors organized by General Andrey Vlasov under Nazi auspices in 1943. In 1970, when Nicholas Bethell was interviewing the editor in chief of *Literaturnaya gazeta* about Solzhenitsyn, Aleksandr Chakovsky remarked acidly, "The play shows Solzhenitsyn for what he is. It is unforgivable." The manuscript was smuggled out to the West and excerpts from it printed in the German *Die Zeit* in November and

December 1969; there were also rumors that it would soon appear in toto "in an émigré journal or in a theater in Paris." When Bethell mentioned those reports to Chakovsky, Solzhenitsyn's critic and rival replied, "Let them print it so people will realize what sort of person he is who slanders his country and defends traitors." Bethell then asked Chakovsky if he would *like* the play to be published abroad; though Chakovsky denied that he would, Bethell came away with the clear sense that "some Soviet officials would be glad about the play's appearance as a further stick with which to beat Solzhenitsyn, and very possibly it was the KGB that actually had sent copies to the West." [5]

At Solzhenitsyn's September 22 confrontation with the board of the Writers' Union, a number of those attending had taxed him with being "anti-Soviet," [6] because of the play: "Baruzdin: Even though Solzhenitsyn protests against the discussion of *Feast of the Conquerors*, we shall have to discuss this play whether he wants to or not." "Kozhevnikov: . . . I have heard Solzhenitsyn renounce the libelous description of Soviet reality in *Feast of the Conquerors*, but I still cannot get over my first impression of this play." "Surkov: I, too, have read *Feast of the Conquerors*. The mood of it is, 'Be damned, the whole lot of you!' " [7] The comments infuriated Solzhenitsyn, who replied, "The play bears the stamp of the desperation of the concentration camp in those years when a man's whole conscious being was determined by his social being, and at a time when the conscious being was by no means uplifted by prayers for those who were being persecuted." Try as he would to rule out consideration of the play in the discussion of whether *Cancer Ward* should be published—the ostensible purpose of the meeting—"Feast of the Conquerors" remained in the back of many minds—very likely the KGB's purpose in distributing its "limited edition" of the play.

A day after Tvardovsky's letter to Fedin was written, the novelist and short-story writer Grigory Svirsky addressed the Party *aktiv* of Moscow writers on January 16, 1968, declared that Russian writers were being crushed by the "militant primitivism" of the Glavlit censorship. "The opinion of the writers' collective today means nothing," Svirsky said. "Metaphorically speaking, the Writers' Union has been engulfed. . . . Above the floodwaters of censorship only the spires emerge." Although the figure of speech might not have been either accurate or appropriate, because what arose above the floodwaters of censorship was surely not *literary* spires, Svirsky rebuked officials for failing to publish many Russian writers, Solzhenitsyn in particular, and noted, "One of the Moscow literary reviews was forbidden to mention Solzhenitsyn's name, even in an article devoted to Soviet literature abroad." Svirsky also attacked the officially inspired slanders against such writers as Solzhenitsyn, Pasternak, Voznesensky, Yevtushenko, Evgenia Ginzburg, and Bulat Okhudzhava, declaring that regime spokesmen were lying when they said "that these writers were not patriots, that they were encouraging reactionary elements." Though his call for literary freedom was "within the Party of which we are the flesh and blood; the Party's interests are our interests," [8] Svirsky was summarily expelled from the Communist Party.

Ten days after Tvardovsky's letter to Fedin, the novelist Veniamin Kaverin also wrote to Fedin, and it is hard to imagine a more painful letter to write or to receive. Kaverin began by reminding Fedin that they had known each other for almost half a century, forty-eight years, that they were friends from childhood, and consequently "have the right as friends to judge one another. It is more than a right, it is a duty." Kaverin rebuked Fedin for having been transformed into a literary bureaucrat far removed from genuine art by the exigencies imposed on a literary bureaucrat, and then condemned him for being cowardly and vicious "in the pointless and tragic history of Pasternak's novel, which did so much damage to our country [so] that you were compelled to make believe that you didn't know of the death of the poet who had been your friend and lived next door to you for 23 years. Maybe the crowd of thousands that accompanied him, that carried him on outstretched arms past your house, could not be seen from your window." Kaverin remarked that Fedin's actions had been absorbed in writers' circles: "Not without reason, on [Konstantin] Paustovsky's 75th birthday, [mention of] your name was greeted with utter silence. Since Solzhenitsyn's *Cancer Ward* has been banned . . . it would not surprise me if when you next appeared publicly . . . you were greeted with catcalls and footstamping." [9]

Kaverin pleaded with Fedin to do what he could to have *Cancer Ward* published so that the logjam of good Russian writing could be released so that the genuine and original works of art which for years have lain in desk drawers because of censorship and prohibition would at last see the light of day. In a *cri de coeur*, Kaverin exclaimed, "Don't you realize that our extraordinary historical experience calls for its own embodiment [in literature] and that you are joining forces with those who, for the sake of their own well-being, are striving to halt this inevitable process?" Warning Fedin that punishing Solzhenitsyn would only provide the novelist with "worldwide notoriety that our opponents will use for political ends," Kaverin concluded darkly, "A writer who puts a noose around another writer's neck is one whose place in the history of literature will be determined not by what he himself may have written, but by what was written by his victim." [10]

In the March 27 *Literaturnaya gazeta*, Chakovsky wrote the first published reply to the many unpublished letters which circulated in the Soviet Union protesting the fates of the trial victims and their defenders and partisans. Chakovsky "affected to be personally in disagreement with the policy of sentencing young rebels to forced labor and suggested, in what was clearly a rhetorical flourish, that they be sent abroad to join the writer [Valeriy] Tarsis and thus be maintained at the expense of the foreign taxpayer instead of 'being fed . . . at public expense in [Soviet] prisons or corrective labor colonies.' "

The comment was not permitted to pass uncontested. The very next day, March 28, Anatoly Marchenko, a former prisoner who had himself served six years in a penal colony and been released two years earlier, wrote an open letter replying to Chakovsky.[11] It was not, of course, published in the Soviet Union, but it did circulate in *samizdat*. Marchenko gave damning evidence of what life in a Soviet penal institution was like and vehemently denied that support of prisoners was a burden to the state; instead, he asserted, the state exploited prisoners so that it profited considerably from their work.

Shortly thereafter, Pavel Litvinov's "White Book" of trial transcripts was completed, and *samizdat* copies were circulated. One of those copies eventually made its way to the West to be published there; [12] soon Litvinov would pay the price for that publication.

Three weeks after Marchenko's letter, on April 18, 1968, Solzhenitsyn addressed another and remarkable letter to the Writers' Union and sent copies to various members of the Union as well as to *Novy mir* and *Literaturnaya gazeta*. In it Solzhenitsyn reported that he had been called to the editorial offices of *Novy mir* and shown a cable sent by the NTS editors of *Grani* to Tvardovsky: "This is to inform you that the Committee of State Security, acting through Victor Louis, has sent one more copy of *Cancer Ward* to the West, in order thus to block its publication in *Novy mir*. Accordingly we have decided to publish this work immediately." Solzhenitsyn was outraged by the prospect of the novel's appearing in *Grani* and even more enraged by the actions of Victor Louis. "Who is Victor Louis," Solzhenitsyn asked in his letter, "what kind of person is he, of what country is he a citizen? Did he really take a copy of *Cancer Ward* out of the Soviet Union, to whom did he give it, and where else are they threatening to publish it? Furthermore, what does the Committee of State Security (KGB) have to do with this?" Solzhenitsyn urged the Secretariat and the Union as a whole to investigate the circumstances of the telegram and of the impending publication of his novel—and asked them to help thwart that publication. Once again he reminded them of "the terrible and dark avenues by which the manuscripts of Soviet writers can reach the West. It constitutes an extreme reminder to us that literature must not be brought to such a state that literary works become a profitable commodity for any scoundrel who happens to have a travel visa. The works of our authors must be printed in their own country and must not become the plunder of foreign publishing houses." [13]

Three days later, on April 21, Solzhenitsyn followed up with a second letter, sent to *Literaturnaya gazeta*, remarking that he had learned that Western publishers were issuing extracts from *Cancer Ward*, and that two such publishers, Mondadori in Italy and the Bodley Head press in Britain were "already fighting over the copyright . . . since the U.S.S.R. does not participate in the Universal Copyright Convention—despite the fact that the author is still living!" [14] Solzhenitsyn insisted that he had given no one permission to submit his manuscript abroad, nor had he given anyone the right to publish it; and certainly he had transferred the copyright for the novel to no one. Solzhenitsyn pointed out that distortion of his text was almost inevitable because of "uncontrolled duplication and circulation of the manuscript"—*samizdat* copies were bound to contain errors and perhaps even deliberate changes, not to speak of what provocative changes might be made by the KGB for its own purposes. Haste in publication would also likely result in poor translation, which he had already experienced in the foreign-language versions of *One Day in the Life of Ivan Denisovich*. Finally, Solzhenitsyn threatened legal action against anyone who distorted his work or made dramatic or film adaptations of it without his express authorization.

It was not until almost three months later that the regime permitted Solzhenitsyn's letter to be made public, and then only as a part of an attack on the novelist:

I have learned from a report in the April 13 *Le Monde* that excerpts and parts of my novel *Cancer Ward* are being published in various places in the West and that a dispute has already arisen between the Mondadori publishing house (Italy) and Bodley Head (Britain) over the copyright to the novel (since the U.S.S.R. is not a party to the international convention on author's rights)—and this while the author is alive!

I declare that none of the foreign publishers obtained the manuscript of this novel, nor the authorization to publish it, from me. Therefore I do not recognize as legal anyone's present or future publication (without my permission), nor do I recognize anyone's publishing rights, and I shall prosecute any distortion of the text (inevitable, given the uncontrolled reproduction and distribution of the manuscript), as well as any willful filming or staging of it.

I have already seen how all the translations of *Ivan Denisovich* were spoiled because of haste. Evidently this fate also awaits *Cancer Ward*. But, over and above money, there is also literature.[15]

Political-police interference in literary and intellectual matters is an old Russian tradition, but the role of Victor Louis, to which Solzhenitsyn called attention, was curious and ambiguous. Solzhenitsyn had good cause to ask who he was; many had. The *New York Times* Soviet analyst and former Moscow correspondent Harrison Salisbury called Victor Louis "the most mysterious man in

Moscow." A Soviet citizen and Moscow correspondent for the *London Evening News*, Louis had been involved in shepherding Valeriy Tarsis around Great Britain and in selling the memoirs of Stalin's daughter in the West to head off publication of Mrs. Alliluyeva's own text. Such actions "suggested to many that he is really the agent for very sophisticated Soviet secret police maneuvers." [16] Anatole Shub, the Moscow correspondent for the *Washington Post* before the Soviet government expelled him, remarked that Louis was, with the Soviet news agency Novosti, the prime source of "official" tips and leaks to foreign newsmen in the Soviet capital. Shub also remarked that Louis was a "Soviet citizen who does not bother to conceal his affiliations. Nominally a correspondent of the London *Evening News*, he is also on the hard-currency payroll of perhaps half a dozen other Western bureaus in Moscow, who chalk him up as 'special research studies.' " [17]

The following year Victor Louis was again to intrude himself into Solzhenitsyn's life. From that intrusion came one of the most skillfully vicious journalistic interviews and cleverest pieces of Soviet apologetics I have ever seen. Though Louis's tone in the published interview is a combination of unction, sarcasm, contempt, and malevolence, it must be read to be appreciated. Louis carefully forwards the regime's explanation that Solzhenitsyn is not quite normal—"obsessed" is the term of choice—that Russians "love a martyr and Solzhenitsyn does not reject the role," and that Solzhenitsyn is really quite well off, living comfortably, even off the fat of the land. The article opens with a description of the novelist in the bucolic setting of a small wooden dacha covered with Russian vines and with a green Moskvich car in the garage. If that's the way he lives, the reader is impelled to ask, how badly can the government be treating Solzhenitsyn? He's really rather well off. Louis then notes that Solzhenitsyn's manuscripts are "as tempting as forbidden fruit . . . copied out again and again in geometrical progress," but that people "who would normally never bother to read a 'medical' novel like *Cancer Ward* read night and day when they are lent a manuscript for 48 hours, hurrying to finish it in time and pass it on to somebody else. Solzhenitsyn knows this very well." [18]

Louis is cleverly implying that people read *Cancer Ward* not for its merits, or because it is Solzhenitsyn's work, but because it is something clandestine, although he ignores what meaning that reason has politically and what it reveals of the people's attitude toward censorship and thought control. Moreover, the book is a "medical" novel, ergo a soap opera, not a serious novel, so why should one bother to read it? Also, Solzhenitsyn himself knows that the book is not really very good or very serious, but is simply exploiting the surreptitiousness of *samizdat* to acquire an otherwise undeserved audience. Louis then continues:

He knows a lot more, too. Like any Soviet citizen who has spent time in a labor camp, he is his own lawyer. If he writes letters, he knows that they will eventually find their way into Western newspapers, but he addresses them to other members of the Writers' Union so that someone out of the hundreds of writer-members will send the letter to its destination.

From a legal point of view, no one can accuse Solzhenitsyn of anything. If, like Tolstoy, he disagrees with the regime, he will not say so openly.

It is hard to accuse him of sending his novels abroad, but he is not at all surprised that they get there. . . .

Solzhenitsyn protested the publication of his manuscripts abroad. This he did with admirable indignation, proclaiming that he would prosecute the publishers.

I do not know whether he did so in the sincere belief that as soon as his protest reached one of the publishers, he would immediately call a halt to the printing; whether he did it out of naïveté or as a calculated protest. Solzhenitsyn knows that Pasternak also protested in vain, and, on the other hand, it is the natural desire of any writer to be published.

In any case, Solzhenitsyn could not be accused, as were Sinyavsky or Daniel, of sending his manuscripts abroad.[19]

By implication, Louis makes Solzhenitsyn seem shifty and shrewd in his literary machinations, and also hypocritical and cowardly: he won't, as did Tolstoy, stand up and be counted for his convictions. Instead, he professes to be innocent both of anti-Soviet sentiments and of forwarding his work abroad for publication, though he is in fact committed to both.

Louis's apologetics for the regime are just as clever. The war and Stalin visited every Soviet family with death and bereavement, he writes, and the "horrors of Beria's concentration camps are, of course, no credit to the state, and most people would prefer to forget the unforgettable." The rhetoric of the last phrase is intended to distract the reader from asking, "Well, if that is the case, why not publish the books? No one will buy them." But Louis cannot let matters rest there. He continues:

"After all," one writer pointed out to me, "in Western Germany nobody encourages novels about the horrors of the Nazi concentration camps, nor in the United States about murdering national leaders." These things are a national shame and people would like to close the dark pages of history.

So why in the Soviet Union, where printing is in state hands, should this type of literature be stimulated, printed, distributed? Why should magazines put salt on open wounds?

Nevertheless, the time Solzhenitsyn spent in camp and in exile shocked him so deeply that he has become singularly obsessed with the subject in his work. Probably this is one of the reasons why, for the time being, his works do not appear in Russian magazines.[20]

Aside from his falsity in suggesting that there has been a dearth of books on the Nazi camps and the Kennedy assassination, and the subtle implication that the West German and American governments are in a position to "encourage" such books, Louis's main effect is to create a lie which will free the present Soviet leadership from any responsibility for the camps. It was all Beria's fault, or Stalin's, and in the remote past anyway; what impels the present leaders not to "put salt on open wounds" is kindness and concern for their people, not any fear of their own complicity being exposed. For equally impersonal and compassionate feelings, the Soviet leaders do not permit Solzhenitsyn to be printed in his own country, not because of censorship but because the novelist is obsessed with such unpleasant themes.

(How important Victor Louis's political connections are can be inferred from the role he played later that year, in September 1969. The top levels of the Soviet government used him to float a trial journalistic balloon about the possibility of a Soviet pre-emptive rocket attack on the Chinese Communist nuclear center at Lop Nor. In a dispatch to the *London Evening News*, Louis wrote that under the "Brezhnev doctrine" which gives the Soviet Union the right to intervene in the internal affairs of other "socialist countries," and which had been used to justify the 1968 Soviet invasion of Czecho-slovakia, the USSR might also attack China. Louis, who had only the week before been the first to report the Russian Premier Aleksey Kosygin's visit to Peking and airport conference with Chinese Premier Chou En-lai, now declared that well-informed sources in Moscow had told him that Soviet nuclear rockets were targeted on the Chinese atomic installations at Lop Nor and that if anti-Mao forces in China produced "a leader who would ask other socialist countries for 'fraternal help,' " [21] the Soviet Union might provide it. Louis's dispatch was an echo of a letter the Kremlin had circu-lated among East European Communist governments and foreign Communist parties earlier in September to canvass "fraternal" atti-tudes toward a surprise strike against Chinese atomic facilities.)

With or without the KGB or Victor Louis's connivance, events in the West now moved swiftly. Excerpts from *Cancer Ward* had appeared in the *London Times Literary Supplement* on April 11, and announcements of the forthcoming publication of the full-length book were made by the Bodley Head publishers in Britain, Monda-dori in Italy, Frederick A. Praeger in the United States, and the NTS's Possev in West Germany. Possev was going to publish the entire novel in Russian although it "had previously refrained . . . because it still hoped that *Novy Mir* might print it." [22]

In May, a few weeks later, Solzhenitsyn sent still a third letter, this time an open letter, to the entire Writers' Union membership, calling to their attention the fact that an entire year had passed since he had addressed his letter to the Writers' Congress, but still his questions remained unanswered. He had since written to the Secretariat and had appeared before it three times in person, but nothing had been accomplished: his works remained unpublished; mention of his name was still interdicted; the slanders against him were still offi-cially promulgated and circulated. He had warned of the danger of publication of his works in the West, and now the Secretariat was faced with the reality of impending Western publication. "What has happened," he wrote in the letter, "compels me to acquaint our literary community with the contents of the attached letters and statements so that the position and responsibility of the Secretariat of the Union of Writers in the USSR will be clear." [23] With this letter Solzhenitsyn also enclosed a copy of his September 12, 1967, letter to the forty-two secretaries of the Writers' Union; his own admittedly incomplete but accurate transcript of his September 22, 1967, session with the Union Secretariat; Voronkov's letter to him of November 25, 1967, inquiring if he had yet reconsidered "clarifying his position on the anti-Soviet campaign surrounding his name"; and last, his own letter of reply dated December 1, 1967.

In 1967, three purge and concentration-camp books had been smuggled to the West via the *samizdat* network: Galina Serebryakova's *Sandstorm*, Lydia Chukovskaya's *The Deserted House*, and Evgenia Ginzburg's *Journey into the Whirlwind*. The last two had ostensibly been published without the connivance of the authors, and presumably therefore neither was—at least openly—punished. Vasily Aksyonov, Evgenia Ginzburg's novelist son, had verified that his mother's book was smuggled abroad in a *samizdat* copy: "Somebody got hold of a copy, took it abroad and sold it for huge sums of money to an Italian publisher. My mother knew nothing about it and was very angry." [24]

The *samizdat* network, the smuggling of manuscripts abroad, and their publication in the West have played an important role in the KGB surveillance of dissidents, although what the KGB's purposes and role in these activities are is difficult to assess. Probably the KGB, for its own quite cogent reasons permits the *samizdat* network to function: to provide a safety valve for some of the intelligentsia's discontents; to have a way of gauging the temper of the dissidents and their ideas; to keep dissidents sufficiently "in the open" so that they can be identified and watched; to have a means at hand through which dissidents can be compromised or provocations created which would involve one or more of them whenever the KGB considered the time propitious. Given the general Russian attitude that "the friend of my enemy is my enemy"—a viewpoint not confined only to the KGB or to the government—there are obvious advantages to the secret police and the ruling circles of the regime in being able to arrange for a *samizdat* manuscript to be published abroad by "nefarious" and "bourgeois" and "émigré" publications. The KGB can thereby plant the material it wishes to have publicized abroad; it can also blacken the reputation and patriotism of those whose manuscripts are so delivered to foreign publishers by reporting the fact to the people back home; it also then has evidence that can be used in cases tried under Articles 70, 190/1 and 190/3 so that the KGB can imprison writers— as it did Sinyavsky and Daniel, or Ginzburg and Galanskov—or send them to psychiatric hospitals—as it did with Yesenin-Volpin or Tarsis. Anatoly Kuznetsov, after defecting to the West, maintained that the KGB deliberately permits the continuing existence of the *samizdat* network and even encourages it—for some of the reasons given above; Kuznetsov insisted that the entire network of publication and distribution could be shut down in forty-eight hours because the secret police know all the individuals and methods involved. On precisely that point, Andrei Amalrik took issue with Kuznetsov:

The KGB would scarcely be able, as you put it, to destroy the *"samizdat"* in two days and play a cat-and-mouse game with it. Perhaps the KGB could arrest dozens of *"samizdat"* distributors in a matter of two hours—and the fact that the KGB does not do this proves, it seems to me, not its playfulness (although a game is being played) but the uncertainty in which the KGB and the regime as a whole find themselves. Apart from this, *"samizdat"* is distributed not among individuals but among thousands.[25]

Albert Parry, in an informed summary of the problems posed by underground publications in the Soviet Union, would seem to agree with Amalrik rather than Kuznetsov and does not believe that the KGB would find destroying the *samizdat* network quite so simple as Kuznetsov believes.[26] Moreover, there are rumors that many younger KGB officials—although what "many" means is subject to the most critical scrutiny and should be—are in sympathy with much of what the *samizdat* network wishes to accomplish, and that is the real reason why the network has not been shut down and those who run it not arrested.

Part III POLITICAL DISSIDENCE

19 The Invasion of Czechoslovakia

> What happened to your nation was not the work of Stalin
> alone. And his accomplices not only are still alive but hold
> responsible positions. They are afraid that, if you are given
> back what was unlawfully taken from you, they may, in time,
> be called upon to answer for their participation in such arbi-
> trary rule.
>
> *Pyotr Grigorenko*

Throughout the winter and spring of 1968 protest began to take
on more radical and explicitly political forms, and anti-Stalinist and
revisionist agitation spread both in the Soviet Union and in the Communist East European countries. Such agitation was particularly rife
in Czechoslovakia, where Solzhenitsyn's letter to the Soviet Writers'
Congress urging an end to censorship had been read to the assembled Czechoslovak Writers' Congress to great acclaim.[1] Soviet ruling circles were increasingly alarmed because they saw the growing
wave of dissent threatening to erode, perhaps even to engulf, the
institutions over which they wielded power. Though there seems to
be no mass disaffection in the Soviet Union, there surely is mass
resistance both to Communism and to the Russians in the countries
of Eastern Europe—and perhaps considerable resistance to both in
some of the Soviet "minority" republics as well. The Kremlin understands and fears the influence of liberalism and revisionism on the
young, the scientists, the technical intelligentsia, and others on whom
it must rely to maintain a complicated industrial society. Nor have
the lessons of Russian history been lost on the Kremlin's rulers;
though the atomic bomb, the rocket missile, and the computer have
changed the nature of warfare and insurrection, they have not forgotten that the Bolsheviks seized Russia from the provisional government with only a few hundred thousand partisans.

The Soviet rulers consequently increased the ferocity of their repression of dissidents, publicly enunciating a new policy at the

235

April Plenum of the Central Committee. The plenary sessions, which took place on April 19 and 20, 1968, "reflected apprehension over unrest in Poland, political reform in Czechoslovakia, and dissidence among Soviet intellectuals." The keynote speech to the Plenum was given by Brezhnev himself, who warned that foreign propagandists were striving "to weaken the unity of the socialist camp and the international Communist movement and simultaneously trying to undermine socialist society from within." [2] The Central Committee forthwith adopted a resolution calling on all Party organizations to "wage an offensive struggle against bourgeois ideology, to stand up actively against attempts to drag views alien to the socialist ideology of Soviet society into individual works of literature, art, etc." [3] Brezhnev declared that foreign enemies ferret out "morally unstable, weak and politically immature people. Sometimes their nets catch people susceptible to self-advertisement, ready to project themselves as loudly as possible not through labor for the benefit of their country, but through any politically dubious means they find at at their disposal and without scorning the praise of our ideological enemies. The Soviet public sharply condemns the disgraceful actions of these deceitful people. Such renegades *cannot expect to go unpunished*." Brezhnev cautioned that the ideological struggle was now the sharpest area of struggle, the front on which no political indifference, passivity, or neutrality would be tolerated: "Our Party has always warned that in the field of ideology there can be no peaceful coexistence." [4]

Perhaps most important of all, the Central Committee officially declared that the "consequences of the personality cult" were now eliminated, and asked for more stringent discipline in resisting the "renewed offensive of bourgeois ideology." If the consequences of Stalinism were officially liquidated, then presumably the heirs of Stalin could continue to repose in their seats of power without trepidation.

What had led to that declaration was evident. In March, ninety-five leading mathematicians had protested vigorously the incarceration of Yesenin-Volpin in a mental institution for the role he had played in challenging the legality of the Sinyavsky-Daniel trial and for actively protesting the Galanskov-Ginzburg trial. In a letter to the Minister of Health, the Procurator General, and the Chief Psychiatrist of Moscow, the mathematicians denounced Volpin's forcible confinement, but when the letter was published by the *New York Times*, fifteen of them withdrew their names from the protest.

In April, just before the Plenum of the Central Committee, a group of Crimean Tatars gathered in the city of Chirchik to celebrate the ninety-fifth anniversary of Lenin's birth on the twenty-first. They were forcibly dispersed by troops and militia, and three hundred of them were arrested. In May, eight hundred Tatars went to Moscow to present the Central Committee with a letter demanding that Tatars be permitted to return to their traditional prewar Crimean homeland.[5] Two months earlier, on the evening of March 17, General Pyotr Grigorenko had addressed a seventy-second birthday celebration for Aleksey Kosterin, a writer who had spent three years in a Czarist prison and seventeen years in a Stalinist concentration camp for having defended the freedom and rights of minority nationalities in the Soviet Union. He told the assembled Tatars not to request but to demand their rights, and not to limit their activities to writing petitions but to use "all the means available to you under the constitution—make good use of the freedom of speech and of the press, of meetings, street processions and demonstrations." Grigorenko also advised them to take over the Tatar newspaper in Tashkent which was run by regime lackeys unsympathetic to the Tatar cause and to replace them with their own partisans—or else simply to start a newspaper of their own. But Grigorenko warned that they were not "dealing only with honest people."

What happened to your nation was not the work of Stalin alone. And his accomplices not only are still alive but hold responsible positions. They are afraid that, if you are given back what was unlawfully taken from you, they may, in time, be called upon to answer for their participation in such arbitrary rule. Therefore, they are doing everything possible to prevent you from succeeding in your struggle. After all, if everything is kept as it is, then it gives the impression that there was no lawlessness in the past.[6]

This was an open call to use the legal instrumentalities presumably guaranteed by the Soviet state and constitution to resist the heirs of Stalin, to expose them and to punish them for the crimes of the past

—in this case a cruel and illegal mass deportation of an entire people. It was the kind of political attack that went far beyond merely literary demands for freedom from "socialist realism." It threatened the central bastions of the leadership's power as well as many of the top leaders personally. It was against just such threats that the April Plenum of the Central Committee was taking action. The Soviet authorities recognized that Grigorenko's advice to the Tatars about the responsibilities of the heirs of Stalin and what ought to be done to and about them could also be understood to apply to all the Russian people, to the other minority nationalities in the Soviet Union, and to East European countries. That such feelings could not be hidden was shortly confirmed when, on June 21, the Tatars, in an open letter, appealed to worldwide public opinion to help them eliminate this "genocide" against their people.

In May, also, a group of 126 Ukrainian scientists, scholars, and other intellectuals protested to Brezhnev, Kosygin, and Podgorny in a document which denounced the regime trial and imprisonment of twenty Ukrainian intellectuals in 1965 and 1966. Those who signed the document called for free and open discussion of ideas and for an end to police persecution and repression. Almost immediately they were met by a Party demand to investigate those who had put their signatures on the document, because they "had provided material for hostile propaganda." [7]

The raucous note of repression sounded by Brezhnev at the April Plenum was shortly echoed—in almost the same words—by various dogmatists in the field of literature. On May 1, *Literaturnaya rossiya* announced that a few days after the Plenum, on April 17, the Secretariat of the board of the Moscow branch of the Writers' Union had considered the question of those writers who had signed petitions in favor of Ginzburg, Galanskov, and other convicted protesters, and had decided that many writers had played an "unsavory role" in doing so, had displayed "inadmissible political dereliction and lack of principle, and lent their names to arm our ideological enemies. The antisocial actions of these writers were aggravated by the fact that their letters appeared in various bourgeois newspapers and foreign radio broadcasts to the USSR." [8] The article went on to say that the direct organizers of those letters were traitors, since the letters had been used to discredit the Soviet way of life and to provoke "certain unstable and politically immature representatives of the Soviet intelligentsia to some sort of anti-Soviet action." Authors who had signed such letters had violated a Writers' Union regulation which required its members "to wage an ideological struggle against bourgeois and revisionist influences," *Literaturnaya rossiya* reminded them. "Anyone who does not fully understand his responsibility to the people in a period of uncompromising conflict between the two ideologies of socialism and capitalism cannot call himself a Soviet writer." [9]

A week later, *Literaturnaya gazeta* reported that an enlarged meeting of the board of the USSR Writers' Union had recently been held—no specific date was given, but probably it was before the Moscow branch's meeting—and in line with the April Plenum of the Central Committee had decided to organize a militant program for mobilizing writers and all the Soviet people to "struggle indefatigably for the purity of Marxism-Leninism and to combat the attempts of hostile propaganda to exert its pernicious influence on unstable and politically immature people." It accused those writers who had signed appeals of defending "renegades justly punished by a Soviet court" and of being politically irresponsible, and warned them that those letters made their way abroad to be used by foreign propagandists to discredit the Soviet system; the propaganda aroused the indignation not only of the entire writers' community but of all the people.[10]

Three days later, *Pravda* carried an article by Sergey Mikhalkov, First Secretary of the Moscow branch of the Writers' Union and also Secretary of the Board of the Soviet Writers' Union, which defended the quality of Soviet literature against foreign charges that it was bankrupt. Mikhalkov explained that the "enemy abroad" had now decided to take the Soviet Union "from the rear. Hesitating at military aggression, which obviously could bring him only crushing defeat, he is concentrating his efforts on ideological aggression." Foreign propagandists were accused of shamelessly bestowing the august title of Soviet writer on "people who have no connection with any literary genre . . . but only with certain articles of the Criminal Code." Mikhalkov berated those who had organized the protest letters in defense of Ginzburg and Galanskov for having taken "advantage of the severe illness and softheartedness of some prominent writer, in other cases [for taking] advantage of ignorance of facts, in still other cases of lack of political understanding or a vague concept of 'humanism in general.' " [11] These "initiators" of the action, Mikhalkov asserted, were only trying to compensate for their lack of artistic talent by creating a political scandal.

Ironically, it was the day after the April Plenum that the *London Times Literary Supplement* published excerpts from Solzhenitsyn's *Cancer Ward*.[12] The following week the Soviet Supreme Court turned down the Ginzburg-Galanskov appeal. On April 18, Solzhenitsyn had sent his letter concerning Victor Louis to the board of the Writers' Union, and on April 21, his letter to *Literaturnaya gazeta* protesting against publication of his novels in the West. Now, at the end of June, *Literaturnaya gazeta* printed an editorial which made clear the implications the Soviet authorities perceived in Solzhenitsyn's work, person, and influence. The Writers' Union weekly noted that "the strength of Soviet writers lies in wholehearted dedication to the ideas of Communism and boundless loyalty to the cause of the Party. This is why the tie between Soviet literature and Communist Party politics evokes such fierce attacks by hostile propaganda." Then the editorial reaffirmed that Soviet writers consistently defend the fundamentals of "socialist realism" and rebuked foreign enemies for trying "to pit the Soviet people against the Party, to sow dissension among the intelligentsia, to divide it into 'right' and 'left,' 'progressives' and 'dogmatists,' to oppose some writers to others." After attacking Valeriy Tarsis as a "graphomaniac and schizophrenic," and Svetlana Alliluyeva as a "homunculus in a flask," it condemned Ginzburg and Galanskov and those who had signed letters and petitions in their behalf, explaining:

Writers who cherish their good name and the honor of their homeland, writers deeply convinced that their work cannot be divorced from the interests of the people and the Party and from the ideas of socialist society—when such writers become involuntary targets of hostile propaganda, they deal fitting rebuffs to their unbidden foreign champions. A whole series of examples can be cited. A few years ago, for instance, our ideological foes failed in an attempt to turn Anatoly Kuznetsov's novel against Soviet rule. This novel, *Continuation of a*

Legend, recounted the story of a young man who, on finishing school, went to work at a construction project and developed spiritually on the job. Employees of a French publishing house took paste, scissors and a dishonest editorial pen, changed the title, printed a spider's web of barbed wire on the cover, and tried to give readers the impression that the action of the book took place not at a construction project but in a concentration camp. Kuznetsov issued a press statement publicly slapping the swindlers' cheeks and instituted legal proceedings against them. The upshot of the trial was that even a bourgeois court was obliged to punish the falsifiers.[13]

The Kuznetsov example was one the Soviet authorities were soon to regret, for when Kuznetsov defected in Great Britain, he was to tell the story in quite a different fashion.[14] Nonetheless, the editorial made the essential point that the Party was aware that literary factions might become political factions, that opposition to the Party policy in letters could easily overflow and become opposition to Party policy as a whole.

The *Literaturnaya gazeta* editorial then turned to Solzhenitsyn, berating him for "attacking the principles that guide Soviet literature," for "violating general norms of behavior" by circulating his letter to the Writers' Congress, for behaving "demagogically" at Union meetings, and for "tendentiously" reporting such meetings in letters sent abroad. It admonished him for having expressed "feigned alarm over the forthcoming publication of *Cancer Ward*" in the West, but its major charge was that the novelist refused to disavow the "enemy provocateurs of our country." [15]

(In passing, *Literaturnaya gazeta* condemned Veniamin Kaverin's letter, which, it said, gave "a perverted interpretation of many events in our literary life in recent years [and] distorted the attitude of some secretariat members toward publication of *Cancer Ward* in the same spirit as characterized the transcript by A. Solzhenitsyn distributed in the West." It then blamed Kaverin for *not* deeming it necessary "to speak out against this hostile 'chorus' " of foreign broadcasts.) [16]

Chakovsky's paper reviled Solzhenitsyn's novels, calling *The First Circle* a "malicious libel" of the Soviet system, *Cancer Ward* "seriously marred ideologically," and "Feast of the Conquerors," the play Solzhenitsyn had repeatedly disavowed, a work in which Solzhenitsyn "presents the Soviet Army that had freed the world from the fascist plague as a horde of blockheads, rapists, marauders and vandals." [17]

The editorial seemed to hint that the novelist might soon be deliberately connected with an "international plot." Ostensibly in reply to Solzhenitsyn's charge that the KGB had confiscated his manuscripts and files, the paper reported that the Soviet Prosecutor's Office had declared that the security services had *not* searched the novelist's Ryazan flat. Instead, "typewritten copies of certain of Solzhenitsyn's manuscripts, without his name, were found in a search of [the apartment of] a certain Citizen Teush in Moscow and were seized, along with other compromising materials; when a customs inspection of a foreign tourist brought to light the slanderous manuscript fabrications about the life of the Soviet land, the course of the investigation instituted by the appropriate agencies led to Teush." Teush was not further identified, but it was stated that Solzhenitsyn had "entrusted the safekeeping of his works to a supplier of anti-Sovietism to the foreign world [and] thereby lost all control over them." [18] It appeared that the KGB was preparing the same kind of case against Solzhenitsyn it had organized against Sinyavsky and Daniel, so that it could bring him to trial and imprison him. Moreover, the explanation offered by Chakovsky's magazine made it seem that the KGB had not arbitrarily invaded Solzhenitsyn's flat and privacy to take his papers, but had instead simply been carrying out the law when a customs inspector discovered someone smuggling manuscripts out of the country. Even then it was not the KGB, presumably, but "appropriate agencies" which had investigated and discovered Teush. It was all very skillful, right down to the manuscripts without Solzhenitsyn's name on them— clandestine productions of a fearful author—and to the nameless "foreign tourist."

Solzhenitsyn's letter to the Writers' Congress had stung the authorities, and the editorial spoke angrily of his having slandered Soviet literature in declaring it to be in the grip of repression and of his having "completely crossed off all the achievements of Soviet literature that have gained worldwide recognition." They were also furious about Solzhenitsyn's call for the Writers' Union to stop helping in the prosecution of writers and to start helping defend them instead. *Literaturnaya gazeta* countered that adding such a clause to the Union statutes "would place the Writers' Union Statutes above statewide laws ensuring equal protection to all Soviet citizens against slander and unjust persecution." [19] Obviously, the authorities were not going to relinquish direction of the very instrumentality they had created to manipulate and control the writers, nor were they about publicly to admit their failure to produce a literature of quality "commensurate with socialism" during the Party's tenure of power.

Two of the foremost dissidents immediately took issue with the *Literaturnaya gazeta* editorial. In a letter dated 27 June–4 July, Lydia Chukovskaya contested the paper's deliberately making itself an accessory of the KGB and the whole apparatus of persecution in dealing with writers and writing, instead of defending writers as it should. Chukovskaya accused the paper of cooperating with the regime in victimizing Solzhenitsyn because the novelist insisted on continuing to expose Stalin and Stalinism, the heirs of Stalin, and the persistence of Stalinist methods and institutions in Soviet life. She condemned the KGB confiscation of Solzhenitsyn's files and manuscripts, and the circulation of a private edition of his play, "Feast of the Conquerors," to a selected audience without the express permission of its author.

In a letter dated June 28, Valentin Turchin wrote directly to *Literaturnaya gazeta* editor in chief Aleksandr Chakovsky, reprimanding him and his paper for a campaign of slander against Solzhenitsyn. Not only had the paper disseminated unsupported charges, literary abuse, outright lies, but it had also committed the crime of slander against Solzhenitsyn that it accused the novelist of. Turchin rebuked Chakovsky for not even believing the lies he printed, but merely following regime orders in publishing materials he himself knew to be false—which is what, Turchin maintained, slander really is. Turchin also attacked the KGB circulation of "Feast of the Conquerors," remarking that Solzhenitsyn himself had never circulated the play, and that had the KGB not confiscated it from the novelist's private files and circulated it in an edition of its own, no one would ever have read it or heard of it. Because Chakovsky was a man skilled in double-speak—"like any Soviet editor"—Turchin charged, he would henceforth refuse to buy *Literaturnaya gazeta,* or to cooperate with it in any way so long as Chakovsky remained its editor.

Two months later, on August 21, 1968, Soviet armies and their East European satellite allies invaded Czechoslovakia and in so doing demonstrated how serious the Kremlin considered the threats of liberalization, revisionism, and reform. Czechoslovak liberalization had been sparked by intellectuals and writers, another example of how a determined minority could help to change the political, economic, and social shape of a nation. It reminded the Soviet leaders of the role Hungarian intellectuals and artists had played in the 1956 revolt in Hungary, and of the efforts of the Polish intelligentsia in the October days of 1956. Only a month before the invasion, in an open letter to three Czechoslovak newspapers and copies to French and British Communist newspapers, as well as the British Broadcasting System, Anatoly Marchenko, author of *My Testimony,* denounced the Kremlin's manipulation of press and public "reactions" to the Czechoslovak reforms. Marchenko stated boldly that he was conscience-stricken because his country was "once more taking on the shameful role of policeman of Europe," and he denied that the Soviet government did in fact speak for the Soviet masses or reflect their attitude toward the Czechoslovak events. Marchenko indicted the whole mechanism of rule and propaganda in the relations between the Soviet people and its leaders, remarking:

For half a year our newspapers have attempted to misinform public opinion in our own country, and, at the same time, to misinform foreign public opinion about our people's attitude toward these events. The newspapers represent the Party leadership's position as the position—even the unanimous position—of all the people. All Brezhnev had to do was pin the labels of "imperialist intrigue!" "menace to socialism," "offensive by anti-socialist elements," etc. on the present events in Czechoslovakia, and in a flash all the press and all the resolutions began a chorus of these phrases, though today as half a year ago, our people basically do not know the real state of affairs in Czechoslovakia. Workers' letters to the papers and resolutions from mass meetings are simply repetitions of the prepared formulas handed down from "above" and not expressions of independent opinion based on knowledge of the concrete facts. Servile voices repeat after the Party leadership: "Waging a determined battle to maintain the socialist order in Czechoslovakia is not only the concern of Czechoslovak Communists, it is our common concern as well." [20]

Marchenko saw that a Soviet invasion was imminent and boldly compared the political pressures the Soviet Union was exerting against the Czechoslovaks to American actions in the Dominican Republic—a policy the Soviet press had denounced a hundredfold as colonialism and capitalist imperialism.

Marchenko dispatched his letter on July 22. A week later he was arrested on a "suspected identity-card violation" and jailed.[21] Shortly thereafter a petition signed by Pavel Litvinov, General Pyotr Grigorenko, Larissa Daniel, I. Rudakov, and I. Belogorodskaya was sent to the Moscow prosecutor's office protesting Marchenko's arrest. At the same time a public protest addressed to the citizens of Moscow was distributed, signed by Litvinov, Mrs. Daniel, Ludmila Alekseyeva, and Viktor Krasin, singling out that portion of Marchenko's letter that was most threatening to the Kremlin:

It is easy to understand why our leaders hurry to intercede for the likes of . . . Novotny: making Party and government leaders responsible to the people is a contagious and dangerous precedent. What if suddenly our own leaders should be called upon to account for those deeds which have shamefully been termed "errors" and "excesses" or, still milder and undefined, "difficulties endured in the heroic past" (when it was a matter of millions of people unjustly condemned and murdered, of torture in KGB cellars, of whole peoples proclaimed enemies, of the breakdown of the nation's farming, and similar *trivia*)? [22]

Such political protest was singularly forceful, specifying the crimes of the heirs of Stalin in no uncertain terms and declaring that no euphemisms could or should be permitted to hide Stalinist crimes or interfere with the proper punishment of those responsible for them. It was insisting on accountability for the past and for assurances of accountability in the present and future. The protest called on the people of Moscow who wanted to help Marchenko to give his arrest publicity: "If you won't want to put up with this tyranny in the future, if you understand that Marchenko is fighting for all of us and that all of us must fight for Marchenko, we ask you to defend him in the ways that you yourselves think necessary." [23]

Immediately following the invasion, an open letter to the Czech and Slovak peoples defending Czechoslovakia was made public and signed by Grigorenko, Aleksey Kosterin, Sergey Pisarev, Ivan Ya-khimovich, and V. A. Pavlichuk. It publicly proclaimed to the Czechoslovaks that the Soviet government and the Soviet Communist Party were interfering in the internal affairs of their country, distorting the reporting of occurrences there, and the protesters declared: "A Party-government leadership which would start a war in Europe, especially a war against a friendly socialist country, would be swiftly discredited and lose the people's confidence." [24]

Regrettably, such was not, in fact, the case. A small number of the Soviet intelligentsia were publicly outraged, perhaps a larger number were privately pained, but the people at large reacted to the invasion either with total indifference or with active hostility toward the Czechoslovaks. A British student in the Soviet Union reported that a friend of his greeted the brief but not prominently placed announcement of the Soviet invasion published in *Pravda* with the remark: "Our bastards [the Soviet leaders] just couldn't let the Czechs go on like that, making something civilized out of socialism." Few such comments were made privately; "as far as the Russian people took any interest in the invasion, the great majority vaguely approved. There was no general anxiety, no shock or outrage, because most Russians felt that their country's foreign policy was in good hands, and the measures taken were certainly justified, and probably just." [25] Indifference, apathy, passivity, and open enmity were the prevailing reactions, the last frequently expressed as simple condemnation of the Czechs: "Those bastards, we freed them from the Germans, spilled our blood for their freedom—and now look: they're going behind our backs to the West Germans again." [26]

The next Sunday, August 25, the small band of brave dissidents who had already taken so many risks took one more. They organized a small demonstration on Red Square in Moscow to protest the invasion. The protesters were Pavel Litvinov, Larissa Daniel, Konstantin Babitsky, Vadim Delone, Vladimir Dremlyug, Viktor Feinberg, and Natalia Gorbanevskaya. The signs and banners they carried read: "Long live a free and independent Czechoslovakia," "Hands off Czechoslovakia," and "Shame on the Occupiers!" The seven demonstrators were almost immediately arrested. Because Gorbanevskaya was a nursing mother, she was released. Three days later she sent an open letter to many newspapers, among them the *London Times* and the *New York Times*,[27] reporting how they had been overwhelmed by the KGB plain-clothes agents on Red Square, agents who were assigned there to await the departure of the Czechoslovak delegation from the Kremlin. The KGB surrounded the seven protestors, shouting: "They're all dirty Jews!" and "Smash these anti-Soviet people!" "We sat quietly and showed no resistance," Gorbanevskaya stated. "They tore the banners from our hands and punched Viktor Feinberg's face bloody and broke some of his teeth. Pavel Litvinov's face was beaten with a heavy bag." [28] The demonstrators were then all hustled into police automobiles, in one of which Gorbanevskaya, who was carrying her three-month-old son, was also beaten.

The underground newspaper *Chronicle of Current Events* reported that there were many other protests against the invasion, including a leaflet that circulated in Moscow criticizing the Soviet occupation of Czechoslovakia.[29] The *Chronicle*'s editors, though in agreement with the substance of the protests, nonetheless counseled both bravery *and* caution:

Everyone who thinks like the heroes of August 25 must follow the promptings of his own mind and choose the proper time and form of protest. There are no general formulas. One thing only is generally understood: "sensible" silence may lead to folly—to restoration of Stalinism. Since the Sinyavsky-Daniel trial in 1966, not a single act of tyranny and coercion by the authorities has escaped public protest or censure. . . . This is a valuable precedent and the beginning of the people's self-liberation from debasing fear and participation in evil.[30]

From October 9 to 11, five defendants—Gorbanevskaya and Feinberg were excluded [31]—were tried under Articles 190/1 and 190/3, charged with systematic slander and "group activities intended to undermine public order." All five were convicted and sentenced. Their final trial statements were courageous and profoundly moving. All proclaimed their innocence, but suffered the sense of futility. Larissa Daniel declared: "I do not doubt that public opinion will support this verdict. We will be depicted as social parasites and outcasts and people of alien ideology." [32] Though Mrs. Daniel deplored the "futility" of what she had done, she explained, "If I had not done this, I would have had to consider myself responsible for the error of the government. Feeling as I do about those who kept silent in a former period, I consider myself responsible." Pavel Litvinov told how he had been followed to Red Square by KGB agents and how after he was arrested, one of them told him, "You fool, if you had kept your mouth shut, you could have lived peacefully." Litvinov glanced at, but did not probe, one of the most profound and usually unspoken dilemmas of the Soviet leadership when he calmly testified:

> The prosecutor says also that we were against the policy of the Party and government but not against the social and state system. Perhaps there are people who consider all our policies and even our political errors as the logical outcome of our state and social system. I do not think so.
>
> I do not think that the prosecutor himself would say this, for he would then have to say that all the crimes of the Stalin era resulted from our social and state system. [33]

(This fundamental criticism of Soviet life and institutions was almost everywhere avoided like the plague, by regime spokesmen and dissidents alike. Ironically, the Party line taken in dealing with this problem was almost "Trotskyist": it called Stalinism a "distortion" instead of seeing it as a direct outgrowth of the Revolution, the institutions imposed on the Soviet Union by the Bolsheviks, and the character of the Bolshevik leadership and of the Russian people.)

Gorbanevskaya, a woman in her early thirties, a philologist and poet, worked for the State Institute of Experimental Design and Technical Research as an engineer and translator. After the Red Square demonstration she was forced to resign her job, and with Viktor Feinberg, she was subsequently sent to a mental institution and declared officially insane.

Babitsky testified that he and his comrades were not enemies of Soviet rule or of "socialism," but "people whose views are to some extent different from those generally accepted, yet who love their country no less than anyone else, love their people no less than anyone else, and therefore deserve respect and tolerance." Delone most clearly stated what the demonstrators sought to accomplish: "Not only the fate of democracy in our country and the hope of preventing a Stalinist restoration is at stake at this juncture, but the freedom of another country's citizens depends on our freedom." But when Delone began, "I am a man to whom any kind of totalitarianism is deeply repugnant," the prosecutor and judge cut him off, the former with a protest, the latter with a warning. It was Dremlyug, however, who was most passionately daring, proclaiming:

Throughout my whole conscious life I wanted to be a citizen, a man who calmly and proudly speaks his mind. For ten minutes on Red Square I was a citizen. Against the background of silence which prevails and which is called the total support of the Party and government's policy, I know that my voice was a dissonance. . . . I believe that all the events described previously are caused by the absence of the right to criticize the government. To make that right legal in the future, I went to Red Square and I would go anywhere else. And in the future I shall continue to protest in every way.[34]

None of the defendants' pleas was effective. Russian armies remained in Czechoslovakia, overthrew the Dubcek government, and reorganized the Party and government to suit the Kremlin. Anatoly Marchenko was sentenced to a year in prison on the trumped-up charges of infringing passport regulations; Pavel Litvinov was exiled to a remote town in Siberia near Chita; and Larissa Daniel was exiled for four years to a village near the Siberian city of Irkutsk where she was reported to be doing hard labor in a sawmill.

Even so ardent and loyal a Soviet apologist as Alexander Werth was shocked by the Soviet invasion of Czechoslovakia—so much that he was moved to change the title of the book he was working on from *Russia at Peace* to *Russia: Hopes and Fears*, and after the invasion he also added an epigraph to the book, a quotation from a letter he had received in September 1968 from a young Russian friend who had written, "Since Prague, our last year's timid hopes of a liberalization of Russia have gone up in smoke, perhaps for a very long time, while our fears of a return to some fiendish kind of Stalinism have grown immeasurably." [35] Werth himself dated the Soviet leadership's decision to "intervene" in Czechoslovakia from early 1968, when Dubcek abolished Czechoslovak censorship, "thus fulfilling that 'incredible' demand Alexander Solzhenitsyn had made, in the case of the Soviet Union, in his famous letter to the Writers' Congress in May 1967. To the Kremlin bureaucrats and those of the Moscow Writers' Union, Dubcek was simply the international equivalent of Solzhenitsyn." By August, the Kremlin "was willing to pay any price for reimposing censorship and for abolishing all freedom of thought in Czechoslovakia, since the Dubcek virus, if not killed, would have spread to the whole of Eastern Europe, and even to Moscow itself." [36]

When the invasion was over, the Soviet leadership, through various Writers' Union officials and other bureaucrats, tried to persuade the intellectuals to put their signatures on a public statement which approved the Soviet invasion, but with the exception of Sholokhov, "not a single writer of any standing signed it. . . . In fact, the vast majority of all writers, technicians and scientists of all levels throughout the Soviet Union refused to sign the declaration, some bluntly—among them Leonov, Tvardovsky and Yevtushenko. . . . Even such very conformist writers as Konstantin Fedin . . . made some excuse for not signing." [37]

Yevtushenko's role during and after the invasion is obscure. He was reported to have sent a telegram to Brezhnev and Kosygin on the very next day after the invasion took place, saying: "I don't know how to sleep. I don't know how to continue living. All I know is that I have a moral duty to express to you the feelings that overpower me." Yevtushenko insisted that the invasion was a tragic error, a blow against the international Communist movement, and a "great gift to all reactionary forces in the world." [38] And he concluded that the Kremlin had taken a step whose consequences it was impossible to measure or to foresee.

20 The Kuznetsov Case

> The Soviet creative intelligentsia—that is, people accustomed
> to thinking one thing, saying another and doing a third—is as
> a whole an even more unpleasant phenomenon than the regime
> which formed it. Hypocrisy and acceptance of things as they
> are foisted on it has become so much a part of it that it con-
> siders any attempt to act honorably as either a crafty provoca-
> tion or madness.
>
> *Andrei Amalrik*

The Czechoslovak invasion, like the Sinyavsky-Daniel trial, was
another watershed; repression and the power of the political police
increased even further, and the imposition of a new orthodoxy was
more stringently enforced. The now emergent neo-Stalinism was
compounded of insistence on ideological purity, of suppression of
protest, of intensified censorship, of most of the old forms of Stalinist control short of ultimate mass violence. Human relations once
more were poisoned by fear and suspicion, by anxiety, caution, and
depression, as the hand of the KGB was increasingly evident in the
affairs of life. The terror the political police wielded against the
liberal intelligentsia, scientists, students, and other dissenters was not
quite the Stalinist kind, but people lost their jobs or were demoted;
students and teachers were expelled from universities or research
institutes; individuals were transferred to remote provinces where
their careers were blighted or their education permanently interrupted. Over everyone hung the old threat of informers who were
part of the KGB apparatus for intimidating anyone who showed
the slightest tendency toward nonconformism.

There is a brilliant rendition of the feel of life during this period
in Moscow and Leningrad by the pseudonymous British "An Observer," [1] who tells of a friend summoned to the secret police and
addressed by a KGB major in civilian clothes:

I'm not going to argue about what *you* think about any trials conducted by a Soviet court or what *you* think the constitution says. Who do you think you are, challenging what has been decided by the responsible people in the Party? I'll tell you: a cheap little sensation-seeking subversive like the rest of them. And *our* decision is this: we are not going to put up with your dirty activities any longer. Traitors like you will never change. You just have to be dealt with so you can never be treacherous again. One more false move and I guarantee the only thing you'll teach your dirty politics to from then on is trees in a nice Siberian forest. We built up this country, made it strong and made it hard —and not for snivelling little intellectual woodworms like you to ruin from the inside. You've had your day; things are getting under control again; in another year or so, I guarantee, all you liberal wreckers with the smart-aleck ideas will be back where you belong. You're no better or safer than all your Sinyavskys and Litvinovs. We gave them what they deserve, and it will be a lot easier to deal with you.[2]

By the end of 1968, the rehabilitation of Stalin, or re-Stalinization, had proceeded apace. Criticism of Stalin's crimes, mass arrests, and deportations, of the murders, purges, and concentration camps, had disappeared from the press and from private conversation. What remained were the tributes to Stalin's role as architect of industrialization and collectivization and to his refurbished role as the great generalissimo during World War II.

Even the liberal writers, in some measure, were unable to free themselves of this terrible contradiction, logical and historical; Ilya Ehrenburg, for instance, had commented:

I knew that a calamity had befallen us and knew at the same time that neither I nor my friends, nor our whole people, would ever disavow [the] October [Revolution], that neither the crimes of individual people nor of groups which had crippled our lives could turn us away from our difficult and great path. There were days when I did not want to live any longer, but even on those days I knew that I had chosen the right way.

After the Twentieth Party Congress, I met acquaintances and friends abroad, and some of them asked me, and also themselves, would that [Congress] not deliver a mortal blow to Communism? They do not understand what I, an old non-Party writer, know: that the idea of Communism turned out to be so strong . . . because we found some Communists who told our people and the whole world about the crimes of the past, about the corruption of the philosophy of Communism, of its principles, of justice, solidarity, and humanism. In spite of everything, our people went ahead with [socialist] construction, and after several years they turned back the Fascist invasion and finished construction of the house in which they live, study, play, argue—boys and girls who never knew the cruel mistakes of the past.[3]

What better argument for Oscar Wilde's contention that nothing succeeds like excess?

As part of the large-scale repression and drive for conformity launched by the regime, a major offensive against the liberal writers and intellectuals was begun by the dogmatists in literature. The conflict, as before, polarized about *Novy mir* and *Yunost* on one side and *Oktyabr* and *Molodaya gvardia* on the other. Before the Czechoslovak invasion the Kremlin seemed to try to maintain some balance between the two camps, but now it was apparent that it had come down hard and definitively on the dogmatist side.

In December, *Oktyabr* published a full-scale attack on *Yunost* with an article signed only with the pseudonym "Literator,"[4] which included the criticisms of a Moscow taxi driver, one Korolev, who complained that *Yunost*'s writers concentrated on the private lives of unimportant people and were basely cynical. (The taxi driver's comments had initially appeared in the trade-union magazine *Sovetskie profsoyuzy*.)[5] Among the special targets of abuse were the poets Yevtushenko and his former wife Bella Akhmadulina. The next issue of *Sovetskie profsoyuzy* published in a letter from Korolev declaring that he had been visited by a "political and moral degenerate named E. Iodkovsky, who had tried to persuade him to withdraw his earlier comments and to allege that the magazine's staff had written those comments and his letter, not he. "Literator" then asked who was behind Iodkovsky. *Yunost*'s editor in chief, Boris Polevoi, denied knowing any of the individuals involved and, in a coldly written rejoinder, struck back:

The attempts by "Literator," a man unknown to me, to settle his literary accounts in the pages of *Oktyabr* with another magazine, which he evidently does not like—evil-smelling hints bordering on political provocation—seem to me to be infinitely removed from all the standards of the Soviet press. . . . I would not wish ever again to read anything like this note, which looks odd in the pages of a Soviet literary journal already 45 years old and in the columns of which many Soviet writers, including the author of these lines, began their careers.[6]

In December, there was no celebration of Solzhenitsyn's fiftieth birthday, though significantly, at a public poetry reading some weeks earlier in Moscow, the chairman asked for questions from the audience of students, and three demanded when they would be permitted to read Solzhenitsyn's novels, or why they would not be permitted to do so. More and more frequently, it was recalled that in the early days of de-Stalinization the saying had been: "Tell me what you think of *Ivan Denisovich* and we will tell you what you are." [7] Once again the novel was proving to be a touchstone.

Two criticisms of *Novy mir* persisted from 1967 through 1969: that the magazine gave a "one-sided" interpretation of Soviet reality and an "impoverished image" of Soviet man; and that the editors refused to accept the criticisms brought against them by "the public." [8] In 1967, the particular work that brought down the wrath of the authorities was Bykov's *The Dead Feel No Pain;* [9] in 1969, it was Voronov's *Youth in Zheleznodolsk.*[10] But *Pravda* was now holding the editorial board more directly responsible for those "incorrect" works which appeared in its pages: "The *Literaturnaya gazeta* article notes correctly that *Novy mir*, which decided to carry this work, shares the responsibility with the author for the novel's errors and weaknesses. This is especially just because *Novy mir* has been criticized more than once in the past for publishing a number of works that contained ideological errors and denigrated our reality." *Pravda* now declared, "The public is entitled to expect that *Novy mir* will finally draw the right conclusions from this criticism." [11]

By the summer of 1969 the tempo and temperature of the campaign had intensified, and the threat was made more imminent by the spring purge of the liberals on the *Yunost* editorial staff. Rumors had been rife all during the first part of the year that Tvardovsky and Polevoi would both be fired from their jobs and the staffs of both magazines purged. Reports had it that the Secretariat of the Writers' Union had demanded Tvardovsky's resignation but that he had refused to tender it.[12] Then, in May, the rumors became fact: three of the leading liberals—Yevtushenko, Aksyonov, and Viktor Rozov [13]—were replaced on the *Yunost* editorial board by four presumably more reliable writers—Anatoly Kuznetsov, Anatoly Aleksin, V. I. Amlinsky, and Kaisyn Kuliev. In July, Daniil Granin was dropped from the editorial board of *Znamya*. The purges of these two magazines seemed to be forerunners of a rearrangement of the *Novy mir* editorial board to give the conservatives control of the magazine and possibly to replace Tvardovsky at the helm.

Despite these forebodings, the May issue of *Novy mir* carried a book review by A. Savin which discussed democratization of the Soviet system. Savin proposed revisionist options for the USSR: a choice of candidates at all elections to the Supreme Soviet; more factory self-management; the right of organized groups to publish petitions in the central press—which would of course give the dissidents a means of becoming a kind of legal opposition—and other similar reforms. Tvardovsky was maintaining not only his reputation but also that of his magazine as a forum for progressive discussion and expanding it beyond the realm of liberal literary debate into a forum for advanced political discussions.[14]

In March there were reports that a new Solzhenitsyn manuscript had been smuggled out of the Soviet Union and, without either the author's knowledge or consent, was being offered to Western publishers. "The novel's virtually untranslatable Russian title, *Arkhipelag Gulag*, suggested that all Russia under Stalin was like a vast sea dotted with islands of concentration camps. Gulag is an acronym for the dread Main Labor Camp Administration." At the same time, a vignette called "The Easter Procession" had reached the West and been published.[15] In it Solzhenitsyn told a "sad little Easter story" about the little church in the writers' colony of Peredelkino.

The young hooligans mocking the tiny Easter procession do not belong to the village: they come from Moscow by train. It is easy on the local line; but it calls for a special effort all the same and the odds are that, as Solzhenitsyn tentatively suggests, they are officially encouraged to turn up and make a nuisance of themselves on Christian occasions. In any case, they represent something undesirable and destructive, destructive not only of the Christian Easter, but also, ultimately, of the regime which allows them to behave this way.[16]

Stories of how Solzhenitsyn was only managing to hang on by his fingernails, of how he was being pressured by the KGB and the Writers' Union, of how his royalties had been cut off, his works forbidden publication, and his name barred from mention in the Soviet press continued to come out of the Soviet Union. As a result, that summer, a plea was sent to Nikolay Podgorny, the Soviet chief of state, signed by such prestigious Western writers as Rolf Hochhuth, Karl Jaspers, Arthur Miller, and Heinrich Böll. It was delivered in a letter to the Russian embassies in Bonn and East Berlin, and said that world public opinion was dismayed to learn that the works of Solzhenitsyn were not being published in his own country when "elsewhere in Europe only the domestically weak military dictatorships of Spain and Greece still practiced censorship because they know no other way of keeping their ragged peoples in check, and when even the Vatican has not put a single book on the index for more than 10 years." [17]

In January 1969, Pyotr Yakir organized an Action Group for the Defense of Civil Rights in the Soviet Union, dedicated to furthering the struggle for civil liberties and the rights of dissidence. Of the small initial group of only fifteen Muscovites, a year later only eight were still free. Yakir's courageous step was followed by a still bolder one; on March 6, 1969, he sent a letter to the Party journal *Kommunist*—because its February issue had been devoted to rehabilitating Stalin as a military leader—calling for the posthumous indictment of Stalin. If posthumous rehabilitations were legal and possible for the victims, Yakir argued, why not posthumous trials, sentences, and punishment for the executioners? Like its predecessor, the ten-thousand-word memorandum on "convergence" circulated in the spring of 1968 by physicist Andrei Sakharov, the Yakir letter seemed to be a collective summary of the ideas of the liberal intelligentsia, the result of group consultation and discussion, even if not collectively composed. It was not, of course, published in *Kommunist*, but was swiftly circulated in *samizdat* and transmitted to the West.[18] Yakir subsequently sent it to the Procurator General of the USSR with a demand that an investigation of Stalin be initiated.

Yakir's letter indicted Stalin on seventeen specific counts, each carefully documented from Soviet sources and the crimes related to the relevant articles in the Soviet penal code. Yakir accused Stalin of abuse of power, mass repressions, torture, violence, and murder.

He showed Stalin responsible for suicides and executions of top Soviet leaders in the Party, government, armed forces, intelligence services, and police. Foreign Communists who had sought refuge in the Soviet Union had also been murdered by Stalin's orders, including such prominent ones as the Germans Hermann Schubert and Heinz Neumann, the Hungarians Bela Kun and Gabor Farkas, the Poles Tomasz Dombal and Yulian Lesczynski (one of the founders of the Polish Communist Party), and even the Swiss Fritz Platten, who had shielded Lenin with his own body during the first attempt on Lenin's life. Yakir also condemned Stalin for the mass repression and deportation of non-Russian peoples during and after World War II, among them the Crimean Tatars, the Balkars, the Chechen-Ingush, and the Kalmyks. He also indicted Stalin for the purges which killed 80 percent of the top officer corps—those who had fought in the Spanish Civil War, top technicians, and leading scholars—resulting in millions of casualties in the first stages of the war. In short, Yakir concluded, Stalin "was the greatest criminal our country has known in its contemporary history."

In April, Yakir and fifty-four other intellectuals sent a three-page appeal to the United Nations Human Rights Commission calling attention to the increased political persecution in the Soviet Union and the gradual return to a Stalinist regime of terror.[19] Two months later, in June, Yakir and ten other dissidents appealed to the World Conference of Communist Parties then meeting in Moscow to help them in the struggle against the restoration of Stalinism in the Soviet Union, but no help was forthcoming either from the UN or the "fraternal" Communist parties.[20]

In the summer of 1969 the Soviet leaders faced still another crisis involving a prominent writer. Anatoly Kuznetsov, appointed in May to the *Yunost* editorial board when the liberals were purged, turned out to be less than reliable for the regime. On July 30, the thirty-nine-year-old novelist, author of *Babi Yar* and *The Fire*, defected in London. Both of these works had come under the attack of dogmatist critics. His *Babi Yar*, like Yevtushenko's poem of the same name (Yevtushenko had written his poem after visiting Kuznetsov in Kiev; "we were standing where hundreds of thousands of people had once writhed and screamed in the throes of death," Kuznetsov wrote after that visit) [21] had been censured for focusing attention on Nazi barbarities against the Jews in Kiev and for portraying Russian and Ukrainian anti-Semitism. It did not, according to the regime's supporters, show the Nazis' crimes against other Soviet nationalities nor show Soviet citizens resisting the Nazis or helping the Jews. (Later, after his defection, Kuznetsov was to publish an uncensored version of *Babi Yar* which included many important segments of the novel cut out before its official Soviet edition, especially those about the role of the NKVD in the destruction of the heart of Kiev, a crime which the Soviet political police endeavored to lay at the feet of the Nazi invaders.) *The Fire* was censured for its portrayal of the negative aspects of Soviet life, especially its unflattering picture of Soviet workers, and its failure to show the social roots of Soviet deficiencies.

Despite such "shortcomings," the regime had considered Kuznetsov a reliable enough defender of its policies to elevate him to the *Yunost* editorial board. In London now, Kuznetsov leveled a series of broadsides against Soviet society which discomfited the Kremlin more than any writings since the defection of Stalin's daughter. In a series of newspaper articles and interviews, he raised a storm by disowning his own books, accusing Soviet censorship of stifling and distorting all the country's creative talents, dismissing "socialist realism," and tearing immense holes in the Potemkin façade of Soviet political and literary life. Kuznetsov confessed to having been a "dishonest, conformist, cowardly author"; [22] he relinquished the name he had been given and had put on his books—Anatoly Kuznetsov—and took the new name A. Anatol, which would henceforce be both his personal and literary signature.

Kuznetsov compared Soviet Russia to Nazi Germany—a comparison always guaranteed to infuriate the Soviet leaders: "As a boy I saw books being burned in Russia in 1937 under Stalin. I saw books being burned in 1942 in occupied Kiev under Hitler." [23] In a radio interview, Kuznetsov explained: "There is in Russia a long tradition of tyranny. You see, if you were born in a concentration camp and your parents were born in a concentration camp and your grandparents were born in a concentration camp you cannot imagine any other life." [24]

Artistic freedom in the Soviet Union, Kuznetsov declared, has been reduced only to the freedom to praise the Soviet system and the Communist Party. Literature was "controlled by people who are ignorant, cynical, and themselves very remote from literature. But they are people with excellent knowledge of the latest instructions from the men at the top and of the prevailing Party dogmas." Russian writers simply had to go along with such idiocy. "If Stalin is on top, then praise Stalin. If they order people to plant maize, then write about maize. If they decide to expose Stalin's crimes, then expose Stalin. And when they stop criticizing him, you stop too." [25] Among writers, Kuznetsov maintained, there was nothing "but murder, suicides, persecution trials, lunatic asylums, an unbroken series of tragedies from Gumilev to Solzhenitsyn." [26] Russia has ancient and deep-rooted traditions of such treatment: "The best Russian writers were always persecuted, dragged before the courts, murdered, or reduced to suicide." [27]

Kuznetsov made public three letters he had sent to the Soviet authorities: one to the government, pleading with it not to persecute or harass his relatives or friends for a defection about which they knew nothing and in which they did not cooperate; the second to the Central Committee, surrendering his membership in the Communist Party because Marxism-Leninism is "utterly obsolete, rigid and naive [and] has led, continues to lead and threatens to go on leading to frightful social tragedies"; and the last to the Soviet Writers' Union, resigning from membership in it because he would not be guided by "socialist realism." [28]

Kuznetsov lamented that he had not been able to pierce the wall of Soviet censorship, though "Yevtushenko managed to achieve a little this way, Solzhenitsyn managed a little more, but even that is all over now. The cracks were noticed and cemented over." He had hidden his own manuscripts in glass jars and buried them almost as soon as he had finished writing them, because "whenever I wasn't there my flat could be broken into and searched, and my manuscripts confiscated, as happened with Solzhenitsyn and many others." [29]

Kuznetsov then recounted the saga of an earlier novel, *The Continuation of a Legend*, depicting the life of hardship and poverty on construction sites in Siberia where he had himself worked. When he submitted the manuscript to the editors of *Yunost*, they told him that they liked the novel but that it would never pass the censorship.

Life in Siberia had to be shown in the brightest colors so that the
young people would go there to work.

But the most important objection was that if my novel were published Western propagandists would seize on it and shout: "Look: here
is an honest piece of reporting from the Soviet Union itself—see how
frightful it is to live there."

True, there was still a possibility of rescuing the novel, they said.
The rules of "socialist realism" permitted an author to reveal a little
of the blemishes in Soviet life, but only if it was clear that they were
minor defects soon to be removed, while the work as a whole must be
infused with optimism and Communist ideology.

If Kuznetsov would agree to make the book more cheerful, give it
a sense of "Communist optimism," the *Yunost* editors promised to
print it. Kuznetsov tried, but could not be cheerful or optimistic
enough, and they finally rejected the manuscript. Some time later,
in 1961, quite by accident, he discovered that his book had been
printed in *Yunost*. "Without my knowledge or agreement, someone
had done the crudest hatchet job on my novel, cutting, rewriting
and adding. The novel had now been given as ideologically optimistic a tone as anyone could wish." [30]

The novel was subsequently translated into thirty languages, and
one day, the French Communist poet and functionary Louis Aragon
sent a copy of the French edition to the Soviet authorities. Entitled
L'Etoile dans le brouillard ("Red Star in the Mist"), it had been
published by the Roman Catholic University of Lyons and translated by Abbé Paul Chaleil, a Jesuit missionary in China who had
been turned over to the Soviets and who had worked as a prisoner-
laborer in Siberia on the same dam that Kuznetsov describes in the
novel. Chaleil had translated Kuznetsov's novel but "had simply not
bothered to translate those chapters which had been forced out of
me," Kuznetsov wrote, "and had merely summarized them with the
comment that they were poorer in quality than the other chapters." [31] Though the French was by far the most skillful translation,
Kuznetsov was called on the carpet and asked to explain how an
"anti-Soviet" book had been published under his name. The Soviet
authorities insisted that he write out a complaint against the French
publisher, and consequently a suit was instituted against the Roman
Catholic Archdiocese of Lyons, charging that the French translation

distorted and falsified the original novel for ideological reasons. A French court ruled against the translation and awarded Kuznetsov damages of a thousand francs. Now, eight years later, a free man in England, Kuznetsov wanted to make amends for what he had been party to, and he asked the French court to reverse its decision.[32]

(Later that year, in December, the American Russian-language quarterly, *New Review*, featured some of the unabridged chapters of his most famous novel, *Babi Yar*. Among the narratives the Soviet censors had excised was the account of a major incident which told how the Soviet secret police deliberately blew up the historic main street of Kiev to provoke the Germans into reprisals against the local population. Hitler's hordes had occupied Kiev in 1941, and in the original version of the novel—before it was censored—Kuznetsov had shown how the local people cooperated with the Germans, removing tank obstacles and scraping Soviet propaganda posters off the walls; some—like Kuznetsov's grandfather—had looked to the Nazis as liberators. These details were also censored. A chapter on the plight of those Soviet prisoners of war who, after they were liberated, were flung into Siberian concentration camps was also excised by the Soviet censors. The Soviet authorities have never admitted their role in destroying the ancient splendor of the center of Kiev, but continue to lay the blame on the Nazi armies.) [33]

Perhaps the most equivocal episodes of Kuznetsov's story of his escape are his deliberate alienation of his young son's affections to "protect" the boy and his paying the price of acquiring his exit visa by pretending to be an informer for the KGB. Kuznetsov admitted that he told the political police a pure fabrication which involved Yevtushenko, Aksyonov, and other liberal writers in a conspiracy to publish an underground magazine—believing, he said, that the story was so outlandish that it would do the writers no harm. But the "crime" of publishing a magazine in the Soviet Union without official permission is punishable by up to seven years of hard labor in a concentration camp.

Upon the publication of his story, Kuznetsov was violently attacked in the press by American playwright Lillian Hellman and American novelist William Styron for having concocted a fiction which endangered his friends. They accused him of betrayal, of worsening the circumstances of Soviet writers, and of being cowardly for not remaining in the Soviet Union to help reform the system as many other Soviet writers were doing. In a reply more sorrowful and chagrined than angry, Kuznetsov suggested that Styron might like to take Sinyavsky's place in the concentration camp and carry on the struggle from there. He added: "My rooms in Tula are vacant. Let him [Styron] take them and live in the Soviet Union for a year and then see what he thinks." [34] Kuznetsov thought that there were many illusions and failures of understanding in the West's view of his native country. "The Soviet Union is a fascist country," he stated. "What is more, its fascism is much more dangerous than Hitler's. It is a country which is living in Orwellian times, but long before 1984." [35] With respect to the suggestion of the American writers that he should have stayed at home to resist, Kuznetsov asked: "Would it have made sense for Thomas Mann to stay in Hitler's Germany? Or for Bertolt Brecht? He did not think so. 'I don't want to go to a concentration camp,' he said firmly." [36]

On July 31, the Secretariat of the board of the Writers' Union expelled Kuznetsov for "betrayal of the homeland, for treason to the cause of socialism, and for political and moral double-dealing." The major attack on Kuznetsov was, too obviously, left to Boris Polevoi, the editor in chief of *Yunost*, to whose editorial board Kuznetsov had so recently been appointed. Polevoi denounced Kuznetsov for having "committed a betrayal, one of the vilest kind. He has deserted to the camp of the enemies of socialism, betraying all his books and all the principles he has proclaimed time and again." To explain his own and *Yunost*'s role in making Kuznetsov's defection possible, Polevoi reported that Kuznetsov had brought them a literary project he wanted to launch; "the most passionate dream of his literary life was the desire to write a novel . . . about the birth of our Party and the activity of the young V. I. Lenin." To do so properly, Kuznetsov claimed that he had to visit London: "For the novel to be alive, for it to be filled with lifelike details, it is necessary for me to go there in person, to look at the houses where Lenin lived and the places where he met with people." Polevoi attempted to convey the notion that Kuznetsov was mentally deranged and morally depraved, accusing him of being the father of an unborn child whose mother Kuznetsov had promised to marry on his return from Britain and whom he had now in effect deserted. (Kuznetsov denied all this absolutely.) Polevoi portrayed Kuznetsov arriving in London and hurrying to Soho to see a striptease and search out a prostitute for his pleasure (both pretexts, Kuznetsov asserted, which he had used to throw off his KGB watchdog and gain enough time and privacy to defect). To counter the dismal portrait Kuznetsov had drawn of the Soviet writer's life—a gauntlet of constant surveillance, censorship, restricted travel, and spying—Polevoi boldly proclaimed, "Who in Britain does not know that Soviet writers travel freely throughout the world, as tourists, as correspondents, and on various public affairs, and that to hide one's works by burying them in the ground is something only a madman would do?" [37] If one must lie, nothing is better than blanket refutation: there is no restriction of travel, no police surveillance of writers, no censorship; *everyone knows* that the Soviet Union is a paradise for writers. Polevoi did his job.

Later in November, Andrei Amalrik spoke out against Kuznetsov, and because he did so in Moscow, not in the security and safety of New York or Connecticut, and because he himself had felt the lash on his own flesh, his words carried special weight. He condemned Kuznetsov for lacking the courage of his convictions and for not promoting greater intellectual freedom, even in the face of Soviet political repression. In a long open letter, Amalrik pointed out that the KGB could take away only a man's *external* freedom, not his *internal* freedom, and he rebuked Kuznetsov for having continually yielded to the demands made on him by the KGB and the censorship although he did not have to. Amalrik told how he himself had preferred expulsion from the university to distorting his own work, and had thereby relinquished his hope of becoming a professional historian. He also had refused to submit his writings to Soviet publishing houses, though he too wanted publication, because he knew his writings would be censored. Several times, the KGB had tried to enlist his services as an informer, but Amalrik had consistently refused their blandishments and coercions until his refusal earned him a stretch of Siberian exile. Amalrik then expanded his indictment of Kuznetsov to all, or at least most, of the Soviet intelligentsia;

But the main thing is that living in this country and continuing to write and doing what I consider correct, I can at any moment again be sent to prison or be dealt with in any other fashion. That is why I think I have the personal right to reproach you.

But perhaps I have no right to do so. Above all because I am almost ten years younger than you and I was only lightly touched by that most terrible (Stalin) period which coincided with your youth and in which you were formed as an individual. Even now the regime exists . . . mainly on the interest from the capital of fear amassed in that period. It is not only a question of the KGB but the fact that the whole atmosphere of Soviet life and Soviet education is such that a man is already conditioned to meet with the KGB and to enter into the same relations with it that you did. . . .

Nonetheless, I do reproach you, not because I want to condemn you personally but because I want to condemn the philosophy of impotence and self-justification which runs through all you have said and written in the West. "I was given no choice," you seem to be saying and this sounds like a justification not only for yourself, but for the whole of the Soviet creative intelligentsia, or at least for the liberal part of it to which you belong. . . .

It sometimes appears to me that the Soviet creative intelligentsia— that is people accustomed to thinking one thing, saying another and doing a third—is as a whole an even more unpleasant phenomenon than the regime which formed it. Hypocrisy and acceptance of things as they are foisted on it have become so much a part of it that it considers any attempt to act honorably as either a crafty provocation or madness.

I do not mean that all those who desire greater freedom for themselves and their country should go to Red Square with banners. However, they ought to reject the customary cynicism which equates truth and lies, and to try to acquire inner freedom. How to do this must evidently be decided by each person himself. Not everyone can come out openly against these conditions in which we live. . . .

But it is always better to be silent than to utter falsehoods, better to refuse to publish any of your books than to put out something which is completely contrary to what one had written in the first place, better to refuse a trip abroad than, for the sake of one, to become an informer. . . .

Judging only by his books, it is impossible to say that Solzhenitsyn is persecuted and tormented. . . . He gives the impression of a man capable of standing out against persecution. He has already once preserved his inner strength in prison and will evidently do so again if he is once more put in jail. From this we can all derive strength.[38]

Nor was Amalrik much kinder to some of the liberal intelligentsia and literati. He remarked in his letter to Kuznetsov, "What gain would there be to our country if Kochetov or Evtushenko were to go to Menton and state that creative freedom exists in the USSR?" "You hint," he wrote, "that several well-known poets were, like yourself, informers [for the KGB]. . . . The important thing is not whether your hints are justified or not but that all this poetic-political deception which flourished in Khrushchev's time and has proved to be not particularly needed by his successors bears as little relation to independent art as the writings of Kochetov. It even appears to me that Kochetov's sincere obscuranticism deserves greater respect than the false rebelliousness of those who, together with vodka and caviar, were for a long time an export necessary to the regime." [39]

Rumors had circulated that Amalrik was himself a KGB agent and that his continued freedom was due only to his cooperation with the political police. His letter to Kuznetsov and its publication, and the publication of his books abroad, were used as the bases for such speculations. Rumors of this kind appeared in several American newspapers, the *Washington Star* in particular.[40] In an open letter, Amalrik attacked the "suspicions, hints, and allusions" directly. He denied that he was or had ever been a police agent, and countered the criticisms of him for rebuking Kuznetsov by saying that if Kuznetsov felt he could only work freely outside the Soviet Union, "it was not only his right but his duty to escape to a place where he could write what he wanted and publish what he wanted." [41] But he did repeat his criticisms of Kuznetsov for having been an informer for the KGB and a "conformer" in the Soviet context.

Amalrik also contradicted the *Washington Star* article about the review of his sentence, which said that his being allowed to return to Moscow was unusual. He gave other examples in which such reviews and returns had taken place—Josif Brodsky, the poet Batshev of the Smog group, Aleksandr Ginzburg, Belogorodskaya—to make his point. He also contended against the notion that if he were not a KGB agent he would have been imprisoned long before for having published his works abroad. In passionate, sagacious terms, he rebuked those who entertain such notions:

My arrest is a kind of litmus paper which is to indicate whether I am a KGB agent or not . . . .

To pose the question in such terms to me seems extremely immoral. My country is not a Roman arena. I am not a gladiator, and the Western world, in the name of which Mr. Bradsher [the *Washington Star* newspaperman who wrote the article] begins to speak with pathos towards the end of his article, is not the Roman plebs, watching excitedly or coolly to see whether the gladiator will really die or whether it is only a circus trick.

When I was writing my books and intending to hand them over for publication I realized that I was risking imprisonment, and I was ready for it and am ready for it now. But I thank God for every day of freedom which is given to me and which I spend at home with my wife. It seems to me that an honourable man who believes in God should not say: "He has not yet been arrested—this is very suspicious," but rather "Thank God he has not yet been arrested, that means there is one more free man on earth."

Mr. Bradsher's anonymous "specialists" have not after all occupied important positions in the secret police of a totalitarian state, and for this reason I think they are scarcely competent to judge who should be arrested straight away and who later. I think that the people in the KGB are reasonably sensible from the police point of view, and they will arrest me when the fuss abroad has died down, and interest in me and my books has fallen away; and they will not try me for my books but will trump up some minor pretext. And after arresting me they will try to blacken my character as they tried to do with all the others. For this reason I think that Mr. Bradsher's article will have delighted the KGB.

As far as the date of my arrest is concerned, a bureaucratic regime does not hurry by its very nature and because it knows that no one will escape it. Marchenko was arrested six months after he had begun circulating his book about Soviet prison camps; Grigorenko seven months after his famous speech at Kosterin's funeral; Bogoraz-Daniel and Litvinov seven months after their appeal "To world opinion"; Yakhimovich 14 months after his letter to Suslov condemning the trials of dissenters; Gorbanyevskaya 15 months after she had taken part in the demonstration in Red Square; and so on. I do not think that they have begun making an exception just for me.[42]

It was an altogether proper rebuke, and, as events were soon to show, Amalrik was prescient: he had understood the regime and the KGB's purposes and methods far better than those who had maligned him.

21 Stalin's New Bust

A writer is above all an artist who is trying to penetrate into
the unknown. He must be honest and objective, and be able to
do his creative work in freedom.

Anatoly Kuznetsov

Soviet authorities were now moving simultaneously on three separate fronts: continuing their crackdown on political dissidents; further restricting literary liberals and liberalism; and carefully refurbishing the image of Stalin, a campaign the Brezhnev-Kosygin
leadership had converted to a genuine re-Stalinization of Soviet life.
The bitter and revealing criticisms of Stalin enunciated at the Twentieth and Twenty-second Party Congresses were past; the press now
carried no attacks on Stalin's crimes or "excesses," and mention of
concentration camps, mass arrests, purges, and forcible transfers of
entire peoples had disappeared. Nor was there any further elucida-
tion of Stalin's mistakes and ineptitudes, his faith in the Hitler-Stalin
Pact, his wartime lack of preparedness, his decimation of the Red
Army officer corps, his uncertain and panicky leadership in the
early days of the Nazi invasion of the USSR. Instead, Stalin's wartime role had been "revaluated" in the spate of wartime memoirs
published for the twenty-fifth anniversary of V-E Day which came
that spring. All paid tribute to the generalissimo's military acumen,
though with less fulsomeness than in the heyday of Stalinism. Excerpts from one such memoir, *Wars and Years*, by Marshal Aleksandr Golovanov, chief of the Red Air Force's long-range bomber
command during World War II, were published in *Oktyabr*—
Kochetov's magazine was one of the leaders in striving to restore
Stalin's reputation—and told how Golovanov had helped to persuade
Stalin to release the gifted aircraft designer Andrey Tupolev from
prison. Tupolev had been arrested in the late 1930s and was still confined in 1943.

"Comrade Stalin, why is that designer sitting?" Marshal Golovanov said he asked. In Russian, the word "sitting" is a euphemism for being imprisoned.

Quite a long silence set in. Stalin, it was evident, was meditating.

"It is said that he had relations with foreign intelligence," Stalin said in a firm and assured tone.

"Do you believe that, Comrade Stalin?" he recalled saying.

"Do you believe it?"

"No, I don't," the marshal said he replied.

"I don't either," Stalin said.[1]

Tupolev was then released from prison. Golovanov used this example to demonstrate that Stalin was open to reasonable persuasion, but the dialogue is revealing, whether altogether true or not, and there are obvious reasons for doubting the accuracy and objectivity of Golovanov's account because of the role he ascribes to himself and because the incident reveals the capriciousness and arbitrariness of Stalin's rule.

Golovanov also asserted that the late Marshal Semyon Timoshenko and Marshal Georgy Zhukov had also "played roles in saving the lives of comrades." [2] In an interview in *Komsomolskaya pravda*, novelist Mikhail Sholokhov declared that he subscribed to the complimentary portrait Zhukov had painted of Stalin in his memoirs, published in 1969, and added: "Stalin's activities in that period must not be belittled or made to appear foolish. First of all, this would be dishonest, and secondly, harmful to the country, to the Soviet people, not because success is never challenged, but because tearing down does not accord with the truth." (Ironically, Sholokhov was having his own troubles in portraying Stalin. Excerpts from his still unfinished novel about World War II, *They Fought for the Motherland*, had appeared in *Pravda* in 1969, but its publication as a book was delayed, presumably because Sholokhov was having difficulty in obtaining the censorship's approval, owing to the book's highly critical references to Stalin.) [3] In addition to the spate of memoirs, a new film was released depicting Stalin as a "wise but firm wartime leader." Finally, the government sponsored a celebration of the former dictator's ninetieth birthday in December 1969.

The second element in the rehabilitation of Stalin was on the surface a minor event, but its symbolic significance sent tremors through all of Soviet society. After his death, Stalin's body had been interred in the Lenin Mausoleum, where it remained in state until 1961, when the Twenty-second Party Congress voted, at Khrushchev's urging, to remove the body from Lenin's tomb. It had subsequently been reburied in a row of graves behind the Lenin Mausoleum with the bodies of other Communist dignitaries.[4] All those graves were marked with busts except Stalin's and that of the recently (December 1969) buried Marshal Klimenty Voroshilov. On June 25, 1970, a larger than life-size gray granite bust by a Stalin Prize winner, sculptor Nikolai Tomsky, was unveiled over Stalin's grave,[5] and at the same time a similar bust was put on Voroshilov's grave. The act was performed without fanfare or publicity, but it was an event which could not escape public attention. Moreover, the bust of Stalin was a soft-focus view of the dictator, portraying the face of a wise, paternal, and benevolent leader rather than the ruthless paranoid and murderer of the "cult of personality."

The small funerary gesture, however uninflated by ceremony or publicity, touched off a wave of rumor and speculation. Did it portend a return to Stalinist terror? Was neo-Stalinism now going to become even more repressive? Was Stalin's historical role now going to be further "revaluated"? On a trip to Moscow at that time, Harrison Salisbury reported that there seemed little likelihood of a resurgence of Stalinism, but there was also little hope for a diminution of the repression. "We are going through a period of difficulty," one writer in Moscow told Salisbury. "But do not overestimate its nature. There is not going to be any resurgence of Stalinism. To be sure, Stalin's reputation is being refurbished a bit. But there is not going to be any terror or any executions. The country will not stand for it."[6] Others explained that the Soviet leadership was so concerned about the threat from China that it felt it could countenance no dissent on the home front. Whether the threat from the East was simply a pretext for additional domestic repression—every Soviet regime had always been able to raise the specter of some foreign "threat"—or truly felt it was impossible to assess. A young government official also remarked: "Our leaders have had no experience in coping with dissent or divisions of opinion. They think the safest thing to do is to suppress it. In fact, they know no other way to deal with it. This is their tragedy. Dissent in this country is not directed against the system. It is directed at making it work better." [7] His comments were pertinent.

(Much later it was reported that a secretary at the Soviet Embassy in Prague had made a speech asserting that the struggle against the "cult of personality," which Khrushchev had begun at the Twentieth Party Congress, had been harmful to the international Communist movement. He was quoted as saying:

Khrushchevism is a poison in the arteries of the movement. This poison must be eliminated if the movement is to recover its health.

Fourteen years have proven the justice of Stalin's thesis concerning the aggravation of the class struggle in the conditions of socialism and concerning the penetration by the class enemy into the Party. By rejecting this thesis the 20th Congress prepared for the penetration of the enemy into the ranks of the Communist Parties.) [8]

All through the summer and fall of 1969 and during the winter of 1970, the position of the liberal writers continued to deteriorate. Kuznetsov's defection had triggered a tightened control of the whole literary field; the two most obvious targets were Aleksandr Tvardovsky and *Novy mir*, and Aleksandr Solzhenitsyn and his writings. In 1966, the *Novy mir* editorial board had been reshuffled, and in summer of 1969 a more serious threat to Tvardovsky and the independence of his magazine was posed. It began with an attack on *Novy mir* for having published an article, "On Traditions and Kinship with the People," [9] written by a former deputy editor of the magazine, A. Dementyev, purged from the editorial board at the end of 1966. The attack was contained in a letter to the editor of *Ogonyok* and signed by eleven conservative writers who, ostensibly, were defending the publication *Molodaya gvardia* against Dementyev's criticism. What was involved, these writers asserted, was a definition of Soviet patriotism. *Molodaya gvardia* declared its goal to be the cultivation in Soviet youth of "feelings of . . . selfless love for [their] socialist fatherland, internationalism and implacability toward every sort of hostile ideological influence." Convinced that "it seems impossible even to question the Party spirit and civic mindedness of such a position," the dogmatists admonished *Novy mir* for its failure to strive toward such appropriate goals:

We assume it is not necessary to tell the reader in detail about the nature of the ideas that for a long time now *Novy mir* has propagated, especially in the criticism department. . . . It was in *Novy mir* that A. Sinyavsky published his "critical" articles, alternating these pieces with the publication of anti-Soviet lampoons. It was precisely in *Novy mir* that blasphemous articles appeared questioning the heroic past of our people and the Soviet Army . . . and scoffing at the growing pains of Soviet society.

The most damning accusation, by Soviet standards, was that "*Novy mir* has long since lost any concept of its true place in the struggle against alien ideology," and that its authors "systematically and deliberately cultivate a tendency to take a skeptical attitude toward the social and moral values of Soviet society, toward its ideals and achievements." [10]

In the July issue of *Novy mir*, its editors attempted a rebuttal, accusing the eleven writers of flagrant demagoguery and crudely concocted denunciations. It noted that the criticism came from writers who "at various times have been subjected to very serious criticism in *Novy mir* for ideological and artistic slackness, poor knowledge of life, bad taste and unoriginal writing." [11] The next step in the running battle was one of the usual ploys, a letter from a Hero of Socialist Labor, M. Zakharov, addressed to Tvardovsky, informing him that literary publications and their editors were in fact answerable not only to the Writers' Union but to their readers; and *Novy mir*'s readers want the magazine "to march in step with all of us. That is why we sometimes criticize such a subtle thing as literature. Don't judge us too harshly for wanting to receive an answer to this criticism. An answer that is to the point, a Party answer—the working class will accept no other." The combination of cloying humility, deliberate and spurious, and naked menace concluded with a thrust at Tvardovsky: "Who gave some of your authors the right to sneer at our people's most sacred feelings?" [12]

In August, *Literaturnaya gazeta* joined the battle, taking up the cudgels against Dementyev's article, defending the eleven writers' letter to *Ogonyok*, and calling for "socialist realism," ideological purity, and Party-minded literature. It damned *Novy mir*'s editors for being evasive, for brushing aside criticism, for ignoring all opinions other than their own, and asserted that their attitude "only corroborates the reproaches for tendentiousness and arrogance that have frequently been leveled against the magazine." [13]

In September, *Pravda* printed an editorial defending Party spirit in literature as the most "reliable weapon in the struggle against the ideological sabotage of world reaction, against all attempts to demoralize Soviet society from within." The real enemy of creative freedom, the Party paper explained, is "anarcho-individualistic influence which leads the artist away from real life, from the social struggle." The Party, *Pravda* declared, would not relinquish its role in guiding the development of literature and the arts.[14]

In October, the poet Robert Rozhdestvensky attacked those writers who would remain above politics, who would try to immerse themselves in, or concern themselves with, their private lives to the exclusion of the "social struggle." Ironically, he told them: "Be happy. Have nothing to do with politics. Live. Think. Exist." Then, one day, someone would knock at one of their doors with a rifle butt, and a stranger would be standing there with a submachine gun who would laugh at their freedom of action because he had his freedom of action, the power of the gun in the hand, the power to destroy them and their private lives. People at large and writers too must make choices, political choices: they must "fight for peace." [15]

In November, ostensibly as a result of the new vigilance imposed on writers because of Anatoly Kuznetsov's defection to the West, the Writers' Union abruptly and swiftly expelled Solzhenitsyn from membership.[16] Simultaneously charges were lodged against Lydia Chukovskaya, Bulat Okhudzhava, and Lev Kopelev in the Moscow section of the Union. (Kopelev, a writer, critic, and specialist in German literature, was the man on whom Solzhenitsyn had based his character Lev Rubin in *The First Circle*. Like Solzhenitsyn, Kopelev had also been in the concentration camps under Stalin.)

In December, Chakovsky wrote an article for *Pravda*, "The Writer in the Contemporary World," castigating "certain writers [who] not only expound views in their works that are hostile to Marxism . . . but also conduct themselves in a way that makes them outright cohorts in the hostile class activities of the ideologists of capitalist society." The reference was not to Solzhenitsyn alone; Chakovsky insisted that Soviet writers had the right "to criticize, to castigate everything negative, harmful and backward in our life," but only "constructive, creative and businesslike criticism" would be considered acceptable.[17]

The same month, the chief editor of *Teatr*, Yuri Rybankov, one of the few liberals remaining in an important editorial post, was dismissed and replaced by Viktor Lavrentiev.[18] *Teatr* had long been under fire from dogmatist playwrights and drama critics for its modernism and downgrading of Party ideology. Rybankov's ouster undoubtedly encouraged the dogmatists to intensify their efforts to unseat Tvardovsky.

Two months later, in February 1970, the long-anticipated reshuffle of *Novy mir*'s editorial board was announced in *Literaturnaya gazeta*.[19] Soviet authorities had at first attempted to persuade Tvardovsky to agree to a retirement notice, probably on the grounds of ill health; but Tvardovsky refused and instead promptly submitted his resignation. The resignation was accepted by the Secretariat of the Writers' Union,[20] but no public announcement was made; instead, his name was simply replaced on the *Novy mir* masthead by his successor's, Vasily Kosopalov. Reliable sources reported that Tvardovsky had resigned because he thought it useless to continue on a board where the liberals who supported him had been forced out and the dogmatists opposing him now controlled the magazine.[21] Four members of the *Novy mir* board—A. I. Kondratovich, Igor Vinogradov, Vladimir Lakshin, and Igor Sats—were replaced by Dmitry Golshov, Oleg Smirnov, Aleksandr Rekemchuk, and Aleksandr Ovcharenko.

In March, the RSFSR Writers' Union elected Sergey Mikhalkov chairman, yet Tvardovsky and Sholokhov retained their posts too, with Mikhalkov assigned the "middle road" between the liberal and dogmatist poles the two of them were supposed to represent.[22]

In May, the director of the Taganka Theater, Yuri Lyubimov, a liberal, was attacked by Mikhail Tsarev, the president of the Russian Theatrical Society, for failing to show proper concern for the ideological battle with the West. About the Taganka repertory, Tsarev remarked that it had included "ideological[ly] dubious plays [which] led to frequent and justified protest from Soviet public opinion." [23] That month, Sholokhov took the occasion to criticize the liberal poets who focused on negative aspects of Soviet life and who read their poems in the United States—a backhanded slap at both Voznesensky and Yevtushenko. He mentioned neither by name, only commented: "In my view, constant opposition, in whatever form it takes, is good for nothing. . . . It smells bad in both creative work and personal conduct." [24]

A month later, on June 21, the Soviet authorities celebrated Tvardovsky's birthday, publicly praising him highly for his poetry. Almost all the papers and literary journals published some tribute to his poetry and the Supreme Soviet awarded him the Order of the Red Banner "for services in the development of Soviet poetry." No word was said about the role he had played as editor of *Novy mir*. Tvardovsky himself declined the honor of a formal celebration, because, it was reported, he was then involved in the protest against the incarceration of Zhores Medvedev in a mental institution.[25] It is likely, too, that Tvardovsky was not in the mood to celebrate his recent departure from the magazine to which he had given so much.

During that fall and winter there were a few blows distributed among the conservatives, chiefly against Kochetov and Ivan Shevtsov for their novels. In November, *Oktyabr* printed the first chapters of Kochetov's novel *What Do You Want?* and then the remainder in three successive issues of the magazine. The novel called for a return to the rigorous discipline of the Stalinist era. In March, 65,000 copies of a new novel by Ivan Shevtsov, *In the Name of the Father and of the Son*, were published, and in the spring a second Shevtsov novel, *Love and Hate*, was issued in an edition of 200,000 copies. All three were dogmatic works full of pro-Stalin sentiments, jingoistic and clumsily "socialist realist," and all three came in for their share of censure for artistic shortcomings, despite their avowed intention of warning Soviet citizens of the dangers of liberalism, revisionism, and intellectualism.

But Kochetov was after bigger game. For one thing, he has a father in his novel explain to his son that the 1930s—the worst period of the Stalinist purge—were really quite a good time because the kulaks had been "liquidated" and "all forms of opposition within the Party destroyed." The younger generation, the father cautions, is too careless: "You believe too much in the peaceloving sirens. Your emblem has become the Biblical dove with the palm leaf in its bill. How did that replace the hammer and sickle? The dove is Biblical, from so-called sacred writing; it is not from Marxism." [26] The villains of the novel are Soviet liberals led astray by Western ideas, duped into being anti-Stalinists. Kochetov's view exemplifies the Brezhnev-Kosygin line: Stalin might have had weaknesses and made errors, but they were by no means as great or numerous as the liberals contended; therefore the sons had better pay more attention to the wisdom of their fathers rather than allow themselves to be seduced by the fashionable foolishness of Western-oriented ideas. Ironically, Kochetov was, in one instance, taken to task for having portrayed only cynics, scoundrels, and riffraff among the young, and also for having failed to show the "leading and organizing role of the Party in the life of our society." [27] Angry protests were heard from the Italian Communist Party paper, *L'Unità*, because Kochetov had written a malicious caricature of its critic Vittorio Strada in the novel. It was Strada to whom Solzhenitsyn had entrusted his letter to the West forbidding publication of his novel *Cancer Ward*.[28] There were similar vicious depictions, only barely disguised, of poets Voznesensky and Bella Akhmadulina in Shevtsov's *In the Name of the Father and of the Son*.

22 The Writers' Union Debacle

I am at peace. I know that I will fulfill my duty as a writer under all circumstances and perhaps with more success and authority after my death than during my life. No one will succeed in barring the road to truth, and I am ready to die in order that it may go forward.

Aleksandr Solzhenitsyn

Summoned to a meeting of the Ryazan branch of the RSFSR Writers' Union on the morning of November 4, 1969, Aleksandr Solzhenitsyn was expelled that same afternoon, following a hearing attended by six of the seven-member total branch membership. Five voted against Solzhenitsyn, and only Solzhenitsyn cast a lone vote for himself. At first there was a single dissenter who said: "I am hesitant. There is a pendulum swing. We go from one extreme to the other. Thus, in the past, Essenin was vilified, then praised to the skies. Do you still remember 1946 [the time of the Stalinist Zhdanov decrees in the arts]? It is hard for me to unravel things. Today we oust Solzhenitsyn and later we will rehabilitate him. I want no part of that." [1] Subsequently the dissenter obediently voted with the others. Also present as an "observer" was Franz Taurin, the assistant secretary of the RSFSR Writers' Union; [2] acting as the Party spokesman, he explained that one of the reasons for strengthening ideological work was the "defection of Kuznetsov." [3] The RSFSR Union was probably used to expel Solzhenitsyn because it was a dogmatist stronghold and because there was opposition to the move in the All-Soviet Writers' Union. The underground *Chronicle of Current Events* reported that it was the Agitprop department of the Communist Party's Ryazan section which actually brought pressure to bear on the local Writers' Union branch to institute the expulsion proceedings against Solzhenitsyn. [4]

The charges leveled at the novelist were the same ones with which the Party and the Writers' Union had been belaboring him since 1966. The essence of the regime's argument against the novelist was that intensified ideological warfare imposed increasing responsibilities on Soviet writers in their work and public conduct, and Solzhenitsyn had not assumed his share of the burden of those important responsibilities. A formal statement contended:

In recent years hostile bourgeois propaganda has actively used A. Solzhenitsyn's name and writing for a campaign of slander against our country. However, A. Solzhenitsyn has not only failed publicly to state his attitude toward this campaign, but has, despite criticism from the Soviet public and repeated recommendations from the USSR Writers' Union, facilitated the whipping up of an anti-Soviet hullabaloo around his name through certain actions and statements of his. The address of A. Solzhenitsyn, who took part in the meeting, indicated that he continues to hold positions unworthy of a Soviet writer.[5]

Other complaints against him were also voiced. He had not taken part in the work of the Ryazan branch of the Writers' Union; he had not made himself available to younger writers and helped them; he had cut himself off from other Union members. The main charge, however, was that he had blackened everything in Soviet life—"He has a black inside"—and because of that, his work was being used to denigrate the Soviet Union. The clearest, if perhaps the most ingenuous, comment came from the regional secretary for Party propaganda, who told Solzhenitsyn: "You deny the leading role of the Party. Everyone marches at the same pace as the Party, but not you." [6] The sound of a different drummer is anathema in the Soviet Union, and, therefore, the Ryazan meeting unanimously noted, "Solzhenitsyn's conduct has been antisocial in nature and is fundamentally at variance with the principles and tasks formulated in the Charter of the USSR Writers' Union." [7] Solzhenitsyn was, consequently, expelled from Union membership.

As always, Solzhenitsyn defended himself vigorously and ably, pointing out that people condemned his writings without ever having read them—several of those at the Ryazan meeting confessed that they had never read the books they were criticizing—and although he had recommended public readings and discussions of his work, they had not been authorized. He maintained that he had answered all the legitimate questions put to him by the Union, that the Union in its turn had swept his questions under the rug; and he tried to explain how his novels had been published abroad:

In the spring of 1968, I wrote to *Literaturnaya Gazeta*, *Le Monde* and *L'Unità* in order to forbid publication of *Cancer Ward* and to deny all rights to Western publishers. The letter was not allowed to go to *Le Monde*, although it was registered. I entrusted the letter to *L'Unità* to the Italian critic Vittorio Strada. The customs confiscated it. I managed to convince the customs officer to send it to *L'Unità* for publication. *L'Unità* published it in June. *Literaturnaya Gazeta* was still waiting.

For nine weeks, from April 21 to June 26, it hid the letter from the public. It was waiting until *Cancer Ward* was published in the West. When the book was published by the Milan publisher Mondadori, in a horrible Russian edition, *Literaturnaya Gazeta* published my letter, accusing me of not having protested vigorously enough. If it had made my letter known in time, this would have been unnecessary. That is proved by the fact that the American publishers decided not to bring the book out when they learned of my objection.[8]

The president of the Ryazan branch interrupted Solzhenitsyn to say that Solzhenitsyn's time was up. The novelist furiously retorted: "To hell with the time limit. This is vital." He asked for ten minutes more and was given three. In a memorable speech, he thereupon summed up:

The crimes of Stalin cannot be hushed up indefinitely. One cannot indefinitely go against the truth. For these are crimes committed against millions of human beings. They demand to be illuminated. What moral influence does hiding them have on the youth? Youth is not stupid. It understands.

I do not disavow one line, one word of my letter to the Writers' Congress. I said in that: "I am at peace. I know that I will fulfill my duty as a writer under all circumstances and perhaps with more success and authority after my death than during my life. No one will succeed in barring the road to truth, and I am ready to die in order that it may go forward."

Yes, I am ready to die and not merely to be expelled from the Writers' Union. Vote. You are the majority. But do not forget that the history of literature will take note of today's meeting.[9]

The expulsion was a foregone conclusion. Franz Taurin told Solzhenitsyn what the regime wanted of him: "The main thing is that you have not hit back at the enemy. No one wants to bring you to your knees. This meeting is an attempt to help you free yourself of everything the West has placed upon your shoulders. The writer Fedin has implored you with all the authority of his great age: Give in! Hit back at the West!" [10] But Solzhenitsyn continued stubbornly to refuse to kiss the rod.

On November 6, his case was reviewed at the section level of the Union in Moscow. Informed of the meeting at the last moment, Solzhenitsyn was unable (and unwilling) to attend.

After the Ryazan vote, Franz Taurin . . . told Solzhenitsyn to attend the Union in Moscow at 3 o'clock the next afternoon. "It's impossible," Solzhenitsyn exclaimed. How could a meeting in Moscow be scheduled only minutes after the Ryazan decision? Surely the secretariat did not *anticipate* the decision of the Ryazan group? If so, said Solzhenitsyn, it had acted unconstitutionally and he would not accept a verbal, non-formal summons.

The next morning, a telegram summoning him officially was sent to Ryazan—to the Union, not to his apartment—and taken to him by hand at 11:20. There was no chance of Solzhenitsyn's reaching Moscow by 3 P.M. The door-to-door journey would take at least four hours, and the trains were delayed by people celebrating the October Revolution.[11]

At the Moscow meeting, Solzhenitsyn's expulsion from the Union was confirmed, and only Aleksandr Tvardovsky spoke up in his behalf. [12] In effect, the expulsion meant that Solzhenitsyn would now be denied all those perquisites which membership in the Union confers: health insurance, pensions, vacations, grants and loans, lecture tours, and other advantages. Most important, the expulsion confirmed formally that as an author in disgrace Solzhenitsyn would henceforth not be published in his homeland.[13] As for the writers themselves, about whom Andrei Amalrik had been so cynical, there was more evidence of failure of nerve. On November 23, 1969, only 7 of Solzhenitsyn's colleagues in the Union had courage enough to ask the Union to reconsider its ouster of the novelist.[14] They were 7 of the 6,790 members of the Writers' Union; but among the 7 were Bulat Okhudzhava, Yury Trifonov, Vladimir Tendryakov, and Grigory Baklanov.[15] Confirmation of the ouster was reported to have gone all the way up to, and been approved by, the Politburo itself.[16]

Four days later, Solzhenitsyn added his own voice to the protest in a letter to the RSFSR Writers' Union. He did more than simply rise to his own defense: he took the offensive against the role played by the Writers' Union and the procedures which most Soviet citizens take for granted as proper. The letter, made available to Western newspapermen by the novelist's acquaintances, minced no words:

Shamelessly flouting your own constitution, you have expelled me in feverish haste and in my absence, without even sending me a warning telegram, without even giving me the four hours to travel from Ryazan to be present. You have demonstrated openly that the decision preceded the deliberations. Was it more convenient for you to invent new accusations against me in my absence? Were you afraid that you would have to give me ten minutes to reply? I am forced to substitute this letter.

Your watches are behind the times. They are running centuries slow. Open your heavy expensive curtains. You do not even suspect that dawn has risen outside. It is no longer that deaf, dim time of no exit that it was when you expelled Akhmatova. It is not even that timid, frigid time when you shouted Pasternak out. Wasn't that shameful enough for you?

Do you want to compound it? The day is near when every one of you will try to find out how you can scrape your signatures off today's resolution. The blind lead the blind. You don't even notice that you are cheering for the side you have declared yourself against. In this time of crisis in our seriously sick society you are not able to suggest anything constructive, anything good, only your hate-vigilance. Your obese articles crawl about. Your mindless works move flabbily. But there are no arguments. Only voting and administration.

Thus neither Sholokhov nor all of you together dared to answer the famous letter of Lidia Chukovskaya, pride of Russian essayists.

For her the administrative pincers are being prepared. How could she dare to allow her unpublished book to be read? Since the higher levels have decided not to print you, crush yourself, choke yourself. Don't exist. Don't let anyone read you.

They are also driving Lev Kopolev to expulsion—a front-line war veteran, already having served a 10-year jail term though innocent.

Now, if you please, he is guilty of standing up for those who are hounded, of going around talking about a holy secret, of violating a confidence with an influential person.

Why do you conduct such conversations which you have to hide from the people? Were we not promised 50 years ago that there would never again be secret diplomacy, secret talks, secret, incomprehensible appointments and reshuffles, that the masses would know and judge everything openly?

"The enemy is listening." That's your answer. These eternal enemies are the basis of your existence. What would you do without your enemies? You would not be able to live without your enemies. Hate, hate no less evil than racism, has become your sterile atmosphere. But in this way the feeling of a whole and single mankind is being lost and its perdition is being accelerated.

And if tomorrow the ice of the Antarctic melted and all of us were transformed into drowning mankind, then into whose nose would you stuff the class struggle? Not to mention even when the remnants of two-legged creatures will roam the radioactive earth and die.

Just the same, it is time to remember that the first thing we belong to is humanity. And humanity is separated from the animal world by thought and speech and they should naturally be free. If they are fettered, we go back to being animals.

Publicity and openness, honest and complete—that is the prime condition for the health of every society, and ours too. The man who does not want them in our country is indifferent to his fatherland and thinks only about his own gain. The man who does not want publicity and openness for his fatherland does not want to cleanse it of its diseases but to drive them inside, so that they may fester there.[17]

Solzhenitsyn's powerful letter was not published inside the Soviet Union, but its appearance abroad, and his expulsion from the Writers' Union, brought a flurry of protests and appeals, even from among those who were often thought to be sympathetic to the Soviet cause. Bertrand Russell wrote directly to Premier Kosygin to advise him that the expulsion of Solzhenitsyn was "in the interest neither of justice nor the good name of the Soviet Union." The international PEN club sent a letter to the Soviet Writers' Union bearing the signatures of Arthur Miller—who had framed the letter —Yukio Mishima, Günter Grass, Heinrich Böll, Friedrich Dürrenmatt, and John Updike, among others, which read, in part:

We reject the conception that an artistic refusal to humbly accept state censorship is in any sense criminal in a civilized society, or that publication by foreigners of his books is ground for persecuting him. . . .

We sign our names as men of peace declaring our solidarity with Aleksandr Solzhenitsyn's defence of those fundamental rights of the human spirit which unite civilized people anywhere.[18]

A letter from thirty-one distinguished writers and intellectuals appeared in the *London Times* appealing to the USSR to stop persecuting Solzhenitsyn and threatened an international cultural boycott. Signed by Hannah Arendt, W. H. Auden, Graham Greene, Rolf Hochhuth and Julian Huxley, among others, it stated, "The treatment of Soviet writers in their own country has become an international scandal," and said that silencing Solzhenitsyn was "in itself a crime against civilization." [19] A French protest in *Le Monde* included the signatures of Jean-Paul Sartre, Vercors, Michel Butor, Christiane Rochefort, and Elsa Triolet:

Is it really necessary that the great writers of the USSR be treated like noxious beings? . . . How could we have believed that today, in the homeland of triumphant socialism, that that which not even a Nicholas II would have thought of doing to Chekhov, when he freely published his *Sakhalin*, would be the fate of a writer who is the most characteristic of the great Russian tradition, Aleksandr Solzhenitsyn, once already a victim of the Stalinist repression and whose essential crime it is to have survived? [20]

Early in December, when Soviet Minister of Culture Yekaterina Furtseva was in Paris, she was questioned so savagely by French journalists about Solzhenitsyn's being silenced and expelled from the Writers' Union that she was prompted to say, in anger, "Let Solzhenitsyn write some good books and they will be published in the USSR." She recommended that Solzhenitsyn "describe Soviet reality with its positive aspects, but not deform those realities." [21] The regime had, obviously, not changed its tune.

That same month Soviet dissidents circulated an unofficial protest signed by thirty-nine of them, including Pyotr Yakir, which said that the expulsion represented "another major manifestation of Stalinism, a reprisal against a writer who embodies the conscience and mind of our people." [22]

The response of the Soviet leaders to Solzhenitsyn's letters and to the appeals and protests in his behalf was swift and unbending. Speaking through the Writers' Union paper, *Literaturnaya gazeta*, they defended the expulsion, promised no compromise or reconsideration, and in a rejoinder by the RSFSR Writers' Union Secretariat denied that Solzhenitsyn had not been given enough time to appear in his own defense. Instead, they maintained that the novelist had "deliberately avoided being present at the meeting and did not take advantage of the opportunity given him." [23] The reply also maintained that the discussions in Ryazan and Moscow, however brief, were more than sufficient, because the criticism of Solzhenitsyn had been going on for years—it specifically noted the May and September 1967 meetings of the Writers' Union board with Solzhenitsyn, and the June 26 *Literaturnaya gazeta* article, "The Ideological Struggle: The Writer's Responsibility"—but had had no effect whatever on Solzhenitsyn. Quite the contrary; Solzhenitsyn had arrogantly ignored the just criticisms by the Soviet "public" and flagrantly violated the regulations of the Writers' Union.

Three serious charges in the *Literaturnaya gazeta* broadside made it conceivable that the authorities might soon bring Solzhenitsyn to trial as they had Sinyavsky and Daniel. First, the authorities made it seem as if Solzhenitsyn was deliberately masterminding the smuggling of his materials abroad. Second, they stressed that his works were being exploited by foreign publications, "among them such openly anti-Soviet, White Guard organs as *Possev* and *Grani*." "We shall note in passing," *Literaturnaya gazeta* remarked, "that the anti-Soviet centers abroad are utilizing the publication of Solzhenitsyn's works not only for the political struggle against our country, but also for the direct financing of various subversive organizations." The article then accused Solzhenitsyn of having his royalties "systematically transferred to the fund of the so-called 'International Rescue Committee,' whose principal task is organizing hostile actions against the USSR and the countries of the socialist commonwealth." Such charges were tantamount to charges of espionage and treason, but the article went still further:

The stream of publications, skillfully organized and directed, has been accompanied by unambiguous compliments from bourgeois commentators and "Sovietologists" who have had no difficulty in detecting in

Solzhenitsyn's works malicious attacks on socialism and the Soviet way of life. The enemies of our country have elevated him to the rank of "leader" of the "political opposition in the USSR," an invention of theirs, and have even proclaimed him a "prophet of things to come."

Espionage, treason, political opposition: the accusations had all the old Stalinist echoes. Solzhenitsyn was then declared to have shown his true colors in his open letter, betraying the fact that he held opinions alien to the Soviet people and their literature, and "thereby confirmed the necessity, justice and inevitability of his expulsion from the Writers' Union." [24]

The final paragraph of the article provided both a threat and an alternative to a Sinyavsky-Daniel type trial: it said simply that Solzhenitsyn was free to leave the Soviet Union. "In the event that Solzhenitsyn should wish to go where his anti-Soviet works and letters always meet with such enthusiasm," *Literaturnaya gazeta* promised, no one would hold him back.[25] It was the same threat that had finally brought Pasternak to his knees, forcing him publicly to condemn the "anti-Soviet" aspects of his novel *Doctor Zhivago*. Like Pasternak, Solzhenitsyn would not accept the invitation to emigrate. According to his friends, he refused to leave his homeland because he considered himself "a Russian writer whose place was in his own land, not abroad working as an anti-Soviet propagandist, no matter how deeply he opposed the present Soviet regime."

Mr. Solzhenitsyn's acquaintances say he is aware that, without soliciting it, he had become the hero of a small but passionate group of intellectuals and literary liberals here. Thus . . . Solzhenitsyn has become a symbol of hope for those who want a more open society in the Soviet Union. Whether he wants such a symbolic role or not, his friends say, it has been forced on him and could affect his decision to remain or emigrate.[26]

A British report remarked:

As with Pasternak, admiration for Solzhenitsyn in the Soviet Union is almost total, extending even to that majority of the population which normally finds it natural or expedient to agree with the party line on dissenting writers. This is partly because of Solzhenitsyn's rocklike integrity and courage, which is so patent that even the ranks of Tuscany cannot forbear to cheer, but more because he exhibits a profound attachment to his native Russia, and this is the one quality which all Russians of otherwise divergent views are prepared to acknowledge as beyond reproach.[27]

A Canadian view noted both strong popular support *for* the censorship and strong popular feeling *against* Solzhenitsyn. That did not contradict the other views expressed, but surely supplemented them:

> To content oneself with the idea that this is a land of strict literary censorship operating in the interests of a totalitarian regime does not get us very far. The trouble is partly that. But just as much that the censorship rests on a very wide base of popular acceptance and on a very deep base of Russian tradition.
>
> Solzhenitsyn's one crime has been to put himself above the unwritten Russian law (Russian not Soviet) which prohibits providing comfort to the enemy. . . . "But he writes against us," a young doctor recently answered when I expressed my own personal disgust with the treatment accorded to Solzhenitsyn.[28]

Most of the protests and appeals from foreigners in behalf of Solzhenitsyn were officially ignored, but Konstantin Fedin did reply to the PEN club telegram from David Carver and Pierre Emmanuel, international secretary and president respectively of the international PEN, angrily rejecting the telegram as "unprecedented interference in the internal affairs of the Writers' Union of the USSR for which the observance of its rules lies exclusively within its competence." [29] Nobel laureate Mikhail Sholokhov took the offensive in addressing a collective farmers' conference, calling Solzhenitsyn a "Colorado beetle" by indirection. "You have done away with pests," Sholokhov told the kolkhozniks, "but unfortunately we [writers] still have Colorado beetles—those who eat Soviet bread but want to serve Western bourgeois masters and send their works there through secret channels. Soviet men of letters want to get rid of them." [30]

In February 1970, the Soviet Union withdrew from the European Community of Writers, which had also objected to the treatment of Solzhenitsyn. Though this organization, led by two Italians, Giuseppe Ungaretti and Giancarlo Vigorelli, was devoted to expanding East–West cultural relations and had been a useful and sympathetic sounding board for Soviet views, it had published a manifesto warning that if Solzhenitsyn were not reinstated in the Writers' Union, it would have no choice but "regretfully to suspend all collaboration" with the Soviet Union. Shortly thereafter, Tvardovsky resigned as vice-president of the organization, and Nikolai Gribachev addressed a long open letter to Vigorelli in which he stated that Solzhenitsyn had been expelled for violating the Writers' Union regulations and that changing the rules to permit his re-entry would be undemocratic. "You, Mr. Vigorelli, shed tears over the fate of Solzhenitsyn," Gribachev wrote. "However, I can tell you this quite honestly, Solzhenitsyn has a good apartment, he is alive and healthy." The upshot was simple and almost inevitable. On February 11, Soviet writers wired the European Community: "Your position rules out the possibility of further cooperation with you." [31]

The underground *Chronicle of Current Events* did manage to communicate some of the Western reaction to Solzhenitsyn's expulsion from the Writers' Union to the Soviet people. In its issue No. 12, February 28, 1970, it quoted (among others) Pierre Emmanuel, the president of the international PEN club and a member of the prestigious French Academy:

Quite justifiably all people are filled with outrage at the events in Greece, but simultaneously their approach to the conditions of the Soviet intelligentsia is inhibited because they consider Russian totalitarianism only an accidental and transient phenomenon. This is an error which only reinforces the machinery of oppression in the East. . . . The very right to think freely is what is denied, in the name of socialism, in the Soviet Union. . . . Censorship and the police . . . prohibit the faithful from praying, philosophers from thinking, and writers from creating. If one inquires into this systematic transformation of a whole generation of talented people into slaves and liars, one is forced into recognizing a slow genocide of the soul. If this regime persists, by the end of the century all Eastern Europe may have become a spiritual desert.

The *Chronicle* also gave Emmanuel's carefully reasoned explanation of why this ouster from the Writers' Union, though not as bad as Sinyavsky's and Daniel's confinement to Siberian labor camps, nonetheless was bad enough: it left Solzhenitsyn exposed, a writer without a profession and its benefits, so that he might be faced with prison as a "parasite," or a psychiatric ward, or any other of the nefarious punishments the regime contrived to impose on writers who did not follow the Party's instructions. "In the [regime's] attempts to humiliate the great writer," Emmanuel commented, "they provoke him by suggesting that he emigrate. But the very purpose of Solzhenitsyn's life is to remain in his own country at any price; there he is asserting his right to die for the truth."

There were no further public attacks on Solzhenitsyn for the time being, and the novelist ignored Sholokhov's suggestion that he emigrate. A few months later, however, in March 1970, Solzhenitsyn took a significant step; a brief announcement in Western newspapers declared that he had retained the Zurich attorney Fritz Heeb to defend his interests abroad and to protect the copyrights of his works.[32] Such a move seemed intended only to protect the novelist's proprietary rights in foreign countries, but in making the move Solzhenitsyn might perhaps be more easily able to control the publication of his writings and the conditions under which they were published. Still, no word of recantation, no disavowal of his books, no attack on the West came from Solzhenitsyn, nor did he consent to those obeisances which might make him *persona grata* to the Soviet authorities, restore him to membership in the Writers' Union, and permit his writing to be published—albeit bowdlerized—in his native land.

In Switzerland, Heeb publicly declared: "Solzhenitsyn has no intention of becoming the easy prey of unscrupulous publishers. He intends to take legal action, if necessary, to prevent the misuse of his name and the unauthorized publication of his work." Heeb also rejected the Soviet charges that the novelist's royalties had gone to "anti-Soviet organizations" as false and malicious.[33]

23 Psychiatric Wards

> With cheerful face,
> Russia falls,
>   As if into mirrors.
> For her son—
>   A dose of stelazine
> For herself—
>   The Potma convoy.
>
> *Natalia Gorbanevskaya*

There was no letup in the persecution of dissidents. More and more often the psychiatric ward and the insane asylum became the government's means to punish them, though exile, prisons, and concentration camps were by no means scanted. In May 1969, General Grigorenko set out for Tashkent, knowing in advance that he would be arrested but nonetheless determined to witness the trial of R. F. Kadiyev, a brilliant Tatar physicist who was being tried with ten other Tatar intellectuals for helping in their people's campaign to persuade the government to permit them to return to their Crimean homeland. Anatole Shub cites Kadiyev as another example of that swift reversal of human fortunes for political reasons endemic in the Soviet Union. The year before, Kadiyev had presented "to an international conference in Tblisi startling new astronomical and space researches confirming and deepening Einstein's theory of relativity. . . . *Za Kommunism*, newspaper of the Dubno Atomic Research Institute, was proudly hailing Kadiyev's feat as recently as November 22, 1968. Today, Kadiyev sits in Tashkent jail." [1] When Grigorenko arrived in Tashkent, he was arrested and kept for ten months without trial in solitary confinement after being committed in October to the hospital for the criminally insane in Kazan. [2] Later that year *samizdat* copies of Grigorenko's notes in prison reported his experiences there at the hands of the KGB in Tashkent: how he had been beaten, put into a strait jacket, been painfully force-fed when he protested his treatment by a hunger strike. In June, Grigorenko was informed that his family—his sick, elderly wife and his invalid son—had been deprived of their pension; and in October, after his wife had traveled nineteen hundred miles to visit him, she was refused even the briefest meeting.[3] In November, Grigorenko was subjected to a psychiatric examination in Moscow, and in February, after a two-day court proceeding, was declared legally insane, a "paranoid." [4] After the psychiatrists had rendered their diagnosis, Grigorenko spoke out: "Until a real stop is put to the abuse of power in our country, every honest person must take part in the fight against it. Of course, if the only 'normal' citizen is one who bows his head to every bureaucrat who exceeds his power, then I am certainly 'abnormal.' " [5]

Circulated with Grigorenko's prison notes was an appeal from his wife, Zinaida, declaring that her husband had been incarcerated for his logic and common sense, that he was perfectly sane, and that he was being threatened with death. She called to all "democratic citizens of the world. Help save my husband. The freedom of one man is the freedom of every man." [6]

During the summer, in August, Anatoly Marchenko was tried in the city of Perm in the western Urals for "slander and anti-Soviet propaganda," and sentenced to two years. The thirty-year-old worker and author had been freed in 1966 and sentenced a second time in 1968 for his protest against Soviet political machinations and press vilification of Czechoslovakia; he was now sentenced a third time.[7]

On December 1, the KGB arrested two young Moscow University students, Olga Ioffe and Irina Kaplun. While searching Miss Ioffe's flat, the KGB discovered several *samizdat* manuscripts, poetry the girl and her father, Y. Ioffe, had written; all were confiscated, as was Miss Ioffe's typewriter. The two young girls were charged with preparing a protest against the celebration of Stalin's ninetieth birthday scheduled for December 21. Both girls had a history of dissidence that went back to 1966, when, with a group of nine other high-school students all under sixteen, they had pasted up leaflets which stated: "There must be no repetition of the Stalin era. Everything depends on us." Three hundred such leaflets were pasted up or mailed to various people in Moscow. The KGB had interrogated the two girls then in an effort to discover if any adults were behind their activities and had counseled them that if they saw things wrong with their country, they ought to come and "see us at the KGB and talk it over with us." They also told Irina Kaplun, whose uncle had been murdered in the Stalin purges in 1938, that she ought to be grateful that the authorities had seen fit to rehabilitate him (in 1956) altogether.[8] On August 20, 1970, Miss Ioffe was committed to an insane asylum as a "chronic schizophrenic." [9]

(One of the problems that terror creates is precisely this geometric progression in making enemies of those related to the people persecuted. When the KGB puts one man in a concentration camp or prison, tortures and starves him, works him to death or puts a bullet in the back of his head, it makes enemies among the man's family and friends; and they are slow to forget and slower still to forgive. Consequently, it is logical that frequently where one finds a dissident, one finds someone personally scarred by the purges and the other crimes of Stalinism. Simply to mention a few examples: Pyotr Yakir's father, Iona Yakir, was killed in the purges of the Red Army; Sinyavsky's father was arrested by the KGB; Aksyonov's mother spent years in Siberian concentration camps; Chukovskaya's husband, an eminent Leningrad scientist, was shot as an enemy of the people; Anna Akhmatova's husband Gumilev was shot in the 1920s, and her son spent years in a concentration camp; Bulat Okhudzhava's father was shot in the great purges and his mother imprisoned for nineteen years in the Arctic labor camps; Yevtushenko's grandfather Yermolay Yevtushenko was arrested for high treason in 1938, and his maternal grandfather, Rudolf Gangnus, was jailed as a Latvian spy. The scars of the dissidents are by no means unique. On the contrary, their heightened sensitivity to Stalinism and repression in general is representative on a more conscious and purposive level of millions of ordinary Soviet citizens whose families or friends suffered in the purges, repressions, mass population transfers, executions, and imprisonments that characterized Stalin's regime.)

Four days after Miss Ioffe's commitment another nineteen-year-old student, Valeria Novodvorskaya, was arrested for distributing leaflets which contained a poem that criticized the Communist Party for the evils it had inflicted on the people and the country. The Serbsky Institute found her unstable, and she was tried in March *in absentia* by a Moscow court, which ordered her committed to the special psychiatric ward of the Kazan prison as a "paranoid schizophrenic." That she had distributed the poem in front of the Palace of Congresses was an added irritation to the KGB.[10]

On December 5, also, the "traditional silent demonstration was held on Pushkin Square" in Moscow. The first of these demonstrations had been organized in 1966 in support of Sinyavsky and Daniel, after their arrest but before their trial. "This time 50 people went out on Pushkin Square to honor the memory of their comrades in camps, prisons and exiles. At six o'clock in the evening, the demonstrators, surrounded by a crowd of plain-clothes sentry guards, bared their heads." [11] The demonstrators were swiftly routed by the KGB, but none was roughed up or arrested, and for the time being it seemed that the KGB were being careful not to provoke further demonstrations, arrests, and trials—and trying to avoid the creation of martyrs that arise from such actions.

Shortly before the celebration of the anniversary of her father's birth, the Presidium of the Supreme Soviet approved a decree stripping Svetlana Alliluyeva of her Soviet citizenship. The action was taken, the decree declared, because of her "misconduct, defaming the title citizen of the USSR," but it said nothing of the fact that Stalin's daughter had burned her Soviet passport publicly in the summer of 1967 after she was severely assailed by Communist political and literary leaders, or that she had also formally renounced her Soviet citizenship in letters to the Soviet consulate in Washington during the summer of 1969.[12]

At the end of the year, Viktor Krasin, one of the most courageous and outspoken of the small band of Moscow dissidents, who was himself a victim of Stalin's concentration camps for having dared to criticize the dictator, and had earlier lost his job as an economist at a Moscow academic institution, was exiled for five years on charges of being "an anti-social parasite," though the law under which he was convicted was already in the process of being rescinded. (In fact, two months later, on February 25, the antiparasite law was replaced by new regulation which forced people to engage in "socially useful work" or face penalties of up to a year in prison or a labor camp. Public announcement of the legal change, however, was not made until May 10.) [13]

Also in December, Anatoly Jakobson, a translator, was arrested at a Red Square demonstration protesting the celebration of the anniversary of Stalin's birth. Arrested with him was the poet Natalia Gorbanevskaya. This time, the KGB did not show her the leniency they had shown after arresting her in 1968 during the demonstration against the Soviet invasion of Czechoslovakia. Instead, they tried her *in absentia*, and with the help of the always cooperative Serbsky Institute committed her to a mental hospital. Though she was pregnant and at first admitted to a maternity hospital, a week later she was transferred to a psychiatric hospital. There she was reminded of a poem sha had written in 1966, after Yury Galanskov had forcibly been committed to the same Kaschenko mental hospital and dosed with the tranquilizer stelazine:

> In the mad house
> Wring your hands,
> Press your white forehead
> Against the wall
> Like a face into a snowdrift.
> Into the hosts of violence
> With cheerful face,
> Russia falls,
> As if into mirrors.
> For her son—
> A dose of stelazine,
> For herself—
> The Potma convoy.[14]

With Grigorenko at the trial of the Tatar intellectuals in Tashkent had been Major Genrigh Altumyan. Both of them had then addressed a protest to the United Nations against Soviet injustices to the Tatars. In July, Altumyan was arrested in Kharkov, and when his apartment was searched, the KGB found *samizdat* copies of Andrei Sakharov's memorandum on "convergence," [15] copies of the *Chronicle of Current Events*, and a copy of Solzhenitsyn's *Cancer Ward*. On orders from the KGB, Altumyan was thereupon dismissed from his job for "links with Yakir and Grigorenko," and in November sentenced to three years in prison.

The underground *Chronicle* continued to report trials in Moscow, Gorki, Kharkov, Riga, Kiev, and in two towns in the Uzbek SSR.

In many of those trials the regime declared defendants "irresponsible," therefore refusing them permission to appear at their own trials—and of course preventing the potentially embarrassing scenes denials of guilt and protests over illegal procedures might cause. Many of the accused were simply remanded to psychiatric hospitals. In one such case involving V. L. Gershuni, a thirty-nine-year-old stonemason and nephew of the founder of the Socialist Revolutionary Party in Russia, the official verdict ignored the testimony of witnesses at the trial. Gershuni was accused of "anti-Soviet slander" under Article 190/1, because he had in his possession a document defending Grigorenko. Though his co-workers testified that he was quite sane, a good worker and a morally sound individual,[16] the court accepted the findings of the Serbsky Institute instead; it recommended that Gershuni be committed to a mental hospital. In protest, Gershuni went on a two-week hunger strike and was subsequently removed to the political prisoners' wing in the infamous Butyrki Prison.

A Gorki University history teacher and three students were also tried in March. They had been arrested the previous summer (1969) for distributing leaflets which opposed the restoration of Stalin, the invasion of Czechoslovakia, the repression of the Crimean Tatars, and the persecution of individuals for their religious beliefs. On April 24, the defendants were found guilty; the teacher and one student were each sentenced to seven years of imprisonment, one student to six years, and the last to five years.[17] One of the students was ordered to have a psychiatric examination, but when his wife, whose parents had been persecuted during the Stalin era, threatened to commit self-immolation if her husband was committed to a mental institution, he was charged as a common criminal instead.

In March, also, three eminent scientists, Andrei Sakharov, Roy Medvedev, and Valentin Turchin, circulated a four-thousand-word appeal for gradual "democratization" of Soviet life. The appeal's basic premise was that freedom of ideas and information is essential to the growth and success of a modern economy. It also promulgated a fourteen-point program which would make information about the state accessible to the public, permit foreign books and papers to be sold, create a public-opinion institute, reform the legal and educational systems, and eventually offer direct elections with a choice of candidates for both Party and government positions. The three scientists also criticized the treatment of dissenters who were trying to reform the Soviet system from within: "How can one justify the detention in prisons, camps and psychiatric clinics of persons who, although in opposition, act entirely within the framework of the law?" [18]

On March 19, S. P. Pisarev, a Communist of fifty-two years' standing, a professional Party worker, and a decorated war veteran and invalid, sent an open letter to the Presidium of the Soviet Academy of Medical Sciences protesting the "mistakes" committed by the Serbsky Institute and explained the reasons for them: the institute "provide[s] a pseudo-scientific sanction for the indeterminate isolation of psychologically healthy people in prison hospitals." He recalled that the Serbsky Institute had been involved in similar activities during the Stalinist period. They had even been exposed in 1956 by a special Central Committee commission which had resulted in hundreds of perfectly sane people being released from psychiatric wards. The commission had concluded that "it was indispensable to reorganize the business of psychiatric commitments and to place the Serbsky Institute together with the prison-psychiatric hospitals of Kazan and Leningrad entirely under the jurisdiction of the Ministry of Health." After two years during which the commission report was not reviewed or made public, it was relegated to the archives, and members and leaders of the commission were removed by the Central Committee on a variety of pretexts. "The guilty parties were not only not punished, but remained at their posts." [19]

Late in April 1970 there were reports of new repressions, chief among them the mass arrest of dissident Tatars who had come to Moscow to demonstrate in front of the Lenin Library during the centennial celebrations of Lenin's birth. Once again, their plea for restoration of their civil rights and return to their Crimean homeland was ignored.[20]

On May 21, the maverick historian and playwright Andrei Amalrik was arrested and removed to Sverdlovsk, where, it was reported, he would probably be tried under Article 190/1 for "defaming the Soviet state." KGB men from Moscow arrested Amalrik at his summer cottage in Ryazan province on the ground that Russian-language copies of his books—*Will the Soviet Union Survive until 1984?* and

Involuntary Journey to Siberia—were being circulated clandestinely in Sverdlovsk.[21]

On the tenth anniversary of Boris Pasternak's death, a brief celebration took place at the poet's graveside outside Peredelkino. Groups of people came to decorate the grave with red and yellow tulips and to await the coming of a group of writers they heard were planning a memorial reading of Pasternak's works. " 'Do you think we will see Aleksandr Isayevich?' a woman asked her husband in a near whisper, referring to Aleksandr Isayevich Solzhenitsyn. . . . He is said to be living and working, shunning publicity, in a dacha not far from here. Mr. Solzhenitsyn, as far as could be determined did not appear. Nor did any other noted literary figures." [22]

On the same day, May 30, Zhores A. Medvedev, the twin brother of Roy Medvedev and a specialist in gerontology, was arrested at Obninsk, a research center sixty-two miles southwest of Moscow.[23] Friends gave the following account of how he was taken into custody by the KGB:

A doctor telephoned and said he wanted to discuss a problem concerning Mr. Medvedev's son with him. Mr. Medvedev said his son was fine and he went fishing. Later in the day, the doctor called again and said it was not his son, but Mr. Medvedev himself who was sought. Mr. Medvedev said he had to leave for Moscow on business. Fifteen minutes later two policemen knocked at the Medvedev apartment. He refused to open. They broke in and forced him into an ambulance.

He was told he needed a psychiatric examination . . . but for several hours after his arrival at the hospital, he was questioned only about his writings.[24]

The writings the authorities found troublesome consisted of one published and two unpublished books. *The Rise and Fall of T. D. Lysenko* had circulated in *samizdat* in part and as a whole for a number of years, and had been rejected by a number of Soviet publishers before a copy made its way abroad. The book was published by Columbia University Press in New York in 1969. It is a critique of the discredited policies of Lysenko and of what Lysenkoism had, under official auspices, done to science and agriculture in the Soviet Union. Carefully documented and objective in tone, it names names and refers to incidents which the heirs of Stalin in biology and genetics, as well as in agriculture, are eager to forget. The two manuscripts were "The International Cooperation of Scientists and Foreign Borders," in which Medvedev charged that the Soviet government ran a "clumsy and degrading system of clearing business, scientific and tourist travel abroad and of issuing passports"; [25] and "The Black Cabinet," named after a secret mail-opening group established in the reign of Catherine the Great, in which Medvedev criticized the Soviet regime's official mail censorship.

Medvedev had been additionally "indiscreet" in circulating an open letter (subsequently printed in the underground *Chronicle of Current Events*, No. 14 [June 30, 1970]) attributing Solzhenitsyn's expulsion from the Writers' Union to the fact that the novelist had defied both Party control and Glavlit, and "in defiance of all logic and common sense" had refused to violate his conscience or betray the truth. Solzhenitsyn had continued in his life and in his writing to expose and fight the "arbitrariness of the Stalin period [which] in disguised form has begun to be manifest once more and the menace of lawlessness and violence [which] has once again come to threaten the land." Medvedev considered Solzhenitsyn's ouster to be only one part of an overall campaign by the heirs of Stalin to intimidate their opponents and to keep all citizens frightened and apathetic.

Medvedev was now confined to the Kaluga mental hospital, where a team of psychiatrists found him normal and said he would be released after a week of observation. Two days after his confinement there was a sharp protest against his detention by some of the most eminent scientists—among them Pyotr Kapitsa and Andrei Sakharov —all members of the prestigious Academy of Sciences, who had made important contributions to research in biology, biochemistry, and nuclear physics. Telegrams were sent to the Kaluga authorities and to others appealing for Medvedev's release. Sakharov termed Medvedev's incarceration "a potential threat to the freedom of science, to Soviet democracy in general," and angrily declared, "I cannot believe that such scandalous illegality can be sanctioned by the highest leadership."

In an open letter, Roy Medvedev announced that his brother had been "forcibly hospitalized" and that Zhores had suffered neither from neurological nor psychiatric disorders. Roy Medvedev charged that Zhores had actually been imprisoned for accusing the regime of widespread mail censorship in violation of the provisions of the Soviet constitution.[26] He also accused the government of a campaign of official harassment against Zhores which had caused him to be dismissed from his research job in 1969 and which had prevented him from finding subsequent employment.

On June 4, a second team of psychiatrists was dispatched from Moscow to examine Zhores for schizophrenia. Among the seven physicians were the director of the Serbsky Institute, Dr. Grigory Morozov, and his assistant, Professor D. R. Lunts. (Lunts was one of those Pisarev had accused of "mistaken diagnoses," and the Central Committee commission of investigation of the Serbsky had verified Lunts's shortcomings. Lunts had sat on a psychiatric screening board which had declared General Grigorenko of unsound mind; according to Grigorenko, Lunts occasionally arrived at the Serbsky in the uniform of a KGB colonel.) [27] After this second examination, Zhores Medvedev was ordered detained for at least one month.

On the next day, June 5, 1970, the Nobel Prize winning physicist Igor Tamm joined the others in vehemently objecting to Medvedev's detention,[28] and a letter of protest signed by twenty scientists and intellectuals [29] was dispatched to the Minister of Health, the Minister of Internal Affairs, and the Procurator General, saying:

Not one honest and principled scientist will be sure of his own security if similar grounds can bring about his own repression. The forced hospitalization of Zhores Medvedev is illegal and provokes anxiety and alarm in the public mind. We, the undersigned, regard his immediate release as necessary. The Ministry of Public Health must state publicly that the incident . . . was a violation of legality and medical ethics. Those guilty must carry the responsibility for depriving Zhores Medvedev of freedom illegally.[30]

The letter insisted that Medvedev had been imprisoned for political reasons because he had "exposed the antiscientific direction of Soviet biology," and also because he had resisted Soviet censorship and governmental bans on contacts with foreign scientists. Moreover, the letter maintained: "The psychiatric health of Z. A. Medvedev has never been in doubt, and we are competent to judge this as people familiar with his works. The forced hospitalization is apparently connected with the public activity of Z. A. Medvedev, which he pursued on strictly legal grounds, although perhaps this activity ran counter to some interests." [31] Unlike Grigorenko, Medvedev was permitted visitors, and Aleksandr Tvardovsky and Vladimir Dudintsev were both reported to have visited him in the hospital. Medvedev was another of the dissidents whose close relatives had been hurt by Stalinism. The Medvedevs' father, a philosophy professor, had been arrested and had disappeared without a trace during the Stalin purges. C. L. Sulzberger believes that his arrest and disappearance had prompted Zhores' study of the Lysenko scandal,[32] but Zhores' own name—the Russian form of Jaurès, the name of the great French socialist—would indicate that perhaps the family had an earlier independent political orientation.

Eleven days later, on June 16, in the novelist's first public identification with the dissidents, Solzhenitsyn joined the attack on Zhores Medvedev's detention. Not only was there an important principle involved, but there was also a personal relationship, probably of some duration. Medvedev had earlier publicly protested Solzhenitsyn's ouster from the Writers' Union in an open letter; he had also in his *samizdat*-circulated essay, "The International Cooperation of Scientists and Foreign Borders," written an account of how Solzhenitsyn's wife, Natalya Reshetovskaya, had in June and July of 1965 been denied a job at the Obninsk Institute of Medical Radiology because she was the novelist's wife. Though the Board of the Institute had voted 18 to 2 to accept Reshetovskaya as a senior research worker, Moscow had intervened. If she worked at the institute, the Solzhenitsyns would then have to be granted housing in Obninsk. To this, Medvedev averred, the KGB was opposed because it had kept Solzhenitsyn carefully isolated (and uncomfortably housed) in Ryazan deliberately and had an organized system of surveillance over him there. If, therefore, the Solzhenitsyns moved to Obninsk, a whole new surveillance system would have to be mounted; in addition, Solzhenitsyn would by the move be put into touch with and perhaps also influence the already restive scientific community there. The Kremlin wanted no such influence brought to bear, so Reshetovskaya was denied the job at Obninsk, and the Solzhenitsyns remained in Ryazan. Now, in a moving statement entitled "This Is How We Live" Solzhenitsyn came to the defense of Medvedev:

This can happen tomorrow to any of us. It has happened to Zhores Medvedev, a scientist, a geneticist, and publicist, a man of subtle, precise and brilliant intellect, a man of good heart. (I know personally of his disinterested help to unknown dying sick people.)

It is precisely for the diversity of his gifts that he has been charged with abnormality: a split personality. It is precisely his sensitivity to injustice, to stupidity, that are made to seem a sick deviation: poor adaptation to the social milieu. Once you don't think as you are ordered to think, you are abnormal! And well-adapted people—they must all think alike.

And there is no restraint of law; even the appeals of our best scientists and writers are bounced back like peas off a wall. . . .

It is time to think clearly. The incarceration of free-thinking healthy people in madhouses is spiritual murder. It is a variant of the gas chamber, and even more cruel; it is a fiendish and prolonged torture of those who are to be killed. Like the gas chamber, these crimes will never be forgotten, and all those who take part in them will be condemned eternally, while they live and after they are dead.

Even in lawlessness, in crime, one must remember the line beyond which a man becomes a cannibal.

It is shortsighted to think that you can live, constantly relying on force alone, constantly scorning the objections of conscience.[33]

The next day Medvedev was released, but only provisionally—the regime reserved the right to recommit him at any time. The release had evidently been engineered at a June 17 meeting attended by Dr. Boris Petrovsky, the Minister of Health; Dr. Grigory Morozov, the psychiatrist who had examined Medvedev—Morozov had said that Medvedev had "pathological psychopathy," but the scientists refused to accept his diagnosis [34]—Mstislav Keldysh, the president of the Academy of Sciences, representing the government; and Sakharov, Mikhail Leontovich, B. L. Astaurov, and a number of other scientists who had earlier supported Medvedev.[35] In persuading the authorities to release Medvedev, the dissidents had enjoyed a success, but it was only a partial victory, for Medvedev's release was evidently contingent on the dissident biologist's refraining from any further scientific or political dissent.[36]

24 The Amalrik Case

Men who are not free . . . always idealize their bondage.
Boris Pasternak

In 1970, William Cole, the former chief of the Columbia Broad-casting System's Moscow bureau, in an unprecedented filmed inter-view with three of the leading dissidents—Yakir, Amalrik, and Bu-kovsky—which he had smuggled out of the Soviet Union, gave the Western world some insights into the position of what Amalrik—and others—had called the Democratic Movement; i.e., the coalesc-ing movement of literary, political, and scientific dissidents and protestors. Bukovsky, who had spent six years in insane asylums, prisons, and concentration camps, gave a picture of how the regime used the psychiatric wards for political confinement:

As a matter of fact, the inmates, the patients of this hospital [the Len-ingrad special psychiatric hospital], are prisoners, people who com-mitted such actions which are considered as crimes from the point of view of the authorities but which do not exist as crimes from the point of view of the law. And in order to isolate them, in order to punish them somehow, these people are declared insane and kept in the ward of the psychiatric hospital.[1]

Bukovsky told how patients were mistreated with various drugs in order to punish them or to keep them docile, and how political pris-oners would often be put in restraints so confining that they lost consciousness.

All three dissidents agreed that the new Democratic Movement's chief target was fear. Yakir held the view that simply informing people, especially outside the Soviet Union, was a way of prevent-ing a rollback to Stalinism. For example, he applauded Pavel Lit-

vinov and Larissa Daniel for giving their protest against the Ginzburg-Galanskov trial to Western reporters, and remarked that their
action "was the first, major step which was a breach with all previous traditions; never before in Russia had there been a case of
people appealing to the West against unlawfulness in our country."
If the Democratic Movement informed people about what was going on, publicizing every illegal act, every arrest, every job dismissal, they might be able to keep Stalinism at bay. Dissidents would
be arrested, but others would take their places: "There are already
many of us, many young people, and no independent-minded people in the Soviet Union will go back to what used to be. They'll
beat us and kill us. All the same people will go on thinking differently." Amalrik put it in a slightly different way, less optimistically
and positively, but his diagnosis was much the same: "No system of
rule by force can exist without people who are ready to submit to
that rule. If we don't want the rule of force to prevail, then we
must all fight against it, not just say that the regime is bad." But it
was Bukovsky who spoke of the struggle against fear in the most
personal and intimate terms:

. . . the fear which has gripped people since the time of Stalin . . .
has still not left people . . . thanks to which this system continues to
exist. . . . It's into the struggle against fear that we put our greatest
efforts, and in that struggle the greatest importance attaches to personal
example, the example which we give people. I personally did what I
considered right, spoke out on those occasions when I wanted to, and
I'm still alive. I'm now sitting here and not in prison. . . . For me and
for many people that's very important. It shows that it's possible to
fight and that it's necessary to fight.[2]

In 1970, the struggle continued unabated. That summer the Kremlin was preparing for the Twenty-fourth Congress of the Communist Party of the Soviet Union, which it would shortly publicly
announce for March 30, 1971, and the leadership was concerned
with laying down the ideological guidelines for it.[3] In August, a
major article in *Pravda* once more defined the Brezhnev-Kosygin
"middle course," on the one hand warning "leftists who strive to
replace the Party by a political organization of petty-bourgeois adventurism and nationalism intended to serve as the tool of a military

and bureaucratic regime"[4] that they would not be tolerated, a warning intended for the hard-line Stalinists at home and for the Maoists abroad; on the other hand, *Pravda* also rebuked the "rightists [who] advocate removing the Party from power and from the leadership of society. Like open anti-Communists they do this under the flag of 'liberalization' and defense of democracy against an illusory Party dictatorship."[5] They, too, would not be tolerated, a rebuke intended domestically for the dissidents of the Democratic Movement and abroad for the Czechoslovak and Yugoslav revisionists.

In October 1970, the Party reprimanded the scientists at the Lebedev Institute for inadequate ideological vigilance,[6] and the reaction the following month had been the organization of the Human Rights Committee by the physicists Andrei Sakharov, Chalidze, and Tverdokhlebov.[7] A week after the committee was founded, *Pravda*'s lead editorial included a sharp reminder that the work of the Party organization at the Lebedev Institute was far below requirements, and warned one and all that the regime would countenance neither compromise nor neutrality in ideology. Local Party organizations were cautioned against allowing any liberal heresies and commanded not to permit even a "shadow of liberalism" in defining their ideological positions.[8]

On November 11, 1970, the Kremlin brought to trial one of the leading dissidents in the country, Andrei Amalrik. Amalrik had for a long time been under police surveillance and suffered continuing harassment. In March the police had searched his tiny Moscow flat and confiscated books and other materials, including a copy of George Orwell's *Nineteen Eighty-Four*.[9] On May 21, Amalrik was arrested at his country cottage in Ryazan and then held for five months incommunicado, not even permitted to see his lawyer or his wife, the Tatar painter Gyusel Makudinova. The day following his arrest, Yakir, Bukovsky, and Yesenin-Volpin protested and called for Amalrik's release. Their protests were followed by others from Dutch writers and an appeal by a group of sixty-four French historians to Mstislav Keldysh, president of the Soviet Academy of Sciences, saying:

We have learnt with great concern of the arrest of our young colleague. The work he has published in the West proves incontrovertibly, in our opinion, that Amalrik is first and foremost a historian.

Despite the objections and comments which his work will no doubt provoke, its strength, originality and subtlety show that we are dealing with a mind of great power.[10]

Amalrik was charged with violating Article 190/1 by disseminating anti-Soviet fabrications or defamations in his book *Will the Soviet Union Survive until 1984?* He was tried in Sverdlovsk, some 850 miles from Moscow, a city closed to foreigners, on the pretext that his book had been clandestinely circulated there. The courtroom too was closed, and the only witness was his wife.[11] Amalrik refused to answer questions put to him by the court, because he maintained that the trial was illegal, but the three-man tribunal found him guilty as charged and sentenced him to three years in a concentration camp.[12] In a speech to the court, Amalrik echoed the courage and determination of such other dissidents as Yakir, Yesenin-Volpin, and Bukovsky:

It seems to me that now the main task of my country is to unburden itself of the heavy weight of the past, and for this criticism is necessary above all, not glorification.

I think that I am a better patriot than those who, loudly declaring their love for the motherland, by love for the motherland mean love for their own privileges.

Neither the witch hunt carried out by the regime, nor this particular example—this trial—arouses in me the slightest respect nor any fear. I understand, however, that such trials are counted on to frighten many, and many will be frightened. But all the same, I think the development of ideological emancipation, having begun, is irreversible.[13]

Amalrik compared the trials of dissidents by the Brezhnev-Kosygin government to the trials of heretics in the Middle Ages, accusing the regime of cowardice, of fearing every thought alien to it. "Recognizing their ideological hopelessness, they cling in fear to criminal codes, to prisons, camps and psychiatric hospitals," he said.[14]

Amalrik had already proved his physical and moral courage on more than one occasion. In 1963 he had been expelled from Moscow University for refusing to rewrite his thesis. As a student of history, he had concluded that the early Russian Kievan state was profoundly indebted to the Normans for its civilization—a view which ran counter to the officially accepted view that Russia owed its civilization only to Russians. In refusing to change his dissertation, Amalrik had wrecked his chances for a job as a professional historian and for an academic degree. Two years later, in February 1965, Amalrik had been approached by the KGB to become an informer and to provide information about his writer and painter friends. He had refused, and three months later was arrested and charged with being a parasite. He was sentenced to two and a half years of exile in Tomsk, in Siberia, on a primitive frozen kolkhoz, where, despite a heart condition, he was forced to do heavy physical labor including the carting of dung. For sixteen months he worked there while friends took the case all the way up to the Supreme Court of the RSFSR, where it was dismissed, and he was permitted to return to Moscow.

During that exile, he wrote two books, *Will the Soviet Union Survive until 1984?*, a brilliant analysis of Soviet prospects for the immediate future, and *Involuntary Journey to Siberia*, based on his experiences on the Siberian kolkhoz, which tells the story of Amalrik's legal resistance to his arrest, trial, and conviction and gives a harsh but piercingly accurate portrayal of the Soviet peasant and countryside, showing the ignorance, hatred, submissiveness, drunkenness, apathy, and incompetence of the peasants as well as their nearly hopeless poverty. In *Will the Soviet Union Survive until 1984?* he indicts the Soviet regime for being mediocre, fearful, backward, and inflexible, and Soviet leaders for a resistance to change which blocks all chance of progress. The chief concern of the regime is simply to maintain itself in power, and as a result it will eventually lose its power, because it lacks the energy, persistence, and intelligence to meet the crucial problems facing the nation. Between 1975 and 1980, Amalrik predicted, the Soviet Union will be involved in a protracted war with China that will permit the boiling ethnic and nationalist hatreds in the Soviet empire to surface and tear it apart.

Amalrik's two books, his telecast with William Cole of the Columbia Broadcasting System, and his letter to Kuznetsov rebuking him for defecting, were all anathema to the regime. His outspoken criticisms, his completely maverick and nonconformist mind and personality offended it. For example, in a nation where spontaneous "demonstrations" are exceedingly rare, Amalrik and his wife had on their own initiative picketed the British Embassy in Moscow in 1968 for supplying arms to Nigeria in the war against Biafra. Gyusel Amalrik's placard read: "Gowon Kills Children; Wilson, Don't Help Gowon!" Andrei Amalrik had deliberately made public his plans to publish his books abroad. He had given them to a Dutch scholar and former Moscow correspondent, K. van het Reve, with instructions to publish them abroad in Amalrik's own name and to have the royalties paid into the Soviet State Bank, not held in escrow for him in a Western bank account, as had been done for other dissident Soviet writers. The books are serious and profound criticisms of Soviet domestic and foreign policy, of the Soviet government, and of the Russian people, written in a coldly fierce, objective style that has something in common with Cartesianism, "perhaps because an ancestor came from France with Napoléon's Grande Armée." [15] Amalrik also takes Anatoly Kuznetsov to task for *not* remaining in the Soviet Union to defend the principles for which he stood and for having, even as a pretext, collaborated with the KGB.[16]

Anatole Shub and his family were friends of the Amalriks when Shub was *Washington Post* correspondent in Moscow. Although Shub called Amalrik the "coolest political mind I encountered in Russia," [17] Amalrik does not seem to be primarily a political person. Henry Kamm, also a friend of the Amalriks when he was a *New York Times* Moscow correspondent, wrote:

> His position is primarily moral. He sympathizes with the aims of the intellectual dissidents but does not sign their protests and petitions; his whole life is a dissent, private and unaffiliated, from a system that holds him but has no place for him.

> [He] is not fighting for a political cause. He is a man struggling for his integrity, his soul, his own truth, in a system that insists that each man must surrender his self and his soul and accept its truth.[18]

But no position could be more alien to the Soviet regime, for what else is the regime built on than the insistence that each man surrender his self and his soul and accept its truth?

Following Amalrik's trial, in December 1970, it was announced that the Ukrainian historian Valentyn Moroz had been tried and sentenced, for "anti-Soviet agitation and propaganda," to nine years in a severe-regimen concentration camp. The first published description of Moroz in the West had appeared in Chornovil's *The Misfortune of Intellect*. A peasant's son, Moroz was born in the village of Volyn in 1936, studied history at Lvov University until 1958, then became a teacher of history and geography in a school for workers' children, and later taught history at a pedagogical institute. Arrested in August 1965 in the first wave of the Brezhnev-Kosygin re-Stalinization, he was tried for "anti-Soviet agitation and propaganda" in January 1966 and sentenced to five years in a severe-regimen concentration camp, one year of which he was to spend in solitary confinement in Vladimir Prison. Released in January 1970, Moroz was soon in conflict with the KGB again. In April 1970, the secret police searched his apartment and confiscated three of his manuscripts—"Moses and Dathan," [19] "In the Snow," and "The Chronicle of Resistance." [20]

In fact, Moroz' chief "crime" seemed to be that he opposed Russification of the Ukraine, the regime's nationalities policy in general, and the overall Stalinist abuse of power. In an essay he wrote in concentration camp which was smuggled out to the West, entitled "Report from the Beria Reserve," [21] Moroz espouses a "socialism with a human face" and describes his fellow prisoners simply as "people who think differently, thinking men whose intellectual world could not be forced into the Stalinist molds which are strictly propagated by the KGB." Moroz condemns the KGB and the Soviet establishment as the true heirs of Stalin: "There have always been and will always be forces in every society for whom the maintenance of the *status quo* means the maintenance of their privileges. Stalin was a typical example in the past as are the present Stalinists who have survived. But time does not stand still, today becomes yesterday and the forces which resist change belong to the past." Moroz attacks Soviet society as an "imperium of cogs," in which Stalinist and neo-Stalinist elements are devoted to producing robot-like conformity to a totalitarian model:

The cog is the cherished ideal of any "totalitarian." An obedient herd of cogs can be called a parliament or a learned council, and you will have no trouble or surprises from them. A cog called a professor or an academician will never say anything new, and if he does produce any surprises, it will not be by new words, but by the lightning chance of his conceptions in the space of twenty-four hours. . . . A cog will emerge from prison and immediately write that he was never there; and what is more he will call the person who demanded his release a liar. . . . The cog will shoot at whomever he is told to and then, on command, campaign for peace. The final and most important advantage is that after people have been turned into cogs, you can blithely introduce any constitution you want to; give people the right to anything. The exquisite point is that it will never enter the cog's head to wield this right.[22]

Moroz believes, however, that a new generation has arisen—the sons—which refuses to be intimidated and turned into cogs—like the fathers—or to accept apathy and indifference. This new generation will resist Stalinist lawlessness and demand the realization in practice of the theoretical guarantees of the Soviet constitution.

On June 1, 1970, Moroz was once more arrested. Tried in a closed-door trial on November 17 and 18, he was sentenced to nine years, six in prison and three in a labor camp with a strict regime, to be followed by five years of exile. In such a severe sentence the heirs of Stalin revealed their concern for what Moroz was saying and doing. In his essay "In the Snow" Moroz gave an interesting and original explanation of the Party leadership's changing policy toward dissident intellectuals. As a case in point he took the Kiev literary critic Ivan Dzyuba. Dzyuba, like Ivan Svetlichny and Moroz himself, had all been arrested before in 1966 and sentenced, but the regime became aware that this made them heroes and martyrs—which the regime did not wish to encourage. "In the Snow" reviews the developments among the Ukrainian intelligentsia during the first half of the 1960s, focusing on a group of writers and academics called the *shestydesiatnyky*, the people of the 1960s. These *shestydesiatnyky*, among them Svetlichny, Dzyuba, and Moroz, by their courageous and intransigent demands for freedom of creative expression, their adamant opposition to Russification of the Ukraine, galvanized many Ukrainians out of their fear and apathy. They accomplished this by refusing to accommodate to Party-imposed "realities." As this movement gathered momentum, the Party leadership realized that it was an error to persecute its leaders. Moroz analyzes the leadership's intentions coolly:

Everything which was brought up against these people [the *shestydesiatnyky*] was nothing but ice which melted in their sparks. The greatest surprise of the decade was that the arrests of 1965 did not stop the Ukrainian renaissance of the time but instead intensified it. The era of the Great Fear was over. The arrests could frighten no one; rather, they produced a considerable interest not only in the Ukraine, but in the entire world. To subject someone to repression under those circumstances would have meant conferring a halo on him and making him a martyr, irrespective of whether the man had suffered or not. That was a miscalculation. . . . They [the regime authorities] tried immediately to rescind that error. Ivan Svetlichny was released from prison, although he was regarded as "the most important" figure. . . . If they couldn't put fear into the people, they'd just have to compromise and disappoint [them].

Moroz then tells the story of Ivan Drach, one of the most important members of the group, who was persuaded to publish a bootlicking article in *Literaturna ukraina* in mid-1966, in order to compromise and denigrate these leaders.

It was necessary to do away with the legend of the *shestydesiatnyky*—these men of new quality—to show that, in fact, there was nothing new about them at all . . . to kill the belief, to extinguish the spark of being possessed, and to set man once again back into a state of nauseous nihilism. It was necessary to deprive the people of an example which had inspired them, to convince them that their god was not a god.

Ivan Dzyuba was another one of the Ukrainian intellectual heroes, his work *Internationalism or Russification* having set ripples off both at home and abroad, so that the regime forbade him to publish and expelled him from the Kiev section of the Writers' Union. But by January 1970, Dzyuba had written a statement which indicated that he had "honorably" compromised with the Party leadership (published in the January 1970 *Literaturna ukraina*). Dzyuba indicated that he had done so because of the "realities," and that those who continued in opposition were guilty of a lack of realism, of political Don Quixotism.

Moroz violently attacked Dzyuba for this capitulation, insisting that often what looked like realism was nothing of the sort, that, in fact, "all discoveries, everything new, the world can thank the Don Quixotes [for]." Dzyuba's compliance had gained him nothing. Though the authorities had permitted Dzyuba to remain in the Ukrainian Writers' Union as a result of his public declaration, that was only a first step; his continued membership would inevitably depend on other steps, and in such circumstances he would never be able to publish anything which stated his real beliefs. Moroz then recalled that Dzyuba's finest hour had been when he had himself behaved like a Don Quixote; on September 4, 1965, Dzyuba, in protest against a wave of arrests in the Ukraine, had walked onto the stage of a Kiev theater and made a flaming appeal to the Party leaders and to the people of Kiev to stop the purge and to support its victims. Though Dzyuba might not see himself as a capitulator, in making his public statement he had helped the regime to destroy another "hero" and in so doing had cooperated with those in power. Moroz believes that all such "realists," who are willing to "compromise with the reality," essentially bow to and serve the dogmatic and chauvinist aims of the Party leadership, which, with such tactical and selective compromises, attempts to achieve the same goals it formerly sought to accomplish with police terror.

A considerable range of views is represented by the dissidents of the Democratic Movement; some of their disagreements polarized around Andrei Amalrik and his essay, *Will the Soviet Union Survive until 1984?* after the underground *Chronicle of Current Events* carried a brief summary of its contents.

The author considers the liberalization of the post-Stalin period to be a sign of the decay of the regime, and sees no forces in our society which are even potentially capable of bringing about a renewal, a democratization of the country. The author predicts disintegration for the state in view of inner contradictions which in his opinion are growing even greater. The author suggests that the basic causes of the coming crash are: the contradiction between the demands of economic development and the ossification of the economic system; the conservatism of the bureaucratic elite; an elite which is increasingly declining in quality . . . ; the absence of positive goals in the lower strata [of society]; the striving toward separateness of the non-Russian nationalities.

Amalrik was accused of "erroneous, mystical and irrational arguments," and of being scornful and contemptuous toward Russia, its people, history, and culture.[23] On March 28, Yakir had taken issue with Amalrik, chiefly concentrating on Amalrik's "underestimation" of the Democratic Movement's strength.[24] Yakir applauded Amalrik's analysis of Soviet society, calling it "the only one of such breadth and logic," but objected: "I cannot fully agree with some of your views, in particular with your forecast of the future of the Democratic Movement. Although at present its social base is indeed very narrow and the movement itself has been forced to operate in extremely difficult conditions, the ideas proclaimed by it have begun to spread widely throughout the country, and that is the beginning of an irreversible process of self-liberation." Many critics had charged Amalrik with Russophobia, but Yakir, though he disagreed with Amalrik's "too one-sided description of the Russian character," [25] refused to make such an accusation himself.

Amalrik evidently felt called upon to defend himself, and, in a reply probably composed toward the end of 1969 or early in 1970, wrote:

It may be that the ordinary Russian, if he were given the chance to read or hear my book . . . would find some passages in it unpatriotic. But I consider the best patriot is not the man who covers over his country's failings but the man who exposes the wounds so that they can be cured. It may be that it is unpatriotic to criticize one's country and to warn it of threatening danger by publishing a book abroad for that purpose. But I have no other possibility. Besides, I think it is time for my country to overcome its national and social inferiority complex. . . .

I love my country, in which I was born and grew up, and I cannot think without tears of its extraordinary fate. To be separated from it would cause me great grief, but with bitterness I confess that I am not enraptured of my country. If I had been able to make a choice before my birth I should have preferred to be born in a small country fighting for its freedom with weapons in its hands, like Biafra or Israel.[26]

The year 1970 ended with two powerful attacks on the liberals. In a long article in *Pravda*, I. Alexandrov, an official whose articles on the danger of "reformism" and "revisionism" in Czechoslovakia in 1968 had preceded the invasion, wrote a sweeping condemnation of the dissidents, including Amalrik (a "half-educated slanderer"), Solzhenitsyn ("Solzhenitsyn has fallen into a dirty refuse pit"), Bukovsky, Tarsis, and Kuznetsov ("marked by a pathological hatred of the Soviet people"), calling them all "a pitiful handful of renegades begging for whisky and cigarettes in exchange for dirty fabrications." [27] On the same day, *Literaturnaya gazeta* published another attack on Yevtushenko, criticizing his work for being "too hasty and superficial," and taking particular exception to Yevtushenko's portrait of Lenin in the poem "Kazan University," in which Yevtushenko had evidently been guilty of the deviation of having Lenin join the revolutionary movement because Czar Aleksandr III had executed Lenin's brother, Aleksandr, for a plot against the Czar's life in 1887. [28]

Part IV

SCIENTIFIC DISSIDENCE

25 The Medvedev Case

> I have heard that a capitalist also likes a good potato. And it goes onto his plate in an indifferent way; it does not care who will eat it.
>
> *Vladimir Dudintsev*

As literary and political opposition grew more outspoken, an increased sense of common interest and purpose was manifest between the literary and scientific intelligentsia, a bridging of the two cultures in the Soviet Union; and joint action to preserve freedom of inquiry, to expand access to information from colleagues and institutions all over the world, and to gain release from the rigidities of Marxist-Leninist dogma and Stalinist bureaucratic control and terror began to be fashioned. Science and scientists had suffered much the same fate during the Stalinist era as art and artists—and for many of the same reasons. Hemmed in by dialectical materialism, as the writers had been, the scientists had tried to ignore, circumvent, or oppose the prevailing Marxist-Leninist canon as the regime tried to impose it on their areas of specialization. In the Stalinist period they had been generally unsuccessful in resisting; Stalin had wielded his terror against scientists and writers alike: if they cooperated, they were well-paid, feted, given expensive research facilities and more than adequate grants and budgets. If they did not cooperate, loss of their jobs, exile, jails, concentration camps, or death awaited them. From the very first, the Party was as hostile or indifferent to non-Party scientists as it was to non-Party writers; and the scientists had neither profound respect for, nor faith in, Party dogma or leadership. The same anti-Semitism, xenophobia, and dogmatism that characterized the Party's dealings with artists applied to its relations with scientists—qualities that were not only expressions of the personality and prejudices of Stalin, but were also deeply rooted in Russian life. Because Albert Einstein and Norbert Wiener, for example, were both Jews and Americans as well as intellectually independent men beyond his reach and influence, Stalin automatically suspected their contributions to the theories of relativity and cybernetics. The "negative qualities" of the Coryphaeus of the Sciences—"a hypertrophied thirst for power, suspicion, cruelty, treachery, vanity, envy, intolerance of brilliant individuals of independent character, and megalomania" [1]—were manifest in the government's and Party's policy toward science and scientists. Leading scientific schools and scientists alike were damned as "bourgeois," "idealist," and "reactionary": among the many prominent physicists and mathematicians so labeled were Abram Ioffe, Lev Landau, Igor Tamm, Nikolay Luzin, Vladimir Fok, and Yakov Frenkel, as well as the psychiatrist Vladimir Bekhterev, the psychologist Kornilov, and the great physiologist Pavlov. [2] Such stereotypical Party epithets were also applied to relativity, psychoanalysis, Werner von Heisenberg's "indeterminacy principle" in quantum mechanics, Linus Pauling's chemical bond, and Mendelian genetics. The labels, of course, were parallel anathemas to the accusations of "formalism," "bourgeois realism," and "ethical socialism" made by the Party commissars in the arts.

As there had been heroes and martyrs in literature—Isaak Babel, Boris Pilnyak, Osip Mandelshtam, Boris Pasternak, and Anna Akhmatova, to name only a handful—so too there were heroes and martyrs in the sciences: geneticists Nikolai Vavilov and S. S. Chetverikov, physicists Pyotr Kapitsa and Lev Landau, the cytologist G. A. Levitsky, the biologist N. V. Koltsov, and many others. Where there are heroes and martyrs, there are—and there were—persecutors and denouncers: in science the numerous equivalents of the Vsevolod Kochetovs, Sergey Mikhalkovs, and Yakov Elsbergs in literature included T. D. Lysenko, V. R. Vilyams, and I. I. Prezent. They were the heirs of Stalin, imposing and carrying out Stalinist policies in the sciences as their counterparts did in the arts. Many individuals were slandered, their careers blighted; many were hounded, exiled, jailed, murdered. Only a few examples will suffice.

Nikolai Vavilov was the Soviet Union's leading geneticist, but the Mendelian theories of inheritance he followed were anathema to the Soviet rulers. They were committed to nurture rather than nature, to shaping a "new socialist man" by creating "socialist institutions" rather than to considering the continuing recalcitrance of genetically transmitted human characteristics and their random mutations. The Mendelian theory, which contends that hereditary qualities are carried in the genes of the chromosomes and that changes are effected by genetic combination or unpredictable and uncontrollable mutation, had been carefully developed speculatively and experimentally by Gregor Mendel, Thomas Morgan, Hugo de Vries, August Weismann, and many others. In the USSR, it was opposed by a school of geneticists led by I. V. Michurin and T. D. Lysenko, who espoused Lamarckianism—that is, a belief in the inheritance of acquired characteristics—and methods of attempting to change the characteristics by changing the environment. Since such a concept dovetailed with Marxist-Leninist notions, it received the approval of the Kremlin and consequently became the official and the sole theory acceptable in Soviet genetics and agrobiology. The gene had not yet been "seen" when the conflict between the two schools came to a head in the 1930s, so Lysenkoists were able to accuse Mendelians of having "invented" it.

Lysenko and his henchmen launched a vicious attack on Vavilov and the Mendelians for being "reactionary," for "sabotage," for being "maidservant[s] of Goebbels' department [for] the fascist distortion of genetics . . . for political aims inimical to the progress of mankind." [3] Medvedev shows how Prezent, one of the most militant and vicious of Lysenko's collaborators, attempted to have M. E. Lobashev and his Leningrad University colleagues expelled from the Party on the grounds of "abetting fascism." One listener at the meeting asked, "How can it be . . . that these comrades . . . spent nearly the whole [of World War II] under arms, fighting fascists, and were decorated with military awards?" Unabashed, Prezent retorted: "This is no argument. They fought fascism *only empirically*." [4] Moved to scorn, Medvedev comments that Prezent and many of his friends "avoided precisely such an empirical fight against fascism during the war." [5] Vavilov and his colleagues were also stigmatized as "enemies of the people," dismissed from their jobs, and mercilessly harried, tried, condemned, and sentenced. In August 1940, Vavilov was arrested by the NKVD,[6] as were his closest friends and collaborators. He was tried by a three-man military collegium in July 1941 and sentenced to death under the catchall Article 58 for having belonged to a rightist conspiracy, spying for Great Britain, sabotaging Soviet agriculture, having connections with reactionary émigrés, and similar charges. After some months in the Saratov prison, his death sentence was commuted to ten-years' imprisonment, but Vavilov could not bear up under the rigors of prison conditions and died in January 1943.

When Vavilov was posthumously rehabilitated, a letter was found in his dossier from secret-police chief Lavrenti Beria to Molotov, then in charge of scientific matters in the Politburo, requesting permission to arrest Vavilov. Such post-Stalin revelations clearly implicated the top leadership in the purges and demonstrated that actions of that kind were taken with the approval and sometimes on the initiative of the very top Soviet leadership.[7]

Another of those struck by the ferocity of the purges was the brilliant Lev Landau, considered by many to be the finest Russian theoretical physicist of his generation. Landau was imprisoned in 1938 by Stalin and charged with being a German spy. After a year in prison, it seemed that he would soon die, and he was saved only by the intervention of Pyotr Kapitsa with Stalin. Evidently Kapitsa threatened to resign from his position as director of the Institute of Problems of Physics unless Landau was released.[8]

Kapitsa had had his own troubles with Stalin. One of the most gifted Russian physicists, he had for a long time lived and taught abroad until, when he was home on a visit, he was prevented by Stalin from returning to Cambridge University in England. In time, Kapitsa was persuaded to work for the regime, and Stalin took great pains to provide money, equipment, and personnel for the Institute of Problems of Physics, to which Kapitsa was appointed as director. After World War II, however, Kapitsa was recalcitrant, refusing to help in the development of Soviet atomic and hydrogen weapons. "To talk of atomic energy in terms of the atomic bomb is like talking of electricity in terms of the electric chair," he told an American reporter in 1948.[9] As a consequence, Stalin kept him under house arrest from 1946 to 1953, and removed him from his position as head of the institute.[10] Not until after Stalin's death was Kapitsa released from house arrest; eventually he was reinstated as head of the Institute of Problems of Physics.

In the more liberal atmosphere of the Khrushchev era, both science and scientists began to flourish. As with the writers, Khru-

shchev was eager to enlist the scientists' loyalties for his own regime, and besides, the scientists had an advantage which gave them
a political leverage denied the writers. The regime needed them
more. In the desire to keep abreast of the rest of the world industrially, technologically, and militarily, the Kremlin was forced to
reconsider its policies with respect to scientific theories and individual scientists. Khrushchev therefore not only continued Stalin's
policy of favoring scientists with money, position, and privilege,
but he was also forced to reconsider the regime's attitude to such an
extent that he permitted greater freedom in many areas of research
and in international travel and communication with foreign scientists, because it was imperative to him and to the nation. Without
accepting the theories of relativity and quantum mechanics, there
was no way to build atomic and hydrogen bombs; without accepting
the principles of cybernetics, computer technology could not be developed for industrial and military uses; without accepting these concepts, Soviet space exploration was impossible. Party leaders, therefore, retreated from dogmatic Marxist-Leninist positions to gain the
practical advantages of science and technology.

The regime gave concessions with reluctance, however. Although
Khrushchev was willing to extend to scientists greater latitude than
they previously had, he restricted freedom to those areas of life
which were of immediate scientific and technical concern. Nor did
Khrushchev altogether abandon Party support for some kinds of
"Party-oriented" science and some scientists—most significantly for
Michurinist genetics and Lysenkoist agrobiology.[11] A renewed attack by scientists against Lysenko, his theories, and his colleagues
was mounted nevertheless. It was led by Zhores Medvedev, a biologist
at the Molecular Radiobiology Laboratory of the USSR Academy
of Sciences Institute of Radiobiology at Obninsk, after Watson,
Crick and Wilkins, Kornberg and Ochoa revolutionized genetics by
cracking the genetic code and making new discoveries in protein
synthesis and the self-reproduction of genetic materials. At that
time, in 1961 and 1962, Medvedev wrote a series of memoranda
which were circulated in *samizdat*, carefully dissecting the theoretical premises of Michurinist biology. The following year, with the
Lysenkoites still in control of most of the professional publications,
Medvedev and a colleague, V. Kirpichnikov, wrote an article, "The

Perspectives for Soviet Genetics," which was published in the Leningrad literary magazine *Neva* [12] and brought him under attack from the entire Lysenkoite establishment. Medvedev was then supported by physicist Andrei Sakharov,[13] who, "in a public speech delivered at a meeting of the USSR Academy of Science made an insulting attack, quite remote from science, against Michurian scientists in the style of the libellous letters circulated by Zh. A. Medvedev" [14] —or so a Lysenkoite reported the occurrence.

Medvedev also received reinforcement from Vladimir Dudintsev, the author of *Not by Bread Alone,* one of the leading novelists of the 1956 "thaw," who wrote an article about a Soviet geneticist and breeder, N. A. Lebedeva, whose work in hybridizing potatoes had been denigrated and whose hybrid varieties had been denied adoption by the Lysenkoist establishment. Written in September and October of 1963, Dudintsev's article continued to be rejected by various Soviet publications for more than a year:

The influential hands of Lysenko, Ol'shansky, Sizov, and others, with the help of agencies controlling the press, prevented its appearance. The means were simple and unfailing, and were based primarily on the editors' cowardice. Although an editor could take personal responsibility for publication, he usually sought approval of a superior. This usually meant that the materials would be brought to the attention of Lysenko's highly placed patrons. As a result, not only would the article fail to see the light of day, but note would also be taken of its author: at the right opportunity, he would be reminded of what he should do. . . .

Dudintsev vividly shows that the representatives of Michurinist biology were in fact a group which, above all, treasured its position and was prepared to bar the road to anything new, useful, and valuable if it contradicted the dogmas of Lysenkoism.[15]

Medvedev approvingly quotes Dudintsev's article for castigating those who called Lebedeva's work "bourgeois, idealistic, harmful to science, categorically unacceptable to us":

It is known that nature provides society with its material treasures in an indifferent way. The only departure from nature's and science's indifference comes about when we ourselves, misguided by irresponsible and illiterate judgments, reject the riches offered through science.

. . . Breeders from bourgeois countries are after Lebedeva's polyploids. . . . Those abroad know what to do with this valuable material.

I have heard that a capitalist also likes a good potato. And it goes onto his plate in an indifferent way; it does not care who will eat it.[16]

Medvedev is perhaps somewhat unfair to the editors, many of whom were undoubtedly cowardly or cautious, but some of whom very likely saw only the hopelessness of combating official policy and the rigorous censorship. However, his accusation may only be a convenient circumlocution, a way of obliquely attacking the leadership and its repressive policies.

In loosening the ideological strait jacket in science as in the arts, the Kremlin had to make sweeping changes in institutions and personnel. Individual Russian scientists, research institutes, publishing houses, periodicals, universities, and textbooks had all suffered under the same yoke as novelists, playwrights, poets, and their equivalent institutions, and the same problems—those of the heirs of Stalin and fathers and sons—arose to plague the Party. Who was to be held responsible for the "errors" and "distortions" in science, for holding back research and development in computers, for failures in genetics and microbiology, for the disastrous results of Lysenkoist techniques in Soviet agriculture? Would the men responsible for the death and imprisonment of such scientists as Vavilov and Landau be exposed, brought to trial, and punished? (In the case of Vavilov the trial plainly led to the highest reaches of the leadership, to Molotov and the Politburo.) Liberalization was mined with all sorts of explosives; here, once more, the heirs of Stalin in science were not simply defending theoretical dogmas against their opponents: they were defending their power, their positions, and their very lives.

It was not until after Khrushchev was deposed that the geneticists at last saw victory in sight. On October 31, 1964, at the end of the month in which Khrushchev was ousted, a group of biologists gathered to celebrate the sixtieth birthday of geneticist B. L. Astaurov. In a toast, Astaurov was both exultant and sad:

We have survived till the hour when real biologists finally feel relief. There is yet nothing concrete, but it is already possible to say that each of us has the kind of feeling experienced by a fisherman when the fish is on the hook and all that is needed is to reel it in. . . . The hour each one present has done so much to bring about has finally arrived. But not an inconsiderable number of our dear comrades who also awaited this hour did not live to see it. And they also have done much, perhaps more than we have, toward its arrival, so that we and you should see the end of the long and difficult road down which our battle was fought. I ask you to rise in memory of our comrades.

Dudintsev, replying to Astaurov's toast, was more skeptical and warned the assemblage, "One fish is on the hook, but how many more are still on the loose . . . ?" [17]

At the beginning of February 1965, Lysenko was removed from his post as director of the Academy of Science's Institute of Genetics, but there was no attendant publicity, no explanation of the causes of his ouster, no overall review of the untoward consequences of the application of his theories to Soviet science, education, and agriculture. Many Lysenkoites continued to hold positions of power and influence in research institutes, laboratories, universities, experimental farms, and soviets. They had "a public forum (*e.g.*, the journal *Oktyabr*)," [18] and they had by no means been driven from the field.

Medvedev's *The Rise and Fall of T. D. Lysenko* is divided into three parts; the third section, covering the years 1962–1966, was written later than the first two parts. All three sections reached the United States in *samizdat* and were published in a single volume in 1969. The entire book was undoubtedly an embarrassment to the Soviet rulers, but the third section very likely was the immediate cause of Medvedev's arrest and confinement in the Kaluga mental hospital the following spring, because it went far beyond a discussion of genetics and biology to probe into the political roots of the Lysenko debacle. It did not confine itself to the Stalin and Khrushchev periods, but examined policy and practice under Brezhnev and Kosygin. In a final chapter entitled "How Did It Happen?" Medvedev asked and answered questions about the most cherished bastions of Party wisdom and control of Soviet society. Medvedev declared that the monopoly of science was a profound sickness in Soviet life arising from erroneous Party classification of sciences as "bourgeois" on the one hand and "socialist" or "proletarian" on the other. False doctrines in science, and by implication in any other area of life, can *"achieve monopolistic position only in state systems that are extremist in nature, as a particular manifestation of many other deviations from the reasonable norms of organized society.*" [19] In biology, Medvedev maintained, Lysenkoism was an outgrowth of the political situation in the USSR, which favored mass repressions by Stalin and the political police in the countryside in a headlong collectivization of the peasantry; culminating in "Khrushchev's decrees which limited the possibilities of individual livestock rearing, agricultural policy was based not so much on concern for an all-around development of agricultural production, but rather on achieving maximum agricultural output at minimum budgetary cost." The Kremlin had chosen deliberately to foster a "progressive science"—whatever that meant—without regard for objective scientific criteria. By keeping peasants "deprived of elementary civil rights (the passportless regime), [and by basing] management . . . on coercion and endless decrees," the Party leaders had installed Lysenkoism as a state-approved agrobiology.[20]

The regime was aided and abetted by a total control of the press which made it possible for the political leadership to impose a single scientific viewpoint on all while simultaneously suppressing completely any contrary views or opposing tendencies. Like Solzhenitsyn, Medvedev struck at the centralized censorship of the Soviet press:

Although great diversity of newspapers and magazines exists, there is a clear-cut centralization and hierarchy, with *Pravda* the main lawgiver. Criticism by other papers of any articles in *Pravda* is practically impossible. Beyond this, censorship stood guard over all officially supported concepts, and even matchbox labels had to pass through it. I know dozens of instances in which censorship stopped articles prepared for the press or already in type which contained direct or indirect criticism of Lysenko. Until Stalin's death all published material was subjected to three stages of censorship: in manuscript, after typesetting and after publication before release. Since 1956, manuscripts have no longer been subjected to censorship, and only the last two stages remain.[21]

Had there been free exchange of opinion in the Soviet Union, Medvedev maintained, Lysenkoism would have lasted less than two years instead of the thirty it did last.

Medvedev also insisted that prolonged domination by Lysenkoism resulted from the isolation of Soviet science and scientists from international science, from foreign scientific institutions and colleagues. Such normal intercourse among individuals and institutions in other civilized nations was looked upon as a "political crime and proof of unreliability" in the Soviet Union.[22] Free interchange between Soviet scientists and their counterparts in other countries is still difficult and must surmount serious regime-imposed obstacles, but the situation has improved somewhat in recent years: scientists are allowed more access to foreign periodicals, international meetings, and encounters with foreign colleagues.

Medvedev also remarked adversely on the political centralization of the administration of Soviet science, higher education, and scientific publication, which tended to foster the imposition of a single standard on the entire country simply by centralizing the control of the disbursement of funds; with the Kremlin controlling the purse strings and paying the piper, the scientists could much more easily be compelled to dance to a single tune.

After the death of Stalin, scientists, like artists, were protesting chiefly against ideological interference in scientific theory and practice and against the bureaucratic control of their specialties by the political authorities. De-Stalinization and liberalization had raised scientists' hopes and expectations in much the same way they had artists', so some of the leading figures in Soviet science were encouraged to speak their minds on a number of the issues which perturbed them. For example, the gifted physicist Igor Tamm, on October 13, 1956, led a rebellion against the automatic election of the "chosen" candidate for the presidency of the Academy of Science. Although his rebellion failed, he did succeed, for a change, in making the election "non-unanimous." [23] In 1962, Kapitsa attacked the regime's efforts to pronounce scientific theories true or false on the basis of Marxist dialectics. Marxist philosophers, he contended, had inveighed against relativity and cybernetics, and if Soviet scientists had heeded them, Soviet nuclear physics and the Soviet space effort would have been stillborn.[24]

Kapitsa also pointed out the disproportion between the numbers of theoretical and experimental physicists in the USSR and implied that this was due in part to the reluctance of physicists to be involved in experimental work, because it required state funds and collective effort which could not elude political supervision and control. Theoreticians could work alone and relatively unhampered, because basically all they needed were paper and a pencil, but experimentalists needed laboratories, equipment, technicians, and funds, all of which could come only from the political authorities.[25] This was a subject Kapitsa returned to again in an important pamphlet, "Theory, Experiment and Practice," written in 1965, originally as an address to the Academy of Science. Kapitsa said that the "gap in the development between [the USSR] and the U.S. has gotten larger instead of being reduced," that the working efficiency of Russian scientists was half that of their American counterparts, and that the gap was widening. Kapitsa despaired of more intensive financial support of research by the political authorities, which in fiscal 1966 was 7.2 billion dollars in the USSR as against nearly 15 billion in the United States, but he thought that Soviet science could be made more productive if fewer creative research scientists were transferred to industry, if new and younger people were brought into research, if more scientists were sent to international conferences on the basis of their professional qualifications, not on the basis of their political reliability. Most important, Kapitsa recommended that research directors be given more freedom in hiring and firing personnel, and greater power to reward productive researchers with money and prestige. Such incentives should particularly be employed in persuading more researchers to switch from theoretical to experimental work, or else the already decreasing number of Russian achievements in research would decrease even more sharply.[26]

At first, the scientists, like the artists, tried to put their own professional houses in order and attempted to free their disciplines from political control. There was, now and again, some joining of artistic and scientific efforts. For example, Dudintsev helped the geneticists in their struggle against the Lysenkoites, and scientists supported modern poetry, abstract painting, and modern sculpture. In 1962, after the debacle wrought by Khrushchev at the Manezh art show, physicists Igor Tamm and Nikolay Semyonov had been among the seventeen signatories of a letter to Khrushchev supporting abstract art.[27] Both Anna Akhmatova and Andrei Voznesensky in the same year made comments indicating that their audience was composed of a good number of the scientific intelligentsia. "Scientists are the most sophisticated, sensitive readers of poetry today," Akhmatova testified.[28] "Voznesensky . . . told a *Times* correspondent that his readers are mainly members of the 'technological intelligentsia': 'There are millions of them in Russia now. Many of them work on sputniks and other enormously complicated machines and they want poetry to be complicated too. They have no use for rhymed editorials." [29] In the spring of 1966, Kapitsa courageously organized an exhibition of the paintings of Alexei Anikeyenok at his own Institute of Problems of Physics, because Anikeyenok, an abstractionist, had not been admitted into the Union of Artists and was therefore not permitted to exhibit his paintings.[30] One element of this increasing support of artists and writers by scientists and of scientists by artists and writers was the fact that more writers and artists were themselves scientists or had a scientific or technical education. For example, Solzhenitsyn was a trained mathematician and physicist, Aksyonov a physician, Yesenin-Volpin a mathematician.

Just as the Sinyavsky-Daniel trial was the watershed for the writers, so it was the watershed for the scientists. As they began to fear re-Stalinization, scientists increasingly joined with artists in public and political protests unrelated to their specialized areas of competence, in an endeavor to hold on to whatever they had gained in the liberalization since Stalin's death. Khrushchev was deposed in October 1964; the following year, in September 1965, Sinyavsky and Daniel were arrested, and in February 1966 they were tried and convicted. Before their arrest, Articles 190/1 and 190/3, though as yet unpublished, had been added to the Criminal Code, but when the code was published, a number of leading Russian scientists, among them Tamm, Sakharov, and Astaurov, addressed a letter to the Supreme Soviet protesting their inclusion in the code. Early in 1966, after the Sinyavsky-Daniel trial, a group of twenty-five intellectuals signed a protest against the rehabilitation of Stalin, including some of the most eminent men in Soviet physics: Tamm, Kapitsa, Sakharov, Lev Artsimovich, and Mikhail Leontovich.[31]

The flurry of trials and repressions thereafter—Ginzburg-Galanskov, Khaustov-Gabay, and Bukovsky-Delaunay—showed that the Brezhnev-Kosygin regime was set on a new dogmatic, neo-Stalinist course. This was confirmed in April after the Central Committee Plenum where it was decided that the "consequences of the personality cult" had officially been eliminated, and where a call was issued for increased vigilance and tightened ideological restraints. A deluge of letters—for the Soviet Union—of protest, appeal, and alarm was addressed to various top leaders and ruling bodies by a wide variety of scientists, the cream of the Soviet scientific elite: Nobel and Lenin Prize winners, senior and junior scientific workers, physicists, mathematicians, biologists, geologists, chemists, physicians, and engineers, joined the writers, historians, economists, actors, critics, and painters in opposing the new turn of affairs. In the various protests, three leaders of the liberal scientists emerged: Kapitsa, Tamm, and Andrei Sakharov, who in their separate and different ways fought against the new restrictions of freedom, sometimes individually, sometimes together. Whether it was all three together protesting Zhores Medvedev's arbitrary confinement to a psychiatric ward, or Kapitsa declaring that the Soviet Union needed more free discussion, more polemics, more airing of ideas even if those ideas were radically wrong,[32] or Sakharov publicly petitioning the Central Committee to dismiss its case against Ginzburg and Galanskov, these prominent scientists were trying to protect those dissidents victimized for their opinions by the Brezhnev-Kosygin repressions.

26 The Sakharov Memorandum

> Any preaching of the incompatibility of world ideologies and nations is madness and a crime. Only universal cooperation under conditions of intellectual freedom and the lofty moral ideals of socialism and labor, accompanied by the elimination of dogmatism and pressures of the concealed interests of ruling classes, will preserve civilization.
>
> *Andrei Sakharov*

The United Nations had declared 1968 "Human Rights Year." In the spring of that year, two major events of Soviet scientific dissent occurred: the publication of the first issue of the *Chronicle of Current Events;* and the *samizdat* circulation of Andrei Sakharov's memorandum on "convergence" of the Soviet and American systems, an essay that was soon smuggled to the West to appear in book form under the title *Progress, Coexistence, and Intellectual Freedom.* Underground publications had begun to proliferate in the Soviet Union after 1958, at first journals like *Phoenix 61, Syntax,* and *Russkoye slovo.* Typewritten on onionskin paper, with several carbons, or occasionally mimeographed or otherwise reproduced, these were generally local, literary, and modernist publications. At the same time, such unofficial literary associations as Smog and the Ryleev Circle, as well as amateur dramatic groups, private art exhibits, and public poetry readings were organized. All these together constituted what Andrei Amalrik was to call the "Cultural Opposition."

After the fall of Khrushchev and as a consequence of re-Stalinization and the regime's tightening grip on cultural and intellectual life, the dissidents' emphasis began to shift from literary to political concerns, from belletristic writing to documentary journalism. In January 1966, a group of two hundred chemistry students at Leningrad University were arrested for having clandestinely published and distributed a paper named *Kolokol* ("The Bell") after Aleksandr Herzen's nineteenth-century publication. The following year the Ukrainian television journalist Vyacheslav Chornovil was arrested and imprisoned for compiling a documentary account of the trials of Ukrainian nationalists. For publishing *Phoenix 66*, Galanskov was tried and sentenced to seven years in February 1968; at the same time Aleksandr Ginzburg was sentenced to five years for assembling a "White Book" on the Sinyavsky-Daniel trial; and in the summer of 1968, Anatoly Marchenko was sentenced to a year for his documentary account of the various prisons and concentration camps he had been confined in during his earlier sentence. Such publications were evidence that in the middle and late 1960s the so-called Cultural Opposition had been politicalized and become what Amalrik was soon to call the "Democratic Movement." [1]

The *Chronicle of Current Events* was one of the most important, though clandestine, voices of that Democratic Movement. Dedicated to the "Human Rights Year in the USSR," the first issue of the *Chronicle* appeared on April 30, 1968, and carried on its front cover a quotation from Article 19 of the United Nations Universal Declaration of the Rights of Man, to which the Soviet Union was a signatory: "Everyone has the right to freedom of opinion and to its free expression; this right includes the freedom to maintain one's own opinion unhindered, and the freedom to seek, receive and disseminate information and ideas by any means and regardless of state frontiers." The first issue devoted itself to the reaction to the Ginzburg-Galanskov trial and reported at length on the protests which the trial had evoked. It also included the text of an appeal against the political trials in the USSR which had been dispatched to the Communist Party Consultative Conference in Budapest. The same issue gave news of political prisoners and described a Leningrad trial during March and April 1968 in which seventeen intellectuals were accused of organizing an All-Russian Christian Union for the Liberation of the People. The format was to prove a model for ensuing issues. The *Chronicle* was to appear thereafter regularly on the last day of every second month, and still continues to be published after three years.[2] Its documentary tone, objectivity, and accuracy were in some ways more politically effective than a more heated polemical tone might have been.

The *Chronicle* has dealt with hundreds of cases in which individuals' civil rights were infringed, as well as with cases in which the rights of small sects and large ethnic groups alike—Crimean Tatars, Uzbeks, Tadjiks, Jews, and Estonians—were violated. It has reported the fate and condition of imprisoned political dissidents, given news of protests and activities of the Democratic Movement, summarized or noted the contents of other underground *samizdat* publications. That the *Chronicle* can continue to publish regularly into its third year is a tribute to the men who run it, their sources of information, and the unity and organization of the dissidents in general. Probably published in Moscow, the paper seems to be the product of top Soviet scientists and technologists. Whoever the specific editors may be, they have had a fairly sophisticated communications network available to them, for the *Chronicle* has carried stories from all areas of the USSR—Moscow, Leningrad, Gorki, Tashkent, Kharkov, Riga, Kiev, Saratov—covering events so close in time that the periodical has surely had sources in all those places as well as means of communication between the sources and the editors of the paper. For one example, the *Chronicle* reported the KGB's search of Amalrik's Moscow apartment on February 27, 1970, in its issue of the very next day, February 28. In that same issue, moreover, it also reported the results of the General Grigorenko trial in Tashkent, which had taken place only the day before. Since the paper's editors have made great efforts to preserve the documentary accuracy of the publication, presumably they have some way of receiving *written* information—texts, facts, documents—from widely placed sources, probably through teletype or computer circuits, though it is possible that other methods—airline couriers, mail, and the telephone system—have been used.

After Human Rights Year (1968) had ended, the *Chronicle* announced that because the job it had set out to do was by no means completed and much remained to be done in the struggle against repression, it would continue publishing. At that time the editors gave a partial picture of how they acquired information and distributed copies:

Although *The Chronicle* is not an illegal publication, the conditions of its work are hampered by peculiar concepts of legality and freedom of information developed over many years by certain Soviet agencies. Therefore, *The Chronicle* cannot, like other newspapers, give its postal address on the last page. Nevertheless, everyone who is interested in seeing that the Soviet public is informed of events in the country can easily transmit information available to him in *The Chronicle*. Give the news to the person from whom you get your copy, and he will pass it on to his supplier, etc. Only do not try personally to reach the top of the chain in order that you shall not be thought to be an informer.[3]

Such caution probably helps to explain why the KGB has evidently not yet been able to infiltrate and close down the *Chronicle*.

Though it is clear that the *Chronicle* is a publication produced by and for an elite minority of academicians and intellectuals, it is also a manifestation of the confidence and courage, the caution and discipline of the intelligentsia in the face of re-Stalinization—and a significant one. Despite the awful power of the KGB and its network of informers, the paper, its editors, its sources, and its readers have remained intact and working. They have continued the long struggle for the rule of law in the Soviet Union—though, at this stage, only by invoking the rights provided for in the Soviet constitution—more honored in the breach than in the observance—and the United Nations' Declaration of Human Rights.

A month after the first issue of the *Chronicle of Current Events*, in June 1968, a ten-thousand-word memorandum by physicist Andrei Sakharov was being widely circulated in *samizdat* among the Soviet intelligentsia. A brilliant young scientist reputed to be the "father of the Soviet hydrogen bomb,"[4] Sakharov had since the early 1960s been one of the leaders of the liberal scientific resistance to re-Stalinization and its bureaucratic and dogmatic manifestations. He had very early come to the support of the biologists in fighting against and eliminating the official Lysenkoist policy in genetics. With Yakov Zeldovich, a fellow physicist, Sakharov had also opposed Khrushchev-imposed changes in the Soviet educational system which required students to spend a considerable portion of their time in field or factory work. Instead, Sakharov and Zeldovich proposed accelerating a course of intensive study for gifted students in mathematics and physics because the most creative work in those fields tended to be accomplished by young men in their early twenties. Now, in his memorandum, Sakharov turned his attention to the broadest, most profound problems facing mankind at large. He believed mankind was on the brink of disaster from thermonuclear war, hunger, overpopulation, destruction of the environment, mass culture, and bureaucratized dogmatism. To solve those problems and thereby to preserve civilization and mankind, Sakharov insisted, the Soviet Union and the United States had to cooperate. Refusal to cooperate and increasing the incompatibility between world ideologies and nations are madness and crimes, and the resulting national hostilities and military competition can lead only to universal suicide.

Sakharov believed that the Soviet and American systems were "converging," each borrowing significant features from the other so that within two decades the USSR would be "democratized" and the United States "socialized." This transformation of the two societies would inevitably minimize their mutual hostility and facilitate the cooperation between the two that is essential if mankind is to prevent catastrophe. The United States and the USSR could then, under United Nations auspices, work together to eliminate or mitigate those problems which afflict the planet.

The most interesting part of Sakharov's essay is devoted to a critique of Soviet policy, practice, and personnel. It covers the whole range of issues the liberal intellectuals had targeted: Stalin and the heirs of Stalin, neo-Stalinism and re-Stalinization, the restoration of truth to Soviet history, intellectual freedom and censorship, anti-Semitism and Great Russian chauvinism, violations of "socialist legality," the "new class" privileges of the ruling elite, and so on. Sakharov identifies Stalin's regime with Hitler's and Mao's; all are "cruel dictatorial police regimes" whose racism, nationalism, militarism, suppression of intellectual freedom, hypocrisy, and demagogy are alike. Stalinism made use of treachery, torture, execution, informing, and denouncing to intimidate millions of people, "the majority of whom were neither cowards nor fools." As a result, at least 10 to 15 million people perished in the torture chambers of the NKVD from torture and execution, in camps for exiled kulaks and so-called semi-kulaks and members of their families and in camps "without the right of correspondence" which were in fact the prototypes of the Fascist death camps where, for example, thousands of prisoners were machine-gunned because of "overcrowding" or as a result of "special orders."

People perished in the mines of Norilsk and Vorkuta from freezing, starvation, and exhausting labor, at countless construction projects, in timber-cutting, building of canals, or simply during transportation in prison trains, in the holds of death ships in the Sea of Okhotsk, and during the resettlement of entire peoples, the Crimean Tatars, the Volga Germans, the Kalmyks, and other Caucasus peoples.

Moreover, Stalin had in the period 1936–1939 slaughtered half of the total membership of the Communist Party; of the 1.2 million members, only 50,000 survived. Sakharov denounced Stalin for inhumane treatment of returning Russian prisoners of war who found that they had only exchanged Nazi camps for Soviet ones, and for the decimation of military leaders and engineers and technicians during the 1930s. He pointed out Stalin's blind faith in Hitler and their pact and Stalin's unpreparedness and ineptitude, and how, in combination, they had led to the debacle of the Nazi invasion of 1941 and its consequences. He attacked the Stalinist collectivization of the countryside: "Unlimited exploitation and predatory forced deliveries at 'symbolic' prices" resulted in "almost serflike enslavement of the peasantry" and crippled Soviet farming and industrial progress. He censured the "criminal exile of entire peoples condemned to slow death." [5]

Sakharov did not confine himself merely to criticizing the past or to poking holes in the historical façade the Stalinists and neo-Stalinists had plastered over the nasty facts; he wanted action taken *in the present* that would be directly threatening to the Brezhnev-Kosygin regime and to all the heirs of Stalin. Sakharov wanted rehabilitation of all the victims of Stalinism, and the NKVD-MGB-KGB archives opened for investigation so that the crimes against the innocent could be openly and publicly documented. He reiterated a demand, evidently first made in 1946 but never fulfilled, for the "symbolic" expulsion of Stalin from the Communist Party for his "crimes." Although Sakharov gave due credit to Khrushchev for instigating de-Stalinization and for freeing and rehabilitating thousands of prisoners, he reminded everyone that "Khrushchev, while Stalin was alive, was one of his collaborators in crime, occupying a number of influential posts." [6] Such an accusation could as justly be brought against Brezhnev, Kosygin, and Party and government leaders throughout the bureaucracy. In addition, Sakharov rejected the idea that the past crimes of Stalinism could be ignored; he declared that "only the most meticulous analysis of the past and its consequences will now enable us to wash off the blood and dirt that befouled our banner," and he called for restricting the influence of neo-Stalinists in political life *in the present* in every possible way.[7]

Essential to Sakharov's argument was his belief in the necessity for intellectual freedom, without which civilization cannot endure. Intellectual freedom means the liberty to get and disseminate information, the right to open and candid debate untrammeled by official censorship, pressure, and terror. Such freedom must be enjoyed by all classes within the society, and Sakharov rejects the notion that the intelligentsia must "subordinate its strivings to the will and interests of the working class (in the Soviet Union, Poland and other socialist countries). What these demands really mean is subordination to the will of the party, or even more specifically, to the party's central apparatus and its officials." Sakharov refuses to accept the current Soviet dogma that these Party officials represent either progress or the interests of the workers; he remarks that they may in fact simply be defending their "own caste interests." [8] He supports Solzhenitsyn's attack on Glavlit and the censorship: "Incompetent censorship destroys the living soul of Soviet literature" and encourages dullness and stagnation in all other areas of intellectual endeavor.[9] He also takes up the cudgels for the dissidents—Grigorenko, Sinyavsky and Daniel, Ginzburg and Galanskov, Bukovsky and Khaustov—recommending that they and all political prisoners be given complete amnesty, not the very limited amnesty the regime granted in celebrating the fiftieth anniversary of the Bolshevik Revolution, and he calls for all political trials to be reviewed and reconsidered. He further deplores the regime's witch hunt among Soviet intellectuals, which forces conformity on them by arbitrary police, judicial, and psychiatric means, as well as by the simple economic method of cutting off their livelihood. Major legislative and organizational changes must be accomplished in Soviet life to remove the various neo-Stalinist manifestations; Sakharov hopes and strives for a development similar to the "bold initiative" of the

Czechoslovaks' effort to give socialism a more human and humane face.

If, in June 1968, Sakharov was hopeful about democratizing the Soviet Union along so-called Czechoslovak lines and about the prospects for a rational reorganization of the USSR according to a Western "social-democratic" model, the Soviet invasion of Czechoslovakia two months later, and the continued and increasing repressiveness of the Brezhnev-Kosygin government could only have been disenchanting.[10]

But Sakharov was not easily discouraged. He continued his efforts, and on March 19, 1970, he sent a letter directly to Brezhnev, Kosygin, and Podgorny calling for an overall democratization of Soviet life, an end to restrictions on freedom of information, and a general turnabout of the government's policy toward the intelligentsia. He warned that the Soviet Union was falling behind the United States in many important fields of science and technology, failing to take advantage of the "second industrial revolution" fueled by advances in computer technology, the production of electric power, chemistry, and drilling for natural gas, so the gap between the two countries was widening. The difficulties, Sakharov contended, could be traced to Stalinist norms and traditions in Soviet public life which, if they were not abandoned, would lead to the USSR's becoming a second-rate provincial power. One neo-Stalinist norm that was an enormous obstacle to scientific and technical progress was the regime's obsessive secrecy: "Real information on our faults and negative phenomena is kept secret because it may be used by hostile propaganda. Exchange of information with foreign countries is restricted on the ground of penetration of hostile ideology. Theoretical conceptions and practical proposals which may seem too bold are suppressed immediately without any discussion under the influence of fear that they may break the foundations." [11] Unless information is circulated freely, Sakharov pointed out, the creative energies and cooperation of the people, especially the intelligentsia, cannot be enlisted; and even the top leadership, continuing to receive false, incomplete, or distorted information, cannot act effectively. Not only must freedom of information be allowed; it must be encouraged. The regime's restrictions, administrative pressures, job dismissals, and trials, which create distrust and lack of understanding, must be eliminated so the nation's creative forces can be mustered for solving social and economic problems.

Sakharov is exceedingly cautious in discussing how democratization is to take place, obviously fearful of alarming the heirs of Stalin. He makes clear that he expects it to be gradual and "at the initiative and under control of the highest authorities," but he is nonetheless concerned to "liquidate the bureaucratic, dogmatic, hypocritical style which is so important now." Sakharov proposes a program for the development of democratization during the next four or five years which would transform Soviet society. First, he recommends that the highest Party and government leaders make public statements declaring their intention to democratize the society and that those statements be properly publicized in the press. Second, he calls for "restricted distribution (through Party and state organs) of information on the state of the country and of theoretical work on public problems. Later this type of material ought gradually to be made available to everyone." He suggests that an institute for the study of public opinion be established with "initially restricted but eventually complete publication of material showing the attitude of the people to the most important problems of internal and external policy." He wants an end to the jamming of foreign broadcasts, free sale of foreign books and periodicals, unrestricted international correspondence and an expansion of tourism, and a Soviet commitment to sign and adhere to the international copyright agreements. Sakharov also would like a reformed judicial system, free from political interference, bias, and corruption; amnesty for political prisoners; publication of the records of political trials; and "public control of the places of imprisonment and political asylums." [12] He asks for the eradication of ethnic designations in Soviet internal passports and the gradual elimination of internal passports altogether. He suggests that greater autonomy and the right to experiment would improve industry and education. But perhaps his most "radical" suggestions are for several candidates to be nominated for various Party and government positions and for greater rights and responsibilities for the Supreme Soviet.

All in all, Sakharov was calling for a transformation of Soviet institutions, a gradual one to be sure, but one which would altogether change the face of contemporary Russia. If the heirs of Stalin were to heed his suggestions, they would move the USSR toward a more humane and effective government, more prosperous and popularly based; but the response to the Sakharov letter—it was, of course, never published in the Soviet Union—was the same old dogmatic reaction.

After the invasion of Czechoslovakia, the upsurge of protest and dissidence was countered by a clear-cut regime program to stifle artistic and scientific dissent. The most striking and publicized cases were those of Zhores Medvedev and Revolt Pimenov in the spring and summer of 1970.[13] Medvedev had not only been a leading figure in the assault on Lysenko and his neo-Stalinist colleagues in the government and in biology, but had also been highly critical of the government's censorship, restriction of travel and international scientific relations, and violations of law. Tamm, Sakharov, Kapitsa, Vladimir Engelhardt, and Astaurov had all appealed for Medvedev's release from psychiatric confinement, as had a host of other scientists and artists, and although they had succeeded in having the biologist released, it was only a partial victory at best, for Medvedev's freedom was contingent on his abstaining from further public dissent. Yet, significantly, the release had been engineered at a face-to-face meeting between scientists and government bureaucrats, between Sakharov, Leontovich, and Astaurov on the one hand, and Dr. Boris Petrovsky, Minister of Public Health, Mstislav Keldysh, president of the Soviet Academy of Sciences, and Dr. Viktor Morozov, the psychiatrist who had examined Medvedev, on the other. In this case, as in those of Grigorenko and Yesenin-Volpin, the regime had seen fit to heed the scientists' advice.[14] Although Sakharov was dismissed from his job in the Soviet nuclear development program and was probably barred from military work after *Progress, Coexistence, and Intellectual Freedom* was published in the West, he continued to do nongovernmental and nonmilitary research at the Lebedev Institute of Physics in Moscow, and he retained his membership in the Academy of Sciences. Moreover, he continued to press for reforms, continued to speak out against the increasing curtailment of freedom.[15]

Revolt Pimenov's arrest took place in July. He was charged under

Article 190/1. Pimenov, born in 1931, was a gifted mathematician, a graduate of Leningrad State University, who had in 1949 been interned in a psychiatric hospital, diagnosed a schizophrenic because he had proffered his resignation from the Komsomol. Pimenov was later pronounced of sound mind, but his release from the mental hospital was made conditional on his withdrawing his resignation. In 1957, he was arrested and tried once again, under Articles 58/10 and 58/11, for disseminating propaganda and for agitation calling for the overthrow, subversion, and weakening of Soviet power, and for circulating literature with such contents, and participating in organizations with similar aims. Pimenov was accused of writing against the Soviet intervention in Hungary in 1956 specifically, and of attempting to form an "anti-Soviet group" among the students at the Leningrad Library Institute. Four young men were tried with him: B. Vail, K. Danilov, I. Zaslavsky, and I. Verblovsky. All were convicted, and Pimenov was sentenced to six years, Vail to three, the others to two years each. But in January 1958, at the instigation of the Leningrad prosecutor's office, all of their sentences were increased: to ten years for Pimenov, six for Vail, five for Zaslavsky and Verblovsky, and four for Danilov. Pimenov was released in the summer of 1963 and put on three years' probation, but his civil rights were restored, so he was able to finish his work as a candidate in mathematics in 1964, and for the doctorate in 1969. Then, in April 1970, the KGB searched his flat and Vail's, appropriating 250 items, including copies of Sakharov's memorandum, Sinyavsky's farewell address, an open letter by Zinaida Grigorenko, manuscripts of Solzhenitsyn's unpublished novels, and the "Two Thousand Words" manifesto by Czech writer Ludvig Vaculik, which had been directed at the neo-Stalinist rule of dictator Antonin Novotny in Czechoslovakia and had been one of the clarion calls for support of the liberalizing reforms of Alexander Dubcek.[16]

Shortly thereafter, Pimenov was called into the office of the Secretary for Ideology of the Leningrad Party Committee, V. A. Medvedev (not to be confused with either Roy or Zhores Medvedev), and was told: "You understand that we don't have to speak about your scientific work. Your scientific successes—they are all good, but there's something else. You're not living right. A whole collection of anti-Soviet literature was taken from you." Pimenov replied that not a single line of what had been taken "called for an overthrow, a weakening or anything detrimental to Soviet authority." To which Medvedev replied that he was not concerned with legal niceties but with where Pimenov acquired an interest in that kind of literature. Pimenov tried to explain:

The reason for all this is that for some time we scientists have lost our sense of personal security. It has been roughly from the end of 1966. Until then somehow there was no fear. But we have since been forced to experience fear. Why? . . .

The threat to personal security explains the studying of politics. All this began with the trials of the writers. The most important element in the trials was how they were conducted. The violation of legal rights drew attention to them and aroused public concern.

Medvedev replied unequivocally:

If you think that we ever will allow somebody to speak and write anything that comes into his head, then this will never be. We will not allow this. Do you want us to change the ideology? Of course, we don't have enough power to force all people to think the same, but we still have enough power not to let people do things that will be harmful to us. There never will be any compromise on the ideological question.[17]

Medvedev's words reflected the general outlook of the heirs of Stalin, and his words troubled the scientific dissidents.

The trial of Pimenov and Vail took place in the Kaluga regional court, near Moscow, on October 20. Five of Russia's foremost scientists—Sakharov, Valentin Turchin, Valery Chalidze, N. Belo-Ozerov, and S. Kovalov—came to Pimenov's defense in a letter to the court expressing their concern about his arrest, asking to be present at the court proceedings, and declaring their uneasiness about the trial's being properly conducted.[18] Chalidze, the compiler of a *samizdat* journal concerning civil liberties in the Soviet Union,[19] also sent a letter to the Leningrad procurator's office and to the Kaluga tribunal in which he pointed out that possession of the Czechoslovak journal *Literarny Listy*, in which Vaculik's "Two Thousand Words" had appeared, was in no way illegal for Soviet citizens.[20] None of these efforts was effective. Pimenov and Vail were convicted of slandering the Russian state, and Pimenov was sentenced to five years of exile in Siberia.

The Pimenov trial was only one manifestation of increasing Party rigor toward scientist dissidents. On October 25, only five days later, the Central Committee of the Communist Party, in an article in the Party bimonthly, *Partinaya zhizn*, rebuked the physicists of Moscow's esteemed Lebedev Institute of Physics for ignoring ideology and called for a campaign to "instill an irreconcilable posture to the ideological notions of anti-Communism and revisionism among scientists." The article attacked the Party cell at the Lebedev, because the physicists "lack permanent ties to the working collective, do not involve themselves sufficiently in disseminating and propagandizing scientific knowledge, do not write and publish enough works on the philosophical problems of the natural sciences, and do not show the necessary steadfastness in the fight against unscientific idealistic conceptions of bourgeois scientists." [21]

The article also addressed itself to a number of other issues which had been raised in the spring by Vitaly Shelest, a physicist in his early thirties who was not only the deputy director of the newly established Institute of Theoretical Physics in Kiev but also the son of the First Secretary of the Communist Party in the Ukraine. Shelest had called attention to several serious shortcomings in Soviet science, particularly the overemphasis in Russian physics on applied research and work on devices as distinct from basic research.[22] Basic research, Shelest said subsequently, in the journal of the Central Committee of the Ukrainian Party, had been submerged by the prominence given to solving practical problems so that Soviet propagandists could say that since Lenin's time two hundred thousand inventions had been registered but only seventy-five discoveries in the basic sciences had been made.[23] Shelest also suggested more extensive and more intensive contacts with Western scientists and the establishment of advanced theoretical study centers such as the Institute for Advanced Studies at Princeton [24] (where Shelest had been a visitor) in the USSR if Soviet physics was not to fall behind. Shelest, in addition, called for more research funds and compared unfavorably Soviet scientific and graduate education with its counterparts in the United States.

A report on Shelest's own Institute for Theoretical Physics in Kiev described the institute as having five departments in Kiev, and one each in Lvov and Uzhgorod.[25] Scientists in the various departments were working on atomic theory, the theories of relativity and gravitation, solid-state theory, and the theory of elementary particles. Shelest proudly noted that sixty of the sixty-seven scientists in the institute were under thirty-five, and also that many Western scientists, from the United States, France, Switzerland, and Italy, had worked there. He also stressed that the institute maintained close ties with a number of foreign research centers: the Center for Theoretical Research in Miami, the Institute for Physics in Turin, the Institute for Physics at the University of Wroclaw (Poland), the Central Institute for Physical Research in Budapest, and so on.

The *Partinaya zhizn* article criticizing the Lebedev Institute was simultaneously a warning and a chastisement for accepting Western "bourgeois" ideas, for contacts with the West, for insufficient "vigilance," but it also agreed that "the efforts of the Institute's collective should concentrate on developing basic research in the most important new areas of physics which are only just beginning to be developed," and recommended encouragement and more rapid promotion of talented young scientists.[26]

The same month that the *Partinaya zhizn* criticism appeared, on November 15, Andrei Sakharov, Andrei Tverdokhlebov, and Valery Chalidze announced the organization of a Committee for Human Rights in the Soviet Union, whose basic principle was: "Maintenance of human rights is important for creating favorable conditions for people's lives, for consolidating peace, and developing mutual understanding." The three physicists promised that their committee would concern itself with "constructive criticism of the contemporary conditions of the system of legal rights of personal freedom in Soviet law," and would be guided not only by the general principles of the United Nations Declaration of Human Rights, but also by the specific character of Soviet law. They forbade membership to individuals who belonged to a political party—presumably the Communist Party—or held government positions, and also ruled out those who participated in "orthodox or opposition political activity." The committee would cooperate with foreign organizations so long as they were nongovernmental and "proceed[ed] from the principles of the United Nations and [did] not pursue the goal of bringing harm to the Soviet Union." [27]

On the same day, six physicists, including Mikhail Leontovich and the three who had organized the committee, made public a letter that they had sent to the Supreme Court of the RSFSR protesting the sentencing and conviction of Revolt Pimenov.[28]

Such activities could not go uncontested, and the Party was swift to show its sharp disapproval. Eight days later, on November 23, *Pravda* printed an editorial calling for a relentless struggle against "bourgeois ideology" which would prevent any "shadow of liberalism [from obscuring] the clarity of ideological positions." [29] The editorial repeated accusations of ideological slackness and apathy at the Lebedev Institute, and on December 2, *Pravda* gave a prominent place to an interview with the head of the Lebedev Party cell, Viktor Silin, who called for intensified vigilance in the "acute ideological struggle in the modern world" and excoriated those who would take non-Party positions. "Anyone who trumpets his non-party attitude plainly and simply makes himself useful to the enemy," Silin declared.[30] Silin did not mention Sakharov, a non-Party man, or his Committee for Human Rights, reserved for non-Party people, nor was the committee given any publicity elsewhere in the Soviet press, but there was no mistaking that they were the targets of Silin's comments and the *Pravda* editorial which preceded them.[31]

On December 17, *Pravda* once more warned the dissidents that the regime would not permit any broadening of their activities, and accused the West of fabricating for its readers the propaganda that there really were some "dissident intellectuals supposedly . . . among Moscow's 'scientific and literary circles.' " [32] Despite such contradictory pronouncements, the regime was aware that the scientific dissidents had taken to heart the open letter of June 20, 1970, circulated in *samizdat* after the Medvedev affair in the spring. The letter had reminded the eminent scientists who had signed the appeal to free Medvedev of the plight of many less prominent and influential dissidents. In the spirit of the Democratic Movement, it suggested equal concern for all people victimized for their beliefs, irrespective of their professional or social standing:

Let us suppose that the martyr of Stalin's torture chambers, Vladimir Gershuni, has no merits whatsoever that are analogous to those of [Zhores] Medvedev. In his personal nobility and his civic valor, however, he is second to none. And even if he were, is this the heart of the matter? All people are equally valuable—in the sense that a human life is priceless. . . . It is indispensable for society to become actively involved in every concrete instance of arbitrary action, regardless of who the "undesirable person" is in any given situation, the famous scholar Zhores Medvedev, or the students Valeria Novodvorskaya, or Olga Ioffe.

A professional group of scholars defends Zhores Medvedev. We welcome all such corporative efforts. This is a wonderful thing. It would not be a bad idea, for example, if writers would follow this initiative and defend their colleagues. We are only emphasizing that those who do not belong to any professional group are in need of the same total and fervent support by society.[33]

Subsequently, a letter was sent to the Presidium of the Supreme Soviet calling for the release of Olga Ioffe, Valeria Novodvorskaya, Anatoly Marchenko, and Major General Grigorenko; it was signed by Sakharov and Chalidze, as well as by Yesenin-Volpin and Pyotr Yakir.[34]

The issues at stake for the Brezhnev-Kosygin regime are now sharply defined. The scientists want numerous changes in Soviet society, democratization and liberalization, a respect for law and for individual rights; they also want to eliminate political and ideological interference in their professional lives and research. They want more communication with Western scientific institutes and colleagues, and freer expression and communication inside the USSR. They want a general relaxation of the repressiveness against domestic dissidence and unorthodox opinion. But all these demands are threats to the heirs of Stalin. The Party has long been aware of the scientists' contempt for ideology and refusal to participate in Party life, and their courage in speaking out. The Party leaders know that they must permit considerable scientific freedom and contact with the West if Russia is not to fall behind technologically and industrially, but they are fearful that contact with foreign projects and individuals will "contaminate" the intellectuals. Consequently, they are constantly urging improved agit-prop work among the scientific intelligentsia to propagate "Marxist-Leninist consciousness," and they have made rigorous efforts to preserve ideological purity and keep scientists from ideological wavering—at least in public. And they continue to strive to keep the intelligentsia and the country at large uncontaminated by foreign, particularly Western, ideas.

Though under pressure from such groups as Sakharov's Committee for Human Rights, the heirs of Stalin recognize that his is a relatively moderate organization, and that there are other scientists and scientific groups who are ready to take more extreme measures. While Zhores Medvedev was being detained, an open letter to the scholars, scientists, and artists of the world was made public, signed by "A Group of Scientists from the USSR Academy of Sciences," which declared that the "experience of the past few years has shown us that to appeal to the conscience or the common sense of our authorities, to urge them to observe legality or to show humaneness is the most assured path to prison or to an insane asylum"; [35] it urged colleagues throughout the world to institute a complete scientific, technical, and cultural boycott of the Soviet Union until Zhores Medvedev was released. Another document, "The Tactical Principles of the Democratic Movement in the Soviet Union," stated that "the legal forms of the movement, having fulfilled their historical role, have basically exhausted themselves"; it called for illegal, underground, and conspiratorial methods of resisting the regime in an effort to further democratization.[36] The Sakharov committee is much less militant than the authors of those documents; it is willing to engage in flexible negotiations with the regime to achieve a gradual, consistent democratization of Soviet institutions and of Soviet life.

The heirs of Stalin are aware of how much political ferment can arise from the creative and reforming zeal and energies of the dissident scientists. They are also cognizant of the importance of the scientists' talents and assiduity for the technical and industrial progress of the nation and that, if the nation is not to be surpassed, they must not alienate the scientific elite. All these factors make the Party leaders and bureaucracy extremely uneasy, for the scientific dissidents and the scientific elite are at best indifferent, and at worst hostile, to their ideology; intelligent, skeptical, better informed and better educated than most Soviet citizens, they are by the very nature of their gifts and the role they play in Soviet society in a position to question, even to threaten, the monopoly of wisdom that the Party arrogates to itself and the monopoly of control over the shaping of Soviet society that is designated by Party propagandists as the "leading role of the Party."

Part V

THE IRON HEEL

27 The Nobel Prize

> For a country to have a great writer is like having another government. That's why no regime has ever loved great writers, only minor ones.
>
> *Aleksandr Solzhenitsyn*

Though he had spoken out and for the first time in the Medvedev case publicly identified himself with the political dissidents, Solzhenitsyn otherwise continued to live a quiet life. After his ouster from the Writers' Union he was forced to move from his house in Ryazan: "The atmosphere . . . is hostile and even dangerous due to threats of violence by local zealots. Since Solzhenitsyn has been denied official authorization to live in Moscow, he has taken refuge in the country house near Moscow of cellist Mstislav Rostropovich." His friends continued to be concerned that he might be brought to trial and imprisoned, like Sinyavsky and Daniel; when, in March 1969, *Grani* published Solzhenitsyn's play *Candle in the Wind*, they were afraid that it offered the Soviet authorities a pretext for accusing Solzhenitsyn of "anti-Soviet" activities, as the Kremlin had Aleksandr Ginzburg and Yury Galanskov, both of whom it had accused of having connections with the NTS. In November 1969, *Die Zeit* also published extracts from an epic poem called *Prussian Nights* which it attributed to Solzhenitsyn, but when Solzhenitsyn's Swiss attorney, Fritz Heeb, approached the newspaper, it agreed to stop publication of the remaining extracts.[1]

Solzhenitsyn was actually then immersed in writing a new historical novel set on "the Balkan front of Czarist Russia in the war years 1914–1916, when the armies of Nechivolodov were fighting the Austro-Hungarians. The author's father fought in World War I as an officer, and, two years ago, when he was beginning his research for the book, Solzhenitsyn drove to Byelorussia in the old Moskvich car he calls 'Denis Ivanovich' because it was bought with the royalties from his novel, *One Day in the Life of Ivan Denisovich*" [2] to acquire some feeling for the setting of the battles he was to portray.

Then, on October 8, the Swedish Academy announced that Solzhenitsyn had been awarded the Nobel Prize for literature for 1970, "for the ethical force with which he has pursued the indispensable traditions of Russian literature." Dr. Karl-Ragnar Gierow, the permanent secretary of the academy, hailed the novelist as a "son of the Russian revolution, of Lenin's revolution," and added that Solzhenitsyn had never surrendered his "spiritual heritage." [3] The Nobel Prize came to Solzhenitsyn twelve years after it had been awarded to Pasternak in 1958—and after Pasternak had been forced by Khrushchev to renounce it—and five years after Sholokhov had received the prize in 1965 and been permitted by Brezhnev and Kosygin to go to Stockholm to accept it. It was also soon revealed that the Soviet rulers had attempted to head off the award of the prize to Solzhenitsyn and had sent Sholokhov to Stockholm in September to lobby against Solzhenitsyn. The effort had achieved the opposite effect altogether and "became instrumental in the Swedish Academy's decision to advance the date of election and thus cut short further interventions." [4]

When informed that he had been awarded the coveted prize, Solzhenitsyn was at first skeptical; he was convinced only when Per Egil Hegge, the Moscow correspondent for both the Norwegian *Aftenpost* and the Swedish *Svenska Dagbladet,* telephoned him and confirmed the report. Solzhenitsyn thereupon dictated a brief statement to Hegge over the telephone: "I am grateful for the decision. I accept the prize. I intend to go and receive it personally on the traditional day in so far as this depends on me. I am well. The journey will not hurt my health." Solzhenitsyn was very cautious, insisting that the Scandinavian newsman take down the words of his statement exactly as he dictated them: "I do not want my words distorted with other interpretations." [5] He also insisted that he would not speak to any other foreign newspapermen, that he wished to remain "inaccessible," and he made Per Hegge promise not to reveal to anyone the private telephone number Hegge had called him on.

When the official notice of the Swedish Academy was delivered to Solzhenitsyn, he replied formally: "I have received your cable and I want to thank you. The decision on the Nobel Prize I regard as a tribute to Russian literature and to our arduous history. On this tradition-rich day I intend to come to Stockholm to receive the prize personally." [6] Solzhenitsyn had been careful in both statements to avoid giving even the appearance of contending with the Soviet authorities, but he had also made clear that if he did not go to Stockholm, it would not be of his own volition.

No sooner had the award been announced than the Soviet authorities began to belittle Solzhenitsyn's stature as a writer and to accuse the Swedish Academy of having "allowed itself to be drawn into an unseemly game which was started by no means in the interest of development of the spiritual values and traditions of literature, but was prompted by speculative political considerations." The Writers' Union Secretariat announced that Solzhenitsyn's works had "long been used by Western reactionary circles for anti-Soviet aims," and that Soviet writers had for a long time so strongly disapproved of both his work and his behavior that they had been moved to expel him from the Writers' Union, a decision "actively supported by the entire public of the country." [7] The literary reactionaries were swift to seize the opportunity to condemn Solzhenitsyn; Leonid Sobolev remarked that he was not surprised by the award, because "the literary and political personality of Solzhenitsyn directed the attention of the Soviet Union's enemies on him," and added that Solzhenitsyn's qualities as a writer had been exaggerated for political purposes.[8] Sergey Mikhalkov insisted that the Swedish Academy's decision was "in no way dictated by concern about Russian literature," [9] and Nikolay Gribachev noted: "The tendentiousness in Solzhenitsyn's creations consists in the rejection of anything positive built by the Soviet people and by socialist society, and in an exaggerated emphasis on the errors and shortcomings which are normal in any great construction." [10] The Writers' Union paper, *Literaturnaya gazeta*, commented on the terms of the award: "It is completely clear that in the given instance, the members of the [Nobel Prize] committee, under the term 'ethical force' had an anti-Soviet tendency in mind." [11]

There were many other such adverse comments, calling the award a "minor event," deliberately sensational, and the recipient a mediocre writer who should not in any way be compared to the great Russian writers.

It will not take too long for the broadest segments of the people to see absolutely clearly the literary and political bankruptcy of Solzhenitsyn's writings. One can think of no other name than blasphemy for some striking analogies drawn by the so-called "specialists on Soviet literature" who bracket [Solzhenitsyn with] the creators of the internationally famous works of Russian and Soviet classical literature. [The award] will repel all those who are fed up with the banal dish of anti-Soviet propaganda.[12]

There were official cries that the Nobel Prize committee had demeaned the prize deliberately for political purposes, primarily because Solzhenitsyn's works "present a distorted picture of Soviet reality . . . permeated with the spirit of anti-Sovietism, anti-Communism, and Western propaganda. [Therefore the committee] uses them as an instrument of the ideological struggle against the Soviet Union."[13] Cold-war adversaries would be delighted by the award. The entire affair was, in fact, "a political provocation, and will be used inevitably for purposes which have nothing in common with literature."[14]

Aleksandr Pogodin, another of the leading literary dogmatists, tried to stress what separated Solzhenitsyn and his works from the "true traditions" of Soviet and Russian literature:

Russian realistic literature was always permeated with the creative spirit, the spirit of progress and the strengthening of the great values of patriotism, love for Russia, deep faith in the Russian people, their greatness, strength, prudence. . . .

Feelings of dejection and inferiority, malice and contempt for man have always been foreign to it, and obviously, it never lowered itself to slandering its own country and people.

Solzhenitsyn, however, denied these values affirmed by classical Russian literature. He attempts to persuade readers that man is evil and insignificant in his essence, and that mutual hostility and hatred have existed in human beings from time immemorial.[15]

A Polish radio commentator was more candid in his analysis of what was at stake when he noted that Solzhenitsyn had clashed with the political leaders of the Soviet state ideologically: "In this context, the fact that he was granted the prize was bound to have a political flavor, although this highest literary distinction should not be linked with politics." [16]

An article by Mikhalkov, "The Writer's Word at the Service of the Times," made plain what the regime required of its writers: "The Soviet writer does not at all resemble his predecessors; he is a writer-warrior, a writer-builder, a direct participant in the historic events that he chronicles." Mikhalkov went on to praise a virtually unknown writer named Anatoly Yemelyanov, whose father died in 1942 fighting the Germans, who himself served in the tank corps, and who was not only the secretary of the Party organization of his kolkhoz, but also a Party instructor and for six years First Secretary of the District Party Committee in the Chuvash Autonomous Republic where he lives. "Where in the West can a writer of this kind be found?" [17] Mikhalkov asked triumphantly, if perhaps rhetorically. The Young Communist League's newspaper attacked the Nobel Prize committee for malicious sensation-seeking too, and condemned Solzhenitsyn's writings as "politically tendentious"—as instruments serving the purposes of "anti-Soviet propaganda":

The tragedy of Solzhenitsyn the writer lies in the fact that, once having put on dark glasses, he deprives himself of seeing all the many-colored life of our country. A man with a pathological sense of his own importance, Solzhenitsyn readily succumbed to the flattery of people who are not choosy about the means they use when the matter at hand is the struggle against the Soviet Union. Thus, what Solzhenitsyn has made out of his isolation is no longer a tragedy but a business. Going back and examining what Solzhenitsyn has written, one can easily see for oneself that the literary element in his works has yielded progressively to the element of political libel—his glory is that of a scandal-monger! [18]

The New York Times also declared that "a special meeting of Communist Party activists of the Writers' Union was reported recently to have called for issuing a 'one-way ticket' to Mr. Solzhenitsyn." [19]

The attack on Solzhenitsyn was, by Soviet standards, relatively restrained and lacked the venomous intensity and political pressure that were directed against Boris Pasternak when he won the Nobel Prize. But it was by no means mild, and it was continuous. Since Solzhenitsyn had already informed the Swedish Academy that he would personally accept the prize and was healthy enough to make the trip, the Soviet leaders had only a limited number of courses of action open to them if they wished to preserve the façade of legality and the fiction of Solzhenitsyn's freedom to do as he wished. They could prevent his going to Stockholm simply by denying him an exit visa, or they could permit him to leave, agreeing privately to let him return only if he did not embarrass them with his acceptance speech there. The latter course involved risks: they knew Solzhenitsyn to be a recalcitrant who in the past had not been amenable to "deals" with the authorities, nor could they rely on his remaining silent or being "discreet" by their standards. Refusing him re-entrance to Russia would mean that they would have to revoke his citizenship or take other extraordinary or extralegal steps that would create bad feeling for them abroad. They would very likely offend public opinion internationally, and Party members and fellow-travelers particularly, whom they were reluctant to alienate further. Already such major Communist parties as the French and Italian, and such Communist or sympathizing writers as Louis Aragon, Heinrich Böll, Alberto Moravia, and François Mauriac, as well as such Communist newspapers as *L'Humanité*, *L'Unità* and *Rinascita*, had hailed the award to Solzhenitsyn. The Soviet rulers chose the simpler, less risky course; they decided not to permit Solzhenitsyn to go to Sweden.

Not only official voices made themselves heard in the Soviet Union, however. On October 11, three days after the award was announced, a typewritten letter acclaiming the decision to give the prize to Solzhenitsyn was circulated in Moscow and distributed to foreign correspondents there. It was signed by thirty-seven prominent dissidents, among them Pyotr Yakir and Zinaida Grigorenko. The letter declared: "We hail the Nobel committee for this decision. The civic inspiration, philosophic depth and high artistic craftsmanship of the works of Solzhenitsyn are recognized by the whole world. [He is] a powerful contemporary writer; the humanitarianism of the positions he has adopted and which he consistently and courageously defends, all this deserves an award of such high distinction." [20] At the end of October, Mstislav Rostropovich addressed a letter to the chief editors of *Pravda*, *Izvestia*, *Literaturnaya gazeta*, and *Sovetskaya kultura* in which he defended the novelist against the attacks of the Soviet press. He pointed out the contradiction in the regime's impugning the integrity of the Swedish Academy in awarding Solzhenitsyn the Nobel Prize and remarked that when the Academy's choice pleased the Kremlin—as it had when the prize was conferred on Sholokhov—it was considered " 'just recognition' of the outstanding world significance of our literature," but when the choice displeased the Kremlin, it was part of a "dirty political game." "And what if next time the prize is awarded to Comrade Kochetov? Of course it will have to be accepted!" Rostropovich indicted the censorship of the arts in general and of Solzhenitsyn in particular:

> In 1948 there were lists of forbidden works. Now oral prohibitions are preferred, referring to the fact that "opinions exist" that the work is not recommended. It is impossible to establish where this opinion exists and whose it is. . . . Who first had the "opinion" that it was necessary to expel Solzhenitsyn from the Writers' Union? . . . Did five Ryazan writer-musketeers really dare to do it themselves without a serious "opinion"?
>
> . . . Obviously it was "opinion" which also prevented publication of Solzhenitsyn's *Cancer Ward* which was already set in type for *Novy Mir.* . . .
>
> I do not speak about political or economic questions in our country. There are people who know these better than I. But explain to me please, why in our literature and art so often people absolutely incompetent in this field have the final word? Why are they given the right to discredit our art in the eyes of our people? . . .
>
> Every man must have the right fearlessly to think independently and express his opinion about what he knows, what he has personally thought about, experienced and not merely to express with slightly different variations the opinion which has been inculcated in him.[21]

Rostropovich's letter was not published by any Soviet publication nor was any official mention of it or answer to it forthcoming from the Soviet leadership.

On November 27, in a meeting with the Swedish ambassador to the Soviet Union, Gunnar Jarring, Solzhenitsyn announced that he would not go to Stockholm to receive the Nobel Prize. He gave the Ambassador a letter for the Swedish Academy which said: "In recent weeks, the hostile attitude toward my prize, as expressed in the press of my country, and the fact that my books are still suppressed—for reading them, people are dismissed from work, or expelled from school—compel me to assume that my trip to Stockholm would be used to cut me off from my native land, simply to prevent me from returning home." Solzhenitsyn expressed his gratitude for having the prize bestowed on him, and declared, "Inwardly I share it with those of my predecessors in Russian literature who because of the difficult conditions of the past decades did not live to receive such a prize or who were little known in their own lifetime to the reading world in translation or to their countrymen even in the original." [22] Solzhenitsyn hoped he would be able to receive the diploma and medal that accompany the prize from a Swedish representative in Moscow, perhaps the Ambassador, if the Nobel Foundation agreed, and he also promised that he would send the written text of the required Nobel lecture within six months of the date of the award.

On December 10, the Nobel prizes were awarded in Stockholm. Despite Solzhenitsyn's absence, Dr. Gierow praised the novelist as coming from "the incomparable Russian tradition. The same background underlies the gigantic predecessors who have derived from Russia's suffering the compelling strength and inextinguishable love that permeates their work." [23] Gierow regretted the reasons for Solzhenitsyn's absence from the ceremonies and announced that the prize would be awarded to the novelist at some agreed-upon but unspecified time and place. Then the American Nobel Prize laureate in economics, Paul Samuelson, told the audience, "If Aleksandr Solzhenitsyn had been here to speak from the heart, all of us would be the better for it; every individual, every country, without exception." [24] The Swedish king and the entire audience stood in a demonstration to applaud the absent Russian novelist.

That same day the news came from Moscow that Solzhenitsyn had agreed to join the Committee for Human Rights which the physicists Andrei Sakharov, Andrei Tverdokhlebov, and Valery Chalidze had founded on November 15 to seek guarantees of personal freedom for Russians, but without activity harmful to the Soviet state. A week after the award ceremonies, a lead article in *Pravda* warned Soviet intellectuals: "The Soviet people will not allow anyone to trample on their historic achievements." *Pravda* denounced the "wretched handful of renegades" who comprised the ranks of the dissidents, singling out Solzhenitsyn, Andrei Amalrik, and Vladimir Bukovsky, and labeling the novelist an "internal emigrant" and one of those dissidents who "hang around foreign press centers begging for whisky and cigarettes in exchange for dirty fabrications." The Party paper proclaimed this wretched handful of renegades was far outweighed by the "hundreds of thousands of devoted Soviet citizens who have built a truly great society, and nobody will succeed in ignoring or belittling this." *Pravda* referred to Solzhenitsyn's writings as "lampoons of the Soviet Union," and asserted, "*The First Circle* and *Cancer Ward,* which blacken the achievements of the heroic victories of our motherland and the dignity of the Soviet people, turned out to be suitable material for the latest anti-Soviet campaign fanned up in the West." [25] The same stress on Solzhenitsyn as a renegade and on his works as "lampoons" of Soviet reality that were being used for anti-Soviet purposes to denigrate Soviet accomplishments continued in the Soviet press right up to the end of the year. The charges were repeated in *Pravda* and in the army newspaper *Krasnaya zvezda,*[26] so there were many who feared that the Soviet leaders might be preparing to act against Solzhenitsyn even more punitively.

Solzhenitsyn's arrest would be the cruel but logical culmination of a three-year effort by the KGB . . . to fabricate a case against him based on Article 70 [which] makes it a crime, punishable by seven years' imprisonment, for a writer deliberately to "disseminate slander" about the Soviet system in Russia or abroad. In order to build a case that could appear plausible in court, the KGB has planted Solzhenitsyn's forbidden manuscripts, together with spurious "authorizations," on many unsuspecting Western publishers.[27]

It did not seem likely that the Brezhnev-Kosygin government would imprison Solzhenitsyn in the near future, but unquestionably it was not considering concessions either to the literary liberals or to the political dissidents, nor was it amenable to any change in Solzhenitsyn's domestic status that would lead to his restoration to the Writers' Union and to the publication of his books in the Soviet Union. In spring 1971, the regime's attitude to Solzhenitsyn's work and person remained implacable. In March, after having finished the first volume of his projected World War I trilogy, *August 1914,* the novelist informed Soviet publishing houses that the manuscript was available, but not a single one replied. He remained on the blacklist. Solzhenitsyn objected to the Writers' Union that no Soviet publisher would accept the novel simply because he had written it; then he decided to publish the book abroad.

Solzhenitsyn had neither authorized nor taken a hand in the publication abroad of his other works, but now he decided personally to take a hand in publishing *August 1914* and authorized its release through a small Paris-based Russian-language publisher, YMCA Press. In an epilogue to that Paris edition (which the June 16, 1971, *New York Times* printed), Solzhenitsyn explained:

This book cannot at the present time be published in our native land except in Samizdat because of censorship objections unintelligible to normal human reason and which, in addition, demand that the word God be unfailingly written without a capital letter. To this indignity, I cannot stoop.

The directive to write God in small letters is the cheapest kind of atheistic pettiness. Both believers and unbelievers must agree that when the Regional Procurement Administration is written with capital letters or K.G.B. or Z.A.G.S. [the secret police or city registration bureau] are written in all caps then we might at least employ one capital letter to designate the highest Creative Force in the Universe. Not to add that on the lips of the people of 1914 the word "god" in small letters grates on the ears and is historically false.

Solzhenitsyn also confided that he thought this his most important work, had been thinking about it and preparing to write it since 1936, when he was completing high school, and had been diverted from it to his other books only by "the peculiarities of [his] career and the richness of contemporary impressions." Though he had gathered material over the years, he had been denied all access to the archives by the authorities, and most of the contemporary witnesses of the events had died, so that perhaps "already it is almost too late. My own life and creative imagination are not sufficient for this 20-year work." But because older Russian writers seemed reluctant to deal with that period, and younger ones would find it even more difficult to re-create that era, he would carry on.

In June 1971 the publication of *August 1914* in Paris was greeted with widespread acclaim. One reviewer of the YMCA Russian edition called the novel "the most important Russian literary work of the 20th century [a book] which both explicitly and implicitly invites comparison with Tolstoy's *War and Peace*." [28] It was a judgment echoed elsewhere.[29] Once again, however, the Soviet leaders attempted, as they had with Svetlana Alliluyeva's *Twenty Letters to a Friend,* to subvert Solzhenitsyn's rights to the copyright and income from his own book. The same Flegon Press in London which had been legally prevented from issuing a pirated edition of the Alliluyeva book was now enjoined by the British courts at the request of Solzhenitsyn's official British publisher, The Bodley Head, to cease the sale of an unauthorized English edition.[30]

In the epilogue to the novel Solzhenitsyn confesses that he is afraid that he may never complete the "cycle of historical novels of which *August 1914* is the first. He fears, too, that he will be prevented from finishing either by a recurrence of cancer, or by the Soviet authorities. . . . Recently Solzhenitsyn told a friend, 'My hands are burning from the works I have not yet completed.' " [31] Yet Solzhenitsyn is a man of courage and determination; he will undoubtedly continue to try to write as his own conscience dictates and in so doing he will remain the conscience of his people, a man struggling against the grim reality of the last line he wrote for *August 1914:* "It is not through our fault that the lie came into being, nor will we be able to put an end to it."

28 The Iron Heel

The lash—
  is a medicine,
although it isn't exactly honey.
The foundation of the state
is direction,
    direction.
                    Yevgeny Yevtushenko

With the memory of the roles writers and intellectuals played in the Hungarian revolt of 1956 reinforced by the consciousness of the contributions of Czechoslovak writers and intellectuals to the liberalization of their country from 1966 to 1968, the Soviet authorities are determined to see that Solzhenitsyn's works, as well as those of a number of other Soviet writers, bring neither increased turbulence at home nor decreased prestige and power for the Soviet Union and its leadership abroad. If they are uneasy about Solzhenitsyn's "blackening the image" of the USSR, about his providing grist for foreign "anti-Soviet" propaganda mills, they are increasingly resentful of the position that Solzhenitsyn, willy-nilly, has come to occupy as the leader of the "domestic opposition." Many would, with justice, confer such a title on Pyotr Yakir or Andrei Sakharov or General Grigorenko, but in some respects Solzhenitsyn speaks for all dissidents in a voice they respect and admire; what he says in his books is given international attention of a kind not usually accorded to their words.

Solzhenitsyn's publications in the West have displeased the Soviet leaders, yet his books have given the novelist a continuing leverage with the regime while making it even more concerned about effectively silencing or controlling him. The Brezhnev-Kosygin regime has not been eager to use the outright and most coercive Stalinist methods of the past against him, but that it is determined to bring the novelist to heel is unquestionable. Soviet leaders have had long —and for the writers, tragic—experience in "handling" literary mavericks (not to speak of other kinds of mavericks) with an arsenal that includes censorship, denial of publication, ostracism, harassment, blackmail, confinement in mental institutions, exile, imprisonment, and execution. The present Soviet authorities have, in general, refrained from using the most violent such measures against writers, especially those with some international reputation. When they thought the occasion required it, however, as in the cases of Sinyavsky and Daniel, for instance, the rulers of the Soviet Union continued to be quite adept at using all the instruments of neo-Stalinist terror. However much Soviet leaders protest to the contrary, and however much they consciously tarnish their reputation when they feel their power seriously challenged or important doctrinal issues at stake (witness the lengths to which they were willing to go in sending armies into Hungary in 1956 and into Czechoslovakia in 1968), they remain extraordinarily sensitive about their "image" abroad. Because they have for decades put themselves forward as the leaders of "progressive" causes and Russia as the "motherland of socialism," because they have built a modern Potemkin façade to dupe and distract the unwary in the rest of the world about the virtues and accomplishments of their system, and because it is important for them to retain the loyalty of their many sympathizers and of Communist Party members abroad, they must pay very careful attention to any Soviet writer or dissident who would disabuse people at home or abroad about Soviet intentions and who would disillusion them about "Soviet reality."

Other reasons, more difficult to define but persistent nonetheless —the relations of Moscow to the Communist International, to take only one obvious and relatively recent example—have their origins far back in Russian history and deep in the Russian psyche, both of which have often revealed the most abject sense of inferiority to the West while simultaneously asserting a compensatory and overweening Slavic feeling of superiority and "manifest destiny." Andrei Amalrik, who has an ironic view of his people, has written: "The idea of justice is motivated [in Russia] by the hatred of everything that is outstanding, which we make no effort to imitate, but, on the contrary, try to bring down to our level. . . . This psychology is, of course, most typical of the peasantry . . . and those of peasant origin constitute the overwhelming majority in our country.[1]

Solzhenitsyn's writings have made him the best-known Soviet literary figure abroad since Boris Pasternak and the same kind of focus of controversy at home. But Pasternak was a more subtle and eccentric writer, less willing and less able to become a leader of a literary or political opposition; he was a man obsessed primarily with his private life and his art,[2] although he was not unaware of how the Soviet state impinged on the lives of individuals, as *Doctor Zhivago* so clearly shows. Solzhenitsyn, on the other hand, writes more simply and straightforwardly and is therefore comprehensible to much wider audiences than was Pasternak. Though each man wrote about the life he knew and lived, each belonged to a different generation, and the experiences of Solzhenitsyn's generation are closer to the present-day Soviet audience, particularly the youth. Whereas the main action of *Doctor Zhivago*, for instance, takes place during the period 1903 to 1929, with a brief epilogue and conclusion set at the end of World War II, Solzhenitsyn's writings have World War II as a background, and most of his works are set in postwar Soviet Russia, and thus have greater impact and appeal for contemporary readers. If, as Anatoly Surkov has said, Pasternak's *Doctor Zhivago* "goes so far as to cast doubt upon the validity of the October Revolution, describing it as almost the greatest crime in Russian history," [3] Solzhenitsyn's works document the bankruptcy of the system which was built on that revolution. In spite of his personal shyness and retiring nature, Solzhenitsyn is a man obsessed by the injustices done to his people and himself, and he is compelled to bear witness to the injuries that have been inflicted on him and that symbolize what the country has endured, and at the same time to try to prevent their repetition. Whereas Pasternak evidently knew when and how to accommodate himself to the regime in order to survive, and was even sufficiently terrorized by Khrushchev to repudiate the Nobel Prize, Solzhenitsyn has so far refused to kiss the rod, has stood his ground; he has accepted the Nobel Prize and resisted the regime's commands in a way that Pasternak, both because of his character and because most of his life was spent under Stalin, could not.

This courageous personal commitment, exemplified in his life and writing, has made Solzhenitsyn a symbol of conscience in the Soviet Union, a rallying point for those who would loosen the reins of tyranny, and a political *cause célèbre* at home and abroad. These roles, domestic and foreign, compounded of reality and myth, have displeased the Soviet authorities. Consequently, the Swedish Academy's award of the Nobel Prize to Solzhenitsyn for carrying on the ethical traditions of Russian literature could only exacerbate their displeasure—and simultaneously give additional leverage, an added measure of personal safety, to Solzhenitsyn. One does not, even in the Soviet Union, jail a Nobel Prize winner with impunity. In the circumstances, Soviet leaders were bound to remember that often repeated saying which swept through the Moscow intelligentsia after the publication of Solzhenitsyn's first novel: "Tell me what you think of *Ivan Denisovich* and I will tell you what you are."

Solzhenitsyn also represents the new Soviet generation, which has not yet risen to the most important seats of power. Born in 1918, he is, unlike Pasternak, altogether a product of the Soviet system, and it is difficult to accuse him of being tainted by a former "bourgeois" life, as was done with Pasternak. He has never been abroad, except during the fighting of World War II, and then only in Poland and East Germany, and has few foreign friends and connections. His war record and his public stance, as well as his books, demonstrate that he is a man who loves his native land with that curious and intense ambivalence that afflicts almost all the best Russian writers—a man who has consciously accepted the role of a conscience for his people and his country.

Whatever the changes in "theory" or in the political exigencies, there are continuous regime hostility to, and repression of, the works of any Soviet writers who criticize any important aspect of Soviet life—especially those who would restore the truth to Soviet history and to the Soviet people's picture of themselves and their lives, as well as those who would jettison or resist the leading role of the Party, who would deny that Marxist-Leninism is a perfect philosophy or that its so-called embodiment in the Soviet system is either perfect or on its way to perfection, or who would defend individuals' rights to private lives and put them beyond the Party's control and indoctrination. The Soviet rulers do need "good" books,

books good enough for their people to want to read, but only such good books as do their bidding. Since Stalin came to power, the Soviet authorities have not been able to elicit such books from their writers, either from those most faithful to their cause or from those alienated from it, because good books cannot be written to order. Given the rulers' insistence on Party tutelage in the arts and their compulsive need to control every aspect of the creative process, their failure is no surprise. The Russian writer can write for the desk drawer, or for an audience abroad—dangerous, frustrating, and in important ways artistically debilitating—or confine himself to that small audience he can reach through the *samizdat* network, with all its myriad shortcomings. All these choices are ultimately unsatisfactory to truly creative Russian artists, yet the regime will permit them no other choice, because it is truly terrified and horrified by freedom to create. The Soviet authorities have seen how often "liberating" literature has had powerful political repercussions antithetical to their interests; liberating literature frequently does just that: it liberates. It is a tribute to their respect for the power of the word that the Soviet rulers watch it so carefully, reward it so well, and praise it so fulsomely—when it does their bidding; but trust it they do not. Year in and year out, therefore, the Soviet rulers fight even the slightest intellectual deviation from their political imperatives: there is always a Party line—and someone is always overstepping it.

The regime's treatment of those who publish abroad is qualitatively different in hostility and repressiveness. The treatment of, say, Solzhenitsyn, Pasternak (for *Doctor Zhivago*), Sinyavsky and Daniel, Yesenin-Volpin, and even Yevtushenko, for publishing his *A Precocious Autobiography* in France without government approval or censorship, has been much more savage than the treatment of Ehrenburg for *The Thaw*, or Dudintsev for *Not by Bread Alone*, or even Viktor Nekrasov for *Both Sides of the Ocean*. Exceptions have been made, evidently for special reasons, for such works published abroad as Evgenia Ginzburg's *Journey into the Whirlwind* and Lydia Chukovskaya's *The Deserted House*, ostensibly because those books were published without the authors' consent, yet many government reprisals against writers are difficult to uncover. Whether this difference derives from a realistic estimate by the regime of the use "hostile" agencies are able to make of such critical works or simply evinces the leaders' rage and frustration against "their own people" being put beyond "their" control is difficult to determine, but both factors probably contribute. The fact that writers elude their control may account for the viciousness the Soviet leaders exercise against the authors of such works and would explain the extra margin of vengefulness in dealing with Solzhenitsyn, Pasternak, and Yesenin-Volpin. In addition, the authorities probably recognize, consciously or otherwise, that their most gifted writers are least susceptible to direction and coercion, with perhaps the signal exception of Sholokhov. Sholokhov's great gifts have continued to be put at the service of the government in recent years—though he has resisted censorship and bureaucratic meddling in his own writing—and he has, as Chukovskaya so acidly reminded him, paid the price for political orthodoxy in the continued failure of his creativity.

Though it may seem hard to accept the fact that sentencing Sinyavsky and Daniel to concentration camps or confining Yesenin-Volpin to an insane asylum or exiling Brodsky and Amalrik to the miseries of hauling manure in primitive kolkhozes is much better than what was meted out to writers under Stalin, such punishments are less harsh than what happened in that time when they were sent to Siberian camps to be worked or starved to death, or were murdered outright. The regime willingness to permit writers like Pasternak, Tarsis, and Solzhenitsyn to emigrate is also a difference in kind, although such permissions were given in the past to a number of writers, Evgeny Zamyatin among them. Does this mean that the Soviet leaders are willing to accept the ill-repute such actions generate in exchange for the advantages of branding exiled writers renegades, traitors, and émigrés before the Russian people? Such a course is likely effective with the Soviet masses, who in their xenophobic paranoia think of the friend of their enemy as their enemy, and who are by and large indifferent or hostile to intellectuals, writers, and students, but is it effective with intellectuals, whose loyalties the regime must retain in order to exploit their skills?

Even if the Soviet rulers permitted a degree of creative freedom they seem never even to have considered, it is unlikely that an important literature would emerge in the USSR for quite a long time.

Such literature requires layer on layer of writers and writing as "seedbed" for great writers and great works. Russian writers are not without gifts, but they have not been permitted to exercise those gifts, to have intercourse with other writers, and to read writings published outside the country, to breathe the air of world culture, for almost forty years. Police terror and censorship have instilled a profound wariness, an internal censorship and inhibition in most Soviet writers that must be difficult to surmount; and if some few do surmount them, it is at the cost of great creative energy which might otherwise go into their work. Stifled since the 1930s, at least two generations of Russian writers have been deprived of their heritage or have surrendered it for a pot of message. As a consequence, who, outside the Communist bloc, has been interested in a Soviet writer or painter or sculptor during the past four decades? There are exceptions—Solzhenitsyn, Pasternak, the sculptor Ernst Nezvestny, the painter Glazounov—but they are rare. In this context, Peter Benno accurately remarks:

This extraordinary Soviet reverence for the servants of the Muses has no small impact abroad, where a Yevtushenko or a Voznesensky, a Dudintsev or a Solzhenitsyn is translated into all the languages of Europe and achieves an international success of the sort that few Western writers, even the most major enjoy. A St.-John Perse or an Auden, for instance, might well envy the number of translations and the general notoriety accorded to the work of Yevtushenko. The wide public success and the profound social impact of post-Stalinist Soviet literature constitute a phenomenon unique in the cultural life of any modern nation.[4]

But such international "interest" is fundamentally political—not literary or cultural—and the "extraordinary Soviet reverence for the servants of the Muses" seems confined to a relatively small portion of the Soviet population, however large it seems in the West. Only in music, of all the creative arts—to distinguish them from the performing arts—where Party censorship and "socialist realism" are more difficult, if not impossible, to impose, have the Soviets been able to produce distinguished art and artists—and the artists have all too often had their work botched and their careers truncated by the stupidity and provincialism of Party bureaucrats. Here, too, Benno's assessment seems substantially apt and just:

Khrushchevian Moscow is very far from being—or ever becoming—another Periclean Athens, Medicean Florence, or Alexandrine Petersburg. Despite the wishful thinking that in both Russia and the West often colors the view of this cultural flowering, in actual fact the literary merit of most (if not all) of the great successes of the post-Stalin era is low by any standards and in particular—to take the example closest in time and culture—by comparison with the works of the generation of Russia's "Silver Age" in the first three decades of the present century.[5]

Not long ago, in a burst of unaccustomed candor, the Soviet novelist Leonid Leonov declared, "People will be writing about the Soviet concentration camps for the next eighty years." Since some eight to fifteen million people were imprisoned and perished in Stalin's camps and since almost no family in the Soviet Union remained untouched, Leonov's prophecy is more than literary hyperbole. Because the victims of the Soviet camps began to be released only after Stalin's death and "rehabilitated" only after the Twentieth Congress in 1956, the first "witness" writing has only begun to emerge—as much of it as can, stifled as it is by Kremlin censorship. That brief period during which Khrushchev lifted the censorship long enough for Solzhenitsyn's *One Day in the Life of Ivan Denisovich* to appear was adequate for verifying and corroborating the powerful repercussions of candor in Soviet life, and to show to what extent Solzhenitsyn spoke to the popular mind and perhaps for the popular heart. Again and again he portrayed the Soviet state as a police state, the Soviet Union as a prison and concentration camp; his works have steadily pointed to the heirs of Stalin as accomplices in Stalin's crimes—crimes which remain unpunished, perpetrated by criminals who are not only still at large but still in power.

Just as the Germans had to come to terms with Hitler and the Nazi crimes, so too the Russians must come to terms with Stalin and the Stalinist crimes. But such a confrontation and resolution are far more difficult to achieve in the Soviet Union, because it won the war and because substantially the same people remain in power. Any genuine revaluation of the Stalinist past must call into question many, if not all, of the underpinnings of Soviet society, particularly the Party's monopoly of power, wisdom, and truth, and it must lead to the trial and punishment of those who were responsible for the crimes against the Soviet people. In such proceedings the heirs of Stalin, from Brezhnev and Kosygin down to the factory informer and the concentration-camp guard, might be held accountable. Thus threatened, they are understandably reluctant to permit, much less encourage, such an accounting, because it would surely have repercussions as great as, and even more far-reaching than those of the Nuremberg trials. Disavowing the Stalinist past and jettisoning Stalin's heritage while holding on to power and privilege are virtually impossible for the heirs of Stalin. For that reason alone, Khrushchev's de-Stalinization had to be rolled back by Brezhnev and Kosygin, who saw the fear and the restiveness in the ranks of the bureaucrats, and who themselves feared that the demoralization of the bureaucracy might have unforeseen and untoward consequences. The stubborn resistance of those who oppose de-Stalinization, liberalization, and reform is not rooted simply in doctrinal differences; it is, in effect, the desperate struggle of the members of a power elite defending their very lives, positions, privileges, and property. Any denigration of Stalin denigrates them, any assault on him or his record is an attack on them and their records, because they were Stalin's men. If he was a criminal, they were his accomplices; if he was inept, they shared his incompetence; if his achievement must be revaluated, so too must theirs. Thoroughgoing de-Stalinization would, consequently, involve naming names and places and dates, and assigning blame; it would involve purges, trials, and punishments on such a scale that it would not only threaten the heirs of Stalin personally, but might overturn the entire edifice of Soviet power.

Many of those in the forefront of the struggle to reform Soviet society are individuals who attack the evils of Soviet institutions and the legacy of Stalinism not only out of a love of truth and justice, but because they themselves have personally endured the lash or have had parents, grandparents, other relatives, or friends who have done so.

Just as World War II left almost no Russian family untouched, so too the ravages of Stalinism, because they occurred on such a massive scale, have left almost no family unscarred. Wherever the KGB arrested, interrogated, tortured, imprisoned, exiled, or executed, it made immediate and probably permanent enemies of the family, relatives, friends, and colleagues of the victims. All these people who survived are eager to see the wrongs of the past redressed, even if they are not eager to redress those wrongs themselves: people who want to be avenged, even if they do not yet feel able to avenge themselves or their kin; people who are the natural constituency of those who are *actively* trying to right the wrongs of the Soviet past, to reform the institutions of Soviet society in the present so that such crimes will be more difficult to perpetrate in the future. It is a constituency far larger than the tiny group of brave dissidents who form the nucleus of the Democratic Movement, though far smaller than many Western observers who hope for liberalization and reform in the USSR imagine, because terror has been part of their inheritance for half a century and more.

The generational conflict between fathers and sons is inextricably bound up with this struggle against the heirs of Stalin. As young Germans were forced to look at their Nazi fathers and ask, "Where were you when . . . ?" so, too, Russian youth have been forced to face their forebears and ask what they were doing during collectivization, the purges, and all the other crimes of the Stalinist era. The regime-promoted explanation—"We didn't know what was happening"—is only the Russian equivalent of the German apologia that no one knew about the concentration camps. Moreover, the Communist equivalent of the Nazi Eichmann argument—"I was a little man and helpless; I only carried out orders"—will no more wash in the Soviet circumstances than it did in the German ones. Moreover, many among the youth know that their fathers *did* know, that by active cooperation, apathy, fear, or indifference they supported and permitted the Stalinist depredations; one of the hallmarks the younger generation sees in the writings of many of the liberal writers—Solzhenitsyn, Ehrenburg, Nekrasov, Chukovskaya —is the public confirmation that the older generation knew and abetted, or knew, and as Ehrenburg publicly confessed, "gritted its teeth and remained silent." Between the two generations there lies the question of "clean hands," and until it is resolved the youth will continue to lack confidence in the probity of their elders. Gaining the confidence of and influencing the youth are consequently essential goals in the battle between the dogmatists and reformists, between the heirs of Stalin and the new generation.

If the heirs of Stalin could persuade the next generation of the rightness of their views, they would be able to keep their power and privilege—and their heads. Ultimately, by co-opting the next generation's members into the hierarchy, they would implicate them in the Stalinist past and the neo-Stalinist present so that the new generation's hands would be dirtied because it was involved with the perpetrators of the crimes of old and with the privileges of the new. The myth of Party infallibility might then persist, and the fundamental institutions of Soviet power could remain intact. The struggle would be postponed a generation; Stalin's, Khrushchev's, Brezhnev's, and Kosygin's heirs would then have to be called to account by *their* sons. So the conflict will continue until the crimes recede so far into the past that their sting is removed while the repressive institutions and their personnel in the present and future gradually change and are responsible for no new great crimes. If that happens, the new heirs will not be held responsible for the accumulated burdens of the past. If it does not, the conflict will go on until those who committed the crimes are called to account, even posthumously.

This life-and-death struggle is intimately involved with writing, because literature has become the arena for telling the truth, for restoring accuracy to Soviet history, which could, as Solzhenitsyn's books already have, call into question all the lies, evasions, hypocrisy, and half-truths with which the regime has endeavored to deal with the injustices of the Soviet past. Restoring the past means not only telling the truth, but it also requires rehabilitating human beings and their reputations, and since that once again raises the issue of who did what to whom, it becomes taboo. The post-Stalin memoirs are almost all attempts to set the record straight, to pin down the facts, to rescue reputations from oblivion or obloquy— too often posthumously. One of the most important audiences is the youth, the sons to whom the fathers are justifying themselves. As General Aleksandr Gorbatov put it when he explained why he had written his memoirs, *Years off My Life*, "The aim of my story is to tell the young generation about these people." By *these people* he meant the Stalinists and their heirs. But the moment truthful revelations of the past began to appear, the heirs of Stalin were faced with all the same problems all over again; wherever they turned, they were threatened by the present and future and hemmed in by the past. Who was responsible for the persecutions of the past? If those who committed such crimes are alive, why have they not been tried and punished? How did such errors and crimes occur under Soviet law and arise out of Soviet institutions in the first place? How, for example, could such a paranoid criminal as Stalin come to power and remain in power in "socialist" circumstances? Is the rise of a Stalin inherent in the system and its logical expression? Once Khrushchev and Mikoyan had made their de-Stalinization speeches at the Twentieth Congress, such questions became inescapable; once one stitch is pulled in the skein, the whole fabric of lies, distortions, and omissions begins to unravel. The assiduously cultivated myth of the Party's infallibility perishes ignominiously, and the Party is revealed as arrogant and ignorant, its top leaders as blindly ruling with the basest motives of lust for power and greed, dancing the *gopka* to the tune that Stalin played, because they were craven and cowardly.

Stalin's heirs have had to postulate answers to such questions, and in the years since his demise—more particularly since the Twentieth Congress—they have enunciated a position. In spite of Stalin, they contend, the Soviet people, led by the glorious Communist Party, have gone ahead to turn the Soviet Union into a "socialist" state, the second most powerful nation on earth, have won the war against the Nazis, have sent rockets to the moon, and have built atomic weapons; in short, though Stalin made "errors" and was the cause of "distortions," the people and the Party in mystically separate ways "built socialism." In order to make such a line of illogic not altogether ridiculous, Party spokesmen have had to refurbish Stalin's reputation, to insist that although he did make errors, he was also responsible for "building Communism" and winning the war and was at heart a good Party man. "Stalin was dedicated to Communism with his whole being. Everything he did was for Communism." [6] Yevtushenko in "The Heirs of Stalin," reveals how emotionally powerful if completely contradictory such an argument is by exempting Stalin and his evils from the achievements of industrialization and winning the war:

> I refer not to the past, so holy and glorious,
> of Turksib,
>   and Magnitka,
>   and the flag raised over Berlin.[7]

In *A Precocious Autobiography*, Yevtushenko says even more revealingly:

I think the broad masses [of the Russian people] sensed intuitively that something was wrong, but no one wanted to believe what he guessed at heart. It would have been too terrible.

The Russian people preferred to work rather than to think and to analyze. With a heroic, stubborn self-sacrifice unprecedented in history they built power station after power station, factory after factory. They worked in furious desperation, drowning with the thunder of machines, tractors, and bulldozers the cries that might have reached them across the barbed wire of Siberian concentration camps.[8]

Yet, if Stalin did succeed in industrializing the nation and in winning the war, what was the price? It is that question, of *the means*, which is carefully avoided by almost all the writers as well as by all the leadership—and it is a question Solzhenitsyn is always asking. Was so much killing and suffering necessary? Couldn't industrialization and winning the war have been accomplished by other means? Solzhenitsyn goes even further, for he shows that the means were not only cruel, but they were also wasteful and inept: labor efficiency was low; materials were wasted; people had no incentive to work; there were no proper arms or leadership during the early stages of the war, nor was there adequate preparation for the war, militarily or diplomatically or industrially; and some of the best people were either killed in purges or imprisoned for arbitrary and often meaningless reasons.

To consider such questions of means would cast doubt on the Party's infallibility and efficacy, so the heirs of Stalin exhort the writers to turn away from poking into the "refuse heaps of history" and to turn to the people's positive achievements: to Turksib and Magnitka, not to Vorkuta and Norilsk. And behind their exhortation is the threat of the KGB and the camps. Literature remains dangerous to them because it offers a forum in which many crucial political, social, economic, and moral issues may be aired and debated. When Solzhenitsyn appeared in that forum, he confronted those issues in straightforward terms, without evasions, plunging to the heart of his country's dilemmas. His love of truth and justice, his defense of literature's right and role in attempting to arrive at and speak of both, were in themselves "opposition," for the Party leaders do not accept any standards or moral authority outside the Party canon. As Robert Conquest aptly phrased it, "Art symbolizes an alternative allegiance" [9]—and alternative allegiances are precisely what the Kremlin will not countenance. Art is not the only expression of nonconformity; miniskirts, long hair, tight trousers or bell-bottoms, and rock-and-roll music can also become ways of asserting individuality, and therefore can come to be considered forms of rebellion and opposition by a regime obsessed with imposing and maintaining conformity and orthodoxy. Literature and the other arts provide métiers which by their very nature deny that the Party has a monopoly on the intellectual and emotional imagination.

It is obviously the social (as opposed to the aesthetic) importance of the artist that draws 14,000 people to a poetry reading or that sells 100,000 copy editions over night. In a country where there are no non-official newspaper editorials, Yevtushenko's "editorials in verse" understandably find an audience and a following which poets in no other country can command. This occurs even when the verse editorials are not explicitly concerned with political or social questions. With official Soviet literature still attempting to reduce the whole of life to the public and collective task of "building Communism"—in other words, to the purposes of the state—a personal lyric or an amorous outpouring is an act of social protest, proclaiming by its mere existence the desirability of the autonomy of the private and intimate life from state control.[10]

If the heirs of Stalin allowed such alternative allegiance, they would deprive themselves of a valuable instrument, for without a politicalized literature to eliminate "subjectivism"—personal emotions and private loyalties—the Party would have one less technique for mobilizing those forces it wishes to exploit in its plans for "constructing Communism."

Another aspect of the quarrel between fathers and sons is the weariness and boredom many of the sons evince in the face of the perpetual plans, demonstrations, meetings, exhortations, the continual invasion of personal and private life. The same quarrel persists between the Writers' Union bureaucratic elders and the younger writers who, as Ehrenburg remarked, "want to write about their inner world, about delicate and controversial subjects. They want new writing; they want satire; and this has very little to do with either the war or the latest computer invented by a Russian engineer of genius." [11] Paeans to Turksib and Magnitka, or to sputnik, are not subject matter that attracts writers; Yevtushenko's comment on what does is probably still more germane: "To a Russian the word 'poet' has overtones of the word 'fighter.' Russia's poets were always fighters for the future of their country and for justice. Her poets helped Russia think. Her poets helped Russia to struggle against her tyrants." [12] It is precisely this role of Russia's writers that the heirs of Stalin would scotch, and precisely the role Solzhenitsyn has taken as his own.

In spite of the courage and eloquence of Solzhenitsyn and that small group of dedicated men who have fought for liberalization of the Soviet police state, the Russian people seem to have remained indifferent. The masses seem as hostile to the Solzhenitsyns, Yakirs, Yesenin-Volpins, and Grigorenkos as the Party press reports. At no point in the alternating freezes and thaws of Soviet life have the Russian masses shown any interest in, or had any influence on, the outcome of the conflicts of power and policy. In fact, in the continuing battle in the top reaches of the Party and government, whether between Malenkov and Beria, or Molotov and Khrushchev, or Khrushchev and Brezhnev—or more accurately perhaps, between the groups those names represent—there has never been the slightest concern on the part of the Kremlin with what the people would say or do, nor have the people shown any desire to play a role in the decisions which so intimately affect their destiny. As Andrei Amalrik noted: "The country passively awaited its fate. While struggle was going on continuously 'at the top,' not a single voice 'from below' was heard challenging the orders which at any given moment were handed down 'from above.' " [13]

True, when bread shortages or price rises have brought rumblings from below, or even such outbreaks as those in Novocherkassk in 1962, the heirs of Stalin have been swift to meet the masses' basic material requirements. The Kremlin knows the dangers that might result from people going angrily out into the streets in bread riots. But for all practical purposes, both the struggle for power in the hierarchy and the struggle for freedom against the hierarchy seem to leave the populace cold. If anything, the common people's anti-intellectual bias and the general chauvinism of Russian culture seem to insulate the people against the criticisms of, and the protests against, evils in Soviet life by writers and intellectuals. How much of this indifference is simply a surface mannerism maintained in order to survive in a police state, and how much profound apathy, it is impossible to tell. One of the traditional reasons intellectuals gave for supporting the Bolsheviks—echoed in Sinyavsky's trial testimony—was that the Bolsheviks got things accomplished despite the passivity and Oblomovism endemic in Russia and particularly among Russia's "tea-drinking intellectuals." But there is also another tradition—of outbursts of mass fury whose bloodshed and cruelties have shocked the world—that characterizes Russian history. Whether such outbursts are able to overthrow a totalitarian government armed with atomic and other modern weapons depends in great measure on why a popular rising would take place, under what conditions, and whether the heirs of Stalin would use all the means at their disposal to put such an insurrection down. Moreover, Amalrik pessimistically maintains, "the idea of self-government, of equality before the law and of personal freedom—and the responsibility that goes with these—are almost completely incomprehensible to the Russian people." [14]

Most citizens in the USSR are economically better off today than they were under Stalin; they have more personal security, and are, in some measure justifiably, proud of the many achievements of Soviet science and industry as well as, quite unjustifiably, proud of the many Soviet *démarches* in the world arena, such as those in Hungary and Czechoslovakia, Cuba and the Middle East. Both kinds of pride are elements of the Great Russian chauvinism which the Soviets have fed for their own reasons, and which is a powerful weapon against such foreign "enemies" as the United States, the entire "West," and China, and against dissident elements domestically.

Again and again those in the West who hoped that economic and cultural liberalization would lead inevitably to greater political freedom and social justice have been disenchanted by the turn of events. The heirs of Stalin are genuinely concerned with modernizing the Soviet economic plant to make it more productive and efficient; but political freedom and social justice are quite another matter. Neither economic efficiency nor a rising living standard will of themselves transform the Soviet system, nor will the multifarious influences of "cultural exchange" as exemplified by Western tourists, jazz, and miniskirts. As Amalrik sardonically comments, "It is possible that we will indeed have a 'socialism' with bare knees some day, but not likely one with a human face." [15]

In politics and literature, the heirs of Stalin will continue to make minor concessions, but when the central bastions of their power are threatened, they will fight tooth and nail to preserve them. Moreover, such concessions as are proffered will not be of fundamental importance until and unless they are embodied in viable institutions under a genuine rule of law. Reforms conceded today can easily be revoked tomorrow. The Soviet system as built by Stalin remains substantially unaltered in its essentials; its institutions, the people who staff them, and the methods they employ remain much the same. Alternations between persuasion and coercion, between the carrot and the stick, will probably continue, because it is difficult to keep large numbers of people hewing to any single Party line in changing circumstances; and the Kremlin will drive them with constant gees and haws, like recalcitrant horses. The state control of the press and publishing will continue, combined with the limitation of imports of foreign books and periodicals, with tightly controlled travel abroad for Soviet citizens and tightly controlled tourism and cultural contacts for foreigners inside the Soviet Union, so that Soviet parochialism, chauvinism, and simple ignorance will be prolonged. In the sciences, the situation will be somewhat eased in order to permit the scientific intelligentsia to "keep up" with such foreign institutions, scientists, and publications as seem necessary for the Soviet Union to keep abreast of industrial, military, and technological developments.

Most of the dissidents and liberals, if not all of them, seem to be interested, not in overturning Soviet institutions, but in reforming them, in imbuing them with a more humane spirit. They apparently have no desire to "return to capitalism"—if such a phrase has any meaning in the Soviet context—nor any genuine belief that such a return would be feasible even if it were desirable. What they want to create is a new socialism by making Soviet practice—now characterized by coercion, arbitrariness, deceit, class conflict, national animosities, calculated injustice—begin to conform to the "socialist" promises of justice, equality, brotherhood, and civility. But the dissidents remained entangled in a web of endeavoring to change the Party, the KGB, the courts, the concentration camps without a thoroughgoing change in Soviet institutions and a confrontation with the heirs of Stalin. Moreover, they all seem to retain—although a number do so for tactical purposes and as a ploy—that strange worship of the Bolshevik Revolution which prohibits or inhibits a rational and objective approach to the system it has created. The attitude toward October 1917 has taken on the form of a religious worship not only of the historical events of that time but of *the Revolution*, as if it were a *Ding an sich*, an icon and a force simultaneously, to be enshrined in religious awe and to be worshiped and used with Machiavellian craft. Some of the psychology involved is revealed, albeit obliquely, by Yevtushenko:

> The first mistake made by Western students of the Russian Revolution is to judge the revolutionary idea not by those who are genuinely loyal to it, but by those who betray it.
> Their other mistake is that they still regard the idea of communism as something imposed by force on the Russian people, without realizing that by now it is a part of the Russian people's flesh and blood.[16]

> But our special Russian character must be kept in mind. Suffering is a sort of habit with us. What seems nearly unendurable to others we endure more easily.
> Besides, we have paid for our ideal with so much blood and torment that the cost itself has endeared it and made it more precious to us, as a child born in pain is more precious to its mother.[17]

But what if the child is stillborn or an abortion or a monster? What if the offspring of the Revolution is truly and inevitably Stalin the cruel paranoid, the "archipelago of Gulag," a cancerous social and political organism gnawed by spreading malignancy? Western students of the Revolution, Yevtushenko notwithstanding, have judged the Revolution not by those who betrayed it, but by those who embodied it in the institutions which have characterized Soviet society for more than half a century—and have condemned it almost unconditionally. Pasternak once, appropriately and pungently, remarked: "Men who are not free . . . always idealize their bondage." It is a remark that almost all Soviet apologists, domestic and foreign, might take to heart and mind.

A new "democratic movement" of sorts has emerged in the Soviet Union in the decades since Stalin's death. Numerically small, it is influential and seems (perhaps only temporarily) to have joined the leaders of political, intellectual, cultural, and scientific dissidence, though not those of religious and ethnic dissidence, into a loosely knit alliance which has several common goals—the rule of law, loosening of censorship, freedom to dissent and freedom to create, downgrading the power of the political police, freer travel and circulation of information, equal treatment for minority nationalities —though by no means a common platform. The regime could very likely crush the movement or decapitate its leadership, but only at a cost it is not presently prepared to pay. It would, at the very least, lose the services of some of its most talented scientists and technicians. It is less concerned with losing the services of its most talented writers, artists, and musicians—hence the stronger measures the regime has taken with respect to them. However, even in suppressing literature the regime's leadership cannot be altogether successful, for, as Richard Pipes has wisely pointed out:

Soviet literature has always managed to preserve, even in the worst years of Stalinism, a modicum of autonomy. The reason for this must be sought not in Stalin's respect for literature, but in the nature of the literary vocation itself. Even when the regime prescribed for the novelist the subjects with which he was to deal and the manner in which he was to do it, it had to allow him a certain amount of latitude in executing the command. After all, if nothing else, the characters, settings and dialogues had to be invented; and where there is freedom of invention there is some freedom.

. . . The freedom of the writer is even greater when he is a poet. . . . A poet who cannot tamper with words cannot write poetry. Thus, as the novelist enjoys over the historian or sociologist some freedom of thematic invention, so the poet enjoys in addition some freedom of linguistic invention. If we consider, furthermore, that most people, censors included, do not understand poetry we will not be surprised that even under the most inauspicious circumstances poets (and to a lesser extent novelists) possess a degree of discretion in the performance of their craft that is not granted to other groups of the intelligentsia.[18]

Yet there are other groups of the intelligentsia to whom the same kinds of freedom are available, particularly those in the more complex and theoretical fields of science and economics, which is why the Party leaders are, and increasingly must be, concerned with incorporating specialists from those arcane areas into top Party counsels.[19] For the Kremlin to take advantage of and keep pace with the development of nuclear weapons, rockets, and space travel, computerization and the more sophisticated methods of economic research and planning, to mention only a few areas, it must have physicists, astronomers, mathematicians, data-processing and linear-programming specialists, input-output economists and econometricians, engineers and metallurgists, chemists and molecular biologists. Those chosen must not only be technically skilled but politically reliable—which means faithful to Party purposes and control. For such reasons alone, the Party leadership is probably not ready or willing to stifle all dissent or criticism, for it must have the competent advice and cooperation of many among the intelligentsia. It probably hopes to permit the dissent as a "safety valve" and a lure, so that the intelligentsia may be persuaded that the regime will listen to its voice, not only in the areas of its expertise, but also when it attempts to achieve the rule of law, the reform of political and juridical institutions, and so on.

Underlying all the problems of the Soviet Union is the "leading role of the Party" in Soviet life. The Communist Party of the Soviet Union is not a political party in any traditional sense. It is a permanent ruling elite which has arrogated to itself mythical and absolute powers of infallibility and historical destiny which no one in the Soviet Union is permitted to gainsay and no institution in the nation is permitted to contest or contradict. The Party, which means the same small group of top leaders, a group that some Soviet students have estimated to number no more than forty thousand, insists that it and only it will determine the purposes, ideals, and quality of the national life. The implications of such a position are profound and far-reaching, for so long as the Party must always be right, none of the major problems facing the USSR can be realistically and practically confronted: not the heirs of Stalin, not fathers and sons, or the modernization of the economy or the liberalization of the political system or the reformation of the judicial system. Only when the Communist Party is understood to be *not* infallible can really important and basic reforms take place.

Almost none of the dissidents have been willing to challenge the Party's primacy head on. Generally, they have skirted the problem of the Party's monopoly of wisdom, speaking very generally of error, miscalculation, deformation, or speaking very specifically about a particular evil—such as Lysenkoism—by blaming it on lower echelons of the bureaucracy but never on top leaders (until after they were ousted) or on the Party as an institution. Some, like Sakharov and his colleagues, have obliquely suggested that it might be good to have several candidates for a single office—a beginning of what might ultimately become a multiparty system—but have always been careful to note that any reforms must be undertaken under the aegis and control of the Party. Perhaps it is impossible, in practical political terms, for dissidents thus to challenge the Party's infallibility; the dissidents are, after all, only a tiny fraction of the nation, only a tiny fraction of the entire Soviet intelligentsia. They are alienated from the workers, the peasants, the military, and the government bureaucracy, so that they have neither a mass base nor political leverage of great strength. Moreover, it is precisely the central bastion that calls down all the repressive power of the regime when it is attacked, for the Party leaders are neither ready to share their power with any other leaders or any other party, nor to have it curbed or limited by any democratic institutions. The Party and its leaders are and intend to remain the sole, authoritarian, and dogmatic rulers of Russia.

The character of the Party leadership must be taken into account. By and large, those who have risen to great power in the Soviet Union have done so as the result of a bureaucratic power which winnows out great originality, intelligence, and individuality. Conformism and the stability which comes from remaining in power are their forte, not the flexibility and change which promote progress. Their system has undoubted advantages—in decisiveness, overall planning, the assignment of priorities, the ability (if not willingness) to introduce new scientific techniques, and so forth—

but its viability depends on that small ruling elite at the top of the pyramid *actually being right.* When those leaders are wrong, as they have so often been, their errors are transmitted down the pyramid of power and immeasurably magnified, because there is no "negative feedback," no way of changing or modifying or opposing the "Party's will" once that will has been defined by the leadership and imposed "from above." The system is that ideological monstrosity "democratic centralism" in practice—once the Party leaders decide on a course of action, everyone must adhere to it without suggestion, criticism, or opposition.

Yet the dissidents, though few in number, are a thorn in the side of the regime because they continue to insist that modernization of the nation—which the Party leaders are eager to achieve—is indissolubly tied to democratization and political reform—which the ruling elite is almost altogether dead-set against. Yet more and more, it becomes evident that if the Kremlin would keep the Soviet Union a first-class power, it must take advantage of the latest fruits of technology; if it would improve the economic and technological viability of its system, it must permit more *scientific* leeway—freer access to foreign information and colleagues, freer foreign travel, the acceptance of many theoretical and practical ideas which are anathema to "orthodox" Marxist-Leninism. Whether such authoritarian dogmatism will be replaced only by authoritarian flexibility is difficult to predict; but in an age when new means of surveillance, computerized memory banks, enormously increased powers of oppression all combine to make authoritarianism technically easier, the prospects are not bright. Liberalization and democratization can come only when the Party monopoly of power and wisdom is shattered in any case, and when changes and reforms are embodied in new institutions. But whence and from whom will the thrust come? the Party? the peasants? the workers? the government bureaucrats? None of these seems even close to assuming the necessary posture. Even among the intellectuals many are alienated and apathetic and would like most of all simply to be left alone, to be allowed to lead their private lives and follow their personal and professional inclinations without government interference.

What was true of Khrushchev's Russia remains true of Brezhnev's and Kosygin's. The time may yet come which many have predicted and yearned for, a time when all the great Russian gifts will be given free rein, but it will not come until the "leading role of the Party" is permanently eliminated, until no party or person is publicly endowed with a monopoly of wisdom, righteousness, or power, until the rule of law is guaranteed in viable and responsive institutions, until the heirs of Stalin have been brought to justice and displaced from power, or have disappeared from the face of the earth.

NOTES, BIBLIOGRAPHY, AND INDEX

Notes

For Russian words and for bibliographical material, this work follows the Library of Congress system of transliteration without diacritical marks, except where general usage or usage in the American press has made another form more familiar.

Chapter 1. *The Web of Politics* (pp. 3–11)

1. Only some of the motivations of the Soviet leaders can be deduced or extrapolated from their public speeches and behavior. At such a time as the Soviet archives are made available to objective historians, the purpose and intent of particular individuals in the leadership, as well as of various elements of Soviet policy, may be greatly clarified.

2. The terms "liberal" and "conservative" are confusing and not altogether precise in the Soviet context. They are, like many of the other commonly used terms—"dogmatist," "revisionist," and so on—essentially a shorthand and metaphors for a broad spectrum of political and literary opinion. See the informed discussion of the literary spectrum in David Burg's "The 'Cold War' on the Literary Front," *Problems of Communism*, Sept.–Oct. 1962.

3. For this reason, Michel Tatu, in *Power in the Kremlin*, seems to believe that Khrushchev's de-Stalinization and liberalization were policies intended chiefly to defeat his rivals for power and that no substantive policy issues were at stake. Since Tatu, the Moscow correspondent of *Le Monde*, was one of the best-informed Western observers and analysts of Soviet affairs, his view must be taken into account.

4. For a more detailed analysis of what this "new course" required in politics, economics, and culture, see the extended discussion in "The Ideology of Agitation," *News from behind the Iron Curtain*, Aug. 1954.

5. *Russia Enters the 1960s: A Documentary Report on the 22nd Congress of the Communist Party of the Soviet Union*, edited and with a commentary by Harry Schwartz, p. 6. Schwartz's introduction is a good summary of some of the political maneuvering between 1953 and 1961. The Soviet paranoia about giving aid and comfort to the enemy is an inextricable characteristic of Soviet policy in all fields.

6. *Ibid.*

7. See the intelligent analysis of the problems of reshaping the working methods and manners of the bureaucracy in "The Bureaucracy Wavers," *News from behind the Iron Curtain*, Jan. 1954, pp. 25–37.

8. Cf. "The Ideology of Agitation," pp. 3 ff.

9. It is also conceivable that the anti-Party group represented the "government" as distinct from the Party, although whether such institutional distinctions are valid in the Soviet context is open to question. Voting against Khrushchev were Malenkov, Molotov, Kaganovich, Bulganin, Voroshilov, Pervukhin, Saburov, and Shepilov. Mikoyan, Suslov, and Kirichenko voted with Khrushchev.

10. Zhukov is said to have put military airplanes at Khrushchev's disposal to bring Central Committee members back to Moscow on time to swing the vote in favor of Khrushchev. The influence of the military on Soviet policy has long been a subject of contention. Party fear of "Bonapartism" has been deeply inbred and in the past seems to have kept the military under tight control. There is some evidence, however, that in the Brezhnev-Kosygin period, the power and influence of the military have increased considerably.

11. Schwartz, *Russia Enters the 1960s*, pp. 4, 17.

12. *Izvestia*, Nov. 18, 1961.

13. Schwartz, *Russia Enters the 1960s*, pp. 124, 100, 97.

14. Part of Khrushchev's effort was devoted to purging the Party. Between the twentieth and twenty-second congresses, Khrushchev reported that more than 200,000 Party members had been expelled (*ibid.*, p. 27).

15. Like "liberalization," "revisionism" in Soviet usage is a most ambiguous term. It is generally used to mean a program or policy which revises the bases of Marxism-Leninism. Communist rulers and their propagandists use the term for opprobrium, for characterizing their opponents and presumably linking them to "reformist" socialists—Second Internationalists as distinct from Third.

16. Schwartz, *Russia Enters the 1960s:* the speeches of Albanian Communist leader Enver Hoxha, pp. 42 ff.; Chou En-lai, pp. 28 ff.; Khrushchev's rejoinder, pp. 148 ff.; and Hoxha's rebuttal of Khrushchev, pp. 147 ff.

17. De-Stalinization in the satellite countries was delayed, in some instances well into 1962 and even later. For example, not until November 1962 were Stalinist Premier Anton Yugov and Party Secretary Vulko Chervenkov purged in Bulgaria; and not until the fall of 1962 was the first symbolic de-Stalinization given visible form in Czechoslo-

vakia with the destruction of the giant Stalin statue which overlooked Prague from Letna Hill, thus beginning the events which were to culminate in the Soviet invasion of Czechoslovakia in August 1968.

18. This policy of permitting each "socialist" nation to find its own road to "socialism" came to be known as "polycentrism." A considerable part of the energy expended by the Soviet leaders in the realm of foreign policy, however, has been devoted to retaining close control over the development of events in the various countries in their orbit. This Kremlin insistence on doing things their way accounts for the Soviet invasion of Czechoslovakia, continued and continuing pressure on Rumania, the war of words—and sometimes guns—with China and its surrogate in Europe, Albania, as well as, in quite another sense, the persistent differences with Titoist Yugoslavia.

Chapter 2. *Engineers of the Soul* (pp. 12–27)

1. For a more detailed discussion of the 1953–1954 "thaw" up to and including the Second Writers' Congress, see Harold Swayze's *Political Control of Literature in the USSR, 1946–1959,* and Abraham Rothberg's "The Literary Volga Flows On," *New Mexico Quarterly,* Winter 1956.

2. *Sovetskaya musika,* Nov. 1953.

3. *Znamya,* Oct. 1953.

4. *Sovetskaya musika,* Nov. 1953.

5. One phenomenon of the struggle between the writers and the regime has been the fact that the writers have, naïvely or deliberately, concentrated their fire on such instruments of Party control of literature as the censorship (Glavlit) or the Writers' Union, as if those organizations functioned independently of Party directives and control. That there is indeed some room for maneuvering in publishing houses or on magazine editorial boards, and even in various branches of the Writers' Union, is obvious, but it is a very narrow area.

6. *Novy mir,* Dec. 1953.

7. *Literaturnaya gazeta,* Jan. 30, 1954.

8. *Pravda,* May 25, 1954.

9. These included Tvardovsky's poetry cycle *Horizon beyond Horizon,* L. Zorin's play *The Guests,* Vera Panova's novel *The Seasons,* and F. Abramov's cutting essay on kolkhoz fiction. Except for Zorin's drama, which appeared in *Teatr,* February 1954, the others appeared in *Novy mir,* in June 1953, November and December 1953, and April 1954 respectively.

10. The Russian poet Ilya Selvinsky attacked Tvardovsky from an-

other viewpoint, remarking that the *Novy mir* editor was altogether a conservative influence on Soviet poetry: "Tvardovsky, Isakovsky, and Surkov are quite sufficient for the Union's leaders. Having once and for all declared this school the universal one, they carefully eschew any deviation whatsoever, calling what is different 'capricious' and what is complex 'chaotic' "; "through the efforts of some comrades the formula Tvardovsky-Isakovsky-Surkov has been propagandized so vigorously that it has almost come to be accepted as a line from the Statutes of the Writers' Union." See Swayze, p. 105, where these passages are quoted from Selvinsky's *Nabolevshy vopros*.

11. For detailed discussions, see Swayze; George Gibian, *Interval of Freedom;* Vera Alexandrova, *A History of Soviet Literature;* and Walter Vickery, *The Cult of Optimism.*

12. Giuseppe Boffa, *Inside the Khrushchev Era*, p. 104. Boffa, himself a member of the Italian Communist Party, lived through this period in the Soviet Union. Because he was a Communist he had better contacts with Russian Party members and even ordinary Russian citizens than most Westerners. Boffa gives some idea, albeit distorted by his Communist convictions, of the shock and turmoil experienced by ordinary Russians and intellectuals as a consequence of de-Stalinization.

13. A tradition of genuine socialist idealism and Marxist humanitarianism has inspired and continues to inspire some Soviet intellectuals. Such sentiments and convictions should neither be scanted nor overlooked in evaluating Soviet events and individuals' motives, but their importance and prevalence should not be overestimated either. A "balanced" view of any particular person or event is always difficult to arrive at.

14. David Burg, "The 'Cold War' on the Literary Front," *Problems of Communism*, Sept.–Oct. 1962, p. 35. Burg, a former Moscow University student and now an analyst of Soviet life and translator of Russian literature in London, has an intimate knowledge of the Soviet cultural scene.

15. A. Kron, "Notes of a Writer," *Literaturnaya Moskva*, II (1956), as quoted by George Gibian in "Ferment and Reaction: 1956–1957," *Problems of Communism*, Jan.–Feb. 1958, p. 23.

16. Writers' reactions to Stalin's denigration, probably like those of the population at large, ran a wide gamut. Aleksandr Fadeyev, long Stalin's spokesman in the arts and General Secretary of the Writers' Union, went home and shot himself (*Izvestia*, May 15, 1956); Ilya Ehrenburg, on the contrary, went home and breathed a sigh of relief (see his *Post-War Years, 1945–1954*, pp. 320 ff). See Pawel Mayewski,

ed., *The Broken Mirror*, Edmund Stillman, ed., *Bitter Harvest*, and Abraham Rothberg, ed., *Flashes in the Night*, for some of the works of such East European writers as Tibor Dery, Gyula Hay, Gyula Illyes, Leszek Kolakowski, Adam Wazyk, Marek Hlasko, Kazimierz Brandys, Zbigniew Herbert, and Milovan Djilas, which were both goad and example to Soviet writers. They were also a reminder that the generally dull writing of the Communist world was by no means due to a lack of individual literary talent.

17. *Oktyabr*, Oct. 1956. Yevtushenko often manifests in his work the kind of Marxist humanitarianism and socialist idealism referred to earlier, but how much is sincere and how much sham is not easy to discern.

18. Yevgeny Yevtushenko, *A Precocious Autobiography*, p. 82.

19. *Novy mir*, Aug., Sept., Oct. 1956. A number of other literary works around which controversy swirled were also published that year, among them Daniil Granin's *A Personal Opinion* (*Novy mir*, September); Semyon Kirsanov's poem "Seven Days of the Week" (*Novy mir*, September); Aleksandr Yashin's short story, "Levers" (*Literaturnaya Moskva*, Vol. II); Yury Nagibin's short story, "Light in the Window," in the same volume of that anthology; and Yevtushenko's poem "Zima Station." But the major issues were joined over the Dudintsev novel.

20. Burg, p. 35.

21. Ilya Ehrenburg, *Liudi, gody, zhizn*, VI, 755.

22. Tom Scriven, "The 'Literary Opposition,'" *Problems of Communism*, Jan.–Feb. 1958, p. 30. Tom Scriven is the pseudonym of an astute and trenchant critic of Soviet affairs.

23. *Ibid.*, p. 32. For this attitude toward bureaucrats, see Nikolay Zhdanov's "Journey Home," *Literaturnaya Moskva*, II (1956), as well as Granin's *A Personal Opinion* and Nagibin's "Light in the Window." It is worth comparing their portrayals with Solzhenitsyn's depiction of Rusanov in *Cancer Ward* and the bureaucrats in *For the Good of the Cause*.

24. They were to continue to raise basic questions about Stalinism and the Soviet system that still have not been laid to rest, as our further discussion attempts to make clear.

25. *Novy mir*, Sept. 1956.

26. *Pravda*, June 17, 1956.

27. *Pravda*, Feb. 21, 1956.

28. Burg, Jan.–Feb. 1963, p. 48, cites this from an unimpeachable but unidentified source who was present at the meeting.

29. Alexander Werth, *Russia: Hopes and Fears*, p. 259.

30. *Literaturnaya gazeta*, Oct. 8, 1957.

31. *Ibid.*, Aug. 28, 1957.

32. *Ibid.*

33. "The Lessons of Stendhal," *Inostrannaia literatura* ("Foreign Literature"), June 1957. This magazine was one of the publications which sprang up during the second "thaw"—among them *Neva, Moskva, Literaturnaya Moskva,* and *Nash sovremennik.* Because it published translations of foreign writing it was of particular interest to Soviet intellectuals. See George Gibian, "Ferment and Reaction," p. 22.

34. *Kommunist,* No. 12 (Aug. 1957).

35. Boffa, p. 104.

36. Werth, pp. 281–283.

37. *Ibid.*, p. 282.

38. There was some speculation that both Surkov and Kochetov had been punished for their roles in the Pasternak affair. The regime was apparently dissatisfied with the repercussions of the way in which the Writers' Union and regime partisans handled Pasternak's winning the Nobel award.

39. See Swayze, pp. 224 ff., for his excellent chapter on "Bureaucratic Controls and Literary Production" in the USSR.

40. As quoted in Swayze, p. 208.

41. *Pravda,* July 2, 1959.

Chapter 3. *The Pasternak Case* (pp. 28–40)

1. The gifted young poet Andrey Voznesensky told Patricia Blake in 1962: "Pasternak was my only master." Miss Blake, in her intelligent and, in places, very moving introduction to *Half-Way to the Moon* (edited in collaboration with Max Hayward) noted (p. 37): For the young writers [Pasternak] "is central to one of their most pressing concerns . . . which is to recreate their own past. Pasternak's forty-seven years of creative work, from 1913 to 1960, bridging as it does the sterile years of Stalinism, represent their link to their literary past. . . . The writers are straining to establish some continuity with their past. . . . By way of Pasternak (and Anna Akhmatova as well) they are returning to masters that are rightfully theirs: Blok, Gumilev, Tsvetayeva, Khlebnikov, Mandelshtam, and, in prose, Babel and Olesha. 'Heredity,' says Voznesensky, 'can sometimes skip a generation.' "

2. See the careful dissection of the regime's campaign against Ivinskaya in Robert Conquest's *The Pasternak Affair: Courage of Genius,* in which the duplicity, myths, and coercion the Soviet authorities used in dealing with Pasternak are anatomized. See also the collection of doc-

uments pertaining to the persecution of Pasternak which Conquest has compiled in the appendices to that book.

3. See text, p. 39, Kornei Chukovsky's comments on Ivinskaya.

4. *New York Times*, Oct. 23, 1967.

5. *Pravda*, June 3, 1954. The article was written by Vladimir Yermilov, an archreactionary critic often to be the regime's spearhead against liberal writers. See Harold Swayze, *Political Control of Literature in the USSR, 1946–1959*, pp. 101–102.

6. Conquest, pp. 59 ff. See above, pp. 31 ff., for the letter's contents and the use made of it.

7. See Max Hayward, "Pasternak's *Dr. Zhivago*," *Encounter*, May 1958, pp. 38–41, for an analysis of the machinations involved and also for a remarkable literary analysis of the novel and why it posed such a threat to the Soviet leaders (pp. 43–48).

8. Gerd Ruge, *Pasternak: A Pictorial Biography*, p. 122, has a photograph of the cablegram. Ruge's book also contains some fine photographs of Pasternak, his friends, and his surroundings.

9. "Judgment on Pasternak: The All-Moscow Meeting of Writers," *Survey*, July 1966, p. 138.

10. New York Public Library fugitive papers entitled "Letter to Boris Pasternak from the Editorial Board of *Novy Mir* Magazine," p. 2.

11. *Ibid.*, pp. 6, 9.

12. "Pasternak's *Dr. Zhivago*," p. 48 and *passim*.

13. "Judgment on Pasternak," p. 138.

14. *Pravda*, Oct. 26, 1958; italics mine.

15. For various views of the value of the novel, see Conquest, pp. 49–58. The reactions to the novel were even more various, however, than even Conquest was able to indicate at that time.

16. *Russian Themes*, pp. 250–263.

17. Tass, Oct. 28, 1958.

18. *Komsomolskaya pravda*, Oct. 30, 1958.

19. *Literaturnaya gazeta*, Nov. 1, 1958.

20. Mihajlov, *Moscow Summer*, p. 132.

21. "Judgment on Pasternak," pp. 144, 136, 137, 138.

22. Tass, Nov. 1, 1958.

23. *London Daily Mail*, Feb. 11, 1959.

24. *Literaturnaya gazeta*, March 31, 1967.

25. Swayze, p. 202.

26. Patricia Blake and Max Hayward, eds., *Half-Way to the Moon*, p. 35.

27. Swayze, p. 202.

28. Alexander Werth, *Russia: Hopes and Fears,* p. 264.

29. See *Literatura i zhizn,* May 30, 1960.

30. Yury Krotkov, "Pasternak's Last Days," *Bulletin of the Institute for the Study of the USSR,* June 1968, pp. 7, 13 ff. Krotkov, a Soviet writer and KGB agent who later defected to the West, was an eyewitness at the funeral. (This periodical is cited hereafter as *Bulletin.*)

31. Mihajlov, *Moscow Summer,* p. 131.

32. Krotkov, p. 11.

33. See Conquest, *op. cit.,* for a discussion of the royalty question distinguished by both political and psychological common sense.

34. Werth, p. 297.

35. Krotkov, p. 8.

Chapter 4. *The Heirs of Stalin* (pp. 41–55)

1. Michel Tatu seems to be of two minds about Khrushchev and de-Stalinization. On one hand, he treats Khrushchev's political maneuvers as arising solely from Khrushchev's desire to retain and aggrandize his own power. On the other hand, Tatu admits, sometimes ruefully, that in order to expand his power at the expense of his colleagues on the Presidium, Khrushchev "had not even hesitated to question some dogmas which were essential to the continuity of the Stalinist leadership and its hard core" (*Power in the Kremlin,* p. 206). It is probably impossible to determine how much of which motivation figured in any particular Khrushchev gambit, but I believe that *both* power *and* policy were involved. This ambiguity in Tatu's approach occasionally leads him to write, for example, that in 1962, "Khrushchev's 'liberalism' on the home front matched his recklessness in foreign policy: that is to say, his liberalism was as aggressive toward his domestic adversaries as the Cuban operation was towards the West" (p. 244). In turning his "aggressive liberalism" against his rivals for power, was not Khrushchev also making institutional and personnel changes which did in some measure liberalize—with or without quotation marks—the country?

2. For the purposes of this book I have chosen not to deal with the present and continuing religious resistance and dissidence in the USSR which, though arising in similar circumstances, are of another kind. They are important phenomena, and combined with ethnic and nationalist opposition, have received and require more extended investigation and evaluation than I am able to give them here.

3. In a superlative essay, "The Political Aspect," reprinted in the

collection *Soviet Literature in the Sixties,* edited by Max Hayward and Edward L. Crowley, Peter Benno declares that the entire issue of de-Stalinization was less a matter of principle than of the loss of power, prestige, and position by Stalin's heirs.

4. Benno, pp. 185–187.

5. *Literatura i zhizn,* Aug. 16, 1959.

6. Benno, p. 181; italics mine.

7. Patricia Blake and Max Hayward, eds., *Dissonant Voices in Soviet Literature,* p. 259.

8. Abram Tertz (Andrey Sinyavsky), *On Socialist Realism,* p. 176.

9. *Literaturnaya gazeta,* Sept. 19, 1961.

10. This version is from Blake and Hayward, eds., *Dissonant Voices,* pp. 260–261.

11. Yevgeny Yevtushenko, *A Precocious Autobiography,* pp. 120–121.

12. *Ibid.,* pp. 116–122.

13. Mihajlo Mihajlov, *Moscow Summer,* p. 34.

14. Schwartz, *Russia Enters the 1960s,* p. 4.

15. Yevtushenko, *A Precocious Autobiography,* p. 97.

16. Patricia Blake and Max Hayward, eds., *Half-Way to the Moon,* pp. 33–36; quoted passage p. 34.

17. *Nedelya,* No. 47 (1961).

18. *London Observer,* May 27, 1962.

19. *Yunost,* Nos. 6–7, 9 (1961).

20. *Izvestia,* April 14, 1962. See also *Znamya,* Nos. 8–11 (1963) and Nos. 1–5 (1964).

21. *Novy mir,* March 1962.

22. "The Boomerang of De-Stalinization," *Bulletin,* Oct. 1962, p. 53.

23. Yuri Idashkin, "If One Stops to Think," *Oktyabr,* Sept. 1962. See also V. Gusaroz, "Success or Failure?" *Zvezda,* Sept. 1962.

24. "Battle in Silence," *Izvestia,* Oct. 28, 1962.

25. "Good Luck, Schoolboy," *Pages from Tarussa* (1961).

26. "An Inch of Land," *Novy mir,* May–June (1959).

27. *Molodoi Kommunist,* No. 2 (1962).

28. *Novy mir,* Oct.–Nov. 1962.

29. *Pravda,* Oct. 21, 1962. The translation is from the *Current Digest of the Soviet Press.*

30. Yevtushenko, *A Precocious Autobiography,* p. 122.

31. Tatu, p. 249; Alexander Werth, *Russia: Hopes and Fears,* p. 265. Poskrebyshev did not die until 1966.

32. In her essay "The Regime and the Intellectuals," initially published in *Problems of Communism,* July–Aug. 1963, and later in revised

form in her book *Khrushchev and the Arts,* Priscilla Johnson gives an outstanding summary and analysis of this period of Soviet cultural affairs, to which I am indebted. The quotation is on pp. 46–47.

33. Benno, p. 189. Benno aptly calls Yevtushenko's poems "editorials in verse."

34. Viktor Nekrasov, *Both Sides of the Ocean,* pp. 18–19, 79, 45 ff.

35. *Izvestia,* Nov. 24, 1962; as translated in *Current Digest of the Soviet Press,* Dec. 26, 1962.

36. *New York Herald-Tribune,* Nov. 31, 1962.

37. Yevtushenko, *A Precocious Autobiography,* p. 78.

38. *Literaturnaya gazeta,* Nov. 24, 1962; as translated in *Current Digest of the Soviet Press.*

39. Greville Wynne, *Contact on Gorki Street,* p. 8.

40. See *Pravda,* Oct. 2, 1963.

Chapter 5. *Denisovich's Day* (pp. 56–60)

1. *Time,* Sept. 27, 1968, p. 25. Even if this story is exaggerated or apocryphal, it does give an indication of the impression the novel and Solzhenitsyn's writing made on Tvardovsky, who was thereafter to become one of the novelist's most loyal promoters and effective defenders.

2. Peter Benno, "The Political Aspect," *Soviet Literature in the Sixties,* ed. Max Hayward and Edward L. Crowley, p. 191, says that Tvardovsky took the book to Adzhubei, Khrushchev's son-in-law, who brought the novel to Khrushchev's attention. Tvardovsky had earlier in his career learned to "go to the top." As a young man he had been accused of writing a "seditious poem," his "The Country of Muravia." The poem was published in 1936, "not [due] to the perversity of fate. It was shown to Stalin, who, to the general astonishment, approved its publication, apparently because he figures in it as the arbiter of his country's fate" (A. Lebed, "Youth as the Mainstay of the Soviet Regime," *Bulletin,* Feb. 1963, p. 22).

3. The number of people purged, imprisoned, and murdered in the Stalin camps has long been a subject of dispute. In *Russia: Hopes and Fears,* the pro-Soviet apologist Alexander Werth claims that "most people in Russia reckon anything between five hundred thousand and five million" were imprisoned (p. 85). But the noted Russian physicist Andrei Sakharov's estimate seems to agree with that of the émigré Menshevik scholar David Dallin that ten to fifteen million people perished in the camps. Solzhenitsyn's estimates in this regard are similar to Sakha-

rov's. See Sakharov, *Progress, Coexistence, and Intellectual Freedom*, p. 111.

4. Benno, p. 191. Tatu corroborates the fact that Kozlov and Suslov had objected to publication of the book at a Politburo meeting held at the end of September when *Denisovich* was on the agenda (*Power in the Kremlin*, p. 248).

5. *New York Times*, November 29, 1962.

6. Gleb Struve asks: "How do we know that Tvardovsky, in submitting the story for the boss's approval, did not point out that if it were not printed in *Novy Mir*, it might find its way abroad and be published there? He might have convinced Khrushchev of the undesirability of this, as well as of the relative innocuousness of Solzhenitsyn's story and the advantages to be gained from its 'de-Stalinizing' aspects. There is no doubt I think that, in some cases at least, the possibility of publication abroad can now be used as an effective argument in promoting the publication of certain works [in the USSR]" ("Soviet Literature in Perspective," *Soviet Literature in the Sixties*, p. 139). Tvardovsky may have pointed out the risk of foreign publication, but Khrushchev would need no help in seeing the political uses of its "de-Stalinizing" virtues by himself. I do not believe, however, that *Ivan Denisovich* is an "innocuous" story, nor does its subsequent influence bear out such a contention. Nor do I believe that Tvardovsky would have been able to persuade Khrushchev that the novel was innocuous; more likely Khrushchev knew the risks he was running and was willing to run them—and probably sure he could hedge his bets en route.

7. Marvin Kalb, Introduction, in Alexander Solzhenitsyn, *One Day in the Life of Ivan Denisovich*, p. 7.

8. Alexander Tvardovsky, Foreword, *ibid.*, p. 13. Khrushchev's words are simpler and more forceful than Tvardovsky's. Was Tvardovsky, a felicitous writer and poet, exercising his usual caution—justifiable in the circumstances—and being deliberately roundabout and obscure?

9. Gulag is an acronym for the Soviet Chief Administration of Corrective Labor Camps, which is in charge of all concentration camps in the USSR. The Soviets have the dubious distinction of having set up concentration camps long before the Nazis. Their first, opened in 1921, at Archangel, was the Kholmogor camp, organized "for the sole purpose of physically destroying the prisoners. It operated successfully for many years and swallowed up many of the Bolsheviks' former allies—members of the non-Bolshevik revolutionary parties" (Mihajlo Mihajlov, *Moscow Summer*, p. 70).

10. Tvardovsky, p. 15.

11. Tatu, p. 282.

12. *Izvestia*, Nov. 18, 1962.

Chapter 6. *The Turning Point* (pp. 61–72)

1. See Albert Boiter, "When the Kettle Boils Over," *Problems of Communism*, Jan.–Feb. 1964, for details.

2. Priscilla Johnson, *Khrushchev and the Arts*, pp. 101–105. The documents which are included in this book, and were compiled by Miss Johnson with Leopold Labedz, are valuable to every student of the period. Khrushchev's comments are reprinted by Miss Johnson from *Encounter*, April 1963.

3. Miss Johnson adduces evidence that Khrushchev's appearance at the Manezh was part of a deliberate provocation organized by the dogmatists in political and cultural life, but the evidence she offers does not seem to me conclusive.

4. *Le Monde*, Dec. 28, 1962.

5. Tvardovsky's interview with American news correspondent Henry Shapiro, *Pravda*, May 12, 1963.

6. Johnson, p. 105.

7. *Pravda*, Dec. 22, 1962. Ilyichev's criticism was chiefly of painting and music, but he did attack Aleksandr Yesenin-Volpin personally and sharply. About Volpin, see text, pp. 147–150.

8. *Time*, Jan. 11, 1963.

9. Peter Benno reports that Serebryakova did not have too bad a time in the camps, "rising to the relatively comfortable position of mistress to at least one commandant" ("The Political Aspect," in *Soviet Literature in the Sixties*, ed. Max Hayward and Edward L. Crowley, p. 196). The words "relatively comfortable" bear a heavier and more ambiguous burden than perhaps Benno intended. Even if what he reports is true, it in no way contradicts the truth of Serebryakova's charges against Ehrenburg. There is an understandable though not commendable desire to criticize the neo-Stalinist and frequently personally abrasive Serebryakova on this and other grounds. Yet no one who spends twenty-one years in Siberian camps has a good time, and to criticize the lengths to which people are driven in such circumstances seems less warranted than criticizing those who drove them to such lengths. Benno remarks that Poskrebyshev was *persona non grata* to Khrushchev and that Serebryakova's use of him as a witness in her attack on Ehrenburg demonstrated that Khrushchev was her real target.

Presumably, in making the attack, Serebryakova had the support of, and was acting as spokesman for Kozlov, Khrushchev's rival in the Presidium (*ibid.*).

10. Johnson, pp. 11–13.

11. The vicious circle which repressive regimes create is tragic. Oppressed minorities generate rebels. In Eastern Europe rightist and proto-fascist regimes produced leftist rebels among many Jews who were the targets of such regimes. Many of these Jews became Communists (others Socialists and Zionists) in such countries as Russia, Poland, Hungary, and Rumania, because anti-Semitism was rampant there. The anti-Semitism of the peoples of the East European countries continued, and they hated those Communists who were Jews doubly—for being both Communists and Jews. By and large, they still do. This, of course, provides a ready-made scapegoat for the Communist regimes as well; although they officially eschew anti-Semitism, they continue to use anti-Semitism for their own purposes, recently disguised, though just barely, under the cover of "anti-Zionism." Their references to Jews as "rootless cosmopolitans" inadvertently reveal their own uneasiness with the "internationalist" traditions of Bolshevism in theory and their "nationalist" and chauvinist practices.

12. Michel Tatu, *Power in the Kremlin*, p. 309.

13. Alexander Werth, *Russia: Hopes and Fears*, p. 182. Anti-Semitism may be more deeply rooted in Marxism than traditional Russian and Ukrainian anti-Semitism would explain in the USSR. Marx himself was a Jewish apostate who identified the Jew with all the evils he perceived in capitalism, and some of his writings display the not unusual ambivalence and self-hatred of the apostate. For example, he wrote: "The social emancipation of the Jew is the emancipation of society from Judaism"; "That which is contained abstractly in Jewish religion—contempt for art, for history, for man as an end in himself—is the actual conscious standpoint and virtue of the monied man"; "What is the worldly cult of the Jew? Bargaining. What is his worldly god? Money" (*Writings of the Young Marx on Philosophy and Society*, trans. L. D. Easton and K. H. Guddat [Garden City, N.Y.: Anchor, 1967], pp. 248, 246, 248).

14. *Literaturnaya gazeta*, Jan. 1, 1963.

15. *Ibid.*

16. Tatu (pp. 300–301) believes that the militant conservative sculptor E. V. Vuchetich was responsible for Kosolapov's dismissal, having gone directly to Khrushchev to complain about an article he, Vuchetich, had written, which, he said, *Literaturnaya gazeta* refused to publish. Vuchetich complained to Khrushchev at the December 17 conference,

the article he had written was printed in the paper the very next day, on the eighteenth, and Kosolapov was fired a week later. Benno (p. 198) says that Chakovsky was a former NKVD agent. Among the six editors dropped with Kosolapov were Yury Bondarev, the controversial author of *Silence;* G. M. Korabelnikov; Boris Leontiev; Vladimir Solukhin; and Yevgeny Surkov (not to be confused with Anatoly Surkov). With Chakovsky came B. Galanov, A. Makharov, Georgy Markov, Yevgeny Osetrov, S. Rostotsky, and Yaroslav Smelyakov.

17. *Pravda,* Jan. 27, 1963; as translated in *Current Digest of the Soviet Press.*

18. Benno, p. 189.

19. Ilya Ehrenburg, *Liudi, gody, zhizn,* VI, 737, 736.

20. Harrison Salisbury, *New York Times,* Oct. 23, 1967.

21. *New York Times,* Feb. 7–8, 1963.

22. Tatu (pp. 301–303) and Johnson (p. 19) demonstrate their grasp of the subtleties of factional in-fighting in analyzing this struggle. Both are out of sympathy with Serebryakova and Yermilov yet give relatively fair weight to their arguments against Ehrenburg.

23. Ehrenburg, *Liudi, gody, zhizn,* VI, 760, 734, 760.

24. *Izvestia,* Feb. 6, 1963. Was it a sign of Ehrenburg's agitation that he confused the date of the issue of *Izvestia* in which Yermilov first attacked him?

25. Tatu, p. 310.

26. *Izvestia,* Jan. 31, 1963.

27. *Literaturnaya rossiya,* Jan. 11, 1963.

28. Ehrenburg, *Liudi, gody, zhizn,* VI, 737–738.

Chapter 7. *Ebb Tide* (pp. 73–84)

1. *Pravda,* March 9, 1963.

2. *Ibid.*

3. *Ibid.*

4. *New York Times,* March 13, 1963. The film was never released to the public. Its title was variously translated as "Lenin's Watchpost," "Lenin's Sentry," "The Guardpost of Lenin," and "Ilyich's Gate."

5. Viktor Nekrasov, *Both Sides of the Ocean,* pp. 92–93.

6. *Pravda,* March 10, 1963.

7. *Ibid.*

8. *Ibid.*

9. Priscilla Johnson, *Khrushchev and the Arts,* p. 25.

10. *Le Monde,* March 12, 1963.

11. Werth, *Russia: Hopes and Fears*, p. 187.

12. Miss Johnson (pp. 25 ff.) cleverly notes that it was Khrushchev himself who had sanctioned publication of Ehrenburg's memoirs—as he had Solzhenitsyn's *Ivan Denisovich*—as part of his de-Stalinization campaign.

13. *Pravda*, March 10, 1963.

14. *Pravda*, Jan. 19, 1957; see also *Kommunist*, No. 12 (1957).

15. *Pravda*, April 27, 1962.

16. *Pravda*, March 10, 1963.

17. The question is whether Khrushchev considered this a "price" or "desirable" in the given circumstances.

18. See Tatu, *Power in the Kremlin*, p. 334.

19. *Pravda*, March 10, 1963.

20. "The Political Aspect," in *Soviet Literature in the Sixties*, ed. Max Hayward and Edward L. Crowley, p. 193.

21. *New York Times*, April 28, 1963.

22. *Pravda*, March 10, 1963.

23. *Ibid*. The constant use of similes and metaphors of combat is characteristic of political exhortation in the USSR. The use of the vocabulary of warfare in literary matters betrays—in this area as in others —the leaders' preoccupation with forceful and combative assertion of their cause, and, if necessary, its imposition by force.

24. Darrell P. Hammer, "Among Students in Moscow," *Problems of Communism*, July–Aug. 1964, p. 13.

25. *New York Times*, March 13, 1963.

26. *Ibid*.

27. *Literaturnaya gazeta*, March 16, 1963.

28. *Pravda*, March 11, 1963.

29. *New York Times*, March 22, 1963.

30. *Ibid.*, March 25, 1963.

31. *London Times*, Dec. 31, 1962.

32. *Literaturnaya rossiya*, April 12, 1963.

33. *Yunost*, April 1963.

34. *Komsomolskaya pravda*, March 31, 1963.

35. *Ibid.*, March 22, 1963.

36. *London Times*, April 20, 1963.

37. *Literaturnaya gazeta*, April 19, 1962.

38. *New York Times*, March 28, 1963.

39. Priscilla Johnson, "The 'New Men' of the Soviet Sixties," *The Reporter*, May 9, 1963, p. 18. Miss Johnson's articles in *The Reporter* are livelier and more replete with insight than even her excellent book.

40. Johnson, *Khrushchev and the Arts*, p. 43.
41. Quoted *ibid.*, p. 54, from *Pravda ukrainy*, April 10, 1963.
42. *Pravda*, June 29, 1963.

Chapter 8. *Matryona's House* (pp. 85–102)

1. Lydia Fomenko, "Great Expectations," *Literaturnaya rossiya*, Jan. 11, 1963.
2. Alexander Solzhenitsyn, "The Incident at Krechetovka Station," *Great Russian Short Novels*, translated and introduced by Andrew R. MacAndrew (New York: Bantam Books, 1969).
3. See "One Day with Solzhenitsyn," an interview by the Slovak journalist Pavel Licko, excerpts of which were published in *Survey*, July 1967, p. 184, for the dating of the story. The original interview appeared in the Slovak paper *Kulturny Zivot* (Bratislava), March 31, 1967.
4. *Novy mir*, December 1962.
5. *Neva*, January 1963.
6. Alexander Solzhenitsyn, "Matryona's House," in *We Never Make Mistakes: Two Short Novels*, p. 62.
7. *Ibid.*, p. 61.
8. *Ibid.*, p. 100.
9. *Literaturnaya rossiya*, No. 3, 1963.
10. *New York Times*, Feb. 1, 1963.
11. *Literaturnaya gazeta*, March 2, 1963.
12. Harrison Salisbury, *New York Times*, Oct. 23, 1967.
13. *New York Herald-Tribune*, March 25, 1963.
14. *Izvestia*, March 30, 1963.
15. *Kortars*, March 1963.
16. *Magyar Nemzet*, Feb. 17, 1963.
17. *Elet es Irodalom*, Feb. 23, 1963.
18. *Ibid.*, March 16, 1963.
19. *Ibid.*
20. *Pravda*, March 27, 1963.
21. *Literaturnaya gazeta*, April 2, 1963.
22. *Komsomolskaya pravda*, March 22, 1963.
23. *Ibid.*, March 29, 1963.
24. *Literaturnaya rossiya*, April 5, 1963. The tone of the meeting is conveyed in the revealing and unwittingly hilarious titles of the speeches: "For a Literature That Inspires Great Feats," "Be as Loyal to the People as a Warrior Is to His Oath," "Hold the Course!" "Always in the Front Lines." The military language was, as usual, ubiquitous.

25. *Literaturnaya gazeta*, March 30, 1963.

26. *Komsomolskaya pravda*, May 11, 1963.

27. *Literaturnaya gazeta*, April 2, 1963.

28. *Oktyabr*, April 1963.

29. Peter Benno, "The Political Aspect," in *Soviet Literature in the Sixties*, ed. May Hayward and Edward L. Crowley, p. 191.

30. *Variety*, April 10, 1963.

31. *Pravda*, April 26, 1963.

32. *Ibid.*, May 12, 1963. See Priscilla Johnson, *Khrushchev and the Arts*, pp. 48–49, about the careful planning involved in the Shapiro interview.

33. *Pravda*, May 12, 1963.

34. *Ibid.*

35. *Ibid.*

36. *Pravda*, May 19, 1963.

37. *Sovetskaya pechat*, May 21, 1963.

38. *New York Herald-Tribune*, June 5, 1963.

39. *Pravda*, June 29, 1963. Though the speech was delivered on June 21, its publication was delayed for eight days.

40. *Ibid.*

41. *Ibid.*

42. *Socialist Herald*, Nov.–Dec. 1963. See Johnson, pp. 95, 101, for other excerpts from this speech.

43. *Pravda*, June 29, 1963. The portrayal of Stalin's separation from the people and the reality of Soviet life is scarifying.

44. *Ibid.*; italics mine.

45. *Ibid.* Some of Khrushchev's stress on the farm situation and the grain shortage, as well as on the confidence of the people in the Party leadership, may have been due to a knowledge that the 1963 harvest was going to be disastrous—as it was. There had been food shortages and price hikes in 1962 which had triggered protests and riots. From 1963 to 1967 the Soviet leaders were forced to buy 29 million tons of wheat from abroad so that there would be no bread shortage in the USSR.

46. *Pravda*, July 20, 1963.

Chapter 9. *For the Good of the Cause* (pp. 103–116)

1. Michel Tatu, *Power in the Kremlin*, p. 353.

2. See the excellent discussion in Priscilla Johnson, *Khrushchev and the Arts*, pp. 62–64, for a detailed analysis of the maneuvers.

3. The conference was cosponsored by UNESCO. The European

Community of Writers was predominantly Italian in make-up, including such well-known Italian writers as Guido Piovene and Giuseppe Ungaretti, but it also had such members as John Lehmann, Angus Wilson, Hans Magnus Enzensberger, Nathalie Sarraute, and Alain Robbe-Grillet. The Secretary-General, Giancarlo Vigorelli, had once delivered himself of the observation, "I am convinced that whoever proclaims himself an anti-Communist thereby assigns himself to the camp of Fascism. One need not be a Communist, but one cannot be an anti-Communist." See Gleb Struve's "Soviet Literature in Perspective," in *Soviet Literature in the Sixties,* ed. Max Hayward and Edward L. Crowley, p. 142.

4. Johnson, pp. 65–70.

5. *Mosty,* No. 10 (1963). See Struve, pp. 139–140.

6. *Izvestia,* Aug. 18, 1963, as translated in Johnson, *Khrushchev and the Arts,* pp. 245–247. The poem was presumably delivered to the printer on June 14, four days before the Central Committee Ideological Plenum opened. It was passed by the censor on August 21, three days *after* it had appeared in *Izvestia,* and was also published in the August *Novy mir* after some six years of circulation underground.

7. *Oktyabr,* October 1963.

8. Alexander Solzhenitsyn, *For the Good of the Cause,* p. 12.

9. *Ibid.,* p. 46.

10. *Ibid.,* p. 60.

11. *Ibid.,* p. 83.

12. *Ibid.,* pp. 85–86.

13. *Ibid.,* pp. 62–63.

14. *Literaturnaya gazeta,* Aug. 31, 1963.

15. *Ibid.,* Oct. 15, 1963.

16. *Literaturnaya gazeta,* Oct. 19, 1963.

17. *Ibid.*

18. *Oktyabr,* Oct. 1963.

19. *Ibid.* The review was, logically, called "Unbending Spirit." A number of other works which deal with concentration camps were published in that period, among them Georgy Shelest's *Notes of Kolyma,* Aleksandr Gorbatov's *Years off My Life,* and Yury Pilar's *Men Remain Men.* The title of Dyakov's story has also been translated as *What I Went Through.*

20. *Kazakhstanskaya pravda,* Oct. 6, 1963.

21. Johnson, p. 72.

22. Conservatives and liberals both make use of "worker" and "Old Bolshevik" ploys to bolster their positions, because people in such categories are given great kudos in Soviet society and are presumed to

have a special wisdom about any and all issues. Letters-to-the-editor columns often serve to air minor conflicts or as places where the regime can launch trial balloons to see what popular reaction will be.

23. *Novy mir*, Oct. 1963.

24. *Literaturnaya gazeta*, Dec. 12, 1963.

25. *Literaturnaya gazeta*, Dec. 26, 1963.

26. *Ibid.*

Chapter 10. *The Lenin Prize* (pp. 117–123)

1. *Literaturnaya gazeta*, Jan. 11, 1964.

2. *Ibid.*, Jan. 18, 1964.

3. *Pravda*, Jan. 30, 1964.

4. *Literaturnaya rossiya*, Jan. 1, 1964. Priscilla Johnson, in "Old Terror and New Doubts," *The Reporter*, December 6, 1962, remarked cogently, "Surely, the people of Russia have a capacity for forgiveness and credulity that is unrivaled anywhere on earth."

5. *Literaturnaya rossiya*, Jan. 1, 1964.

6. *Ibid.*, Jan. 10, 1964.

7. *Izvestia*, Jan. 15, 1964.

8. *Ibid.*

9. *Izvestia*, Dec. 29, 1963.

10. *Literaturnaya rossiya*, Jan. 31, 1964.

11. *Novy mir*, Jan. 1964. Lakshin's long and carefully thought-out article, "Ivan Denisovich, His Friends and Foes," was the kind of strong defense of Solzhenitsyn that made Priscilla Johnson remark that Tvardovsky hoped that, in the light of the Sino-Soviet conflict's increasing virulence, Khrushchev might find it politically opportune to give the Lenin Prize to *Ivan Denisovich*, and in so doing give the liberal writers an opportunity to recover some lost ground in their battle with the dogmatists.

12. *Literaturnaya rossiya*, Jan. 11, 1964.

13. *Novy mir*, Jan. 1964.

14. *Ibid.*

15. *Literaturnaya gazeta*, Feb. 8, 1964.

16. *Literaturnaya rossiya*, March 6, 1964.

17. *Pravda*, April 11, 1964.

18. *New York Times*, Dec. 31, 1963.

Chapter 11. *The Brodsky Case* (pp. 127–133)

1. The Brodsky trial transcript was smuggled out of the USSR, but it is an incomplete transcript obviously taken down surreptitiously by someone in the courtroom. Parts of it were subsequently published in the *New Leader*, Aug. 31, 1964, pp. 6–17.

2. *New York Times*, Aug. 31, 1964.

3. Yury Krotkov, *I Am from Moscow*, pp. 203–204.

4. "The Trial of Josif Brodsky," *New Leader*, Aug. 31, 1964, p. 9.

5. Krotkov, p. 203.

6. "The Trial of Josif Brodsky," p. 10. The Soviets' use of such terms as "impermissible" and "cannot be" conveys a dogmatic and skewed vision of reality which I believe most Westerners will find difficult to comprehend.

7. Identical methods of using works which the authors had disavowed and which the police then made available to opposition critics or prosecution witnesses in order to influence their attitudes toward the accused characterized the Sinyavsky-Daniel trial and Solzhenitsyn's confrontation with the Soviet authorities.

8. "The Trial of Josif Brodsky," p. 11.

9. *Ibid.*, pp. 7, 8. The term "administrative measures" is a Soviet euphemism for political police action which includes discharging people from their jobs, harassment, arrest, torture, imprisonment, exile, and murder.

10. *Ibid.*, p. 14.

11. *Time*, July 3, 1964.

12. *New York Times Book Review*, Feb. 23, 1965.

13. The poems were translated by Nicholas Bethell, who subsequently became one of the translators of Solzhenitsyn's works.

14. *New York Times*, July 16, 1967. Harrison Salisbury reported that Brodsky had been released and was working in Leningrad.

15. *Russia: Hopes and Fears*, p. 323.

16. *Ibid.*, pp. 322–323.

17. See Andrei Amalrik's *Involuntary Journey to Siberia* for his similar and grueling experience in hauling dung in a kolkhoz.

18. Patricia Blake, "In Soviet Literary Life, the Hazards Endure," *New York Times Book Review*, July 21, 1964.

19. S. L. Shneiderman, "Trial in Leningrad," *Congress Bi-Weekly*, Oct. 12, 1964, p. 7.

20. "The Trial of Josif Brodsky," pp. 10, 13.

21. Shneiderman, p. 7.

Chapter 12. *Changeover* (pp. 134–150)

1. Priscilla Johnson believes that the liberal writers may have been promised that Solzhenitsyn would subsequently be awarded the prize (*Khrushchev and the Arts*), p. 77. If such a promise was made, I suspect that it was insincere; it was a temporary sop which the regime did not in the long run intend to offer, because Solzhenitsyn's work remained potentially too threatening to the heirs of Stalin for the foreseeable future.

2. *Izvestia*, March 8, 1964.

3. *New York Times*, April 15, 1964.

4. *Ibid.*, May 24, 1964.

5. *Sovetskaya kultura*, May 5, 1964.

6. *Literaturnaya gazeta*, June 9, 1964.

7. *Pravda*, June 17, 1964.

8. *New York Times*, June 26, 1964. Rehabilitations of writers, like those of political figures, were part and parcel of the de-Stalinization and liberalization campaigns—and they ran the same risks of endangering the heirs of Stalin, for the same questions were bound to be asked: Who was responsible?

9. *Novy mir*, April 1964.

10. *Izvestia*, April 25, 1964.

11. *Izvestia*, Sept. 6, 1964.

12. See, for example, the fulsome eulogy by Galina Serebryakova in *Literaturnaya rossiya*, April 17, 1964.

13. *Pravda*, Oct. 17, 1964.

14. Michel Tatu, *Power in the Kremlin*, p. 398.

15. He had alienated many of the best scientists, particularly the biologists, by his advocacy and support of Lysenko and Michurinist techniques in agriculture. See text, pp. 316 ff.

16. Albert Boiter, "When the Kettle Boils Over," *Problems of Communism*, Feb. 1964, pp. 41–43.

17. Tatu, p. 389. Not only had Khrushchev acted in opposition to one of the cardinal tenets of postwar Soviet foreign policy—adamant opposition and hostility to West Germany—but he had behaved "impermissibly" in bypassing the Foreign Ministry by sending his son-in-law to do some probing in Bonn.

18. *New York Times*, Jan. 7, 1971. Djilas does not clarify what he means by "mass repressions." If he meant that there would have to be trials, sentences, and imprisonments of those heirs of Stalin responsible

for the crimes of the Stalinist era, such trials and punishments would be likely.

19. The facts concerning Solzhenitsyn's royalty payments are difficult to ascertain. Evidently he was permitted to receive royalties from those of his works published in the USSR and other Communist countries in East Europe. He was also allowed to accept Western royalties for *One Day in the Life of Ivan Denisovich,* which had been published abroad with government sanction, but reports (*Time,* March 23, 1970, p. 25) indicated that even those royalties might have been cut off. Rumor had it that Solzhenitsyn was living on the largesse of other, like-minded Russian intellectuals, and it was certain that some of them, like the cellist Mstislav Rostropovich, had helped in quite practical ways.

20. "*Samizdat* is a play on the word *Gosiuzdat,* a telescoping of *Gosudarstvennoye Izdatelstvo,* the name of the monopoly-wielding State Publishing House. The *sam* part means self, so that the word translates as: 'We publish ourself'—that is, not the state, but we, the people." See Albert Parry, "Samizdat Is Russia's Underground Press," *New York Times Magazine,* March 15, 1970.

21. See text, pp. 316 ff., for an extended discussion of Lysenkoism and its political repercussions.

22. *Novy mir,* Jan. 1965; as translated in "Soviet Literature: To Be or Not to Be?" *Bulletin,* June 1965, p. 34.

23. *Pravda,* Jan. 29, 1965. See also Timothy McClure's "The Politics of Soviet Culture," *Problems of Communism,* March–April, 1967, pp. 30–31, for a sensible grouping of the liberals and conservatives in the spectrum of Soviet literary life.

24. *New York Times,* Jan. 30, 1965.

25. *Literaturnaya gazeta,* Jan. 21, 1965.

26. *Ibid.;* italics mine.

27. *New York Times,* Jan. 30, 1965.

28. *Literaturnaya rossiya,* Feb. 2, 1965.

29. *Pravda,* Feb. 21, 1965.

30. *New York Times,* March 29, 1965.

31. *Pravda,* March 28, 1965.

32. *New York Times,* March 29, 1965.

33. McClure, p. 33.

34. *Ibid.*

35. *Pravda,* May 9, 1965.

36. *New York Times,* Aug. 23, 1965.

37. *Pravda,* Aug. 27, 1965.

38. *Kommunist,* April 13, 1965.

39. *Pravda*, Sept. 9, 1965.

40. Tass, Sept. 21, 1965.

41. *New York Times*, Dec. 18, 1965.

42. Aleksandr Yesenin-Volpin, *A Leaf of Spring*, p. 3.

43. *Ibid.*, pp. 49–50. The poem was written in 1946!

44. *Pravda*, December 22, 1962.

45. *Pravda*, Dec. 27, 1962.

46. *Ogonyok*, Jan. 20, 1963.

47. David Burg, "The 'Cold War' on the Literary Front," *Problems of Communism*, July–Aug., 1962, pp. 7–8.

48. *A Leaf of Spring*, p. 5.

Chapter 13. *The Sinyavsky-Daniel Case* (pp. 151–167)

1. *Izvestia*, Jan. 12, 1966.

2. Max Hayward, ed., *On Trial: The Soviet State versus "Abram Tertz" and "Nikolai Arzhak,"* rev. ed., p. 23. This volume contains an incomplete record of the trial taken down by a courtroom witness and smuggled out of the USSR. The introduction and appendix by Max Hayward, the latter of which contains the complete text of the Zoya Kedrina article among other documents, are very useful.

3. *Literaturnaya gazeta*, Jan. 22, 1966.

4. Hayward, ed., *On Trial*, pp. 163, 168.

5. *Zvezda*, Oct. 1965.

6. Tass, Nov. 30, 1965.

7. Hayward, ed., *On Trial*, pp. 41–42, 44.

8. *Ibid.*, p. 26.

9. See *ibid.*, p. 117.

10. Tass, Feb. 11, 1966.

11. Hayward, ed., *On Trial*, p. 98. The traditional apathy of the Russian intelligentsia, "Oblomovism," haunts many among the Russian leadership and intellectuals. It is a part, but only one part, of a much larger and more complicated problem in Soviet life and history: Do the considerable industrial advances finally justify the ruthless methods of Stalinist dictatorship? Was such progress possible only by such means? Such questions haunt all considerations by reflective Russians as well as by many Westerners.

12. *Ibid.*, p. 149.

13. *Ibid.*, pp. 61, 83–84.

14. *Ibid.*, p. 160.

15. *New York Times*, Feb. 14, 1966.

16. *Le Monde,* April 17, 1966.

17. *New York Times,* Feb. 20, 1966.

18. *L'Unità,* Feb. 16, 1966.

19. *Daily Worker,* Feb. 16, 1966.

20. *New York Times,* Feb. 17, 20, 1966.

21. Tass, March 5, 1966.

22. *New York Times,* March 5, 1966.

23. *Paese sera,* March 17, 1966.

24. *New York Times,* March 5, 1966.

25. *New York Herald-Tribune,* March 27, 1966.

26. *New York Times,* April 4, 1970.

27. *Literaturnaya gazeta,* April 17, 1965.

28. *Pravda,* Jan. 30, 1966.

29. *Voprosy istoriy,* No. 5 (1965).

30. See V. Khvostov and A. Grilev, "On the Eve of the Great Fatherland War," *Kommunist,* No. 12 (1968), for the fully developed Party line on how Stalin prepared the nation for World War II.

31. *New York Times,* April 2, 1970.

32. Hayward, ed., *On Trial,* p. 285.

33. Alexander Werth, *Russia: Hopes and Fears,* p. 297. Chukovskaya's short novel, *The Deserted House,* never published in the USSR, is perhaps the only work of fiction in post-Stalinist literature to equal the force, honesty, and merit of Solzhenitsyn's *One Day in the Life of Ivan Denisovich.*

34. Hayward, ed., *On Trial,* pp. 287, 289.

35. Werth, p. 185.

36. Hayward, ed., *On Trial,* p. 290.

37. Werth, p. 277; italics mine.

38. Hayward, ed., *On Trial,* p. 291.

39. *Atlas,* March 1968.

Chapter 14. *The Aftermath* (pp. 168–182)

1. *New York Times,* Feb. 20, 1966.

2. Reuter's, Feb. 6, 1966.

3. See text, pp. 226 ff., for further discussion of Victor Louis's ambiguous role in Soviet literary affairs.

4. Reuter's, Feb. 10, 1966.

5. *New York Times,* Feb. 9, 1966.

6. *Sunday Times* (London), Feb. 13, 1966.

7. *Pravda,* Feb. 21, 1966.

8. *New York Times*, Feb. 22, March 18, May 3, July 29, 1966.

9. *New York Herald-Tribune*, Jan. 4, 1966.

10. *Le Monde*, Jan. 4, 1966.

11. *New York Times*, April 6, 1966.

12. *Suchanost*, Jan. 1965.

13. Under the title *Bereh chekan* ("Prolog"), 1965, in New York.

14. *Pravda ukrainy*, March 17, 1966.

15. *New York Times*, April 14, 1966.

16. *Novy mir*, April 1966.

17. *New York Times*, April 20, 1966.

18. *Yunost*, No. 4 (1966).

19. See *New York Times*, May 4, 1966.

20. *Ibid.*, Jan. 27, 1967.

21. In the conflict concerning *Yunost*, Bykov defended the publication by remarking: "Literature is not a headache pain pill to kill pain immediately, but rather a vitamin pill that has gradual effect" (*New York Times*, March 6, 1966).

22. Tass, April 16, 1966.

23. *Krasnaya zvezda*, Oct. 15, 1966.

24. Requiring prisoners to write their autobiographies over and over again was—and remains—a standard KGB interrogation technique. Its purpose is not only to gather information but to involve the prisoner in contradictions, provide the KGB with the kind of biographical "facts" which it can use to incriminate prisoners and to rig evidence for show trials.

25. *London Daily Mail*, April 26, 1966.

26. *New York Times*, April 21, 1966.

27. Andrei Amalrik, *Involuntary Journey to Siberia*, pp. 122, 32, xiv, 32.

28. *Ibid.*, p. 122.

29. Pavel Litvinov, *The Demonstration in Pushkin Square*, pp. 13–15.

30. Even such spurious and repressive legalism was looked on by some as an advance over the arbitrariness of the Stalinist era.

31. "Truth and Freedom in *Novy mir*," *Rinascita*, May 7, 1966.

32. *Literaturnaya gazeta*, March 8, 1967, announced *Novy mir*'s plans for 1967.

33. *Novy mir*, Jan. 1967.

34. Yury Krotkov, "Signs of the Times," *Bulletin*, April 1968, p. 17.

35. Ilya Ehrenburg, *Post-War Years*, pp. 158–167.

36. Ilya Ehrenburg, *Liudi, gody, zhizn*, VI, 596, 598.

37. *Ibid.*, VI, 599, 602.

38. *Pravda*, Feb. 21, 1956.

39. "Soviet Reality and the Writer's Conscience," *Bulletin*, April 1968, p. 10.

40. Krotkov, "Signs of the Times," pp. 12, 14.

41. *Ibid.*, pp. 15, 16.

42. *Yunost*, Jan. 1967.

43. *Pravda*, Jan. 27, 1967.

44. *Ibid.*

45. *Pravda*, March 29, 1967.

46. *Pravda*, April 8, 1967.

47. Alexander Werth, *Russia: Hopes and Fears*, p. 274.

Chapter 15. *The Alliluyeva Case* (pp. 183–191)

1. Andrei Amalrik, *Will the Soviet Union Survive until 1984?*, p. 7.

2. Published in Russian in the NTS magazine, *Grani*, No. 52 (1967). See also *Times Literary Supplement*, Feb. 8, 1968, for an English summary of the contents. Ginzburg had in 1965 circulated a typewritten journal called *Syntax*, later also published in *Grani*, No. 58 (1968). See Amalrik, *Will the Soviet Union Survive until 1984?*, pp. 7 and 91; and Keith Bosley and Dmitry Pospielovsky, eds., *Russia's Underground Poets*, for selections from *Phoenix*, *Syntax*, and other fugitive journals.

3. Smog is thought to be an acronym either for *Samoye Molodoye Obschchestvo Geniyev*, meaning "The Youngest Society of Geniuses," or the first initials of the four Russian words *smelost, mysl, obraz, glubina*, meaning "boldness," "thought," "image," and "depth."

4. Pavel Litvinov, *The Demonstration in Pushkin Square*, p. 65.

5. Viv Broughton, *Peace News*, Feb. 2, 1968; quoted in Alexander Werth, *Russia: Hopes and Fears*, pp. 308–309.

6. Litvinov, pp. 65, 64.

7. *Chronicle of Current Events*, No. 1 (April 30, 1968) (hereafter referred to as *Chronicle*). This underground newspaper, probably edited and distributed by a network of scientific and technical intelligentsia, began to publish in the spring of 1968, devoting itself to the defense of legal rights in the USSR and the exposure of injustice. See text, pp. 328 ff.

8. *Le Monde*, Dec. 7, 1967.

9. *Twenty Letters to a Friend*. See the story of her slow discovery of her desire to defect and live in freedom in *Only One Year*.

10. *New York Times*, April 27, 1967.

11. *New York Daily Worker*, May 16, 1967.

12. *Za rubeshom*, No. 23 (June 2, 1967). Most of this article was reprinted two days later, June 4, in *Izvestia*.

13. Chalmers Roberts, *Washington Post*, Aug. 4, 1967.

14. *Pravda*, May 27, 1967.

15. *Komsomolskaya pravda*, May 31, 1967, entitled its article on the affair "Svetlana's Dollars." *Literaturnaya gazeta*, June 7, 1967, proclaimed that "Svetlana . . . became merchandise to be sold just like a book." And *Za rubeshom*, June 2, 1967, in its treatment of the issue, dubbed "God Seeker after Dollars," condemned Mrs. Alliluyeva for religiosity and greed, imputing her defection to those motives.

16. *Christian Science Monitor*, Aug. 23, 1967.

17. "To Boris Leonidovich Pasternak," *Atlantic Monthly*, June 1967, pp. 133, 134, 136. Alliluyeva's ingenuousness, a kind of adolescent gushing, is sometimes an embarrassment. One symptom of it is the curious interjection in contexts where they seem to have no relevance of remarks about a man's physical attractiveness: to Sinyavsky, for example, "You were not the most handsome man in the world"; of her second husband, "He was not much to look at." There is much less of this, fortunately, in *Only One Year* than in *Twenty Letters to a Friend*.

18. "To Boris Leonidovich Pasternak," p. 139. Alliluyeva's references to the political police and to Soviet official xenophobia were bound to be anathema to the official leadership's sensibilities.

19. *Toronto Daily Star*, May 20, 1967.

20. Chalmers Roberts, *Washington Post*, Aug. 4, 1967.

21. *Only One Year*, pp. 336, 338.

22. Chalmers Roberts, *Washington Post*, Aug. 4, 1967.

23. UPI, Aug. 25, 1967. See also *Christian Science Monitor*, Aug. 23, 1967.

Chapter 16. *Solzhenitsyn and Glavlit* (pp. 192–203)

1. *New York Times*, Oct. 23, 1967. Harrison Salisbury reports this, evidently from personal knowledge, but he gives no sources.

2. *Ibid.* The letter was dated May 16, 1967. With great prudence, Solzhenitsyn focuses only on censorship of fiction; he says nothing about other kinds of writing.

3. Alexander Solzhenitsyn, *Cancer Ward*, p. vii. Even the apologist Alexander Werth is forced to admit, if only in a footnote, that Glavlit is stifling and that "undoubtedly the worst censorship in the world is to be found today in the Soviet Union" (*Russia: Hopes and Fears*, p. 279).

4. Solzhenitsyn, *Cancer Ward*, pp. viii–ix.

5. *Ibid.*, p. x.

6. *Ibid.*, pp. x–xi. Among the works Solzhenitsyn specified were: *Cancer Ward*, which cannot be published as a whole or in part; a play, "The Reindeer and the Little Hut," accepted by the Sovremennik Theater in 1962 but refused performance; a screen play, "The Tanks Know the Truth"; a drama, "The Light That Is in You"; and a group of short stories called "The Right Hand"; the series, "Small Bite," had all been unable to find producers or publishers. Stories published in *Novy mir* had never been reprinted and had everywhere been rejected for book publication.

7. Solzhenitsyn, *Cancer Ward*, p. ix.

8. Werth, p. 281.

9. *Pravda*, May 26, 1967.

10. Werth, pp. 185–186.

11. By Aleksandr Korneichuk in *Izvestia*, September 3, 1967, and by Anatoly Surkov and Konstantin Simonov in *Literaturnaya gazeta* of the same date.

12. Werth, pp. 189–190.

13. *Pravda*, Oct. 26, 1967.

14. Pavel Litvinov, *The Demonstration in Pushkin Square*, p. 73.

15. *New York Times*, Dec. 27, 1967.

16. Litvinov, p. 60.

17. *Ibid.*, pp. 99–100; italics mine.

18. *Ibid.*, pp. 102–103.

19. *Ibid.*, pp. 113, 115.

20. *Ibid.*, p. 127.

21. *Ibid.*, pp. 132–133. Accusing foreign reports of "distortion" and "hostility" is one way in which dissidents attempt to prevent the regime from linking them with the "foreign enemies" of the USSR. Such dissociation is not always successful.

22. The talk took place on June 12.

23. Solzhenitsyn, *Cancer Ward*, pp. xiii–xiv.

24. *Ibid.*, pp. 559, 540, 550, 551. To a Western intellectual some of this dialogue sounds like farce or *opéra bouffe*, but regrettably it was in deadly earnest.

25. *Ibid.*, p. 543.

26. *Ibid.*, p. 547.

27. The former head of the KGB, Vladimir Semichastny, had attacked Solzhenitsyn precisely on those grounds (*ibid.*, p. 548).

28. *Ibid.*, pp. 555, 558.

29. *Ibid.*, p. 552.
30. *Survey*, April 1968.
31. *Ibid.*
32. *Ibid.*

Chapter 17. *Trials and Transcripts* (pp. 204–217)

1. Pavel Litvinov, *The Demonstration in Pushkin Square*, p. 135; italics mine.

2. *Ibid.*, p. 137.

3. *Ibid.*, p. 167.

4. See Abraham Brumberg, *In Quest of Justice*, pp. 101–102, for the entire list of names. Brumberg's is a very valuable collection of documents on trials and dissidents in the Soviet Union.

5. *Ibid.*, pp. 102–104.

6. *New York Times*, Jan. 13, 1968.

7. These included Galanskov's letter to Mikhail Sholokhov after the Twenty-third Party Congress and Andrey Sinyavsky's essay "On Socialist Realism."

8. *Grani*, No. 62 (1966). The anonymous author reads off a martyrology of those Soviet writers "who were tortured, killed or shot, who starved or were frozen to death in Stalin's concentration camps." Among them he mentions specifically Pilnyak, Gumilev, Mandelshtam, Babel, Voronsky, Tabidze, as well as those who, like Bulgakov and Platonov, died unpublished.

9. *Novoye russkoye slovo*, June 6, 1968.

10. Brumberg, p. 110.

11. *Ibid.*, p. 120.

12. *New York Times*, Feb. 28, 1968.

13. *Ibid.*, March 8, 1968.

14. *Literaturnaya gazeta*, Dec. 27, 1967.

15. See *New York Times*, Dec. 28, 1967.

16. *Novoye russkoye slovo*, Feb. 25, 1968.

17. Harry Schwartz, *Russia Enters the 1960s*, pp. 127, 98. Khrushchev neglects to mention that at the time of the Yakir arrest and execution, he himself referred to Yakir as "riff-raff who wanted to let in the German fascists." See Robert Conquest's *The Great Terror*, p. 225.

18. Yuli Kim, the popular singer, is married to Yakir's daughter Irina.

19. See *London Times*, Feb. 15, 1968; *Washington Post*, Feb. 18, 1968; and *New York Times*, Feb. 15 and 18, 1968.

20. Among the books Yakir specifically mentioned were Konstantin

Simonov's war diaries and Evgenia Ginzburg's *Journey into the Whirl-wind*.

21. *Possev*, No. 8, 1968. The letter is worth reading *in toto* for the same literary honesty and felicity that characterize Chukovskaya's brilliant short novel, *The Deserted House*.

22. *Possev*, No. 8, 1968.

23. *New York Times*, Feb. 18, 1968.

24. *Ibid.*, April 16, 1968.

25. *Message from Moscow*, pp. 67–68. This sharply observed and written book by a pseudonymous British "An Observer" is a splendid introduction to contemporary Soviet life.

26. See Brumberg, pp. 340–349, for some feeling of the viciousness and ugliness of this campaign as demonstrated in the dismissal proceedings against a schoolteacher who signed one of the protests. One can smell the very "odor" of the way terror operates in a relatively undramatic context.

27. *New York Times*, May 5, 1968.

28. *Literaturnaya rossiya*, May 1, 1968.

29. *Ibid.*

30. Brumberg, p. 365.

31. *New York Times*, April 12, 1968.

32. *Literaturnaya gazeta*, April 3, 1968.

Chapter 18. *Solzhenitsyn's Ordeal* (pp. 218–232)

1. The letter was not published in the Soviet Union and was smuggled out to the West to appear in the October 1968 issue of *Possev*.

2. Alexander Solzhenitsyn, *Cancer Ward*, p. 544.

3. Nicholas Bethell, "Solzhenitsyn Can Still Write—He Just Can't Publish," *New York Times Magazine*, May 1970, p. 74.

4. Solzhenitsyn, *Cancer Ward*, p. 556.

5. Bethell, p. 56.

6. On a visit to Yale University in 1964, Chakovsky said, revealingly: "You know there is an English proverb, 'Wrong or not, it's my country!' I'm a patriot." This attitude is characteristic of the regime stalwarts. The term "anti-Soviet" has thereby been made to bear all sorts of burdens by the regime's proponents; anything the regime deems to be "objectively" harmful to Soviet interests, however "subjectively" motivated or intended, is by definition "anti-Soviet." Chakovsky very likely did not know that the quotation he was using was American, not British, and very likely did not know the whole Stephen Decatur quo-

tation—"Our country! In her intercourse with foreign nations, may she always be in the right; but our country right or wrong"—which provides an added irony. See Peter Khiss's report, "Russian Writers Joust with Yale," *New York Times*, Dec. 2, 1964.

7. Solzhenitsyn, *Cancer Ward*, pp. 544, 551, 552.

8. *Le Monde*, April 28–29, 1968.

9. *Possev*, No. 7 (1968). From beginning to end this is an extraordinarily touching letter to an old friend from whom the writer has become estranged—right down to Kaverin's addressing Fedin by his diminutive, Kostya. It is also, not incongruously, far more savage and less politic than Tvardovsky's letter to Fedin.

10. *Possev*, No. 7 (1968).

11. Max Hayward, Introduction to Anatoly Marchenko's *My Testimony*, pp. ix–x.

12. The trial transcripts were published in English under the title *The Demonstration in Pushkin Square*.

13. Solzhenitsyn, *Cancer Ward*, p. 559.

14. *Ibid.*, p. 560.

15. *Literaturnaya gazeta*, June 26, 1968. The article was titled "The Ideological Struggle, the Writer's Responsibility," and was a full-scale attack on Solzhenitsyn.

16. "Review of the Week," *New York Times*, May 5, 1968.

17. Anatole Shub, *The New Russian Tragedy*, p. 32. The comments on Victor Louis appear in an excellent chapter on how the Soviet government controls and warps the activities of foreign journalists in the USSR.

18. Victor Louis, "Solzhenitsyn Lives Martyr's Role," *Washington Post*, March 16, 1969.

19. *Ibid.*

20. *Ibid.*

21. *New York Times*, Sept. 18, 1969.

22. *Ibid.*, May 1, 1968. Raymond Anderson, Moscow correspondent for the *Times*, noted that "Possev distributes its books and periodicals among Russian émigrés and smuggles them, mostly in onionskin micro-editions, into the Soviet Union," so that *samizdat* produces a printed feedback from the West into the USSR.

23. *Novy zhurnal*, No. 93 (1968).

24. Alexander Werth, *Russia: Hopes and Fears*, p. 292.

25. Andrei Amalrik, "An Open Letter to Kuznetsov," *Survey*, Winter–Spring, 1970, p. 99.

26. Albert Parry, "*Samizdat* Is Russia's Underground Press," *New*

York Times Magazine, March 15, 1970. Parry lists (p. 72) a number of the Russian émigré publications which regularly print *samizdat* materials: *Possev* ("Sowing"), a monthly, and *Grani* ("Frontiers"), a quarterly, both published in Frankfort, West Germany, by the NTS; the weekly *Russkaya mysl* ("Russian Thought"), published in Paris; and the daily *Novoye russkoye slovo* ("New Russian Word") and the quarterly *Novy zhurnal* ("New Review"), both published in New York.

Chapter 19. *The Invasion of Czechoslovakia* (pp. 235–250)

1. *New York Times,* July 3, 1967.
2. *New York Times,* April 11, 1968.
3. Tass, April 11, 1968.
4. *Sovetskaya rossiya,* April 13, 1968.
5. Descendants of the thirteenth-century Tatar invaders, the Crimean Tatars were exiled from their autonomous Black Sea Crimean Republic toward the end of World War II, accused of having collaborated with the German invaders. They were rehabilitated almost two decades later, on September 5, 1967, but the half-million Tatars remained scattered throughout Central Asia and Siberia, the Kremlin having denied them permission to return to their homes and having refused to reconstitute their republic.
6. Abraham Brumberg, *In Quest of Justice,* pp. 211–212.
7. *New York Times,* May 3, 1968.
8. *Literaturnaya rossiya,* May 1, 1968.
9. *Ibid.*
10. *Literaturnaya gazeta,* May 8, 1968.
11. *Pravda,* May 11, 1968.
12. *Times Literary Supplement,* April 11, 1968.
13. *Literaturnaya gazeta,* June 26, 1968.
14. See text, pp. 259 ff.
15. *Literaturnaya gazeta,* June 26, 1968.
16. *Ibid.*
17. *Ibid.*
18. *Ibid.*
19. *Ibid.*
20. *Novoye russkoye slovo,* Sept. 3, 1968.
21. Marchenko was arrested on July 29, the same day his letter was transmitted to the Czechoslovak Embassy in Moscow.
22. *Novoye russkoye slovo,* Sept. 3, 1968.
23. *Ibid.,* Sept. 18, 1968.

24. *Grani,* No. 67 (1968).

25. "An Observer," *Message from Moscow,* pp. 33, 41. For a more detailed reaction, see pp. 27–43.

26. *Ibid.,* p. 42.

27. *New York Times,* Aug. 29, 1968.

28. *Novoye russkoye slovo,* Nov. 3, 1968.

29. *Chronicle of Current Events,* No. 3 (Aug. 31, 1968).

30. *Ibid.*

31. Both were sent to psychiatric hospitals instead of being tried.

32. *Washington Post,* Sept. 29, 1968.

33. *Ibid.,* Oct. 15, 1968.

34. *Possev,* Jan. 1969.

35. Alexander Werth, *Russia: Hopes and Fears,* p. 9, the title page.

36. *Ibid.,* pp. 332, 10.

37. *Ibid.,* p. 336.

38. *Washington Post,* Sept. 29, 1968.

Chapter 20. *The Kuznetsov Case* (pp. 251–267)

1. "An Observer," *Message from Moscow,* pp. 44–90.

2. *Ibid.,* p. 63.

3. Ilya Ehrenburg, *Liudi, gody, zhizn,* IV, 192. Ehrenburg's *People, Years—Life* was written and published in six volumes, which are included in his *Selected Works, Sobranie soschenyi,* Volumes VII and IX, each of which contains three volumes of the memoirs. The edition was published by Khudozhestvennaya Literatura, Moscow, 1966–1967.

4. *Oktyabr,* December 1968.

5. *Sovetskie profsoyuzy,* April 1968.

6. *Yunost,* Jan. 1969.

7. Anatole Shub, *Washington Post,* Dec. 12, 1968.

8. *Izvestia,* March 30, 1967.

9. *Pravda,* Jan. 27, 1967.

10. *Literaturnaya gazeta,* March 5, 1969.

11. *Pravda,* March 6, 1969.

12. *Le Monde,* May 28, 1969.

13. *New York Times,* July 22, 1969. A fourth editor was said to have resigned for nonpolitical reasons.

14. *Novy mir,* May 1969.

15. *Time,* March 21, 1969, pp. 28–29.

16. Edward Crankshaw, *Toronto Globe and Mail,* April 8, 1969.

17. *New York Times,* Aug. 14, 1969.

18. See *Le Monde,* March 17, 1969, for most of a French text of the

letter; also the *Christian Science Monitor,* March 25, 1969, for excerpts in English.

19. *Washington Post,* April 23, 1969.

20. *Ibid.,* June 4, 1969.

21. *New York Times,* Aug. 1, 1969.

22. *Sunday Telegraph* (London), Aug. 3, 1969.

23. *Ibid.*

24. Columbia Broadcasting System, Sept. 3, 1969.

25. *Sunday Telegraph* (London), Aug. 3, 1969.

26. *Ibid.,* Sept. 28, 1969. Two summers earlier there had been reports that friends feared for Solzhenitsyn's safety because young toughs in Ryazan had threatened the novelist with bodily harm. His friends tried to persuade Solzhenitsyn to leave Ryazan and settle in one of the writers' colonies, but he refused (*New York Times,* July 14, 1967).

27. *Sunday Telegraph* (London), Aug. 3, 1969.

28. *Ibid.*

29. *Ibid.*

30. *New York Times,* Aug. 7, 1969.

31. *Ibid.*

32. *Ibid.,* Aug. 8, 1969.

33. See the revised edition of Kuznetsov's novel *Babi Yar, passim.*

34. *New York Times,* Aug. 24, 1969.

35. *Sunday Telegraph* (London), Sept., 1969.

36. *New York Times,* Aug. 24, 1969.

37. *Literaturnaya gazeta,* Aug. 6, 1969.

38. *Washington Post,* Nov. 23, 1969.

39. "An Open Letter to Kuznetsov," *Survey,* Winter–Spring, 1970, pp. 101–102. Is Amalrik referring here to Yevtushenko and Voznesensky, among others?

40. *Washington Star,* Nov. 26, 1969.

41. "I Want to Be Understood Correctly," *Survey,* Winter–Spring, 1970, p. 104.

42. *Ibid.,* pp. 108–109. The letter is deeply moving and should be read in its entirety.

Chapter 21. *Stalin's New Bust* (pp. 268–276)

1. *News York Times,* June 7, 1970.

2. *Ibid.*

3. *Ibid.,* June 25, 1970.

4. *Ibid.,* June 26, 1970. See the newspaper's Associated Press photograph of the bust with its kindly serene face. The other Communist

notables buried there are Yakov Sverdlov, the first president of the USSR; Felix Dzerzhinsky, head of the secret police under Lenin; Mikhail Frunze, an early military leader; Mikhail Kalinin, president under Stalin; and Andrei Zhdanov, Stalin's deputy and ruler in Leningrad during World War II.

5. *Time*, July 6, 1970, p. 31.

6. *New York Times*, May 27, 1970. The continued and continuing passivity and apathy of the Soviet people at large toward the changes at the top do not give much credence to the last sentence, nor does the comment as a whole offer any reasons for the refurbishing of Stalin or any estimate of its consequences.

7. *Ibid.*

8. *Le Monde*, Jan. 12, 1971.

9. *Novy mir*, April 1969.

10. *Ogonyok*, July 26, 1969.

11. *Novy mir*, July 1969.

12. *Sotsialisticheskaya industria*, July 31, 1969.

13. *Literaturnaya gazeta*, Aug. 27, 1969.

14. *Pravda*, Sept. 12, 1969.

15. *Izvestia*, Oct. 11, 1969.

16. See text, pp. 277 ff.

17. *Pravda*, Dec. 18, 1969.

18. UPI, Dec. 9, 1969.

19. *Literaturnaya gazeta*, Feb. 11, 1970.

20. *Sunday Telegraph* (London), Feb. 15, 1970.

21. *New York Times*, Feb. 15, 1970.

22. *Ibid.*, March 29, 1970. Mikhalkov is another of the dogmatist literary bureaucrats and writers said to have been "co-opted" by the KGB. See the *Sunday Telegraph* (London), Sept. 20, 1970.

23. *New York Times*, May 14, 1970.

24. *Ibid.*, June 25, 1970.

25. See text, pp. 296–300.

26. *Oktyabr*, Sept. 1969; as quoted in *New York Times*, Sept. 20, 1969.

27. *Literaturnaya gazeta*, Feb. 11, 1970.

28. See text, p. 279. Also see text, p. 177.

Chapter 22. *The Writers' Union Debacle* (pp. 277–288)

1. *Le Monde*, Nov. 12, 1969.

2. Reuter's, Nov. 5, 1969.

3. *Christian Science Monitor*, Nov. 26, 1969.

4. *Chronicle of Current Events*, No. 12 (Feb. 28, 1970).

5. *Literaturnaya gazeta*, Nov. 12, 1969.

6. *Le Monde*, Nov. 12, 1969.

7. *Literaturnaya gazeta*, Nov. 14, 1969.

8. *Le Monde*, Nov. 12, 1969. In the United States, E. P. Dutton and Frederick Praeger both agreed to drop publication plans for *Cancer Ward* in compliance with Solzhenitsyn's wishes (*New York Times*, May 15, 1968).

9. *Le Monde*, Nov. 12, 1969.

10. *Ibid.*

11. Nicholas Bethell, "Solzhenitsyn Can Still Write—He Just Can't Publish," *New York Times Magazine*, May 1970, p. 42. With the new calendar, the October Revolution is now celebrated in November.

12. *The Economist*, Nov. 15, 1969. Of the twenty-two writers present at the Moscow meeting, none resisted effectively enough to prevent the condemnation of Solzhenitsyn from being "unanimous" (*Le Monde*, Dec. 2, 1969)

13. See the illuminating, carefully documented chapter, "Bureaucratic Control and Literary Production," in Harold Swayze, *Political Control of Literature in the USSR, 1946–1959*, pp. 224–258, for the flow of rewards administered by the Union. In 1970, when Nicholas Bethell was in Moscow, he reported, "At first, some feared that Solzhenitsyn, now no longer a member of his Union, could be charged with 'parasitism' or compelled to work as a manual laborer. But this is not so. He remains a member of 'Litfond,' the writers' social security organization, and so can still call himself a professional writer and even use the Writers' Club" (Bethell, p. 44). Similar treatment was accorded Pasternak when he was expelled from the Writers' Union.

14. *Time*, March 23, 1970.

15. *New York Times*, Nov. 23, 1969.

16. *Time*, Nov. 21, 1969.

17. *New York Times*, Nov. 15, 1969.

18. *Ibid.*, Nov. 5, 1969.

19. *London Times*, Dec. 18, 1969; *New York Times*, Dec. 19, 1969.

20. *Le Monde*, Nov. 19, 1969.

21. *New York Times*, Dec. 26, 1969.

22. *Ibid.*, Dec. 21, 1969.

23. *Literaturnaya gazeta*, Nov. 26, 1969.

24. *Ibid.*

25. *Ibid.*

26. "News of the Week in Review," *New York Times*, Nov. 30, 1969.

27. *Manchester Guardian*, Dec. 20, 1969.

28. David Levy, Moscow correspondent, *Montreal Star*, Nov. 28, 1969.

29. Tass, Nov. 25, 1969.

30. *Washington Post*, Nov. 28, 1969.

31. *New York Times*, Feb. 19, 1970.

32. *Ibid.*, March 11, 1970.

33. *Time*, March 23, 1970, p. 25.

Chapter 23. *Psychiatric Wards* (pp. 289–300)

1. Anatole Shub, *The New Russian Tragedy*, pp. 22–23.

2. *New York Times*, Feb. 27, 1970.

3. *Time*, April 6, 1970.

4. *New York Times*, Feb. 27, 1970.

5. *Time*, April 6, 1970.

6. *Ibid.*

7. *New York Times*, Aug. 28, 1969.

8. *Chronicle*, No. 11 (Dec. 31, 1969).

9. Reuter's, Aug. 21, 1970.

10. *Chronicle*, No. 13. No specific date appears on this issue, but it was probably printed the last week of April 1970. Reuter's (May 21, 1970) reports that it dated from April 28. The poem was printed in English in the *Chicago Tribune*, May 21, 1970.

11. *Chronicle*, No. 11 (Dec. 31, 1969).

12. *New York Times*, Jan. 22, 1970.

13. *Ibid.*, Dec. 27, 1969; May 10, 1970.

14. *Ibid.*, July 10, 1970. A number of Gorbanevskaya's letters about her experiences in the psychiatric hospital were smuggled out of the USSR and published in the NTS journal *Possev*.

15. Published in English as *Progress, Coexistence, and Intellectual Freedom*.

16. *Chronicle*, No. 13 (April 1970). It was admitted that Gershuni had been critical of the Brezhnev-Kosygin conduct of Soviet foreign and domestic policies.

17. *New York Times*, April 28, 1970.

18. *Time*, April 6, 1970.

19. *Chronicle*, No. 13 (April 1970). For protesting against the Doctors' Plot in Stalin's time, Pisarev had been confined for two years, a year and a half of which he spent in the Leningrad Prison psychiatric ward. Although diagnosed "schizophrenic" by the Serbsky Institute, he was rehabilitated in 1956 and officially "proclaimed sane."

20. Associated Press, April 27, 1970.

21. *New York Times,* May 22, 1970.

22. *Ibid.,* May 31, 1970.

23. *Ibid.*

24. *Ibid.,* June 14, 1970.

25. *Ibid.*

26. *Ibid.,* June 5, 1970, June 14, 1970, June 2, 1970.

27. *Chronicle,* No. 11 (Dec. 31, 1969).

28. *New York Times,* June 6, 1970.

29. *Christian Science Monitor,* June 19, 1970.

30. *Washington Post,* June 6, 1970.

31. *New York Times,* June 6, 1970.

32. *Ibid.,* June 7, 1970.

33. *Ibid.,* July 17, 1970. Solzhenitsyn knew Medvedev through his wife Natalya Reshetovskaya, who had worked at Obninsk as a chemist before regime pressures forced her out. And Medvedev had written an account of her ouster in his *samizdat* essay, *"The International Cooperation of Scientists and Foreign Borders."* See text, p. 299.

34. Reuter's, June 17, 1970.

35. *Manchester Guardian,* June 18, 1970.

36. *Daily Telegraph* (London), June 18, 1970.

Chapter 24. *The Amalrik Case* (pp. 301–312)

1. The interviews were telecast on July 29, 1970. Amalrik, Bukovsky, and Yakir spoke in Russian and were simultaneously translated into English.

2. *Ibid.*

3. *New York Times,* Dec. 8, 1970. The Twenty-third Party Congress, the first Brezhnev-Kosygin congress, was held from March 29 to April 8, 1966, and had set the Five-Year Plan for 1966–1970. The Twenty-fourth Congress was expected to set the new 1971–1975 plan.

4. *Pravda,* Aug. 11, 1970. The article, by V. Afanasyev, was given considerable prominence.

5. *Ibid.*

6. *Partinaya zhizn,* No. 21 (1970).

7. *New York Times,* Nov. 16, 1970.

8. *Pravda,* Nov. 23, 1970.

9. *New York Times,* May 22, 1970.

10. Peter Reddaway, *London Times,* Oct. 10, 1970.

11. For reports of the trial, see *Frankfurter Allgemeine Zeitung,*

Nov. 4, 1970; Agence France Presse, Nov. 5, 1970; UPI and Reuter's, Nov. 11, 1970; and the *New York Times*, Nov. 12, 1970.

12. *Sunday Times* (London), Nov. 22, 1970.

13. *New York Times*, Nov. 15, 1970.

14. *Ibid.*

15. Anatole Shub, *The New Russian Tragedy*, p. 38. Shub has a good chapter, "Pictures at an Exhibition," pp. 37–50, showing how the KGB harassed the Amalriks and tried to intimidate their visitors, especially foreign guests.

16. See text, pp. 263–267.

17. Shub, p. 38.

18. Henry Kamm, "Portrait of a Dissenter," Preface to Andrei Amalrik, *Will the Soviet Union Survive until 1984?*, pp. viii, xii. With Shub's portrait of the Amalriks, see also Kamm's essay and Sidney Monas' "Amalrik's Vision of the End," an afterword to *Will the Soviet Union Survive until 1984?* for a combined and intelligent view of Amalrik the man and his ideas. See also Max Hayward's Introduction to Amalrik's *Involuntary Journey to Siberia*, pp. vii–xiii.

19. This is a reference to the Biblical Dathan, who was part of a plot with Korah and Abiram to overthrow Moses. See Numbers 16.

20. "The Chronicle of Resistance against Denationalization of the Ukraine" is the full title, and it was circulated in a *samizdat* edition, probably during the summer of 1970.

21. The report appeared in the émigré journal *Suchanost*, Nos. 3 and 6 (1968), in Munich, West Germany, and later in Polish translation in the anthology *Ukrainia, 1956–1968* (Paris: Kultura, 1969), pp. 211 ff.

22. Valentyn Moroz, "Report from the Beria Preserve," in *Ukrainia, 1956–1958*, pp. 220, 227.

23. *Chronicle*, No. 12 (Feb. 28, 1970).

24. *Chronicle*, No. 13 (April 28, 1970).

25. Peter Reddaway, *London Times*, April 27, 1970.

26. "I Want to Be Understood Correctly," *Survey*, Winter–Spring, 1970, pp. 102–110.

27. *Pravda*, Dec. 17, 1970. I. Alexandrov is thought to be a nom de plume for a high Party or government official.

28. *Literaturnaya gazeta*, Dec. 17, 1970.

Chapter 25. *The Medvedev Case* (pp. 315–327)

1. Zhores Medvedev, *The Rise and Fall of T. D. Lysenko*, p. 5.

2. *Ibid.*, p. 7.

3. *Ibid.*, pp. 49–50.

4. *Ibid.*, p. 50.

5. *Ibid.*, pp. 267–268.

6. See *ibid.*, pp. 67–77, for Medvedev's coolly told but morally fiery account of Vavilov's arrest, trial, and fate. See another account in his notes, pp. 261–262.

7. *Ibid.*, pp. 261–262.

8. *New York Times*, July 9, 1964, quotes an article Landau wrote for *Komsomolskaya pravda* in which he tells the story.

9. Richard Lauterbach, "Russia's Kapitza," *Science Illustrated*, March 1948, p. 24.

10. Mihajlo Mihajlov, *Moscow Summer*, p. 97.

11. See Michel Tatu, Power in the Kremlin, pp. 337 ff., for a political account. See also Albert Parry's *The New Class Divided*, pp. 69–87.

12. *Neva*, No. 3 (March 1963).

13. Not to be confused with the biologist V. V. Sakharov.

14. *Selskaya zhizn*, Aug. 29, 1964, as quoted in Tatu, p. 379.

15. Medvedev, p. 224.

16. *Ibid.*, p. 225.

17. *Ibid.*, pp. 226, 227.

18. *Ibid.*, p. 240.

19. *Ibid.*, p. 246; the italics are Medvedev's.

20. *Ibid.*, p. 248.

21. *Ibid.*, p. 249.

22. *Ibid.*, p. 251.

23. *New York Times*, Nov. 23, 1959.

24. *Ibid.*, April 15, 1962. See also *Ekonomicheskaya gazeta*, as quoted in Parry, p. 41.

25. See Peter Kapitsa, *On Life and Science*, pp. 197–201.

26. "Science in the U.S. Far Ahead, Says Top Russian," *Business Week*, Dec. 24, 1966, pp. 74–75.

27. When sculptor Ernst Neizvestny attempted to defend himself against Khrushchev's vicious assault on him and his work by saying, "You may not like my work, but it has the warm support of such eminent Soviet scientists as Kapitsa and Landau," Khrushchev cut him off with the comment, "That's not why we admire Landau and Kapitsa." See Priscilla Johnson, *Khrushchev and the Arts*, p. 11.

28. Olga Carlisle, "Poems of Anna Akhmatova," *Atlantic Monthly*, Oct. 1964, p. 61.

29. Patricia Blake and Max Hayward, eds., *Half-Way to the Moon*, p. 9.

30. *New York Times,* June 4, 1966.
31. UPI, March 15, 1966; *Washington Post,* March 19, 1966.
32. *Yunost,* Jan. 1967.

Chapter 26. *The Sakharov Memorandum* (pp. 328–345)

1. Andrei Amalrik, *Will the Soviet Union Survive until 1984?,* pp. 7–13. Amalrik divides the Democratic Movement into three strands: Marxist-Leninists who would restore "Leninist norms" to Soviet life; Christians who call for a return to Christian moral principles for Russia; and liberals who would like to reform the society in the style of a Western social democracy. In the first group Amalrik includes such men as Aleksey Kosterin, Ivan Yakhimovich, and Pyotr Grigorenko; in the second, men like I. Ogurtsov and Anatoly Levitin; in the last, individuals like Pavel Litvinov and, "with some reservations," Andrei Sakharov.

2. As of June 1971.

3. For materials on the *Chronicle of Current Events,* I am indebted to several good studies done by the Radio Free Europe Research Section from 1968 onward and to D. Pospielovsky's "Two Years of the *Chronicle of Current Events,"* a Radio Liberty Research Bulletin, April 1, 1970. Amnesty International in London began to offer English translations of the *Chronicle* in 1972 on a subscription basis, but too late to be of use to me in this volume.

4. The English edition of Andrei Sakharov's memorandum, *Progress, Coexistence, and Intellectual Freedom,* has useful notes and a commentary by *New York Times* Soviet affairs specialist Harrison Salisbury. He writes: "What happened was this: while the Beria teams pushed ahead toward the production of fission weapons (the A-bomb, an achievement which they attained late in 1949), Sakharov and Tamm (principally Sakharov) leapfrogged ahead toward the hydrogen weapon. Many Soviet scientists contributed to the Russian H-bomb but Sakharov's contribution was the greatest" (pp. 11–12).

5. *Ibid.,* pp. 52, 54.
6. *Ibid.,* p. 55.
7. *Ibid.,* p. 56.
8. *Ibid.,* p. 30.
9. *Ibid.,* p. 62.

10. See an intelligent summary of the pros and cons of the possibilities of "convergence" between the Soviet Union and the United States in *Time,* Jan. 12, 1970, pp. 18–19.

11. *Newsweek*, April 13, 1970. The letter was also signed by Valentin Turchin and Roy Medvedev (p. 34).

12. *Ibid.*

13. See text, pp. 319–324 and pp. 337 ff.

14. On March 9, 1968, ninety-five mathematicians protested Yesenin-Volpin's arrest and succeeded in winning his release. For the names and the protest letter, see Abraham Brumberg, ed., *In Quest of Justice*, pp. 173–174.

15. See *New York Times*, June 11, 1970, for a review of dissident activities.

16. See the *Paris Herald-Tribune*, Sept. 22, 1970; the *Washington Post*, Sept. 22, 1970; and the *New York Times*, Oct. 8, 1970.

17. Pimenov's work was in general relativity and he had written a book, *Kinematic Spaces*, translated into English and published by Consultants Bureau in New York. The verbatim account of the interview appeared in the *Chronicle*, No. 15 (Aug. 31, 1970), and was circulated among Western journalists. Extracts later appeared in the *New York Times*, Oct. 8, 1970.

18. Reuter's and *New York Times*, Oct. 12, 1970.

19. Chalidze's work is called "A Collection of Selected *Samizdat* Texts on Social Problems," five issues of which have been described in the *Chronicle of Current Events*, Nos. 10, 11, 13, and 14.

20. Agence France Presse, Oct. 12, 1970.

21. *Partinaya zhizn*, No. 21 (Nov. 1970). See also *New York Times*, Oct. 26, 1970.

22. *Literaturna ukraina*, May 5, 1970.

23. *Pid praporom leninizmu*, No. 17 (1970).

24. *Literaturna ukraina*, Aug. 21, 1970.

25. *Ibid.*

26. *Partinaya zhizn*, No. 21 (Nov. 1970).

27. *New York Times*, Nov. 16, 1970.

28. *Ibid.*

29. *Ibid.*, Nov. 24, 1970.

30. *Ibid.*, Dec. 3, 1970.

31. In May 1969, a group of fifteen dissidents formed the Action Group for the Defense of Civil Rights in the Soviet Union. This group was openly critical of the Soviet system and appealed to the United Nations Human Rights Commission for help in stopping the persecution and arrests of Soviet dissidents, but the United Nations took no action, and since then many members of this group have been arrested.

32. *New York Times*, Dec. 18, 1970.

33. *Chronicle*, No. 14 (June 30, 1970). Gershuni was arrested in 1949, allegedly for participation in an anti-Stalin youth group. He was tortured, then imprisoned in the same camp as Solzhenitsyn. Rearrested in 1969, presumably for "anti-Soviet slander," he was put into the psychiatric ward of Butyrki Prison. Novodvorskaya and Ioffe were also in special psychiatric hospitals for their activities as political dissidents.

34. See *Possev*, No. 11 (1970), p. 62, for the text of the letter.

35. *Ibid.*, pp. 61–62. Sakharov and Chalidze had written in their letter to the Presidium that the recent release of two young dissidents "raises our hopes that we can appeal not only to the legality, but also to the humaneness of the authorities" (*ibid.*).

36. *Chronicle*, No. 14 (June 30, 1970).

Chapter 27. *The Nobel Prize* (pp. 349–359)

1. *Time*, March 23, 1970, p. 25.

2. Nicholas Bethell, "Solzhenitsyn Can Still Write—He Just Can't Publish," *New York Times Magazine*, May 1970, p. 37.

3. *New York Times*, Oct. 9, 1970 (from Stockholm).

4. Marc Slonim, *New York Times Book Review*, Nov. 8, 1970.

5. *Atlas*, Dec. 1970, as translated from the *Oslo Aftenpost*.

6. *New York Times*, Oct. 9, 1970 (from Moscow).

7. Tass, Oct. 9, 1970.

8. Radio Moscow, Oct. 9, 1970.

9. *New York Times*, Oct. 15, 1970.

10. Radio Moscow, Oct. 19, 1970.

11. *New York Times*, Oct. 15, 1970.

12. Novosti news agency; as quoted in "News of the Week in Review," *New York Times*, Oct. 24, 1970.

13. Radio Moscow (in Czech), Oct. 17, 1970.

14. Reuter's, Oct. 9, 1970.

15. Radio Moscow, Oct. 16, 1970.

16. Radio Warsaw, Oct. 23, 1970.

17. *Sovetskaya rossiya*, Oct. 14, 1970.

18. *Komsomolskaya pravda*, Oct. 17, 1970.

19. *New York Times*, Nov. 27, 1970.

20. *Ibid.*, Oct. 12, 1970.

21. *Ibid.*, Nov. 16, 1970.

22. *Ibid.*, Dec. 1, 1970.

23. *Ibid.*, Dec. 11, 1970.

24. Anthony Lewis, *New York Times*, Dec. 12, 1970.

25. *New York Times,* Dec. 18, 1970.

26. Reuter's, Dec. 27, 1970.

27. *Time,* Dec. 28, 1970, p. 18.

28. Anatole Shub, *London Observer,* June 19, 1971.

29. See Patricia Blake, "News of the Week," *New York Times,* July 11, 1971, for example, who writes that "the novel will inevitably and quite properly enter into literary history as the modern *War and Peace.*"

30. The rights were sold to The Bodley Head through Solzhenitsyn's Zurich attorney, Fritz Heeb. See *New York Times,* Aug. 9, 1971, and *Publishers' Weekly,* Aug. 16, 1971, p. 37.

31. Patricia Blake, "News of the Week," *New York Times,* July 11, 1971.

Chapter 28. *The Iron Heel* (pp. 360–382)

1. Andrei Amalrik, *Will the Soviet Union Survive until 1984?,* p. 35.

2. Pasternak himself seems to have shared that "passive submissiveness to blind elemental power" that Max Hayward so astutely remarked of his creations in *Doctor Zhivago.* See Hayward's "Pasternak's *Dr. Zhivago,*" *Encounter,* May 1948, p. 44.

3. *L'Unità,* Oct. 22, 1957; as quoted in Robert Conquest's *The Pasternak Affair: Courage of Genius,* p. 66.

4. Peter Benno, "The Political Aspect," in *Soviet Literature in the Sixties,* ed. Max Hayward and Edward L. Crowley, p. 179.

5. *Ibid.*

6. *Pravda,* April 22, 1962.

7. *Pravda,* Oct. 21, 1962; as translated in the *Current Digest of the Soviet Press,* Oct. 31, 1962, p. 5.

8. Yevgeny Yevtushenko, *A Precocious Autobiography,* p. 17.

9. "Khrushchev and the Intellectuals," *East Europe,* Feb. 1964, p. 13.

10. Benno, p. 184.

11. Alexander Werth, *Russia: Hopes and Fears,* p. 188.

12. Yevtushenko, *A Precocious Autobiography,* p. 89.

13. Amalrik, *Will the Soviet Union Survive until 1984?,* p. 6.

14. *Ibid.,* p. 33.

15. *Ibid.,* p. 29.

16. Yevtushenko, *A Precocious Autobiography,* p. 39.

17. *Ibid.,* p. 42.

18. Richard Pipes, "Russia's Exigent Intellectuals," *Encounter,* Jan. 1964, p. 84. Pipes's is an excellent and wry essay on the traditional

roles and functions, strengths and weaknesses, of the Russian intelligentsia.

19. In the postwar period, Jews were gradually eliminated from important jobs in the military, intelligence, and foreign services of the Soviet Union. But keeping those areas *Judenrein* and free of dissenters has become an increasingly difficult task for the Soviet rulers, because the complex technical advances in such fields as nuclear physics, space science, and computerization have made it necessary to employ technically competent people, not merely people the regime considers "politically reliable." Because so many of the most gifted scientists in physics, chemistry, advanced mathematics, and astronomy in the USSR are Jewish, there has been an ironic reversal of Party and government policy with respect to allowing Jews to enter into important military, technical, and intelligence jobs once again.

Selected Bibliography

Western scholarship on the Soviet Union has been remarkable for its breadth and profundity. In spite of the most rigorous censorship of all time, in spite of virtually hermetically sealed borders, in spite of few colloquies and courtesies normal to international scholarly exchange, the Soviet Union has not been able to keep Western scholars from investigating and analyzing most aspects of Soviet life. Everyone studying or writing or endeavoring to make policy should be grateful for such an impressive body of factual and interpretive material.

Indispensable in research are a number of publications, chiefly the *Current Digest of the Soviet Press, Problems of Communism, Soviet Studies, Soviet Survey, East Europe*, the *Russian Review*, the *Bulletin of the Institute for the Study of the USSR*. Also essential are the reporting and news analyses of such newspapers and magazines as the *New York Times*, the *Washington Post, The Observer*, the *London Times*, the *Manchester Guardian, Le Monde, L'Express, Die Zeit, Neue Zürcher Zeitung, Time, Newsweek, Encounter*. Especially helpful are the publications, information files, and libraries available to scholars at Radio Liberty and Radio Free Europe, the Slavonics division of the New York Public Library, the Foreign Broadcast Information Service, and various other Western information services, official and unofficial. Of special and considerable use are a number of Russian émigré publications, such as *Grani, Novy zhurnal, Novoye russkoye slovo*, as well as such other émigré publications as the Polish *Kultura* and the Czechoslovak *Svědectvi*.

Publications and radio broadcasts from countries in the Soviet orbit, particularly those of Poland, Czechoslovakia, and Hungary, are often exceptionally revealing and provide a rich source of fact and opinion, as do those of China, Yugoslavia, and Albania, and the publications of the Western Communist parties, such as the *Daily Worker, L'Humanité, L'Unità, Rinascita,* and *The Worker,* provide still another dimension often available nowhere else.

Sources of quotations and of translated materials are given in the notes. In some instances, private sources cannot be disclosed. This is a selective bibliography intended for those English-speaking readers who wish to pursue their study of Soviet life and literature more extensively.

Akhmadulina, Bella. *Fever and Other Poems.* New York: Morrow, 1969.

Akhmatova, Anna. *Selected Poems.* New York: Oxford University Press, 1969.

Aksyonov, Vasily. *It's Time My Friend, It's Time.* London: Macmillan, 1969.

Alliluyeva, Svetlana. *Only One Year.* New York: Harper & Row, 1969.

——. *Twenty Letters to a Friend.* New York: Harper & Row, 1967.

Amalrik, Andrei. *Involuntary Journey to Siberia.* New York: Harcourt Brace Jovanovich, 1970.

——. *Will the Soviet Union Survive until 1984?* New York: Harper & Row, 1970.

Blake, Patricia, and Max Hayward, eds. *Dissonant Voices in Soviet Literature.* New York: Pantheon, 1962.

——. *Half-Way to the Moon.* New York: Holt, Rinehart & Winston, 1964.

Boffa, Giuseppe. *Inside the Khrushchev Era.* New York: Marzani & Munsell, 1959.

Bondarev, Yury. *Silence.* London: Chapman and Hall, 1965.

Bosley, Keith, and Dmitry Pospielovsky, eds. *Russia's Underground Poets.* New York: Praeger, 1970.

Brodsky, Josif. *Elegy to John Donne and Other Poems.* London: Longmans, Green, 1967.

Brumberg, Abraham, ed. *In Quest of Justice.* New York: Praeger, 1970.

Bulgakov, Mikhail. *The Master and Margarita.* New York: Grove, 1967.

Chornovil, Vyacheslav. *The Chornovil Papers.* New York: McGraw-Hill, 1968.

Chukovskaya, Lydia. *The Deserted House.* New York: E. P. Dutton, 1967.

Conquest, Robert. *The Great Terror.* New York: Macmillan, 1968.

——. *The Pasternak Affair: Courage of Genius.* Philadelphia: J. B. Lippincott, 1962.

——. *The Politics of Ideas in the USSR*. New York: Praeger, 1967.

——. *Power and Policy in the USSR*. New York: St. Martin's, 1961.

Crankshaw, Edward. *Khrushchev: A Career*. New York: Viking, 1966.

Daniel, Yuli. *This Is Moscow Calling*. London: Collins & Harvill, 1968.

David-Poynter, R. G., ed. *For Freedom: Theirs and Ours*. New York: Stein & Day, 1969.

DeMauny, Erik. *Russian Prospect*. London: Macmillan, 1969.

Deutscher, Isaac. *Russia in Transition*. New York: Coward-McCann, 1957.

Djilas, Milovan. *Anatomy of a Moral*. New York: Praeger, 1957.

——. *Conversations with Stalin*. New York: Harcourt, Brace & World, 1962.

——. *The New Class*. New York: Praeger, 1957.

Dombrovsky, Yuri. *The Keeper of Antiquities*. London: Longmans, Green, 1969.

Dudintsev, Vladimir, *A New Year's Tale*. New York: E. P. Dutton, 1960.

——. *Not By Bread Alone*. New York: E. P. Dutton, 1957.

Ehrenburg, Ilya. *Chekhov, Stendhal, and Other Essays*. New York: Knopf, 1963.

——. *Eve of War, 1933–1941*. (*People, Years—Life*, Vol. IV.) London: MacGibbon and Kee, 1963.

——. *People and Life: 1891–1921*. New York: Knopf, 1962.

——. *Post-War Years: 1945–1954*. Cleveland: World, 1967.

Fedin, Konstantin, *Early Joys*. New York: Vintage, 1960.

Gibian, George. *Interval of Freedom*. Minneapolis: University of Minnesota Press, 1960.

Ginzburg, Evgenia. *Journey into the Whirlwind*. New York: Harcourt, Brace & World, 1967.

Gorbatov, Aleksandr. *Years off My Life*. New York: W. W. Norton, 1965.

Hayter, William. *The Kremlin and the Embassy*. New York: Macmillan, 1966.

Hayward, Max, ed. *On Trial: The Soviet State versus "Abram Tertz" and "Nikolai Arzhak."* Rev. ed. New York: Harper & Row, 1967.

Hayward, Max, and Edward L. Crowley, eds. *Soviet Literature in the Sixties*. London: Methuen, 1965.

Hindus, Maurice. *House without A Roof*. New York: Doubleday, 1961.

Hollo, Anselm, ed. *Selected Poems of Andrei Voznesensky*. New York: Grove, 1964.

Hopkins, Mark. *Mass Media in the Soviet Union*. New York: Pegasus, 1970.

Houghton, Norris. *Return Engagement*. New York: Holt, Rinehart & Winston, 1962.

Huxley, Julian. *Soviet Genetics and World Science*. London: Chatto & Windus, 1949.

Hyland, William, and Richard Shyrock. *The Fall of Khrushchev*. New York: Funk & Wagnalls, 1968.

Johnson, Priscilla. *Khrushchev and the Arts*. Cambridge: MIT Press, 1965.

Joravsky, David. *Soviet Marxism and Natural Science*. New York: Columbia University Press, 1961.

Kapitsa, Peter. *On Life and Science*. New York: Macmillan, 1968.

Katayev, Valentin. *The Grass of Oblivion*. New York: McGraw-Hill, 1969.

——. *The Holy Well*. London: Harvill, 1967.

——. *The Small Farm in the Steppe*. London: Lawrence & Wishart, 1958.

Kaverin, Veniamin. *Open Book*. London: Lawrence & Wishart, 1958.

Kazakov, Yuri, *The Smell of Bread*. London: Harvill, 1965.

Krotkov, Yuri. *I Am From Moscow*. New York: E. P. Dutton, 1967.

Kuznetsov, Anatoly. *Babi Yar*. Rev. ed. New York: Farrar, Straus & Giroux, 1970.

Laqueur, Walter. *The Fate of the Revolution*. New York: Macmillan, 1967.

Litvinov, Pavel. *The Demonstration in Pushkin Square*. Boston: Gambit, 1969.

Mandelshtam, Nadezhda. *Hope against Hope: A Memoir*. New York: Atheneum, 1970.

Marchenko, Anatoly. *My Testimony*. New York: E. P. Dutton, 1969.

Marshall, Herbert, ed. *Voznesensky: Selected Poems*. New York: Hill & Wang, 1966.

Mayewski, Pawel, ed. *The Broken Mirror*. New York: Random House, 1958.

McLean, Hugh, and Walter Vickery, eds. *The Year of Protest, 1956*. New York: Vintage, 1961.

Medvedev, Zhores. *The Rise and Fall of T. D. Lysenko*. New York: Columbia University Press, 1969.

Mihajlov, Mihajlo. *Moscow Summer*. New York: Farrar, Straus & Giroux, 1965.

——. *Russian Themes*. New York: Farrar, Straus & Giroux, 1968.

Nekrasov, Viktor. *Both Sides of the Ocean*. New York: Holt, Rinehart & Winston, 1966.

——. *Front-Line Stalingrad*. London: Harvill, 1962.

——. *Kira Georghievna*. New York: Pantheon, 1961.

An Observer. *Message from Moscow*. New York: Knopf, 1969.

Panova, Vera. *The Span of the Year*. London: Harvill, 1957.

Parry, Albert. *The New Class Divided*. New York: Macmillan, 1966.

Pasternak, Boris. *Doctor Zhivago*. New York: Pantheon, 1958.

——. *Essay in Autobiography*. New York: Fernhill, 1959.

——. *In the Interlude: Poems, 1945–1960*. London: Oxford University Press, 1962.

Paustovsky, Konstantin. *The Story of a Life*. New York: Random House, 1964.

——. *Years of Hope*. New York: Pantheon, 1968.

Payne, Robert. *The Three Worlds of Boris Pasternak*. New York: Coward-McCann, 1961.

Platonov, Andrei. *The Fierce and the Beautiful World*. New York: E. P. Dutton, 1970.

Reddaway, Peter, ed. *Soviet Short Stories*. Vol. II. Baltimore: Penguin, 1970.

Rigby, Thomas H., ed. *Stalin*. Englewood Cliffs, N.J.: Prentice-Hall, 1966.

Rosenfeld, Barbara and Stephen. *Return from Red Square*. Washington: Robert B. Luce, 1967.

Rothberg, Abraham. *Aleksandr Solzhenitsyn: The Major Novels*. Ithaca, N.Y.: Cornell University Press, 1971.

——. ed. *Flashes in the Night*. New York: Random House, 1958.

Ruge, Gerd. *Pasternak: A Pictorial Biography*. New York: McGraw-Hill, 1959.

Sakharov, Andrei. *Progress, Coexistence, and Intellectual Freedom*. New York: W. W. Norton, 1968.

Salisbury, Harrison. *American in Russia*. New York: Harper, 1955.

Schwartz, Harry, ed. *Russia Enters the 1960s: A Documentary Report on the 22nd Congress of the Communist Party of the Soviet Union*. Philadelphia: J. B. Lippincott, 1962.

——. *The Soviet Economy since Stalin*. Philadelphia: J. B. Lippincott, 1965.

——. *Tsars, Mandarins, and Commissars*. Philadelphia: J. B. Lippincott, 1964.

Sholokhov, Mikhail. *One Man's Destiny*. New York: Knopf, 1967.

Shub, Anatole. *The New Russian Tragedy*. New York: W. W. Norton, 1969.

Slonim, Marc. *Modern Russian Literature*. London: Oxford University Press, 1953.

——. *Russian Theater: From the Empire to the Soviets*. Cleveland: World, 1961.

Snow, C. P., and Pamela Hansford Johnson, eds. *Stories from Modern Russia*. New York: St. Martin's, 1962.

Solzhenitsyn, Aleksandr. *Cancer Ward*. New York: Farrar, Straus & Giroux, 1969.

——. *The First Circle*. New York: Harper & Row, 1968.

——. *For the Good of the Cause*. New York: Praeger, 1964.

——. *The Love-Girl and the Innocent*. New York: Farrar, Straus & Giroux, 1969.

——. *One Day in the Life of Ivan Denisovich*. New York: E. P. Dutton, 1963.

——. *We Never Make Mistakes: Two Short Novels*. Columbia: University of South Carolina Press, 1963.

Stillman, Edmund, ed. *Bitter Harvest*. New York: Praeger, 1959.

Swayze, Harold. *Political Control of Literature in the USSR, 1946-1959*. Cambridge: Harvard University Press, 1962.

Tarsis, Valeriy. *The Gay Life*. London: Harvill, 1968.

——. *The Pleasure Factory*. London: Harvill, 1967.

——. *A Thousand Illusions*. London: Harvill, 1969.

——. *Ward 7*. New York: E. P. Dutton, 1966.

Tatu, Michel. *Power in the Kremlin*. New York: Viking, 1969.

Tertz, Abram (Andrey Sinyavsky). *Fantastic Stories*. New York: Pantheon, 1963.

——. *The Makepeace Experiment*. New York: Pantheon, 1965.

——. *On Socialist Realism*. New York: Pantheon, 1961.

Ulam, Adam. *The New Face of Soviet Totalitarianism*. Cambridge: Harvard University Press, 1963.

Van der Post, Laurens. *Journey into Russia*. London: Hogarth, 1964.

Vladimirov, Leonid. *The Russians*. New York: Praeger, 1968.

Voznesensky, Andrei. *Antiworlds and the Fifth Ace*. Rev. ed. New York: Basic Books, 1967.

Werth, Alexander. *Russia: Hopes and Fears*. New York: Simon & Schuster, 1969.

Whitney, Thomas. *Russia in My Life*. New York: Reynal, 1962.

Wynne, Greville, *Contact on Gorki Street*. New York: Atheneum, 1968.

Yesenin-Volpin, Aleksandr. *A Leaf of Spring*. New York: Praeger, 1961.

Yevtushenko, Yevgeny. *Bratsk Station and Other New Poems*. New York: Anchor-Doubleday, 1967.

——. *A Precocious Autobiography*. New York: Dutton, 1963.

——. *Selected Poems*. Baltimore: Penguin, 1962.

Index

Library of Congress Cataloging in Publication Data
(For library cataloging purposes only)

Rothberg, Abraham.
  The heirs of Stalin.

  Bibliography: p.
  1. Russia—Politics and government—1953–   2. Russia—Intellectual life—1917–   I. Title.
DK274.R63   320.9'47'085   77-164643
ISBN 0-8014-0667-6